INVENTING THE
AMERICAN PRESIDENCY

William N. Young
1989

INVENTING THE AMERICAN PRESIDENCY

EDITED BY THOMAS E. CRONIN

University Press of Kansas

© 1989 by the University Press of Kansas
All rights reserved

Published by the University Press of Kansas (Lawrence, Kansas 66045), which was organized by the Kansas Board of Regents and is operated and funded by Emporia State University, Fort Hays State University, Kansas State University, Pittsburg State University, the University of Kansas, and Wichita State University

Library of Congress Cataloging-in-Publication Data

Inventing the American presidency/edited by Thomas E. Cronin.
    p. cm.
  Bibliography: p.
  Includes index.
  ISBN 0-7006-0405-7 (alk. paper)—ISBN 0-7006-0406-5
(pbk. : alk. paper)
    1. Presidents—United States. 2. Executive power—United States.
3. United States—Politics and government. I. Cronin, Thomas E.
JK516.I57 1989
353.03'13—dc20   89-16492
                                                              CIP

British Library Cataloguing in Publication Data is available.

Printed in the United States of America
10 9 8 7 6 5 4 3 2 1

CONTENTS

THE CONTRIBUTORS

THOMAS E. CRONIN is McHugh Professor of American Institutions and Leadership at The Colorado College. He is the author of *The State of the Presidency; U.S. v. Crime-in-the-Streets;* and *Direct Democracy: The Politics of the Initiative, Referendum and Recall* and is a coauthor of the text *Government by the People.* He was the 1986 winner of the American Political Science Association Charles E. Merriam Award "for significant contributions to the art of government."

MICHAEL NELSON is a professor of political science at Vanderbilt University. A former editor of the *Washington Monthly,* he is a coauthor of *Presidents, Politics and Policy,* an editor of *Presidential Selection* and *The Presidency and the Political System,* and the editor of the *Congressional Quarterly's Guide to the Presidency.*

SHLOMO SLONIM is the James G. McDonald Professor of American Studies at Hebrew University, Jerusalem. He has written numerous articles and is editor of several volumes in American constitutional history, including *The Constitutional Bases of Political and Social Change in the United States.*

JOHN R. LABOVITZ, an attorney, is a partner in the District of Columbia law firm of Steptoe and Johnson. Counsel to the Impeachment Inquiry Staff of the House Judiciary Committee in 1974, he had responsibility for legal and constitutional issues concerning grounds for impeachment of President Nixon. He helped draft the proposed articles of impeachment. He is the author of *Presidential Impeachment.*

DAVID GRAY ADLER is an associate professor of political science at Idaho State University and is the author of *The Constitution and the Termination of Treaties.* A former journalist, Adler is the author of several articles and essays on the conduct of foreign policy and constitutional principles.

ROBERT J. SPITZER is an associate professor and chair of the Political

Science Department at the State University of New York College at Cortland. He is the author of *The Presidency and Public Policy; The Right to Life Movement and Third Party Politics;* and *The Presidential Veto.* He is a member of the New York State Bicentennial Commission and is the author of several articles on the American presidency.

ROBERT SCIGLIANO is a professor of political science at Boston College. A political theorist as well as a student of the Constitution and the judiciary, he has written extensively on the presidency, the Constitution, and representation and is the author of *The Supreme Court and The Presidency.*

GLENN A. PHELPS is an associate professor of political science at Northern Arizona University. A coauthor of *Contemporary Debates on Civil Liberties,* he has written extensively on George Washington as leader and president.

JOHN C. KORITANSKY is professor and chair of political science at Hiram College. He is the author of *Alexis de Tocqueville and the New Science of Politics: An Interpretation of Democracy in America;* he has also written several articles and papers on American political thought and executive power.

BRUCE MIROFF is a professor of political science at the State University of New York at Albany. He is the author of *Pragmatic Illusions: The Presidential Politics of John F. Kennedy* and numerous articles on the presidency and political leadership. He is currently writing *The Tribe of the Eagle: American Images of Political Leadership.*

GARY J. SCHMITT, a political scientist, has served as a research associate at the University of Virginia's White Burkett Miller Center of Public Policy, as a senior staff member of the President's Foreign Intelligence Advisory Board, and in 1988–1989 as a visiting fellow at the journal *The National Interest.* He has also written on executive privilege.

RALPH KETCHAM, recently honored as one of the outstanding university teachers in the United States, is a professor of American Studies at the Maxwell School of Citizenship and Public Affairs of Syracuse University. He is the author of *Presidents above Party; The First American Presidency, 1789–1829; Benjamin Franklin;* and *James Madison: A Biography.* He is also the author of *From Colony to Country: The Revolution in American Thought, 1750–1820.*

PREFACE

The American presidency is a unique, necessary, yet always potentially dangerous institution. The framers of the Constitution knew this, and we appreciate it as well today.

The invention of the American presidency is sometimes described as one of the most fateful developments in American history. By no means, however, was it inevitable. The framers could have strengthened their existing government under the Articles of Confederation, as indeed, the Continental Congress instructed them. Many of the framers recognized the need for further centralization, yet centralization and the invention of a chief executive were not one and the same.

At Philadelphia the framers recommended both a more centralized national government and a relatively independent executive. The creation of the presidency, like the development of the Constitution, was the result of the collective experience and wisdom of the nation. The founders carefully took into account their own experiences, both good and bad, under the Confederation, under the crown, under royal governors, in their newly independent states, and with George Washington during the Revolution. The founders also read about other systems—those of antiquity and those described in legal commentaries and theoretical treatises. Thus experience, political theory, and political history were all very relevant to their undertaking. Still, the creation of the national executive involved imagination, vision, and risk taking, moving beyond the lessons of history and political thought.

The framers wanted a more authoritative and decisive national government, yet they were keenly aware that the American people were not about to accept too much centralized power vested in a single person. Their challenge was to invent an executive office that would be strong enough to provide effective governance without threatening the newly developed and most cherished republican forms of government.

Everyone assumed that George Washington would become the first president. His deft handling of power during his command of the Revolutionary forces constituted reassurance to the framers that his performance in office would be appropriately restrained. But the framers wanted to invent an office that would last well beyond the stay of Washington. They wanted to provide for emergency leadership, for an executive who could negotiate treaties and enforce the laws, yet they wanted also to ensure that presidential power would be accountable to Congress and the people.

This book, through fourteen interpretative essays, tells the story of the invention of the American presidency. The aim of this volume is to provide the essential historical and political analyses of who and what shaped the presidency. These essays also examine what was decided in Philadelphia and why. Why have a presidency? Who could be elected, how, for how long a tenure, and with what responsibilities and powers? What were the key debates then, during the early years, and what are the enduring debates that remain even now?

This volume is divided into three parts: these treat the *structure* or design of the presidency, the *powers* and roles granted to the presidents, and the significant *precedents* set by early presidents. Throughout, these essays examine the heated debates that surrounded the invention, as well as the enduring debates about the proper place of the presidency in our constitutional and political systems.

Plainly, to understand the contemporary United States presidency, it is first necessary to understand its creation, the early intentions for it, and how its precedents took shape. Controversies have always been triggered by the exercise of executive power. This has been the case in every society. The American experiment is no exception.

The presidency is indeed unique, necessary, and always a potentially dangerous institution. That is why we try to understand the history and the exercise of presidential power. These essays are inevitably interpretative and, in places, argumentative. At least a couple of the authors, such as David Gray Adler and Bruce Miroff, oppose a spacious reading of the Constitution's provisions on the presidency. They want an effective presidency but one that is accountable, and they read the Constitution's provisions for the presidency in a narrower or stricter way than others do. On the other hand, Robert Scigliano and, perhaps to a lesser extent, Gary J. Schmitt and John C. Koritansky, read these same provisions more broadly and look also to presidential precedents, and thus hold a more capacious view of a president's inherent powers and responsibilities. Thus, readers should peruse these chapters with a critical eye not only as to the debates among the framers but also with an appreciation of the on-going debates among contemporary scholars.

In some respects the Constitutional Convention of 1787 is still in session. Much of what the delegates debated then is still being debated today. The debates may have changed their focus, yet the presidency is clearly still a much-debated institution. This is as it should be.

Half of the pieces that follow have appeared in print previously; in some cases, they have been revised here. The original publication is noted in the notes at the end of each chapter. I am indebted to the journals and scholars and, in one case, to Yale University Press for permission to reprint them. I am even more indebted to those who have prepared the original, fresh chapters that appear here.

Readers should read the sections of the United States Constitution and the amendments that speak to the role and the powers of the presidency. These are placed after this introduction because they should be read at the outset. Further, five of Alexander Hamilton's key *Federalist* essays, which explain and defend the work of the framers at Philadelphia, are located in the appendix. They, too, could be read at the outset. Hamilton wrote to persuade his fellow citizens that the presidency was necessary and that it would be a responsible institution. He may have overstated his case in places, yet his analysis is about as close an understanding of the mood of the framers on this subject as we have. Moreover, his views are elegantly stated.

Readers should be duly warned that problems sometimes arise as to what the framers of the Constitution intended. We can often examine the debates at the Constitutional Convention of 1787, the writings in *The Federalist,* the criticisms and commentary of the Antifederalists, debates and decisions at the ratifying conventions of the states, and even the early actions and interpretations of the founding presidents and members of Congress, and through rigorous analysis, be able to determine what the framers intended or at least expected. Yet on some points we must appreciate that the framers themselves did not regard the debates at Philadelphia or other early writings as the final word on the meaning of the Constitution. Men like Alexander Hamilton and James Madison occasionally changed their minds over the course of these early years of the Republic. On a few points the Constitution is either silent or vague because had the framers been more specific it might have stirred up opposition to the document they dearly hoped would win ratification. Doubtless, too, many of the founders expected those who would come later to interpret for themselves the spacious words of the Constitution. Most assuredly, this is precisely what justices of the Supreme Court, members of Congress, presidents, and scholars such as those included in this volume regularly do. The Constitution is a wonderful document, yet it is a broad charter—a general guide rather than a detailed encyclopaedia for future behavior. Whether we like it or not, in part we have an unwritten Constitution whose history is the history of judicial review and of continuous reinterpretation by presidents and members of Congress.

Americans have always had a fundamental ambivalence toward executive power. They admire strong presidents, yet they fear the abuse of power. These essays will readily inform, yet they will also appropriately alert readers about the potential abuses of unchecked presidential power. And they should serve as well to make us think anew about what kind of presidential leadership is needed for our times.

Thomas E. Cronin
Colorado Springs, Colorado, 1989

RELEVANT SECTIONS OF AND AMENDMENTS TO THE CONSTITUTION OF THE UNITED STATES

ARTICLE I — THE LEGISLATIVE ARTICLE

SECTION. 1. All legislative Powers herein granted shall be vested in a Congress of the United States, which shall consist of a Senate and House of Representatives.

SECTION. 2. The House of Representatives shall be composed of Members chosen every second Year by the People of the several States, and the Electors in each State shall have the Qualifications requisite for Electors of the most numerous Branch of the State Legislature. . . .

The House of Representatives shall chuse their Speaker and other officers; and shall have the sole power of impeachment.

SECTION. 3. The Senate of the United States shall be composed of two Senators from each State, [chosen by the Legislature thereof,] for six Years; and each Senator shall have one Vote. . . .

The Vice President of the United States shall be President of the Senate, but shall have no Vote, unless they be equally divided.

The Senate shall chuse their other Officers, and also a President pro tempore, in the Absence of the Vice President, or when he shall exercise the Office of President of the United States.

The Senate shall have the sole Power to try all Impeachments. When sitting for that Purpose, they shall be on Oath or Affirmation. When the President of the United States is tried, the Chief Justice shall preside. And no person shall be convicted without the Concurrence of two thirds of the Members present.

Judgment in Cases of Impeachment shall not extend further than to removal from Office, and disqualification to hold and enjoy any Office of honor, Trust or Profit under the United States: but the Party convicted shall nevertheless be liable and subject to Indictment, Trial, Judgment and Punishment, according to Law. . . .

SECTION. 7. All Bills for raising revenue shall originate in the House of Representatives; but the Senate may propose or concur with Amendments as on other Bills.

Every Bill which shall have passed the House of Representatives and the Senate, shall, before it become a Law, be presented to the President of the United States; If he approve he shall sign it, but if not he shall return it, with his Objections to that House in which it shall have originated, who shall enter the Objections at large on their Journal, and proceed to reconsider it. If after such Reconsideration two thirds of that House shall agree to pass the Bill, it shall be sent, together with the Objections, to the other House, by which it shall likewise be reconsidered, and if approved by two thirds of that House, it shall become a Law. But in all such Cases the Votes of both Houses shall be determined by yeas and Nays, and the Names of the Persons voting for and against the Bill shall be entered on the Journal of each House respectively. If any Bill shall not be returned by the President within ten Days (Sundays excepted) after it shall have been presented to him, the Same shall be a Law, in like Manner as if he had signed it, unless the Congress by their Adjournment prevent its Return, in which Case it shall not be a Law.

Every Order, Resolution, or Vote to which the Concurrence of the Senate and House of Representatives may be necessary (except on a question of Adjournment) shall be presented to the President of the United States; and before the Same shall take Effect, shall be approved by him, or being disapproved by him, shall be repassed by two thirds of the Senate and House of Representatives, according to the Rules and Limitations pre-scribed in the Case of a Bill.

SECTION. 8. The Congress shall have Power To Lay and collect Taxes, Duties, Imposts and Excises, to pay the Debts and provide for the common Defence and general Welfare of the United States; but all Duties, Imposts and Excises shall be uniform throughout the United States;

To borrow Money on the credit of the United States;

To regulate Commerce with foreign Nations, and among the several States, and with the Indian Tribes;

To establish a uniform Rule of Naturalization, and uniform Laws on the subject of Bankruptcies throughout the United States;

To coin Money, regulate the Value thereof, and of foreign Coin, and fix the Standard of Weights and Measures;

To provide for the Punishment of counterfeiting the Securities and current Coin of the United States;

To establish Post Offices and post Roads;

To promote the Progress of Science and useful Arts, by securing for limited Times to Authors and Inventors the exclusive Right to their respective Writings and Discoveries;

To constitute Tribunals inferior to the supreme Court;

To define and punish Piracies and Felonies committed on the high Seas, and Offences against the Law of Nations;

To declare War, grant Letters of Marque and Reprisal, and make Rules concerning Captures on Land and Water;

To raise and support Armies, but no appropriation of Money to that Use shall be for a longer Term than two Years;

To provide and maintain a Navy;

To make Rules for the Government and Regulation of the land and naval forces;

To provide for calling forth the Militia to execute the Laws of the Union, suppress Insurrections and repel Invasions;

To provide for organizing, arming, and disciplining, the Militia, and for governing such part of them as may be employed in the Service of the United States, reserving to the States respectively, the Appointment of the Officers, and the Authority of training the Militia according to the discipline prescribed by Congress;

To exercise exclusive Legislation in all Cases whatsoever, over such District (not exceeding ten miles Square) as may, by Cession of particular States, and the Acceptance of Congress, become the Seat of the government of the United States, and to exercise like Authority over all Places purchased by the Consent of the Legislature of the State in which the Same shall be, for the Erection of Forts, Magazines, Arsenals, dock-Yards, and other needful Buildings: — And

To make all Laws which shall be necessary and proper for carrying into Execution the foregoing Powers, and all other Powers vested by this Constitution in the Government of the United States, or in any Department or Officer thereof. . . .

ARTICLE II — THE EXECUTIVE ARTICLE

SECTION. 1. The executive Power shall be vested in a President of the United States of America. He shall hold his Office during the Term of Four Years, and, together with the Vice President, chosen for the same Term, be elected, as follows

Each State shall appoint, in such Manner as the Legislature thereof may direct, a Number of Electors, equal to the whole Number of Senators and

Representatives to which the State may be entitled in the Congress; but no Senator or Representative, or Person holding an Office of Trust or Profit under the United States, shall be appointed an Elector.

[The Electors shall meet in their respective States, and vote by Ballot for two Persons, of whom one at least shall not be an Inhabitant of the same State with themselves. And they shall make a List of all the Persons voted for, and of the Number of Votes for each; which List they shall sign and certify, and transmit sealed to the Seat of the Government of the United States, directed to the President of the Senate. The President of the Senate shall, in the Presence of the Senate and House of Representatives, open all the Certificates, and the Votes shall then be counted. The Person having the greatest Number of Votes shall be President, if such Number be a Majority of the whole Number of Electors appointed; and if there be more than one who have such Majority, and have an equal Number of Votes, then the House of Representatives shall immediately chuse by Ballot one of them for President; and if no Person have a Majority, then from the five highest on the List the said House shall in like Manner chuse the President. But in chusing the President, the Votes shall be taken by States, the Representation from each State having one Vote; A quorum for this purpose shall consist of a Member or Members from two thirds of the States, and a Majority of all the States shall be necessary to a Choice. In every Case, after the Choice of the President, the Person having the greatest Number of Votes of the Electors shall be the Vice President. But if there should remain two or more who have equal Votes, the Senate chuse from them by Ballot the Vice President.][1]

The Congress may determine the Time of chusing the Electors, and the Day on which they shall give their Votes; which Day shall be the same throughout the United States.

No Person except a natural born Citizen, or a Citizen of the United States, at the time of the Adoption of this Constitution, shall be eligible to the Office of President; neither shall any Person be eligible to that Office who shall not have attained to the Age of thirty five Years, and been fourteen Years a Resident within the United States.

[In Case of the Removal of the President from Office, or of his Death, Resignation, or Inability to discharge the Powers and Duties of the said Office, the Same shall devolve on the Vice President, and the Congress may by Law provide for the Case of Removal, Death, Resignation or inability, both of the President and Vice President, declaring what Officer shall then

---

[1] Superseded by the Twelfth Amendment.

act as President, and such Officer shall act accordingly, until the Disability be removed, or a President shall be elected.]²

The President shall, at stated Times, receive for his Services, a Compensation, which shall neither be encreased nor diminished during the Period for which he shall have been elected, and he shall not receive within that period any other Emolument from the United States, or any of them.

Before he enter on the Execution of his Office, he shall take the following Oath or Affirmation: — "I do solemnly swear (or affirm) that I will faithfully execute the Office of President of the United States, and will to the best of my Ability, preserve, protect and defend the Constitution of the United States."

SECTION. 2. The President shall be Commander in Chief of the Army and Navy of the United States, and of the Militia of the several States, when called into the actual Service of the United States; he may require the Opinion, in writing, of the Principal Officer in each of the executive Departments, upon any Subject relating to the Duties of their respective Offices, and he shall have Power to grant Reprieves and Pardons for Offences against the United States, except in Cases of Impeachment.

He shall have Power, by and with the Advice and Consent of the Senate, to make Treaties, provided two thirds of the Senators present concur; and he shall nominate, and by and with the Advice and Consent of the Senate, shall appoint Ambassadors, other public Ministers and Consuls, Judges of the supreme Court, and all other Officers of the United States, whose Appointments are not herein otherwise provided for, and which shall be established by Law; but the Congress may by Law vest the Appointment of such inferior Offices, as they think proper, in the President alone, in the Courts of Law, or in the Heads of Departments.

The President shall have Power to fill up all Vacancies that may happen during the Recess of the Senate, by granting Commissions which shall expire at the End of their next Session.

SECTION. 3. He shall from time to time give to the Congress Information of the State of the Union, and recommend to their Consideration such Measures as he shall judge necessary and expedient; he may, on extraordinary Occasions, convene both Houses, or either of them, and in Case of Disagreement between them, with Respect to the Time of Adjournment, he may adjourn them to such Time as he shall think proper; he shall receive Ambassadors and other public Ministers; he shall take Care that the Laws be faithfully executed, and shall Commission all the Officers of the United States.

SECTION. 4. The President, Vice President and all civil Officers of the United States, shall be removed from Office on Impeachment for, and Conviction of, Treason, Bribery, or other high Crimes and Misdemeanors.

---

²Superseded by the Twenty-fifth Amendment.

AMENDMENT XII (1804) — ELECTION OF THE PRESIDENT

The Electors shall meet in their respective states, and vote by ballot for President and Vice President, one of whom, at least, shall not be an inhabitant of the same state with themselves; they shall name in their ballots the person voted for as President, and in distinct ballots the person voted for as Vice President, and they shall make distinct lists of all persons voted for as President, and of all persons voted for as Vice President, and of the number of votes for each, which lists they shall sign and certify, and transmit sealed to the seat of the government of the United States, directed to the President of the Senate; — The President of the Senate shall, in the presence of the Senate and House of Representatives, open all the certificates and the votes shall then be counted; — The person having the greatest number of votes for President, shall be the President, if such number be a majority of the whole number of Electors appointed; and if no person have such majority, then from the persons having the highest numbers not exceeding three on the list of those voted for as President, the House of Representatives shall choose immediately, by ballot, the President. But in choosing the President, the votes shall be taken by states, the representation from each state having one vote; a quorum for this purpose shall consist of a member or members from two-thirds of the states, and a majority of all the states shall be necessary to a choice. And if the House of Representatives shall not choose a President whenever the right of choice shall devolve upon them, before the fourth day of March next following,[3] then the vice President shall act as President, as in the case of the death or other constitutional disability of the President. — The person having the greatest number of votes as Vice President, shall be the Vice President, if such number be a majority of the whole number of Electors appointed, and if no person have a majority, then from the two highest numbers on the list, the Senate shall choose the Vice President; a quorum for the purpose shall consist of two-thirds of the whole number of Senators, and a majority of the whole number shall be necessary to a choice. But no person constitutionally ineligible to the office of President shall be eligible to that of Vice President of the United States. . . .

AMENDMENT XX (1933) — THE LAME-DUCK AMENDMENT

SECTION 1. The terms of the President and Vice President shall end at noon on the 20th day of January, and the terms of Senators and

---

[3] Modified by the Twentieth Amendment.

Representatives at noon on the 3d day of January, of the years in which such terms would have ended if this article had not been ratified; and the terms of their successors shall then begin.

SECTION 2. The Congress shall assemble at least once in every year, and such meeting shall begin at noon on the 3d day of January, unless they shall by law appoint a different day.

SECTION 3. If, at the time fixed for the beginning of the term of the President, the President elect shall have died, the Vice President elect shall become President. If a President shall not have been chosen before the time fixed for the beginning of his term, or if the President elect shall have failed to qualify, then the Vice President elect shall act as President until a President shall have qualified; and the Congress may by law provide for the case wherein neither a President elect nor a Vice President elect shall have qualified, declaring who shall then act as President, or the manner in which one who is to act shall be selected, and such person shall act accordingly until a President or Vice President shall have qualified.

SECTION 4. The Congress may by law provide for the case of the death of any of the persons from whom the House of Representatives may choose a President whenever the right of choice shall have devolved upon them, and for the case of the death of any of the persons from whom the Senate may choose a Vice President whenever the right of choice shall have devolved upon them.

SECTION 5. Sections 1 and 2 shall take effect on the 15th day of October following the ratification of this article.

SECTION 6. This article shall be inoperative unless it shall have been ratified as an amendment to the Constitution by the legislatures of three-fourths of the several States within seven years from the date of its submission.

AMENDMENT XXII (1951) — NUMBER OF PRESIDENTIAL TERMS

SECTION 1. No person shall be elected to the office of the President more than twice, and no person who has held the office of President, or acted as President, for more than two years of a term to which some other person was elected President shall be elected to the office of President more than once. But this Article shall not apply to any person holding the office of President when this Article was proposed by the Congress, and shall not prevent any person who may be holding the office of President, or acting as President, during the term within which this article becomes operative from holding the office of President or acting as President during the remainder of such term.

SECTION 2. This Article shall be inoperative unless it shall have been ratified as an amendment to the Constitution by the legislatures of three-fourths of the several States within seven years from the date of its submission to the States by the Congress.

AMENDMENT XXV (1967) — PRESIDENTIAL DISABILITY, VICE-PRESIDENCY VACANCY

SECTION 1. In case of the removal of the President from office or of his death or resignation, the Vice President shall become President.[4]

SECTION 2. Whenever there is a vacancy in the office of the Vice President, the President shall nominate a Vice President who shall take the office upon confirmation by a majority vote of both houses of Congress.[5]

SECTION 3. Whenever the President transmits to the President pro tempore of the Senate and the Speaker of the House of Representatives his written declaration that he is unable to discharge the powers and duties of his office, and until he transmits to them a written declaration to the contrary, such powers and duties shall be discharged by the Vice President as Acting President.[6]

SECTION 4. Whenever the Vice President and a majority of either the principal officers of the executive departments or of such other body as Congress may by law provide, transmit to the President pro tempore of the Senate and the Speaker of the House of Representatives their written declaration that the President is unable to discharge the powers and duties of his office, the Vice President shall immediately assume the powers and duties of the office as Acting President.

Thereafter, when the President transmits to the President pro tempore of the Senate and the Speaker of the House of Representatives his written declaration that no inability exists, he shall resume the powers and duties of his office unless the Vice President and a majority of either the principal officers of the executive department or of such other body as Congress may by law provide, transmit within four days to the President pro tempore of the Senate and the Speaker of the House of Representatives their written declaration that the President is unable to discharge the powers and duties of his office. Thereupon Congress shall decide the issue, assembling within forty-eight hours for that purpose if not in session. If the Congress within twenty-one days after receipt of the latter written declaration, or, if Congress is not in session, within twenty-one days after Congress is required to assemble, determines by two-thirds vote of both Houses that

[4]Superseded by the Twelfth Amendment.
[5]Superseded by the Twenty-fifth Amendment.
[6]Modified by the Twentieth Amendment.

the President is unable to discharge the powers and duties of his office, the Vice President shall continue to discharge the same as Acting President; otherwise, the President shall resume the powers and duties of his office.

PART 1
STRUCTURE

1

QUALIFICATIONS FOR PRESIDENT

MICHAEL NELSON

No person except a natural born Citizen, or a Citizen of the United States, at the time of the Adoption of this Constitution, shall be eligible to the Office of President; neither shall any Person be eligible to that Office who shall not have attained to the Age of thirty five Years, and been fourteen Years a Resident within the United States.
—*Article II, section 1*

Because the presidential qualifications clause was not debated at the Constitutional Convention, scholars have despaired of knowing why the framers stipulated that the president must be a natural-born citizen who has resided in the United States for at least fourteen years and reached the age of thirty-five. "The deliberations of the Constitutional Convention of 1787 furnish no clues to the underlying purpose" of the qualifications clause, wrote Charles Gordon in a 1968 article, easily the best treatment of the subject. Stated qualifications for the president "were recommended as a seeming afterthought in the report from the Committee on Postponed Matters and Unfinished Business near the end of the Convention," Joseph Kallenbach noted in 1961; "they were accepted without debate or explanation." Charles Thach, author of the 1923 classic work *The Creation of the Presidency,* referred simply to "the silent insertion of the clause in a committee where matters could be managed quietly."[1] Leading recent works on the constitutional presidency or on presidential selection have entirely ignored the qualifications clause.[2]

In truth, the recorded debates on presidential qualifications at the Constitutional Convention are meager and generally unilluminating. Such discussion as there was came on a proposed property requirement that the convention rejected. The delegates labored through late May, June, July, and most of August without any apparent interest in establishing qualifications for the president. Then, on August 20, Elbridge Gerry moved that the Committee of Detail recommend such qualifications. Two days later, it did:

the president "shall be of the age of thirty five years, and a Citizen of the United States, and shall have been an Inhabitant thereof for Twenty one years." On September 4, a revised recommendation was made by the new Committee on Postponed Matters: "No person except a natural born citizen or a Citizen of the U— S— at the time of the adoption of this constitution shall be eligible to the office of President; nor shall any person be elected to that office, who shall be under the age of thirty five years, and who has not been in the whole, at least fourteen years a resident within the U— S." No debate or explanation accompanied Gerry's motion or either committee's recommendations, the second of which was approved by the convention on September 7, unanimously and without debate. The Committee of Style, executing its general charge "to revise the style of and arrange the articles which had been agreed to" for a final draft of the Constitution, altered the presidential-qualifications clause into its present form.[3]

Considering the scarcity of evidence from the convention debates, can anything be said about the origin of paragraph 5? Some evidence has been uncovered—an exchange of letters between John Jay and George Washington, a newspaper article or two from the period, a fleeting reference in *Federalist* number 64—but as we have seen, none of these has emboldened scholars to move beyond their conclusion that the presidential-qualifications clause is a puzzle.

In truth, much can be learned by formulating the issue of presidential qualifications more specifically, then extending the search for evidence more widely. Instead of simply asking about the origin of paragraph 5, it is prudent to ask two questions. First, Why did the convention state any qualifications at all for president? Second, Why did it state the qualifications it did? As for relevant evidence, considerable insight can be gained by viewing the presidential-qualifications clause "synoptically," as part of the entire constitution, rather than as something proposed and enacted purely on its own terms.[4] The convention discussed other proposals and made other decisions that shaped its consideration of presidential qualifications. Some of these had to do with qualifications for legislative offices; some, with broader aspects of the presidency, Congress, and the powers of the new national government. All of the considerations that shaped the writing of paragraph 5 were political, both philosophically and pragmatically.

In the first section of this essay, I offer a narrative account of the debates on qualifications for all offices that took place at the convention. Two analytic sections follow: one devoted to explaining why the convention established qualifications for president, the other to explaining how it arrived at age, residency, and citizenship as its categories and at thirty-five years of age, fourteen years of residence, and natural-born citizenship (except for foreign-born citizens who were alive at the time) as its particulars. In the conclusion I briefly assess the place of philosophy and pragmatism in the process of writing the constitution.

THE DEBATES ON QUALIFICATIONS

The Virginia Plan, which was drafted by James Madison as a working agenda for the convention and introduced by Governor Edmund Randolph on May 19, the first day of substantive business, stated no qualifications for the "National Executive." He (or they—the issue of whether the executive should be unitary or plural was not settled until floor debate began the next day) would be chosen by the legislature for "the term of _____ years . . . , and to be ineligible a second time." In provisions for members of both "the first branch of the National Legislature" (later called the House of Representatives), who were "to be elected by the people," and "the second branch" (the Senate), who were "to be elected by those of the first," it was stipulated that they were "to be of the age of _____ years at least."[5]

Accepting the Virginia Plan as a basis for discussion, the convention reconstituted itself as a Committee of the Whole on May 30 and began to debate the individual provisions of the plan. On June 12, five days after the delegates had decided that the Senate should be chosen by the state legislatures rather than by the House, a motion to strike the age requirement for senators failed by a vote of three states in favor, six opposed, and two divided. (Throughout the convention, the delegates voted by state.) Instantly a motion to set the standard at thirty years passed by a vote of 7 to 4. No debate accompanied either motion or a later one, on June 25, to reaffirm the thirty-year age requirement for senators, which passed unanimously. But some evidence of the delegates' thinking was revealed on June 22, when George Mason moved that twenty-five years be established as the minimum age for members of the House of Representatives. Mason argued that "every man carried with him in his own experience a scale for measuring the deficiency of young politicians; since he would if interrogated be obliged to declare that his political opinions at the age of 21. were too crude & erroneous to merit an influence on public measures." To this, James Wilson rejoined, first, that he "was agst. abridging the rights of election in any shape" and, second, that "there was no more reason for incapacitating *youth* than *age,* when the requisite qualifications were found." The twenty-five year age requirement for representatives passed, 7 to 3 to 1.[6]

Not until July 26 was the issue of qualifications for the president raised for the first time. Mason, who exactly one month earlier had expressed, in passing, a desire to attach a property-owning qualification to the Senate, now moved that "certain qualifications of landed property & citizenship of the U. States in members of the Legislature" be required. (Mason also moved that "all such persons as are indebted to, or have unsettled accounts with the United States" be barred from the legislature. This part of his motion was rejected 9 to 2, probably in response to the argument of Wilson and others that a venal government could keep its accounts with certain citizens unsettled just to exclude them from office.) Charles Pinckney and Charles Cotesworth Pinckney together added to Mason's motion in the form of an amendment a property requirement for judges and the president.[7]

At the time the Constitution was being written, it was common to have property qualifications for executives ranging from £500 for New Hampshire's governor to £10,000 for South Carolina's and usually including a stipulation that some or all of the property be landed.[8] Most delegates seem to have had no objection to the principles underlying Mason's motion, namely, that officeholders should be wealthy enough to be secure from the temptation to financial corruption, to identify with the fundamental property rights that government was meant to protect, and to have a substantial economic stake in the communities they represented. But some delegates spoke out against the motion. Gouverneur Morris argued, "If qualifications are proper, he wd. prefer them in the electors rather than the elected." John Dickinson agreed that if "the freeholders who were to elect the Legislature . . . should be corrupt, no little expedients would repel the danger." He also "doubted the policy of interweaving into a Republican constitution a veneration for wealth."[9]

Madison, agreeing with Morris's argument but recognizing that the setting of standards for voter eligibility was a jealously guarded state prerogative, spoke for the purpose of modifying but not rejecting Mason's motion for a property requirement. He urged that to require "landed" property of officeholders would be insensitive to "the growing commercial and the manufacturing classes" (unless the requirement was very low, in which case it would be meaningless). He also noted from experience that "men who had acquired landed property on credit, got into the [state] Legislatures with a view of promoting an unjust protection agst. their Creditors." Madison's motion to strike the word "landed" passed 10 to 1.[10]

What remained of Mason's motion—that the president, legislators, and judges must be citizens and property owners—passed 8 to 3. Interestingly, speakers in the debate referred only to legislative offices, not to judgeships or the presidency. Nor was anything said about the part of Mason's motion that established a citizenship qualification for the president and other officials.[11]

Along with the Committee of the Whole's previously adopted motions to require that representatives and senators be at least twenty-five and thirty years of age, respectively, the citizenship and property qualifications were forwarded on July 26 to the Committee of Detail, which had been formed for the purpose of incorporating these and other decisions of the convention into a fresh working draft of the Constitution. The five-member committee worked for ten days in near secrecy, then reported back to the convention on August 6. Some of the delegates' earlier decisions on qualifications the committee took literally, notably those pertaining to the minimum ages of legislators. In other cases, the committee followed the charge from the convention to fix the details of its decisions: a representative "shall have been a citizen of the United States for at least three years before his election"; a senator, for four years. There also were elements of the committee's report that altered the convention's earlier votes. No property or citizenship qualifications were stated for president or judges (or any other qualifications, for that matter); as for legislators, Congress itself was given "authority to establish such uniform qualifications of the members of each House, with regard to property, as to the said Legislature shall seem expedient." Finally, the committee created a new qualification, again for legislators only: each representative and senator "shall be, at the time of his election, a resident of the State [in] which he shall be chosen."[12]

The new residency requirement was the first issue to rouse the delegates. Several positions emerged when it was debated on August 8 as part of their larger discussion of the House of Representatives. Gouverneur Morris again urged constitutional silence: the word "resident" was subject to varying interpretations, which invariably were applied in particular cases on partisan, not objective, grounds; besides: "Such a regulation is not necessary. People rarely chuse a nonresident." In the case of the House, which was to represent people, not places, the latter consideration was especially pertinent. Some delegates agreed with one or another of Morris's arguments but saw the solution in changing "resident" to "inhabitant," a word that Roger Sherman regarded as "less liable to misconstruction" and that Madison "would not exclude persons absent occasionally for a considerable time on public or private business." John Rutledge thought a simple residence requirement was insufficient: he urged that the standard be seven years of residence. "An emigrant from N. England to S. C. or Georgia would know little of its affairs and could not be supposed to acquire a thorough knowledge in less time."[13]

In the end, Mason and Hugh Williamson, in separate statements, captured the common sentiment of the convention. Without any residence requirement, Mason argued, "Rich men of neighbouring States, may employ with success the means of corruption in some particular district and thereby get into the public Councils after having failed in their own State. This is the practice in the boroughs of England." But, argued

Williamson, there was no need to make the requirement lengthy: "New residents if elected will be most zealous to Conform to the will of their constituents, as their conduct will be watched with a more jealous eye." Rutledge's motion, even when he reduced it to require three-year residence, failed 2 to 9. So did a motion for a one-year requirement (4 to 6). In the end, the only modification to the Committee of Detail's recommendation that a representative must live in the state whose people elected him was the substitution of "inhabitant" for "resident": it passed unanimously. On August 9, having aired all the issues it deemed relevant in the debate on the House, the convention, unanimously approved a similarly modified inhabitancy requirement for senators.[14]

The Committee of Detail's proposed citizenship requirement for representatives was debated briefly on August 8, but the issue was joined with greater intensity the next day, in connection with the Senate. The decision on representatives was quick. A motion by Mason to raise the standard from three years to seven years of citizenship was made, then defended by its author on the grounds that although he welcomed immigrants, he "did not chuse to let foreigners and adventurers make laws for us," did not want to leave the door open for "a rich foreign Nation, for example Great Britain, [to] send over her tools who might bribe their way into the Legislature for insidious purposes," and did not regard three years of citizenship as "enough for ensuring that local knowledge which ought to be possessed by the Representative." The motion passed, 10 to 1.[15]

The citizenship issue took center stage on August 9, in connection with the Committee of Detail's recommendations for Senate qualifications. Gouverneur Morris, "urging the danger of admitting strangers into our public Councils," moved that a fourteen-year citizenship requirement be substituted for the committee's proposal of four years. Support for his motion emerged along two main lines. The first was simple suspicion of foreigners. "Admit a Frenchman into your Senate, and he will study to increase the commerce of France," argued Morris: "An Englishman, he will feel an equal bias in favor of that of England." Morris also suggested that to allow recent immigrants to hold office would be to follow the example of "some tribes of Indians, [which] carried their hospitality so far as to offer to strangers their wives and daughters" for "carnal amusement." Mason added, "Were it not that many not natives of this Country had acquired great merit during the revolution, he should be for restraining the eligibility into the Senate, to natives."[16]

A second argument for a lengthy citizenship requirement rested on certain distinctive features of the Senate. Charles Pinckney suggested the special importance of barring foreigners' influence from that branch of the legislature with "power of making treaties & managing our foreign affairs." (As yet, the delegates had not decided to give the power to negotiate treaties to the president.) The Athenians, he added darkly, "made it death for any stranger to intrude his voice into their legislative proceedings." Williamson added, "Bribery & Cabal can be more easily practised in the choice of the Senate which is to be made by the Legislatures composed of a few men, than of the House of Represents. who will be chosen by the people."[17]

Opponents of Morris's proposed fourteen-year citizenship requirement for senators argued that the proponents' fears were unfounded. Not only would state legislatures not elect "any dangerous number" of foreign senators, said Madison, but no foreign government seeking to infiltrate Congress would use its own people as agents. "Their bribes would be expended on men whose circumstances would rather stifle than excite jealousy & watchfulness in the public." Madison added that citizenship requirements should not be a constitutional matter: the convention's earlier decision to give Congress the power to regulate naturalization placed such a requirement squarely in the category of legislative judgment. But the argument most fervently pressed by opponents of the motion had to do with its assumptions about immigrants. Oliver Ellsworth, Benjamin Franklin, Randolph, Madison, and Wilson chorused that foreign governments would scorn the United States for its hypocritical illiberality; "meritorious aliens" would be discouraged from emigrating; and recent immigrants—the very people whose choice of the United States is a "proof of attachment which ought to excite our confidence & affection"—would "feel the mortification of being marked with suspicious incapacitations." "We found in the Course of the Revolution, that many strangers served us faithfully," said Franklin, "and that many natives took part agst. their Country."[18]

Morris's motion for fourteen years failed, 4 to 7; subsequent motions for thirteen years and ten years failed by an identical vote. Then Rutledge made the argument that prevailed: "Surely a longer time is requisite for the Senate, which will have more power," than for the House, with its seven-year citizenship requirement. A motion that nine years of citizenship be required for eligibility to the Senate passed 6 to 4 to 1.[19]

But the issue was not settled. A counterattack on the lengthy citizenship requirement instantly was launched, established a beachhead, and then was massively thwarted. Wilson began on August 9 by pressing for a reconsideration of the seven-year requirement for the House. The next day, the delegates approved without debate his motion to restore the Committee of Detail's figure of three years. The vote was 6 to 5, so close that it prompted a subsequent 9 to 2 decision to take up the question again after the weekend, on August 13.[20]

The Monday debate was dominated by a furious offensive by Gerry and Williamson. Gerry, claiming to speak for many in Massachusetts, said that he "wished that in future the eligibility [to the House] might be confined to Natives." Williamson thought nine years of citizenship for representatives would be better than seven, much less three. Gerry's reasoning was by now familiar—"Persons having foreign attachments will be sent among us & insinuated into our councils"—but Williamson raised a new concern: "He wished this Country to acquire as fast as possible national habits. Wealthy emigrants do more harm by their luxurious examples, than good, by the money, they bring with them."[21]

Alexander Hamilton rose to make Madison's arguments from the week before—that "the advantage of encouraging foreigners was obvious" and that "embarrassing the Govt. with minute restrictions" was unsound constitutional practice—and Madison and Wilson echoed him. Wilson even withdrew his three-year proposal in favor of Hamilton's motion, seconded by Madison, to have the Constitution require of representatives "merely Citizenship & inhabitancy," leaving Congress to decide any future details. But Hamilton's motion failed, 4 to 7, as did Wilson's modified proposal for a four-year requirement (3 to 8). Then Williamson had his turn at nine years (the motion failed 3 to 8), before the delegates gave up and left the House requirement at seven years.[22]

Morris now moved that "any person now a citizen" be exempted from the seven-year citizenship requirement for representatives. Various state constitutions accorded all the rights of citizenship to immigrants after a short period of residency; the new constitution, John Mercer, Madison, and Wilson argued (Madison with special intensity), should not and perhaps legally could not create new and opprobrious limits. Again, however, fears of foreign influence carried the day. "Greater caution wd. be necessary in the outset of the Govt. than afterwards," said Mason, contemplating a first Congress dominated by recent immigrants still loyal to their former countries. "All the great objects wd. be then provided for." If allowed, the "great Houses of British Merchants would spare no pains to insinuate the instruments of their views." Besides, said Rutledge, "It might as well be said that all qualifications are disfranchisemts. and that to require the age of 25 years was a disfranchisement." Morris's motion to protect current citizens from the seven-year House citizenship requirement failed, 5 to 6. So, without debate, did Daniel Carroll's motion to reduce the requirement to five years (3 to 7 to 1). The House qualifications clause—twenty-five years old, seven years a citizen, and an inhabitant of the electing state—then was passed "nem.con."[23]

Having debated qualifications for the House, the delegates showed no interest in Wilson's motion to reduce the nine-year citizenship requirement for senators to seven years. Not even a vote was recorded—the motion simply "was disgd. to." Then, again without debate, the Committee of Detail's modified recommendation for Senate qualifications—thirty years of age, nine years a citizen, and an inhabitant of the electing state—was approved, 8 to 3.[24]

In the midst of the convention's long and heated debate on residency and citizenship requirements for the House and Senate, time was set aside to consider property qualifications for members of all three branches. On August 10, Charles Pinckney complained that the Committee of Detail had not responded to the convention's July 26 injunction to include such a provision in its draft of the Constitution. He did not like the Committee of Detail's recommendation that Congress be empowered to set the property standard, Pinckney said, mainly because the first Congress to be elected under the Constitution might be dominated either by wealthy or by poor members, either of whom would enact a distorted standard. (Again, nothing was said about the president or judges.) Pinckney had seconded the July 26 motion, and he still "thought it essential that the members of the Legislature, the Executive, and the Judges—should be possessed of competent property to make them independent & respectable." He said that his personal preference was for a minimum requirement of $100,000 for the president and $50,000 for legislators and judges, but that he would only move that they "should be required to swear that they were respectively possessed of a clear unincumbered Estate to the amount of _____ in the case of the President, &c &c."[25]

Rutledge, the chairman of the Committee of Detail, seconded Pinckney's motion and apologized that the committee had made no recommendations on property "because they could not agree on any among themselves, being embarrassed by the danger on one side of displeasing the people by making them high, and on the other of rendering them nugatory by making them low." But Ellsworth, a member of the committee, disagreed: "to have either *uniform* or *fixed* qualifications" would, in the former case, ignore regional variations and, in the latter, assure obsolescence. Franklin then attacked the very idea of property qualifications: "Some of the greatest rogues he was ever acquainted with, were the richest rogues."[26]

Pinckney's motion "was rejected by so general a *no*, that the States were not called." But Franklin's argument had unleashed the furies. Madison now urged the delegates to strike as excessive the very committee proposal to let Congress state property qualifications for its members that Pinckney had thought too modest. "Qualifications founded on artificial distinctions may be devised, by the stronger [faction] in order to keep out partizans of a weaker faction," he argued: such had been the case with the British parliament. Gouverneur Morris then put Madison's objection in the form of a motion. It failed, 4 to 7, but only because some delegates wanted to pass a stronger motion that would deny Congress the right to establish any qualifications at all for its members. They prevailed, by a vote of 7 to 3.[27]

Religious faith, like property holding, was a requirement for the office of governor in several but not all states at the time of the Constitutional Convention. Some state constitutions prescribed an adherence to Christianity; others, to Protestant Christianity. North Carolina insisted that its governor be loyal to church and state—no one could hold the office who denied the existence of God, the truth of Protestantism, or the divine authority of scripture or who subscribed to religious principles that were inimical to the peace and safety of the state. In part, these provisions simply reflected conventions of the time; in part, they codified the widely held belief that no oath of office could be taken seriously unless the pledger believed in an ultimate day of judgment.[28]

But the issue of a religious qualification for officeholders was not raised at the convention until August 20, and then only for the purpose of forbidding it. On that day, Charles Pinckney offered a number of suggestions for consideration by the Committee of Detail, including: "No religious test or qualification shall ever be annexed to any oath of office under the authority of the U. S." The committee had not acted favorably by August 30, when its proposal to require that all state and national officials take oaths to support the constitution came up for consideration, so Pinckney took his motion to the convention itself in the form of an amendment to the oath requirement: "but no religious test shall ever be required as a qualification to any office or public trust under the authority of the U. States." Sherman said he "thought it unnecessary, the prevailing liberality being a sufficient security agst. such tests." But Luther Martin, in a postconvention report to the Maryland legislature, fumed that "there were some members *so unfashionable* as to think, that a *belief of the existence of a Deity,* and of a *state of future rewards and punishment* would be some security for the good conduct of our rulers, and that, in a Christian country, it would be *at least decent* to hold out some distinction between the professors of Christianity and downright infidelity or paganism." If there were such members, they were silent: Pinckney's motion passed with no one dissenting.[29]

August 20, the day of Pinckney's initial motion on religious tests, was a day of numerous and miscellaneous motions for consideration by the Committee of Detail. Among them was one by Gerry "that the Committee be instructed to report proper qualifications for the President, and a mode of trying the Supreme Judges in cases of impeachment."[30] Gerry's coupling of two unrelated issues suggests that he may simply have been looking for gaps to fill in the by now well-developed plan of government the convention was writing. But as we shall see, the timing of his motion and of the committee's quick response makes plausible the argument that there now existed in the delegates' minds a need for presidential qualifications that had not existed before. In any event, no debate or discussion accompanied Gerry's motion, which was forwarded to the committee.

On August 22 the Committee of Detail recommended that the Constitution include a requirement that the president be at least thirty-five years old, a United States citizen, and an inhabitant of the United States for no fewer than twenty-one years.[31] The structural parallel between this set of requirements and the qualifications clauses for representatives and senators is obvious, although in the case of the president, simple citizenship and long inhabitancy were demanded, rather than long citizenship and simple inhabitancy. As with Gerry's original motion of two days earlier, however, no debate or vote occurred when the committee made its recommendation.

On September 4, the newly-formed Committee of Eleven (better known as the Committee on Postponed Matters) made a revised recommendation. Now the president would have to be either a "natural born" citizen or "a Citizen of the U— S— at the time of the adoption of this Constitution." He also would have to be fourteen years (rather than twenty-one) a "resident" (not inhabitant) of the United States. Finally, these qualifications, and the unaltered age requirement of thirty-five years, were to be applied at the time that "any person be elected to that office." The convention approved this version unanimously and without debate. In the final copy-edited version of the Constitution that was reported to the convention by the Committee of Style on September 13, the wording of the qualifications clause had undergone some slight revision—notably, the requirements once again were tied to the right of a person to "be eligible to the office"— but no delegate took issue with it.[32]

QUALIFICATIONS FOR PRESIDENT

Why did the convention decide, late and without explanation, to enumerate the qualifications for president?

Both the delegates' longstanding practice during the convention of not setting qualifications for president and their ultimate decision to do so seem to have manifested a consistent principle: a constitution that stated qualifications for those who fill an office need not state qualifications for the office itself; but a constitution that stated no qualifications for the electors must do so for the elected. In the case of Congress, the need for a qualifications clause for members was agreed upon literally from the first day of substantive business, when the convention accepted the Virginia Plan. (Gouverneur Morris later argued: "if qualifications are proper, he would prefer them in the electors rather than the elected"; but although Madison said he agreed in principle, he and virtually all the other delegates disagreed on prudential political grounds: "he was aware of the difficulty of forming any uniform standard that would suit the different circumstances

& opinions prevailing in the different States.")[33] Conversely, in the case of judges, ambassadors, consuls, ministers, heads of departments, "inferior officers," and other public officials mentioned in the Constitution, no qualifications ever were stated or even proposed. None were needed, the delegates seemed to assume, because these positions would be filled by other constitutional officials for whom qualifications had been established.

The presidency received more varied but no less principled treatment from the delegates. During most of the convention they remained wedded to the idea, initially stated in the Virginia Plan, that the chief executive should be chosen by the legislature. Because age, citizenship, and residency requirements had been set for senators and representatives, the delegates saw no need to establish any for the president. Constitutionally qualified legislators could be counted on not to select an unqualified president.

But the delegates did not rest easy with their decision. The convention reconsidered the presidential selection process again and again. The problem for most delegates was, not legislative selection per se, but a corollary decision that, inevitably in their view, flowed from it: the president, if chosen by Congress, must be restricted to a single term. Otherwise, said Mason, there would be too strong a "temptation on the side of the Executive to intrigue with the Legislature for a re-appointment," using political patronage and illegitimate favors to buy votes in Congress. But many delegates came to believe that ineligibility was too high a price to pay for legislative selection: to deny a president the opportunity for reelection would tend, as Morris put it, to destroy the great incitement to merit public esteem by taking away the hope of being rewarded with reappointment. Adding to this intellectual dissatisfaction was a practical concern: How would Congress vote for president? If the House and the Senate were to vote concurrently or by state, the small states would dominate the process, alienating the delegates from large states. But if, as was ultimately decided, the two houses were to vote jointly—one legislator, one vote—the small states saw reason to fear for their interests.[34]

By midsummer, the tide of opinion in the convention clearly had turned against election of the president by Congress. Although it took until September for the framers to agree on an acceptable, nonlegislative alternative, one thing was clear: whoever chose the president, it would not be an electorate for which the Constitution stated qualifications. Hence, the logic of Gerry's motion on August 20 to establish qualifications for president, of the two committees' prompt responses, and of the convention's willingness to adopt a presidential-qualifications clause without controversy.

The delegates' rule of reason on qualifications, then, was applied consistently and uncontroversially to the presidency. As long as legislators, for whom age, residency, and citizenship requirements were stated, were the electors, there was no need to state qualifications for the president; but once the selection of the president was turned over to some other electorate, then qualifications must be established. Such qualifications also would have to be high, in the delegates' terms, because of another set of decisions by the convention and a second principle the delegates deemed relevant. The other set of decisions was to divest the Senate of its sole power, assigned to it during most of the convention, "to make Treaties; send Ambassadors; and to appoint the Judges of the Supreme Court."[35] Late in the convention, in an effort to shore up support for the constitution in the large states whose interests were represented in the House, the Senate's role in treaties and appointments was reduced to confirmation. The presidency then was assigned the responsibilities of negotiation and appointment, which enhanced its constitutional powers significantly. Now the second principle of constitutional qualifications applied: the greater the powers of the office, the higher the qualifications for it must be. Just as would-be senators were forced to meet stiffer requirements for eligibility than were contenders for the House (an axiom stated numerous times during the debates), so would the newly empowered president have to be more qualified than would senators.

AGE

Having decided to establish qualifications for president, the convention never seems to have considered using different categories than those designated for Congress: age, residency, and citizenship. As we will see, within the latter two categories, the delegates altered the character of the congressional qualifications substantially because of unique characteristics they saw in the presidency, but not when it came to age.

Age was the most widely accepted qualification to specify for officeholders. It was the only one mentioned in the Virginia Plan and the only one to prompt no objections during the debates. When it was decided to set a minimum age for the president, thirty-five years no doubt seemed logical: twenty-five for representatives, five additional years for the more powerful senators, another five years for the still more powerful president. Perhaps it is solely coincidence that in July, debating presidential re-eligibility, Wilson used thirty-five as the age of his hypothetical president: "If the Executive should come into office at. 35 years of age, which he presumes may happen & his continuance should be fixt at 15 years. at the age of 50. in the very prime of life, and with all the aid of experience, he must be cast aside like a useless hulk."[36]

The *Federalist,* generally scanty and unrevealing in its treatment of qualifications (it is silent on residency, for example), not only says more about age than any other requirement; it also gives full and honest reflection of the reasoning of the delegates. In number 62, Madison or Hamilton, explaining why qualifications for the Senate are higher than the House, cites "the nature of the senatorial trust, which, requiring greater extent of information and stability of character, requires at the same time that the senator should have reached a period of life most likely to supply these advantages." In number 64, which contains the only passage in the *Federalist* that mentions any presidential qualifications, John Jay argues in connection with the treaty power that "by excluding men under thirty-five from the first office, and those under thirty from the second, it confines the electors to men of whom the people have had time to form a judgment, and with respect to whom they will not be liable to be deceived by those brilliant appearances of genius and patriotism, which, like transient meteors, some times mislead as well as dazzle."[37]

RESIDENCY

The debates on the residency (or inhabitancy—for all the quibbling over the two terms, their meanings are indistinguishable) requirements for members of Congress reveal a consensus within the convention that voters and their chosen legislators should know each other well. Delegates acknowledged, when debating the Committee of Detail's recommendation that representatives and senators be required to live in the states they represented, that seldom would a nonresident be chosen. But they worried about the possibility that, as Mason warned, "Rich men of neighbouring States, may employ with success the means of corruption" to get elected.[38] Concerned but not preoccupied with this possibility, the convention established the residency standard for members of Congress but rejected motions to attach a length requirement.

As with age, once the decision to state qualifications for president had been made, the convention's decisions on Congress provided the model. In the president's case, the concern about residency was more serious, since the only nonresidents of the president's constituency were foreigners or recent expatriates. Not only was the prospect of having such a person occupy the presidency more alarming than having, say, a Virginian represent North Carolina in Congress, but also the War of Independence had produced two especially suspect classes of nonresidents. Foreign military leaders who had come from Europe to help in the Revolution and remained after victory were one such class, notably Baron von Steuben, the Prussian officer who had trained the rank-and-file troops at Valley Forge, endeared himself to them, and even supported their alarming (to most of the delegates) actions in Shays's Rebellion. The other class consisted of Tory sympathizers who had fled to Britain during the war and now had returned. To exclude both groups and, more generally, to express the greater seriousness of presidential qualifications, the delegates attached a substantial length to the residency requirement: twenty-one years in the original Committee of Detail proposal, fourteen years in the revised recommendation of the Committee on Postponed Matters, which ultimately was approved by the delegates.[39]

It is impossible to say with assurance where the twenty-one year figure came from, but it is easy to explain why it was reduced to fourteen years. A twenty-one-year requirement would technically have excluded three of the delegates from eligibility to the presidency, a fourteen-year requirement would have excluded none.[40]

CITIZENSHIP

The written record of the convention barely conceals the passion the delegates brought to their discussions of a citizenship qualification. Not only did they debate the issue longer than any other proposed requirement, but they were also more inclined to tamper with the Committee of Detail's recommendation.

As we saw, the rationale for a lengthy citizenship requirement for legislators was twofold. First, there was the fear, often and fervently expressed, that, as Gerry put it, "persons having foreign attachments will be sent among us and insinuated into our councils, in order to be made instruments for [foreign powers'] purposes." Such apprehensions are understandable in any new nation, but as Madison pointed out, a foreign government bent on subversion would hardly pursue its strategic aims by sending over its own citizens to run for Congress. The second reason (if reason it be called) was rampant xenophobia on the part of many delegates. Immigrants were "adventurers," "tools," "strangers," "dangerous." The Athenians had killed foreigners who spoke at their meetings; to allow aliens into Congress would be like inviting them to sleep with one's wife.[41]

As with the age and residency requirements, the citizenship requirement for legislators was paralleled in the presidential-qualifications clause the committees wrote after the delegates had decided to abandon the policy of legislative selection of the executive. But unlike age and residency requirements, a citizenship requirement probably would have been established for the president even if legislative selection had been preserved.

The presidency they were creating was, the framers realized, the closest analog in the new constitution to a king, just by being a separate, unitary executive. Even before the convention had assembled, Steuben had disseminated a rumor that Nathaniel Gorham, a convention delegate from

New Hampshire who had been president of Congress under the Articles of Confederation, had approached Prince Henry of Prussia about serving as America's king. Similar stories involved the ascendancy of King George's second son, Frederick, Duke of York. During the summer, these rumors gained new currency. The story spread that the convention, whose deliberations were secret, was advancing the plot behind closed doors. So vexatious did the situation become that the delegates momentarily lifted the veil with a leak to the *Pennsylvania Journal*:

> [August 22] We are informed that many letters have been written to the members of the Federal Convention from different quarters, respecting the reports idly circulating that it is intended to establish a monarchical government, to send for [Frederick] &c. &c.—to which it has been uniformly answered, "though we cannot, affirmatively, tell you what we are doing, we can, negatively, tell you what we are not doing—we never once thought of a king."

However effective their squelching of this rumor might be, the delegates knew that the plain fact of an independent executive in the Constitution would prompt further attacks upon its latent monarchical tendencies. If nothing else, they could defuse the foreign-king issue by requiring U.S. citizenship.[42]

Another reason for setting a special citizenship requirement for the presidency was the office's power as commander in chief. With troops at his disposal, it was feared, a foreign subversive, as president, could seize tyrannical power for himself, or alternatively, lay down arms in front of an invading army. John Jay, in New York, sent a letter to this effect to George Washington, president of the convention, on July 25: "Permit me to hint whether it would not be wise and reasonable to provide a strong check on the admission of foreigners into the administration of our National Government, and to declare expressly that the commander in chief of the American Army shall not be given to, nor devolve, upon, any but a natural born citizen."[43]

One cannot be certain when Washington, a former commander in chief himself, read Jay's letter or what effect it had. The record does show, however, that on September 2, Washington replied to Jay: "I thank you for the hints contained in your letter."[44] Two days later, the Committee on Postponed Matters recommended that the president be "a natural born citizen or a citizen of the US at the time of the adoption of this Constitution," a sharp departure from the Committee of Detail's recommendation, made on August 22, that the president merely be "a Citizen of the US."

The provision for "natural born Citizen" probably was aimed at immigrants, although the term is so unusual as to be vague. It is without "conspicuous colonial precedents," Charles Gordon has noted, but it had deep roots in British common law. In medieval times it had embodied the doctrine of jus soli: a natural-born citizen was one born within the realm (on the soil, so to speak). But with increased commerce and travel, Parliament, starting in 1350, seemed to expand the definition of natural born to incorporate the doctrine of jus sanguinis. Now babies born of British citizens abroad or at sea were included as well. One can presume only that Jay and the delegates meant to apply the evolved, broader common-law meaning of the term when they included it in the presidential-qualifications clause. Certainly Jay did not mean to bar his own children, born in Spain and France while he was on diplomatic assignments, from legal eligibility to the presidency.[45]

That living citizens of any nativity were included in the ranks of eligible presidents may have been a concession to the eight delegates who had been born abroad. It may also have reflected the framers' uncertainty about what United States (as distinct from state) citizenship was or when such a thing first had existed. These were issues they deliberately avoided during the convention for fear of provoking hostile reactions from the states during the ratification debates.

The *Federalist* is singularly unhelpful in illuminating the origins of the natural-born citizenship requirement for president. Number 64 mentions the minimum-age standard as being relevant to the president's activities in foreign affairs, but it is utterly silent on citizenship—this in a paper written by Jay! Number 62 offers a reasoned defense of the nine-year qualification for senators, but whether Hamilton or Madison was the author, their remarks at the convention were spirited in opposition to the position stated here: "The term of nine years appears to be a prudent mediocrity between a total exclusion of adopted citizens, whose merits and talents may claim a share in the public confidence, and an indiscriminate and hasty admission of them, which might create a channel for foreign influence on the national councils." And considering Madison's passionate opposition to the long and retroactive citizenship requirement for representatives, it is interesting to see him trumpet in number 52 the openness of the House "to merit of every description, whether native or adoptive."[46]

PHILOSOPHY AND PRAGMATISM

Paragraph 5, the presidential-qualifications clause, owes its origin to the dynamic interplay between political philosophy and political pragmatism that characterized the entire convention. An axiom of good government—that if a constitution does not state qualifications for the electors, then it must do so for the elected—seems to have led the delegates to insert such a clause in the first place. But it was practical politics—namely, the desire not to arouse state resistance to the proposed constitution, that led them not to define eligibility for voters. Philosophical concerns were the basis for the rule that legislative selection and presidential reeligibility were incompatible and for the decision that reeligibility was more important. Again, however, a pragmatic consideration—namely, the difficulty of establishing a legislative selection process that did not favor either the large or the small states—was part of that decision.

Philosophy and pragmatism also were interwoven in the delegates' choice of qualifications. The connection between age and maturity, the principle that voters and their representatives should know each other by having lived together, the desire to protect the nation's independence and sovereignty within the halls of government by excluding any but citizens—these were carefully conceived (if disputable) tenets of good government. But by excluding wartime immigrants and Tory expatriates, a long residency requirement for president served the practical end of not raising unnecessary fears among the ratifying electorate. And to stipulate natural-born citizenship squelched doubts that a foreign prince might be imported to rule.

Finally, pragmatism no doubt contributed to the omission of certain specific qualifications for president from the Constitution. Not to state a property requirement seemed the best way to avoid a controversy between landed interests on the one hand and commercial and manufacturing classes on the other hand that also would have aggravated tensions between North and South, coast and inland, town and country. No doubt any attempt to define a religious qualification in a particular way would have alienated many who wanted it defined differently.

The writing of paragraph 5 illustrates the insight that the delegates to the Constitutional Convention were politicians in the fullest sense of the word. They wanted to develop a plan of republican government that would "bolster the 'National Interest'" by being strong enough to protect liberty but not so strong as to jeopardize it. But they also wanted something they could sell to the people and to the states that would have to ratify their plan if it ever were to go from parchment to practice. The dual requirement for sound political philosophy and shrewd political pragmatism underlay all their efforts.[47] It also provided a necessary, if not sufficient, condition for their success.

NOTES

An earlier version of this chapter appeared in *Presidential Studies Quarterly*, Vol. 17, Spring, 1987. It is reprinted here by permission of the author.

1. Charles Gordon, "Who Can Be President of the United States: The Unresolved Enigma," *Maryland Law Review,* Winter, 1968, p. 132; Joseph E. Kallenbach, *The American Chief Executive: The Presidency and the Governorship* (New York: Harper & Row, 1961), pp. 156–71; Charles C. Thach, Jr., *The Creation of the Presidency, 1775–1789* (Baltimore, Md.: Johns Hopkins University Press, 1923). In this essay, I do not consider the legal issues raised by paragraph 5; see Gordon, "Who Can Be President," and Edward S. Corwin, *The President: Office and Powers, 1787–1957,* 4th ed. (New York: New York University Press, 1961), chap. 2. Nor do I discuss social and cultural barriers to the presidency; see Erwin Hargrove and Michael Nelson, *Presidents, Politics, and Policy* (Baltimore, Md.: Johns Hopkins University Press, 1984), chap. 5.

2. See, e.g., Richard M. Pious, *The American Presidency* (New York: Basic Books, 1979); Christopher H. Pyle and Richard M. Pious, *The President, Congress, and the Constitution* (New York: Free Press, 1984); Joseph M. Bessette and Jeffrey K. Tulis, eds., *The Presidency in the Constitutional Order* (Baton Rouge: Louisiana State University Press, 1981); Stephen J. Wayne, *The Road to the White House,* 2d ed. (New York: St. Martin's Press, 1984); and Nelson W. Polsby and Aaron Wildavsky, *Presidential Elections,* 6th ed. (New York: Charles Scribner's Sons, 1984).

3. Max Farrand, ed., *The Records of the Federal Convention of 1787,* 4 vols. (New Haven, Conn.: Yale University Press, 1911), 2:344, 367, 498, 536, 598. Quotations are almost entirely from James Madison's notes. I have preserved his spelling, punctuation, and use of the third person.

4. Jeffrey Tulis, "The Two Constitutional Presidencies," in *The Presidency and the Political System,* ed. Michael Nelson (Washington, D.C.: Congressional Quarterly Press, 1984), p. 60.

5. Farrand, *Records,* 1:21, 20.

6. Ibid., pp. 217–18, 408, 375.

7. Ibid., p. 428, 2:116–17, 121–26.

8. Kallenbach, *American Chief Executive,* p. 157.

9. Farrand, *Records,* 2:121, 123.

10. Ibid., pp. 123–24.

11. Ibid., pp. 124–25.

12. Ibid., pp. 134, 178–79.

13. Ibid., pp. 216–19.

14. Ibid., pp. 218–29, 239.

15. Ibid., p. 216.

16. Ibid., pp. 235–39, 242.

17. Ibid., pp. 235, 239.

18. Ibid., pp. 235–39.

19. Ibid., pp. 238–39.

20. Ibid., p. 251.

21. Ibid., p. 268.

22. Ibid., pp. 268–69.

23. Ibid., pp. 270–72.

24. Ibid., pp. 272–73.

25. Ibid., pp. 248–49.

26. Ibid., p. 249.

27. Ibid., pp. 249–51. The issue of Congress' right to *set* property qualifications for its members is different from the right of each house of Congress to *judge* the qualifications of its members, a right that each house has. Both provisions were included in the Committee of Detail's draft.

28. Kallenbach, *American Chief Executive*, pp. 157–58.

29. Farrand, *Records*, 2:342, 458, 3:227.

30. Ibid., 2:344.

31. Ibid., p. 367.

32. Ibid., pp. 498, 536, 598.

33. Ibid., pp. 123–24, 201–6.

34. Ibid., 1:68, 2:53; see also Hargrove and Nelson, *Presidents, Politics, and Policy*, pp. 15–18, 32–33; and James L. Sundquist, *Constitutional Reform and Effective Government* (Washington, D.C.: Brookings Institution, 1986), pp. 24–30.

35. Farrand, *Records*, 2:169.

36. Ibid., pp. 102–3.

37. Alexander Hamilton, James Madison, and John Jay, *The Federalist Papers* (New York: New American Library, 1961), pp. 376, 326, 391.

38. Farrand, *Records*, 2:218.

39. Thach, *Creation of the Presidency*, p. 137; Corwin, *The President*, pp. 32–34.

40. Pierce Butler, James McHenry, and Alexander Hamilton. Hamilton had been a resident for fifteen years in 1787.

41. See notes 16, 17, 18, and 21.

42. Richard B. Morris, *Witnesses at the Creation: Hamilton, Madison, Jay, and the Constitution* (New York: New American Library, 1985), pp. 190–91; Cyril C. Means, Jr., "Is Presidency Barred to Americans Born Abroad?" *U.S. News & World Report*, Dec. 23, 1955, pp. 26–30.

43. Farrand, *Records*, 3:161.

44. Ibid., 3:76.

45. Gordon, "Who Can Be President."

46. *Federalist*, pp. 390–96, 376, 326.

47. John P. Roche, "The Founding Fathers: A Reform Caucus in Action," *American Political Science Review* 55 (Dec., 1961): p. 799.

2

DESIGNING THE ELECTORAL COLLEGE

SHLOMO SLONIM

> The Electors shall meet in their respective States and vote by Ballot for two Persons, of whom one at least shall not be an Inhabitant of the same State with themselves. And they shall make a List of the Persons voted for, and of the Number of Votes for each; which List they shall sign and certify, and transmit sealed to the Seat of the Government of the United States, directed to the President of the Senate. . . . The Person having the greatest Number of Votes shall be President.
>
> —*Article II, section 1*

With the bicentennial of the Constitution, attention was once again focused on the drafting of that remarkable instrument of government. Among the provisions of the Constitution deserving of closer examination is the one dealing with the electoral college, the system devised by the founding fathers for the election of a chief executive.[1] No other constitutional provision gave them so much difficulty in its formulation. The subject of the method of electing a president was brought up in the Constitutional Convention on twenty-one different days and occasioned more than thirty distinct votes on various phases of the subject. Over the years, no other provision has drawn so much criticism or provoked so many constitutional amendments as has the electoral-college clause. Close to seven hundred proposals to amend the Electoral College scheme have been introduced into Congress since the Constitution was inaugurated in 1789. The most recent effort to revise the system for electing a president was undertaken in 1979, when a constitutional amendment, moved by Senator Birch E. Bayh, Jr., of Indiana and endorsed by President Jimmy Carter, to institute the popular election of the president, was soundly defeated.[2]

Two main interpretations have been put forward to explain the adoption of the electoral-college provision. On the one hand, the Progressive school, represented by such writers as J. Allen Smith and Charles A. Beard, maintained that the complicated indirect method instituted for selecting a chief executive was a reflection of the founders' deep distrust of democracy. The framers, according to that view, deliberately precluded the popular choice of the president to ensure that the leveling force of the masses would not threaten the rights of the propertied minority. That economic-determinist thesis has, in turn, been vigorously challenged by political scientist John P. Roche, who has asserted that the electoral college was but a last-minute compromise designed to allow the Constitutional Convention to wind up its business. It was merely a "jerry-rigged improvisation . . . subsequently . . . endowed with a high theoretical content. . . . No one seemed to think well of the college as an institution. . . . The future was left to cope with the problem of what to do with this Rube Goldberg mechanism."[3]

Roche's antideterminist interpretation clearly denies an overall design to the electoral college; it was in the nature of a makeshift contraption. That is not, however, the way contemporaries viewed the electoral college. According to Abraham Baldwin, delegate for Georgia (as reported by John Pickering), "late in their session the present complex mode of electing the President and Vice-President was proposed; that the mode was perfectly novel, and therefore occasioned a pause; but when explained and fully considered was universally admired, and viewed as the most pleasing feature in the Constitution." And Alexander Hamilton, in *Federalist* number 68, wrote: "The mode of appointment of the Chief Magistrate of the United States is almost the only part of the system, of any consequence, which has escaped without severe censure, or which has received the slightest mark of approbation from its opponents. . . . I venture somewhat further, and hesitate not to affirm that if the manner of it be not perfect, it is at least excellent." Max Farrand, in his succinct work *The Framing of the Constitution of the United States,* sums up the attitude of the framers toward the electoral college: "For of all things done in the convention the members seemed to have been prouder of that than of any other, and they seemed to regard it as having solved the problem for any country of how to choose a chief magistrate."[4]

The true rationale and purpose of the electoral-college scheme can best be unraveled by a close examination of the Constitutional Convention debates. By following the tortuous course the framers took during the summer months of 1787, we can gain insight into the influences that led them to institute such a complex procedure for selecting a president. The records of the convention debates also shed light on the extent to which the founding fathers were consciously guided by such factors as prevailing political theories and past republican practices—ancient or modern. In particular, how prominently did the state constitutional precedents figure in the deliberations at Philadelphia? Did the other well-known clashes at the convention—large states versus small states, federalists versus nationalists, slaveholders versus nonslaveholders—inform the electoral-college debates? A detailed analysis of the 1787 discussions should also help to explain why the electoral-college scheme encountered so little criticism in the state ratifying conventions.[5]

Both the Virginia Plan and the New Jersey Plan, the foundation documents of the Constitution, called for the election of the executive by the legislature, as was the practice in all but three of the states. In two of the three states where the choice was by popular election, in the event that no candidate received a clear majority, the choice would fall on the legislature. During the debates the delegates frequently referred to this pattern of state practice.[6]

That both the Virginia Plan and the New Jersey Plan endorsed selection by the legislature did not mean that they were at one on the mode of election. The legislature, in each case, was a very different body. Whereas the Virginia Plan provided for a popularly elected legislature, with the representation of each state being proportional to the size of its population, the New Jersey Plan proposed that the legislature remain (as under the Articles of Confederation) the representative body of the states, with each state entitled to one vote. Thus, while the Virginia Plan called for a "National Executive" to be chosen by the "National Legislature," the New Jersey Plan envisaged a "federal Executive" to be appointed by "the U. States in Congs." In effect, therefore, at the very outset of the convention, the large states and the small states were at loggerheads over the method of selecting an executive no less than they were over the composition of the legislature.[7]

When, on June 1, the convention moved to debate the scheme outlined in the Virginia Plan for the selection of the executive (the New Jersey Plan was first submitted on June 15), three distinct, but interrelated, issues arose for discussion: (1) the mode of election; (2) the term of office; and (3) the question of reeligibility. The three issues formed a sort of tripod on which an imbalance on one side would disrupt the balance of the whole. Because the executive was to be elected by the legislature, it was deemed essential that he not be eligible for reelection, for reeligibility would compromise his independence; but if he was to serve only one term, then it ought to be a reasonably lengthy one. The relationship between reeligibility and the term of office was stressed throughout the debate. James Wilson favored a three-year term "on the supposition that a re-eligibility would be provided for." This was endorsed by Roger Sherman who was "agst. the doctrine of [compulsory] rotation as throwing out of office the men best qualified to execute its duties." George Mason, on the other hand, favored "seven years at least" and a prohibition on reeligibility "as the best expedient both for preventing the effect of a false complaisance on the side of the Legislature towards unfit characters; and a temptation on the side of the Executive to intrigue with the Legislature for a re-appointment." In short order the convention, by a vote of 8 to 2, endorsed Mason's viewpoint (moved by Charles Pinckney) and decided that the executive should be chosen by the legislature for a seven-year term without the right of reelection.[8] This was but the first of many times that the convention would settle for this formula.

In the course of the debate, two diverse, even conflicting challenges were directed at the proposed scheme. Wilson, a delegate from Pennsylvania and "a nationalist of the nationalists," advocated the popular election of the executive. That system of electing "the first magistrate," he declared, though "it might appear chimerical," was really "a convenient & successful mode," as the experience of New York and Massachusetts had proven. On the next day, June 2, Wilson submitted a motion to divide the states into districts, the voters in each district to choose electors who, in turn, would select the "Executive Magistracy." (The intervention of electors did not, apparently, make it any less "an election by the people" in Wilson's eyes.) In supporting his proposal, Wilson argued for "an election without the intervention of the States." His suggestion evoked interest but also considerable skepticism. Thus Mason said he favored the idea but thought it "impracticable." Similarly, Elbridge Gerry of Massachusetts said he "liked the principle" but feared that "it would alarm & give a handle to the State partizans, as tending to supersede altogether the State authorities."[9]

And indeed, at that very sitting, one of the convention's foremost "State partizans," John Dickinson of Delaware, moved "that the Executive be made removable by the National Legislature on the request of a majority of the Legislatures of individual States." "He had no idea of abolishing the State Governments as some gentlemen seemed inclined to do. . . . He hoped that each State would retain an equal voice at least in one branch of the National Legislature." James Madison and Wilson both objected to Dickinson's motion on the ground, *inter alia,* "that it would leave an equality of agency in the small with the great States."[10]

Neither Wilson's nor Dickinson's motion was received with much sympathy (the votes were 2 to 8 and 1 to 9, respectively). But these divergent suggestions reflected a contrast of views on the measure of state control that should be exercised in the selection of the executive. In the eyes of such a nationalist as Wilson, even election by the legislature detracted from the national independent stature of the executive, whereas for Dickinson the states were not accorded adequate control over the nation's chief executive officer. The two viewpoints, in one shape or another, arose repeatedly during the numerous discussions the convention was to hold on the mode of electing an executive. Dickinson's comment on the composition of the legislature foreshadowed, at this early stage of the discussions, the growing dissatisfaction of the smaller states, with their diminished role in the organs of government.[11]

On June 15 (some two weeks after Dickinson's address), William Paterson presented the New Jersey Plan to the convention, and the issue of the small states versus the large states was joined. The controversy was not settled until July 7, after three weeks of protracted discussions. The Connecticut Compromise, which emerged, resolved the issue of the composition of the legislature.[12] But had it equally settled the procedure for the election of the executive? At first glance it would appear that it had done so, since the convention's earlier decision to provide for election of the executive by the legislature remained intact. Delegates could not but realize, however, that the new legislature was a creature very different from the body that had previously been entrusted with the task of selecting an executive. For one thing, the upper house now represented the states. Further, as a result of the principle of equality of representation in the upper house, the smaller state would exercise willy-nilly an inordinate influence on the selection of a chief executive. It is perhaps not surprising, therefore, that no sooner had the convention adopted the Connecticut Compromise than the issue of the mode of electing the chief executive arose once again.

On July 17, Gouverneur Morris, one of the "leading conservatives" of the convention and probably its "most brilliant member," criticized the earlier decision to leave the selection of the nation's chief magistrate in the hands of the legislature. He moved to insert, in place of "National Legislature," "citizens of U.S."

He will be the mere creature of the Legisl: if appointed & impeach-able by that body. He ought to be elected by the people at large, by the freeholders of the country. . . . If the people should elect, they will never fail to prefer some man of distinguished character, or services; some man . . . of continental reputation. If the Legislature elect, it will be the work of intrigue, of cabal, and of faction.[13]

Wilson supported Morris's motion for popular election and dismissed the argument that a majority of the people might be unable to agree on any one candidate. In such event, he said, the expedient used in Massachusetts could be employed, with the legislature choosing between the leading candidates. "This would restrain the choice to a good nomination at least, and prevent in a great degree intrigue & cabal." In response, Pinckney of South Carolina highlighted the fears of the smaller states:

[He] did not expect this question would again have been brought forward; An Election by the people being liable to the most obvious &

striking objections. They will be led by a few active & designing men. The most populous States by combining in favor of the same individual will be able to carry their points.

Sherman of Connecticut also voiced the concern of the small states:

The sense of the Nation would be better expressed by the Legislature, than by the people at large. The latter will never be sufficiently informed of characters, and besides will never give a majority of votes to any one man. They will generally vote for some man in their own State, and the largest State will have the best chance for the appointment.[14]

The smaller states clearly were concerned that in a straight-out popular election the larger states would overwhelm them. The smaller states had not fought for equality in one branch of the legislature only to see control of the executive go by default.

Mason of Virginia (a large state) did not share the fears of the small states. Nonetheless, he was sharply critical of the suggestion for the nationwide popular election of the executive. He graphically portrayed the inability of the people to select a national figure:

He conceived it would be as unnatural to refer the choice of a proper character for chief Magistrate to the people, as it would, to refer a trial of colours to a blind man. The extent of the country renders it impossible that the people can have the requisite capacity to judge of the respective pretensions of the Candidates.[15]

This passage is frequently cited as evidence of the framers' lack of faith in democracy. If the words are examined in their context, however, it is evident that Mason was not challenging the *right* of the people to choose but, rather, their *ability* to do so, given the size of the electoral district within which they would have to exercise that right. The vast expanse of the United States, the difficulty of communication, and the unfamiliarity of the general populace with national personalities—all militated against an informed choice. In fact, as noted above, Mason had earlier expressed himself in favor of popular election, but he considered it "impractical," for the reasons, no doubt, that he now enumerated by reference to "the extent of the Country." As Cecelia M. Kenyon, in discussing the stand of the Antifederalists, has written:

This belief that larger electoral districts would inevitably be to the advantage of the well-to-do partially explains the almost complete lack of criticism of the indirect election of the Senate and the President. If the "middling" class could not be expected to compete successfully with the upper class in Congressional elections, still less could they do so in state-wide or nation-wide elections. It was a matter where size was of the essence. True representation . . . could be achieved only where electoral districts were small.

It was in this sense that Mason, for one, found fault with nationwide elections of the executive. Under the circumstances, the popular election of the executive would have the trappings of representative democracy but not the essence.[16]

The final speaker on Gouverneur Morris's proposal for the popular election of the executive was Hugh Williamson of North Carolina, who added a new slant to the discussions. He reiterated the point made by the earlier speakers that "the people will be sure to vote for some man in their own State, and the largest State will be sure to succede." He went on to say, "This will not be [Virginia] however. Her slaves will have no suffrage." Williamson was referring to a key advantage that the slave states presently enjoyed in the projected lower house, in which slaves counted three-fifths for purposes of representation. If a system for the direct popular election of the executive were instituted, the slave states would stand to lose that advantage because only the enfranchised white population could actually vote, and the increment derived from the slaves would be lost. In effect, the adoption of the Connecticut Compromise had forged a natural alliance between the small states and the slave states in reserving decisions for the legislature as currently constituted. The slave states would gain an advantage in the lower house, and the smaller states would gain one in the Senate (small slave states, such as the Carolinas, had a double advantage). It is hardly surprising, therefore, that Morris's motion for popular election was rejected by a vote of 1 to 9, with only his own state, Pennsylvania, voting in favor. Luther Martin of Maryland then proposed that the executive be chosen by electors appointed by the state legislatures. The proposal was defeated by a vote of 2 to 8. The election of the executive by the legislature was thereupon unanimously reendorsed.[17]

At this point, however, the convention took a peculiar step. As matters stood on July 17, the executive was (1) to be elected by the legislature, (2) to serve for seven years, and (3) to be ineligible for a second term. The latter two provisions were designed to ensure the executive's independence of the legislature. But now, William Houstoun of Georgia moved that the clause on ineligibility be struck out. Morris supported the motion because ineligibility, he argued, "tended to destroy the great motive to good behavior, the hope of being rewarded by a re-appointment. It was saying to him, make hay while the sun shines." The argument apparently impressed the other delegates, who proceeded, by a vote of 6 to 4, to strike out the ineligibility clause. Such a move, however, meant that one leg of the tripod was out of balance, since the legislature was now in a position to exert undue influence on the executive, who was beholden to it for reelection. By the same token, because the executive could serve more than once, a term as long as seven years was no longer warranted. Various delegates thus suggested the substitution of a shorter term. Others, however, maintained that the only way to ensure the executive's independence was to provide that he serve "during good behavior." The latter proposal was vigorously condemned by Mason, who "considered an Executive during good behavior as a softer name only for an Executive for life . . . the next would be an easy step to hereditary Monarchy." The motion for instituting "good behavior" was defeated by a vote of 6 to 4, and the seven-year term was retained by the same margin. Clearly, the delegates were much troubled by the difficulty of maintaining the balance of the tripod arrangement. Endowing the legislature with authority to reelect the executive would compromise the latter's independence and pose problems in fixing the term of office. All this prompted thoughts that only by removing the selection of the executive from the legislature could the tripod be secured firmly. This idea, among others, surfaced in the full-dress debate on the issue held on July 19.[18]

Martin of Maryland opened the discussion with a proposal that the clause barring a second term be reinserted. He was supported by Edmund Randolph of Virginia, who stressed the need to ensure the executive's independence. "If he ought to be independent, he should not be left under a temptation to court a re-appointment. If he should be re-appointable by the Legislature, he will be no check on it." Randolph warned the smaller states that reeligibility would work to their disadvantage, in particular, since the executive would undoubtedly court the larger states to ensure his reelection.[19]

Gouverneur Morris vigorously challenged Martin's proposal. Once again, Morris advocated the popular election of the executive, coupled with a right of reeligibility. "If he is to be the Guardian of the people let him be appointed by the people." In a lengthy address he extolled the virtues of popular election: "The Executive Magistrate should be the guardian of the people, even of the lower classes, agst. Legislative tyranny, against the Great & the wealthy who in the course of things will necessarily compose—the Legislative body. . . . The Executive therefore ought to be so constituted as to be the great protector of the Mass of the people." He recommended biennial elections of the executive, and in conclusion, he noted that popular election would make the plan of the constitution "extremely palatable to the people." Both Rufus King of Massachusetts and Paterson of New Jersey also endorsed popular election but feared that the people might not be able to settle on any one man. To obviate this difficulty they suggested "an appointment by electors chosen by the people for the purpose." At this point Wilson remarked that he "perceived with pleasure that the idea was gaining ground, of an election mediately or immediately by the people." Only Gerry spoke out against popular election, regarding it as "the worst [mode] of all." "The people are uninformed," he declared, "and would be misled by a few designing men." But even Gerry endorsed the notion of electors, except that he would entrust their selection to the state executives rather than to the state legislatures.[20]

Madison inveighed strongly against any role by the legislature in the selection of the executive since such an arrangement would tend to "establish an improper connection between the two departments." During the debate of two days earlier, he had argued against reelection by the legislature: "A dependence of the Executive on the Legislature, would render it the Executor as well as the maker of laws; & then according to the observation of Montesquieu, tyrannical laws may be made that they may be executed in a tyrannical manner." In the current debate Madison expressed doubts whether "an appointment in the 1st. instance even with an ineligibility afterwards would not establish an improper connection between the two departments." Inevitably, it would produce "intrigues and contentions." He therefore favored lodging the appointment in some other source. "The people at large was in his opinion the fittest in itself." Madison acknowledged, however, "one difficulty . . . of a serious nature attending an immediate choice by the people: The right of suffrage was much more diffusive in the Northern than the Southern States; and the latter could have no influence in the election on the score of the Negroes. The substitution of electors obviated this difficulty and seemed on the whole to be liable to the fewest objections."[21]

Madison's reference to the disparity of eligible voters between the North and the South highlighted, of course, the advantage the latter enjoyed under the three-fifths rule. The use of electors on something less than a directly proportionate scale would help preserve the relative advantage of the South (and of the smaller states). In this spirit, Oliver Ellsworth of Connecticut moved that in place of "appointmt. by the Natl. Legislature" there be inserted "to be chosen by electors appointed by the Legislatures of the States in the following ratio": each state with less than 100,000 population—one vote; between 100,000 and 300,000—two votes; and above 300,000—three votes. Since the ratio was 1:3, no southern or small state had cause to feel disadvantaged, and it is not surprising, therefore, that the convention summarily proceeded to endorse the system of electors by a vote of 6 to 4. For the first time in the course of the deliberations, the legislature had been excluded from the process of selecting the executive. And with the removal of the legislature, the convention felt free to restore the reeligibility clause. The term of office was fixed at six years, and members of the legislature were forbidden to serve as electors.[22] Now the provision for choosing an executive was, in certain key features, approaching the ultimate form that would emerge from the convention.

But barely three days later, on July 23, doubts were expressed with regard to the system of electors just adopted. Houstoun "urged the extreme inconveniency & the considerable expense, of drawing together men from all the States for the single purpose of electing the Chief Magistrate." Obviously, it was envisaged that the electors under the scheme adopted would assemble in some central location to cast their votes. On the next day, July 24, Houstoun moved that the system of electors be abandoned in favor of restoring to the legislature the choice of the executive. "He dwelt chiefly on the improbability, that capable men would undertake the service of Electors from the more distant States." Houstoun was supported by Williamson, who argued that "the proposed Electors would certainly not be men of the 1st. nor even the 2d. grade in the States. These would all prefer a seat in the Senate or the other branch of the Legislature." Interestingly, Gerry dismissed Houstoun's fears and urged the retention of the system of electors "The best men," he declared, would be honored to be electors, since "the election of the Executive Magistrate will be considered as of vast importance and will excite great earnestness." Nonetheless, Houstoun's motion was carried by a vote of 7 to 4.[23]

Thereupon Martin and Gerry moved to reinstate the ineligibility clause. Any involvement of the legislature in the selection of the executive would compromise his independence, they maintained. "The longer the duration of his appointment the more will his dependence be diminished," said Gerry. "It will be better then for him to continue 10, 15, or even 20—years and be ineligible afterwards." Others proposed an eight- or eleven-year term of office. King recommended a twenty-year term, since "this is the medium life of princes." In a footnote Madison remarked, "This might possibly be meant as a caricature of the previous motions in order to defeat the object of them." Williamson favored a seven-year term without eligibility for reelection, but he would not object to a ten- or twelve-year term. "It was pretty certain he thought that we should at some time or other have a King; but he wished no precaution to be omitted that might postpone the event as long as possible."[24]

Once again the convention was thrown into disarray in its efforts to settle on a system for electing the executive that would not leave him overly dependent on the legislature. Balancing the tripod—the mode of election, the term of office, and reeligibility—was proving to be an extremely difficult task. Gerry summed up the frustration of the delegates when he said, "We seem to be entirely at a loss on this head." He recommended that the problem be referred to the Committee of Detail, which was to be set up. "Perhaps they will be able to hit on something that may unite the various opinions which have been thrown out." Wilson, acknowledging "the difficulties & perplexities into which the House is thrown," proposed a scheme whereby a small group, drawn by lot from the legislature, would retire to make the choice "and not to separate until it be made." "By this mode intrigue would be avoided . . . and . . . dependence . . . diminished." Gouverneur Morris warned the convention against denying the executive a right of reelection. "He will be in possession of the sword, a civil war will ensue." Wilson's proposal, he said, was worth considering. "It would be better that chance sd. decide than intrigue." Regardless, the delegates were not inclined to accept Wilson's novel suggestion precisely because it left too much to chance.[25]

On the next day, July 25, Ellsworth moved that the executive be selected by the legislature except when the incumbent stood for reelection. In that case the choice would fall to electors appointed by the state legislatures. Thereupon Madison delivered a lengthy address on the subject: "There are objections agst. every mode that has been, or perhaps can be proposed. The election must be made either by some existing authority under the Natil. or State Constitutions—or by some special authority derived from the people—or by the people themselves." The legislature, he declared, was "liable to insuperable objections." Besides compromising the independence of the executive, conferring the choice on the legislature would (1) "agitate & divide the legislature"; (2) lead to intrigues between the executive and "the predominant faction" within the legislature; and (3) result in foreign meddling in the election. He was also opposed to entrusting the selection of the national executive to the states, whether the choice devolved on their legislatures or on their executives. In conclusion, said Madison, the choice lay between direct elections and the use of electors. In the latter case, "as the electors would be chosen for the occasion, would meet at once, & proceed immediately to an appointment, there would be very little opportunity for cabal, or corruption. As a further precaution, it might be required that they should meet at some place, distinct from the seat of Govt." But since that mode had just been rejected, there was little purpose in proposing it anew. There remained "election by the people or rather by the qualified part of them at large. With all its imperfections he liked this best." He recognized, however, that there were two serious difficulties with this method. "The first arose from the disposition in the people to prefer a Citizen of their own State, and the disadvantage this wd. throw on the smaller States." Madison expressed the hope "that some expedient might be hit upon that would obviate" that possibility. "The second difficulty arose from the disproportion of qualified voters in the N. & S. States, and the disadvantages which this mode would throw on the latter." The latter handicap, he surmised, would be overcome with the passage of time as the population of the South increased. In any case, "local considerations must give way to the general interest." Madison declared that as a southerner "he was willing to make the sacrifice."[26]

Madison's remarks served to highlight the underlying causes of the opposition to the popular election of the executive—the disadvantage from which both the smaller and the southern states would suffer. The fact was confirmed when, immediately after Madison had concluded his remarks, Ellsworth (one of the authors of the Connecticut Compromise) declared, "The objection drawn from the different sizes of the States, is unanswerable. The Citizens of the largest States would invariably prefer the Candidate within the State; and the largest States wd. invariably have the man." The same theme was taken up by Williamson, who said "an election of the Executive by the Legislature . . . opened a door for foreign influence. The principal objection agst. an election by the people seemed to be, the disadvantage under which it would place the smaller States." He suggested that as a "cure," each person should vote for three candidates, two of which would presumably be from states other than his own "and as probably of a small as a large one."[27]

Both Gouverneur Morris and Madison liked Williamson's idea. Morris suggested that "each man should vote for *two* persons one of whom at least should not be of his own State." Madison endorsed Morris's amendment and said that the effect would be that "the second best man in this case would probably be the first, in fact." He expressed fears, however, that after having voted for his favorite candidate, each citizen would throw away his second vote on some obscure person "in order to ensure the object of his first choice. But it could hardly be supposed that the Citizens of many States would be so sanguine of having their favorite elected, as not to give their second vote with sincerity to the next object of their choice."[28]

Dickinson suggested a means to combine popular election and selection by the legislature. He declared that he "had long leaned towards an election by the people which he regarded as the best and purest source." The difficulty arose "from the partiality of the States to their respective Citizens." But could this "partiality" not be put to use in the search for an executive magistrate? Let the citizens of each state select their favorite son, and from the thirteen candidates thus nominated, let the legislature, or the electors appointed by it, make the final choice.[29] Because Dickinson did not submit a formal proposal, his scheme never came to a vote. But it did raise the possibility of dividing the nominating and selection procedure so that the legislature would make the final choice from a list of candidates nominated in the states. The procedure was clearly patterned on the contingency arrangements under the Massachusetts and New Hampshire constitutions in the event that no gubernatorial candidate received a popular majority.

The complexity of the task involved in formulating a mode of election was never better demonstrated than at this stage of the debate, which extended over several days. The convention voted down seriatim various ideas that had been put forward during the course of the debate. Thus Ellsworth's suggestion that in cases where an incumbent was standing for election, the choice be left to state-appointed electors rather than to the national legislature was turned down by a vote of 4 to 7. And Williamson's popular-election proposal (as amended), whereby each person would vote for two candidates, one of whom would not be a citizen of his own state, was defeated by the narrow vote of 5 to 6. A motion by Charles Pinckney for a system of rotation, so that no person could serve as executive for more than six years out of twelve, was defeated by the same close margin.[30] The convention adjourned on July 25 without having decided on either the term of office or the matter of reeligibility The only element that now stood was the decision to have the legislature make the choice.

On the next day, July 26, Mason delivered a lengthy oration in support of restoring once again the seven-year term, coupled with ineligibility. He emphasized "the difficulty of the subject and the diversity of the opinions concerning it [that] have appeared. Nor have any of the modes of constituting that department been satisfactory." Earlier in the debate, Pierce Butler of South Carolina and Gerry of Massachusetts had both vigorously challenged the idea of the popular election of the executive. "The Govt. should not be made so complex & unwieldy as to disgust the States. This would be the case, if the election shd. be referred to the people," declared Butler. According to Gerry, the proposal for "popular election in this case" was "radically vicious. The ignorance of the people would put it in the power of some one set of men dispersed through the Union & acting in Concert to delude them into any appointment. He observed that such a Society of men existed in the Order of the Cincinnati." Mason, in challenging the various proposals that had surfaced, also repeated his earlier opposition to popular election. Such an election would mean "that an act which ought to be performed by those who know most of Eminent characters, & qualifications, should be performed by those who know least." He was also unable to support Williamson's suggestion that each person vote for several candidates since he was convinced that it "would throw the appointment into the hands of the Cincinnati," as Gerry had observed. The suggestions that the choice be made by the state legislatures or by special electors had all been found wanting. Nor had the idea of a "lottery" produced "much demand" for its "tickets," said Mason. He concluded, therefore, that "an election by the Natl Legislature as originally proposed, was the best" (that is, for a single term of seven years). In opposing reelection he declared:

Having for his primary object, for the pole star of his political conduct, the preservation of the rights of the people, he held it as an essential point, as the very palladium of Civil liberty, that the great officers of State, and particularly the Executive should at fixed periods return to that mass from which they were at first taken, in order that they may feel & respect those rights & interests, Which are again to be personally valuable to them.[31]

These remarks prompted a rare comment by Benjamin Franklin:

It seems to have been imagined by some that the returning to the mass of the people was degrading the magistrate. This he thought was contrary to republican principles. In free Governments the rulers are the servants, and the people their superiors & sovereigns. For the former therefore to return among the latter was not to *degrade* but to *promote* them—and it would be imposing an unreasonable burden on them, to keep them always in a State of servitude, and not allow them to become again one of the Masters.

In response, Gouverneur Morris said:

In answer to Docr. Franklin, that a return into the mass of the people would be a promotion. instead of a degradation, he had no doubt that our Executive like most others would have too much patriotism to shrink from the burden of his office, and too much modesty not to be willing to decline the promotion.

At the same time, Morris pronounced himself opposed to the whole paragraph on the selection of the executive if reeligibility were denied. Despite that objection, the convention adopted Mason's proposal by a vote of 7 to 3 to 1 and reendorsed selection by the legislature, for a seven-year term, without the right of reelection. This formula was taken up in late July by the five-member Committee of Detail for incorporation into the draft constitution that it was to prepare.[32]

Although the convention had decided on election by the legislature, no one had broached the question of whether it was to be by a joint ballot of both houses (voting together) or by each house acting separately. In the eight states in which the legislature chose the executive, the election was by both houses jointly. Other state officials, however, were chosen according to the regular legislative procedure, with each house exercising a veto. The latter arrangement for the selection of a president would give the states, especially the smaller states, substantial leverage in the choice of the executive. One document by the Committee of Detail in the Farrand collection hints that the committee experienced considerable difficulty in settling the matter. Randolph, a member of the committee, had originally written that the executive shall be elected "by joint ballot." Subsequently, "joint" had been crossed out, and Randolph had added to an emendation of South Carolina's John Rutledge the words "& in each Ho. havg a Negative on the other." However, the final report of the Committee of Detail, issued on August 6, reverted to the simple form that had been adopted by the convention plenum, namely, "He shall be elected by ballot by the Legislature." The relevant provision (X) on the election of an executive (for the first time labeled "The President of the United States") read as follows: "He shall be elected by ballot by the Legislature. He shall hold his office during the term of seven years; but shall not be elected a second time."[33]

When the convention on August 7 took up the committee's report, the issue of electing the president arose in the discussion of the procedures of the legislature (for the first time called the "Congress"). According to Article III of the draft constitution, each house "shall, in all cases, have a negative on the other." Mason expressed doubts regarding "the propriety of giving each branch a negative on the other 'in all cases.'" He assumed that there were some cases in which no negative was intended, "as in the case of balloting for appointments." Morris moved to insert "legislative acts" in place of "all cases." Sherman objected that such wording would "exclude a mutual negative in the case of ballots." Nathaniel Gorham of Massachusetts supported election by joint ballot and cited the difficulties experienced in his own state in selecting officers because of separate balloting by each house of the state legislature. "If separate ballots should be made for the President, and the two branches should be each attached to a favorite, great delay, contention & confusion may ensue." Wilson also advocated a joint ballot, "particularly in the choice of the President. Disputes between the two Houses, during & concerng the vacancy of the Executive, might have dangerous consequences," he declared. Nonetheless, Morris's motion failed to carry by a tie vote, 5 to 5. In the meantime, however, Madison argued that a provision spelling out a negative by one house on the other was in any case unnecessary since the same was implied by the very existence of a bicameral legislature. Madison's motion to strike out the reference to a mutual negative in the legislature carried by a vote of 7 to 3.[34] Since the powers of each house were left unchanged, the vote in effect postponed a decision on the matter of legislative balloting for the office of president.

When on August 24 the convention took up the provision on the election of the executive in the report of the Committee of Detail, the delegates were once again divided on the procedure of balloting by the legislature. The previous week, on August 17, a similar clash had arisen over the appointment of the treasurer by the legislature (as envisaged under the report of the Committee of Detail). Gorham had moved to insert "joint" before "ballot." "Mr [Roger] Sherman opposed it as favoring the larger States." Nonetheless, Gorham's amendment was upheld by a vote of 7 to 3. Now Rutledge moved to make the election of the executive also by "joint" ballot "as the most convenient mode of electing." But, as on the previous occasion, Sherman objected to the motion "as depriving the *States* represented in the *Senate* of the negative intended them in that house." Gorham again responded that "it was wrong to be considering, at every turn whom the Senate would represent. The public good was the true object to be kept in view." His words, in turn, drew the following retort from Jonathan Dayton of New Jersey: "It might be well for those not to consider how the Senate was constituted, whose interest it Was to keep it out of sight.—If the amendment should be agreed to," he declared, "a *joint* ballot would in fact give the appointment to one House. He could never agree to the clause with such an amendment."[35] At this point, Daniel Carroll of Maryland, with the support of James Wilson, vainly tried to have election "by the people" inserted in place of "by the Legislature." The motion was quickly dismissed by a vote of 2 to 9.

Reverting to the proposal for a joint ballot, David Brearley of New Jersey, in opposing the proposal, reminded the delegates that "the argument that the small States should not put their hands into the pockets of the large ones did not apply in this case." This was a reference to the demand of the larger states that money bills originate in the House of Representatives and not be subject to amendment in the Senate. That arrangement had formed an essential part of the Connecticut Compromise. In effect, Brearley was arguing that, unlike money bills, which affected the larger and wealthier states more directly and which were, therefore, left to the determination of the lower house, the selection of an executive concerned all states, smaller no less than larger, and was therefore a legitimate subject for Senate control. In contrast, Wilson "urged the reasonableness of giving the larger States a larger share of the appointment, and the danger of delay from a disagreement of the two Houses." He also pointed out that the Senate had a privileged position in other spheres, "balancing the advantage given by a joint balot in this case to the other branch of the Legislature." Madison pointed out that even with a joint ballot, the larger states would still not exercise influence commensurate with their size. "The rule of voting will give to the largest State, compared with the smallest, an influence as 4 to 1 only, altho the population is as 10 to 1." This, declared Madison, "cannot be unreasonable as the President is to act for the *people* not for the *States*." But the most telling speech in favor of a joint ballot was delivered by John Langdon of New Hampshire. In his home state, he declared, "the mode of separate votes by the two Houses was productive of great difficulties. . . . He was for inserting 'joint' tho' unfavorable to N. Hampshire as a small State." The proposal for a joint ballot of both houses was accepted by a vote of 7 to 4, with two small states (New Hampshire and Delaware) breaking ranks and voting with the large states. The smaller states did not concede defeat, however. Immediately after the vote, Dayton of New Jersey, seconded by Brearley of the same state, moved to insert after "Legislature" the words "each State having one vote." The motion failed, by the close vote of 5 to 6.[36] (Delaware, in this instance, sided with its natural allies, the smaller states.)

It was now Gouverneur Morris's turn to express displeasure at the decision of the convention. The executive, he complained, can never be truly independent if he is chosen by the legislature. "Cabal & corruption are attached to that mode of election: so also is ineligibility a second time . . . rivals would be continually intriguing to oust the President from his place." He proposed that as a means of guarding against "all these evils," the president "be chosen by Electors to be chosen by the people of the several States." His motion was defeated by the close vote of 5 to 6 in one vote and by a split vote, 4 to 4 to 2 (1 absent) on a second try.[37]

But the convention was apparently still not satisfied with the arrangements it had settled on for choosing the president. Although it had confirmed election by the legislature in joint ballot, it was not yet ready to determine with finality the term of office or the reeligibility issue. Those matters were postponed, at the suggestion of the New Jersey delegation, to the next day, August 25.[38] The matter was not broached then, however, and apparently the convention preferred to let the issue ride.

The convention's continuing vacillation and soul-searching on the whole subject was subsequently revealed when on August 31 the delegates took up for consideration Article XXIII of the draft constitution. That provision described the procedures for instituting the government, including a direction to Congress to "choose the President of the United States." Morris moved to strike those words out of the provision, "this point, of choosing the President not being yet finally determined." The clause was struck out by the rather surprising vote of 9 to 1 to 1 (one state divided). Clearly the convention had not yet pronounced the last word on the method of selecting a president. The delegates, even at this late stage, were still groping for a solution free of the serious shortcomings raised against every single method proposed to date. At the conclusion of the day's session, the issue of the election of a president, together with all other pieces of unfinished business, were referred to a committee composed of a representative from each state. Apparently the convention was hoping that the members of the committee, as Gerry had put it, would be able to come up with something that would "unite the various opinions which have been thrown out."[39]

The Brearley Committee on Unfinished Parts (named thus after its chairman) completed its work on procedures for electing an executive in four days and reported back to the convention on September 4. The result was the electoral college.[40] It was striking in its innovation and remarkable for having combined all the salient features of the numerous plans proposed during the debate while having overcome the deficiencies of each. First, it removed the choice of president from the Congress and conveyed it to an independent, ad hoc body whose sole function was the selection of a chief executive. The independence of the president was thus assured, while cabal and foreign influence were safely excluded, and the president was free to run for reelection without fear that his independence would be compromised. Yet at the same time, and this was the critical point, in terms of numbers, the electoral college was an exact replica of Congress, since each state was entitled to as many votes in the electoral college as it had in Congress, with even the smallest state entitled to at least three votes; moreover, the southern states would enjoy the bonus of the three-fifths rule. The smaller and the southern states thus would continue to enjoy the relative advantage they possessed in Congress itself, either in the Senate or in the House of Representatives, or in both. In mathematical terms the advantage in the first Congress (with sixty-five members in the House of Representatives and twenty-six in the Senate) was as follows:

$$\text{Delaware (smallest state)}$$
$$\frac{1+2=3}{65+26=91}$$

$$\text{Virginia (largest state)}$$
$$\frac{10+\ 2=12}{65+26=91}$$

Thus, as a result of the Electoral College, the ratio was 1:4 rather than 1:10 as it would have been had size of population been the sole criterion.[41]

In effect, the electoral college was simply a special congress elected to choose a president, without the shortcomings of the real Congress. Since the electors would never assemble together at one national site but would meet to vote "in their respective States" and immediately thereafter disband, there was no danger of corruption, plotting, or cabal. As Gouverneur Morris indicated, "The principal advantage aimed at was that of taking away the opportunity for cabal." To prevent the larger states from dominating the selection process, each elector was to vote for two persons, one of whom, at least, was not to be a citizen of his own state. At the same time, since a majority was required for the selection of the president, no elector would be prone to throw away his second vote. Thus the outcome would be, not simply the selection of thirteen favorite sons, but a genuine possibility that a national figure would be chosen on the first round. In the event that no candidate received an absolute majority in the electoral college, the Senate would choose the president (from the five highest on the list). In effect, the smaller states were to get two bites of the cherry under the new plan. First, they would retain their numerical advantage in the electoral college. Second, if no candidate should succeed in obtaining an absolute majority, the choice would devolve on the Senate, where again the smaller states would have a built-in advantage. As noted above, this contingency arrangement was derived from the constitutions of Massachusetts and New Hampshire.[42]

The presentation of the electoral-college scheme to the convention excited considerable surprise. "Mr Randolph & Mr Pinkney wished for a particular explanation & discussion of the reasons for changing the mode of electing the Executive." Gouverneur Morris served as the committee's spokesman in explaining the "reasons" for the new proposal: (1) "The danger of intrigue & faction if the appointmnt. should be made by the Legislature." (2) "The inconveniency of an ineligibility" were the choice to remain with the legislature. (3) "The difficulty of establishing a Court of Impeachments, other than the Senate," which would be an improper body to judge the executive if he were to be chosen by the legislature. (4) "No body had appeared to be satisfied with an appointment by the Legislature." (5) "Many were anxious even for an immediate choice by the people." (6) "The indispensable necessity of making the Executive independent of the Legislature.—As the Electors would vote at the same time throughout the U. S. and at so great a distance from each other, the great evil of cabal was avoided."[43]

In response, Mason expressed his satisfaction that the plan "had removed some capital objections, particularly the danger of cabal and corruption." It was liable, however, "to this strong objection, that nineteen times in twenty the President would be chosen by the Senate, an improper body for the purpose." Randolph "dwelt on the tendency of such an influence in the Senate over the election of the President in addition to its other powers, to convert that body into a real & dangerous Aristocracy." Pinckney and Rutledge also argued that conferring the choice on the Senate, even in the ultimate resort, was likely to compromise the president's independence. Sherman apparently sensed that some delegates were objecting to the Senate because of the influence of small states there. He "reminded the opponents of the new mode . . . that if the Small States had the advantage in the Senate's deciding among the five highest candidates, the Large States would have in fact the nomination of these candidates." Nonetheless, when Mason moved that the choice be made from the top three rather than the top five, the smaller states objected. Sherman declared he "would sooner give up the plan." Apparently, the smaller states reasoned that a choice out of five rather than three would allow them some prospect to land a candidate of their own. Other delegates stressed that in fact, the choice would most likely be made in the electoral college, and there would be no need to resort to the Senate. "The increasing intercourse among the people of the States," declared Baldwin, "would render important characters less & less unknown; and the Senate would consequently be less & less likely to have the eventual appointment thrown into their hands." Wilson also stressed that "Continental Characters will multiply as we more & more coalesce, so as to enable the electors in every part of the Union to know & judge of them." Gouverneur Morris similarly believed the matter would be settled by the electors and would never reach the Senate. Madison considered it "a primary object to render an eventual resort to any part of the Legislature improbable." He referred to two features of the plan that made such an eventuality unlikely. First, given the reluctance of the large states to see the choice fall to the Senate, their "concerted effort . . . would be to make the appointment in the first instance conclusive." Second, the fact that the vice-president, unlike the president, could be selected without a majority would deter electors from wasting their second votes and would heighten the chance that the choice would be made in the electoral college.[44]

The delegates, it appears, were impressed with the electoral-college scheme, which so successfully blended all the necessary elements to ensure a safe and equitable process for electing a president and which reserved considerable influence for the states. They beat back, by large majorities, every attempt to upset the plan and to restore to the legislature the selection of the executive. There was, however, considerable sentiment against leaving the ultimate choice in the hands of the Senate. Mason regarded it as "utterly inadmissible. He would prefer the government of Prussia to one which will put all power into the hands of seven or eight men, and fix an Aristocracy worse than absolute monarchy." Mason was vigorously supported by Wilson, who complained that under the Constitution too much power was concentrated in the Senate. As a means of avoiding resort to the Senate, Mason proposed that the candidate who received the highest number of ballots in the electoral college be pronounced president, whether or not the vote constituted a majority. Wilson proposed that the final choice be accorded to the whole legislature, rather than to the Senate alone. The convention, however, rejected both proposals, just as it rejected numerous other proposals that tended to alter the finely tuned instrument that had evolved. The electoral college constituted a package deal in which diverse interests and safeguards were neatly balanced. Even the slightest change was likely to undermine the entire structure and to make the machinery inoperable. The delegates were not prone to tamper with the delicate compromise. Only in the matter of the Senate as the venue of ultimate resort were the delegates ready to accept change. Sherman, alert to objections that the Senate represented a center of "aristocracy," proposed that the House of Representatives be substituted for the Senate in the ultimate resort, with voting by states, not per capita. Since this proposal, in contrast to the other suggestions, preserved state power, the amendment was readily accepted by a vote of 10 to 1. Another amendment readily accepted (this time unanimously) was a clause barring "a member of the Legislature of the United States, or who holds any office of profit or trust under the United States" from serving as an elector. An incidental by-product of the new scheme was the emergence of the office of vice-president, which was designed to take care of the electors' second vote. Some delegates voiced opposition to the creation of the office, and others protested that the vice-president's appointment as ex-officio president of the Senate would violate the principle of the separation of powers. But once again the vast majority wished to preserve the electoral-college plan intact, and the office of vice-president and his role in the Senate were overwhelmingly confirmed.[45]

The records of the convention demonstrate that the protracted discussion over the mode of electing an executive was but a continuation of the struggle that had marked the debate on the composition of the legislature. The smaller states were no more prepared to concede to the large states the domination of the process of selecting a chief executive than they were prepared to allow them to dominate the legislature. From a truly "nationalist" choice, as envisaged under the Virginia Plan, the United States executive was transformed, in the give-and-take of the debates at Philadelphia, into a "federal" institution in which the rights and interests of the states, particularly the smaller states, would also be safeguarded.[46] The compromise that marked the creation of the electoral college is thus revealed as simply a second round of the Connecticut Compromise in settling differences between the large and small states.

This second stage of the running battle between the large and the small states was distinguished from the first in several ways. The dispute over the mode of electing an executive never assumed the same dimensions of crisis that nearly disrupted the convention with respect to the issue of the composition of the legislature. Of that confrontation Gouverneur Morris said that "the fate of America was suspended by a hair."[47] After having backed down on the issue of the legislature, the large states were neither able nor willing to create a new impasse. Nevertheless, a major and prolonged struggle (down to the wire) ensued over the system to be instituted for choosing an executive.

Second, the small states were not the only ones to feel directly affected by the various schemes proposed. Once the Connecticut Compromise had accorded the smaller states a handsome increment in the Senate, they understandably refused to contemplate removal of the choice from the legislature. But the slave states were no less reluctant to agree to such a move since it would dissipate the advantage they had secured in the lower house through the three-fifths rule. As a result, a natural alliance existed between the two groups—the slave states and the smaller states—in reserving the decision to the national legislature. However, according the legislature such a role would inevitably have compromised the executive's independence, something that tended to violate the principle of the separation of powers, regarded as sacrosanct by the founding fathers. To overcome this deficiency, it was decided that the executive's term of office would be relatively long (seven years) and that he would be ineligible for reelection. Those conditions, however, were found wanting in other respects, so that the delegates kept probing and testing for an alternative to the triangular arrangement—choice by the legislature, long term, ineligibility.

Now it was the turn of the small states to make a valuable concession, which represents a third noteworthy aspect of the electoral-college compromise. Given the equality of both houses in the legislature, the Senate would be free to exercise a veto in the choice of the executive. In the interest of preventing deadlocks, however, several smaller states resolved to endorse a joint ballot of both houses in selecting an executive. Unlike the Connecticut Compromise, in which the concession of the smaller states was limited to granting the lower house the right to initiate money bills, in this instance the concession was significant and meaningful. It paved the way for a transference of the responsibility of choosing the executive from the legislature to some outside body. The most logical outside body was the people, in direct popular elections. Such a step, however, would have canceled the advantages enjoyed by the smaller and the slave states in the legislature. In response, the Committee on Unfinished Parts invented the electoral college—an ingenious means of preserving the built-in advantages of those states while removing the choice from the legislature. The electoral college represented a congress away from home for the express and limited purpose of choosing the nation's chief magistrate. The institution of the electoral college represented the first, indeed the primary, compromise in the arrangements for selecting an executive. National and federal elements were neatly balanced therein. But it was only part of the package. In the event that the electoral college should fail to come up with a sufficiently national choice, the Senate (ultimately the House of Representatives), as the constitutive body of the states, would choose. In effect, therefore, in the event that the electoral college should become a mere nominating body under the domination of the large states, the smaller and the slave states would be well placed to exercise a controlling voice over the final election in the Senate (House of Representatives).[48] (Although the three-fifths rule did not operate at this point, the slave states retained influence by virtue of the number of southern states present.)

The records of the convention indicate that many delegates favored the direct popular election of the executive but, for three reasons noted, were unable to institute such a system. The most prominent advocates of direct elections were those who campaigned for a strong executive—Wilson, Gouverneur Morris, and Madison. Their motives possibly were mixed. They were opposed to lodging the choice in the legislature because the executive's independence would be compromised. They were also concerned about the disproportionate influence of the smaller states in that body. As Martin told the Maryland legislature, "Those who wished as far as possible to establish a *national* instead of a *federal* government, made repeated attempts to have the President chosen by the people at large." Democratic doctrine—the belief that the executive should represent the mass of the people—also seems to have been a factor. In the end the proponents of direct elections achieved partial success. Although the election of the president was not to be a direct act of the people, the state legislatures would be free, if they wished, to confer the choice of electors upon the people themselves. Indeed, that seems to have been the expectation of the framers. For this reason Madison, in one of the last sessions of the convention, described the election of the president as one "by the people."[49]

Only a few delegates—most notably Mason, Gerry, and Butler—were opposed in principle to direct election of the executive. But such opposition reflected, as least in the case of Mason, not mistrust of representative democracy, but a conviction that the extent of the country and the difficulty of communication did not permit the informed selection of a national candidate. True representation could work only over a small area where the people could be acquainted firsthand with the candidates. An attempt to apply representative democracy on a national scale was a distortion of the principle and would simply lead to the manipulation of elections by nefarious characters. The ultimate solution of state electors was, from that standpoint, a sound means of giving expression to the popular will, and it was viewed in that light by the Antifederalists in the state ratifying conventions.

What clearly emerges from the foregoing is that contrary to the claim of the Progressive historians, antimajoritarianism was by no means the primary motivation behind the creation of the electoral college. Nor was it, as Roche would have it, simply the product of a last-minute accident of history. Design and purpose guided the creation of the electoral college. At the same time, however, it would be wrong to suggest that the electoral college was based on some grand concept of political theory. Also, there is no evidence that the convention was inspired in the matter by classical or medieval precedents. Not once did the delegates refer to the procedures that had prevailed in ancient Rome or Greece or in republican Venice. (The Federalist Papers, equally, do not mention any such historical forerunners of the electoral college.) The delegates were confronted with a practical problem arising from the constellation of clashing forces at Philadelphia, and they devised a practical solution—an ad hoc congress that would faithfully reflect the pattern of weighted voting that was an integral part of the operation of the real Congress. The precedents guiding their deliberations were all drawn from practices of the states.[50]

Two alternatives presented themselves: the indirect method of selection by the legislature and the direct method of popular choice (qualified by a contingency procedure entailing a legislative role). The latter method represented too national a choice for some; the former, while it offered a satisfactory federal solution, clashed with accepted republican principles. Concepts that had come to be viewed by many as essential components of representative government—separation of powers, limited terms of office, reeligibility, rotation in office, and devices for minimizing electoral corruption—were analyzed and weighed in the search for an unassailable solution. Thus, if political theory did not inform the creation of the electoral college, it provided the essential backdrop to the evolution of this new instrument of government. The device of a congress away from home represented, in sum, an adaptation of state experience modified by the need to resolve the central dispute at Philadelphia, namely the large state–small state controversy. Concessions to the federal impulse were reflected in the manner in which the composition of the electoral college was fixed; in the option accorded the state legislatures to appoint the electors; and in the ultimate choice being bestowed upon the House of Representatives, voting by states. These features stamped the compromise nature of the electoral college and assured its acceptability both within the convention and without. For in the eyes of its admirers, the electoral college represented a brilliant scheme for successfully blending national and federal elements in the selection of the nation's chief magistrate.

NOTES

This chapter was previously published as "The Electoral College at Philadelphia: The Evolution of an Ad Hoc Congress for Selection of a President," *Journal of American History* 73 (June, 1986). It is reprinted here by permission of that journal and of the author.

1. Constitution of the United States, Art. II, sec. 1.
2. Max Farrand, ed., *The Records of the Federal Convention of 1787*, 4 vols. (New

Haven, Conn.: Yale University Press, 1937), 2:501, 3:166, 329, 458, 459. According to Farrand, "Whatever difficulties might have been encountered in other directions, they paled into insignificance in comparison with the problem before the convention of determining a satisfactory method of electing the executive" (*The Framing of the Constitution of the United States* [New Haven, Conn.: Yale University Press, 1913], p. 160). See also Max Farrand, "Compromises of the Constitution," *American Historical Review* 9 (Apr., 1904): 486; Herman V. Ames, *The Proposed Amendments to the Constitution of the United States during the First Century of Its History* (Washington, D.C.: Government Printing Office, 1897), pp. 75–76; Senate Document no. 93, 69th Cong., 1st sess. (1926); Senate Document no. 163, 87th Cong., 2d sess. (1963); Senate Document no. 38, 91st Cong., 1st sess. (1969); Richard A. David, Congressional Research Service of Library of Congress, Report no. 85–36 Gov.; *Congress and the Nation*, vol. 5: *1977–1980* (Washington, D.C.: Congressional Quarterly Press, 1981), pp. 941–43; U.S. Congress, Senate, Committee of the Judiciary, *Direct Popular Election of the President and Vice President of the United States*, 96th Cong., Apr. 9, 1979; and *Public Papers of the President of the United States, Jimmy Carter 1977*, bk. 1, Mar. 22, 1977 (Washington, D.C.: Government Printing Office, 1980), pp. 481–85.

3. J. Allen Smith, *The Spirit of American Government: A Study of the Constitution: Its Origin, Influence and Relation to Democracy* (New York: Macmillan, 1907), pp. 135–36, 165; Charles A. Beard, *An Economic Interpretation of the Constitution of the United States* (New York: Macmillan, 1913), pp. 161–62; John P. Roche, "The Founding Fathers: A Reform Caucus in Action," *American Political Science Review* 55 (Dec., 1961): 799–816, esp. 810–11. Roche was not the first to highlight the compromise nature of the electoral college. See Farrand, "Compromises of the Constitution," pp. 479–89; Farrand, *Framing of the Constitution*, pp. 166–67; and Charles Warren, *The Making of the Constitution* (Boston: Little, Brown, 1928), pp. 621–23. Neither of the last two writers has accepted the assertion that in the eyes of the framers the electoral college was a "jerry-rigged improvisation." See the comments of Gouverneur Morris and James Madison in Farrand, *Records*, 3:405, 458, 464.

4. Farrand, *Records*, 3:132, 403; E. M. Earle, ed., *The Federalist* (Washington, D.C.: National Home Library Foundation, 1938), p. 441; Farrand, *Framing of the Constitution*, p. 175.

5. See the statements of James Wilson and Rufus King in Farrand, *Records*, 3:166, 461. See also that of Madison at the Virginia ratifying convention in Jonathan Elliot, ed., *The Debates in the Several State Conventions, on the Adoption of the Federal Constitution*, 5 vols. (Philadelphia: J. B. Lippincott, 1881), 3:494. See also Cecelia M. Kenyon, "Men of Little Faith: The Anti-Federalists on the Nature of Representative Government," *William and Mary Quarterly* 12 (Jan., 1955): 13.

6. Farrand, *Records*, 1:20–22, 242–45. In both plans the term of office was left blank and reeligibility was ruled out. The election of the executive by the legislature was provided for under the constitutions of Delaware, Georgia, Maryland, North Carolina, New Jersey, Pennsylvania, South Carolina, and Virginia. (In every instance of a bicameral legislature the executive was chosen by joint ballot. Other officers of government, however, were chosen by regular legislative procedures, allowing each house to exercise a veto on the choice of the other. On occasion that procedure produced deadlock and crisis.) The popular election of the executive was provided for under the constitutions of Massachusetts, New Hampshire, and New York. Under the last, a simple plurality was sufficient for election, and there was no provision for a contingency choice. But in

the first two, in the absence of a popular majority for any one candidate, the lower house chose two out of the top four candidates, and the upper house made the final choice out of the two selected. Benjamin Perley Poore, comp., *The Federal and State Constitutions, Colonial Charters, and Other Organic Laws of the United States,* 2 vols. (Washington, D.C., 1877). Contingency proposals surfaced frequently during the convention debates, and of course, the electoral-college scheme contains such an arrangement.

7. During the course of the convention, two further plans were presented: the Pinckney Plan (May 29) and the Hamilton Plan (June 18). Under the former the executive would be chosen annually by both houses of the legislature in joint session; under the latter the executive would be selected by electors chosen by the people and would serve during good behavior. Neither plan figured in the convention debates and neither was ever voted on. The Hamilton Plan was not even moved to committee: see Farrand, *Records,* 1:292, 2:135, 3:606, 617.

8. Ibid., 1:68–88, 3:132, 167; Roche, "Founding Fathers," p. 810; George Bancroft, *History of the Formation of the Constitution of the United States of America,* 2 vols. (Boston: Little, Brown, 1889), 1:166.

9. Charles C. Thach, Jr., *The Creation of the Presidency 1775–1789: A Study in Constitutional History* (Baltimore, Md.: Johns Hopkins University Press, 1923), p. 85; Farrand, *Records,* 1:68, 69, 77, 80. This was the first of many times in the debate that the use of electors was proposed. Ultimately, of course, the convention adopted a system of indirect election in the form of the electoral college. One can speculate on the precedents for the introduction of an intermediate step in the selection of an executive. In the Massachusetts ratifying convention, former Governor James Bowdoin declared, "This method of choosing was probably taken from the manner of choosing senators under the constitution of Maryland": Elliot, *Debates,* 2:127–28. Under that constitution the people chose electors, who, in turn, selected the fifteen members of the state Senate for a five-year term. In Federalist no. 63, Madison gave high praise to that feature of the Maryland constitution. See also Ames, *Proposed Amendments,* pp. 75–76. For Elbridge Gerry's role in the convention see George Athan Billias, *Elbridge Gerry, Founding Father and Republican Statesman* (New York, 1976), pp. 153–205, 331–39.

10. Farrand, *Records,* 1:78, 85, 86, 87, 244.

11. Ibid., 77, 78, 81, 87. Delaware, John Dickinson's state, alone favored his proposal. There is evidence that even before a quorum had assembled at the Constitutional Convention, the smaller states were already evincing anxiety about the outcome. See the letter of George Read of Delaware to Dickinson on May 21, 3:25–26. Subsequently Dickinson endorsed the election of the executive "by the people which he regarded as the best and purest source" (ibid., 2:114). Clearly, Dickinson's present move was designed to ensure a federal system of government in which the role of the states would not be entirely eclipsed.

12. Ibid., 1:242–45, 549–51.

13. Thach, *Creation of the Presidency, 1775–1789,* p. 35; Farrand, *Framing of the Constitution,* p. 21; Farrand, *Records,* 2:22, 29.

14. Farrand, *Records,* 2:29–30.

15. Ibid., p. 31.

16. Kenyon, "Men of Little Faith," p. 13. This analysis is reflected in Wilson's argument in the Pennsylvania ratifying convention on the method of electing a president (Farrand, *Records,* 3:167). See also Billias, *Elbridge Gerry,* p. 160. George Mason's record, both before and during the convention, demonstrates that he was a foremost champion of democratic causes (Farrand, *Records,* 1:48, 2:201–3,

273–74, 370, 637); Alfred H. Kelly and Winfred A. Harbison, *The American Constitution: Its Origins and Development* (New York: W. W. Norton, 1970), p. 120.

17. Farrand, *Records,* 2:22, 32.

18. Ibid., pp. 23, 33, 35, 36.

19. Ibid., pp. 52, 54–55.

20. Ibid., pp. 52–54, 55–56, 57.

21. Ibid., pp. 34, 56–57.

22. Ibid., pp. 50, 57, 58, 59, 60, 61, 63–64, 69.

23. Ibid., pp. 95, 97, 99, 100, 101. A possible explanation for the sudden change of heart on the scheme of electors may lie in the fact that a move to accord New Hampshire and Georgia two electors each, instead of the one that each state had been allotted, failed; ibid., pp. 60–61, 63–64.

24. Ibid., pp. 98–99, 100–101, 102.

25. Ibid., pp. 97, 102, 103, 105, 106. On the difficulties encountered by the delegates at this point, compare the descriptions by Robert A. Dahl and George Bancroft. Dahl observed: "Almost to the end, it [the convention] would move toward a solution and then, on second thought, reverse itself in favor of some different alternative. . . . The Convention twisted and turned like a man tormented in his sleep by a bad dream as it tried to decide" (*Pluralist Democracy in the United States: Conflict and Consent* [Chicago: 1967], p. 84). Bancroft wrote: "The convention was now like a pack of hounds in full chase, suddenly losing the trail. It fell into an anarchy of opinion and one crude scheme trod on the heels of another" (*History of the Formation of the Constitution,* 2:170). Some writers have suggested that Wilson's notion of a choice by lot was drawn from the example of the ephori elections in ancient Greece. See John Fiske, *The Critical Period of American History, 1783–1789* (Boston, Mass., and New York: Houghton-Mifflin, 1895–1901), p. 281; and Richard M. Gummere, *The American Colonial Mind and the Classical Tradition* (Cambridge, Mass.: Harvard University Press, 1963), p. 186.

26. Farrand, *Records,* 2:107–11.

27. Ibid., pp. 111, 113.

28. Ibid., pp. 113–14 (emphasis added).

29. Ibid., pp. 114–15.

30. Ibid., pp. 107, 111–12, 115. A rotation requirement in the office of governor was present in eight state constitutions.

31. Ibid., pp. 112, 114, 118–20.

32. Ibid., pp. 116, 117, 120–21, 128 (emphasis in original).

33. Ibid., pp. 145, 185.

34. Ibid., pp. 177, 193, 196–97.

35. Ibid., pp. 314–15, 401, 402 (emphasis in original).

36. Ibid., 1:524, 526, 2:397, 402–3 (emphasis in original). Although the executive in New Hampshire was elected by popular vote, other officers were selected by the legislature, with each house voting separately.

37. Ibid., 2:397, 404.

38. Ibid., pp. 397–98, 404.

39. Ibid., pp. 103, 472, 473, 480, 481.

40. According to Charles Warren, the reason for the success of the committee was that it consisted of "almost the ablest men from each State" (*Making of the Constitution,* p. 621 n. 1). See also Roche, "Founding Fathers," p. 810.

41. Constitution of the United States, Art. 1, secs. 2, 3. In the 1790 census, Delaware had a population of 59,000 while that of Virginia was 692,000. In the 1792 elections, Virginia elected nineteen members to the House of Represen-

tatives whereas Delaware continued to elect only one. Since the electoral-college total was 132, the resultant ratio was Delaware, 3:132; Virginia, 21:132. Thus the ratio was 1:7 rather than 1:12, as the population figures would warrant. (These figures allow 3 votes for every 5 blacks under the census.) U.S. Bureau of the Census, *Historical Statistics of the United States, Colonial Times to 1970* (Washington, D.C.: Government Printing Office, 1975), pt. 1, pp. 24, 36, and, pt. 2, pp. 1074, 1085. Representation in the House was apportioned on the basis of 30,000 population per seat (Constitution of the United States, Art. 1, sec. 2).

42. Farrand, *Records,* 2:501.

43. Ibid., p. 500.

44. Ibid., pp. 500, 501, 507, 511, 512–13, 514, 523; Bancroft, *History of the Formation of the Constitution,* 2:177. The remarks by Abraham Baldwin, Wilson, Gouverneur Morris, and Madison demonstrate that a considerable body of opinion at the convention did not share Mason's view that "nineteen times in twenty" the selection would be made in the Senate (House). Roche's claim that "no one seriously disputed [Mason's] point" is thus unsupportable. Moreover, as Madison notes, certain features of the electoral-college scheme were specifically designed to heighten the prospects of a final choice in the college. On this point see Warren, *Making of the Constitution,* p. 629. But cf. Farrand, *Framing of the Constitution,* p. 167; and Farrand, *Records,* 3:405.

45. Farrand, *Records,* 2:507, 511, 512, 513, 514, 515, 517–21, 522–23, 525–29, 532, 536–38. Gouverneur Morris quipped that the vice-president "will be the first heir apparent that ever loved his father" (ibid., p. 537).

46. See the subsequent comment of Jonathan Dayton, delegate from New Jersey: "The States, whatever was their relative magnitude, were equal under the old Confederation, and the small States gave up a part of their rights as a compromise for a better form of government and security; but they cautiously preserved their equal rights in the Senate and in the choice of a Chief Magistrate" (ibid., 3:400–401). See also the remarks of Gouverneur Morris, ibid., 405; and of Rufus King, ibid., 462.

47. Ibid., p. 391.

48. At various times the contingency arrangement, with the House of Representatives voting by states, has been depicted as the key element of compromise in the electoral-college scheme. See, for instance, Farrand, "Compromises of the Constitution," pp. 487–88; and Farrand, *Records,* 3:458, 461, 464. However, as noted, this is only part of the package. The first and fundamental element of compromise lay in the composition of the electoral college. As summed up by Baldwin, "The Constitution in directing *Electors* to be appointed throughout the United States equal to the whole number of the Senators and Representatives in Congress . . . had provided for the existence of as respectable a body as Congress, and in whom the constitution on this business has more confidence than in Congress" (ibid., p. 382). See also the remarks of Gouverneur Morris, ibid., p. 405; and of King, ibid., p. 461.

49. Ibid., pp. 217, 330, 422–23, 2:587, 1:50 (emphasis in original). See also *Federalist Papers* nos. 60 and 68.

50. King commented, "The members of the convention in settling the manner of electing the Executive of the U.S. seem to have been prejudiced in favor of the manner, to which they were accustomed, in the election of the Governor of their respective States" (ibid., 3:459). Also, as indicated earlier, the notion of establishing an electoral college may well have been drawn from the precedent of the Maryland senate; see Elliot, *Debates,* 2:127–28.

3

PRESIDENTIAL TERM, TENURE AND REELIGIBILITY

THOMAS E. CRONIN

The executive Power shall be vested in a President of the United States of America. He shall hold his Office during the Term of four Years, and, together with the Vice President, chosen for the same Term, be elected as follows.

—*Article II, section 1*

Once the framers of the Constitution had agreed there would be a national executive, they next had to determine the powers of the office and also how long this official would serve. How long the executive would serve obviously had a bearing on how powerful or independent the office would be, and this became the source of considerable debate in Philadelphia and later at ratifying conventions in the states. The framers also had to decide whether an incumbent president could be eligible for reelection.

Although presidential tenure and reeligibility were not the most important topics at the federal convention, still they understandably provoked extended and often heated debate. Antifederalists and other critics immediately pointed to these decisions and complained that the proposed four-year term and the notion that a president might be reelected and reelected and reelected posed a serious threat to the liberties of the newly independent states. Naysayers and reformers of varying partisan camps have ever since been trying to lengthen, shorten, or restructure presidential tenure.

Today the term of four years enjoys widespread acceptance, yet this was hardly a settled question in 1787. Most Americans today also accept the legitimacy that a successful first term deserves at least a second presidential term. However, present day Americans are divided, as early Americans also were, about whether a president should be eligible beyond a second term. The framers were silent, at least in the Constitution, on the matter of how many terms a president might serve. That, presumably, was for the voters and the electors to decide. This changed 144 years later when, as a result of the Twenty-second Amendment, Americans, through their national and state legislatures, fundamentally altered the intent of the framers in this regard.

The questions of term length and reeligibility were important in 1787, and they remain so today. These structural considerations help define the constitutional authority and boundaries of the office. They also help shape and limit presidential power; a president with a ten- or fifteen-year term would be accountable to Congress, the voters, and the Constitution in different ways from a president with a four-year term. A president who is unable to run for reelection might be a different kind of president from one who has the unrestricted privilege of doing so once, twice, and even more.

Nearly a dozen former presidents have advocated a lengthened six- or seven-year term, usually specifying that it should be a single term. Some presidents, including Ronald Reagan, have urged that the Twenty-second Amendment be repealed. Generally, views about a six-year nonrenewable term and about the Twenty-second Amendment reflect attitudes about how powerful the presidency should be, as well as related constitutional principles. Views on these subjects are also often related to one's views of who is president and who is likely to control the White House in the near term. Scholars and practitioners alike are unable to predict with any certainty what the consequences and secondary effects of these structural considerations might be, yet there is agreement that these are not inconsequential matters—especially as the presidency looms ever more central in American politics and government.

TERM LENGTH AND REELIGIBILITY
OF GOVERNORS, 1776–88

When political independence from England was declared in 1776, Americans favored strong legislatures and weak executives. In the years before the Revolution, the Crown-appointed royal governors had often provoked widespread popular mistrust. Legislatures spoke for the people and their liberties, or so at least most Americans believed.

The early state constitutions, reflecting a belief in limited government, provided for state executives that were dependent on the legislature. Short terms, usually of one year, were the norm. The legislatures, not the people, elected the state's chief executive in almost every state. Only in Massachusetts and New York did the voters have the right to elect the governor. Later, a few other New England states permitted this as well. Yet even in these states, the decision reverted to the state legislature if a majority choice did not emerge in the popular vote.

Only Delaware, New York, and South Carolina chose their governors for terms of more than one year. South Carolina allowed a single two-year term. Delaware permitted a single three-year term. New York, which favored a slightly stronger executive than other states, provided for a three-year term with unlimited reeligibility. Reflecting the widely held belief that rotation in office was essential if freedom and liberty were to be preserved, about half of the states limited tenure in office by imposing various restrictions upon the executive's reeligibility for additional successive terms.

The architects of the state constitutions, who were consistent with their evolving notions both about separation-of-powers doctrine and executive power, believed long terms and the lodging of independent power and trust in the executive would pose a threat to liberty. Memory of the hated royal governors encouraged the subordination of the governors to the legislature. "Americans in 1776 thought it was easy to keep the legislature a truly popular agency, but they knew of no way of holding a powerful governor to their will," wrote the historian Allan Nevins. "They were unable to distinguish properly between a Crown governor and a popularly-elected one, and had not learned the value of concentration of responsibility."[1]

These experiments at the state level taught early Americans about the pitfalls of overreliance on legislatures. In practice, both the legislators and the voters grew to value continuity in their state executive offices. Except for Georgia, where governors came and went with great frequency, the states averaged less than four governors apiece in the formative 1776–88 period. Two states, New Jersey and New York, retained the same governor throughout this long stretch. Massachusetts had only two governors during these same years, and other states had only three. Their terms may have been short and their powers constitutionally limited, yet the apparent benefits of having continuity and stability in the state executive position plainly were acknowledged. These new republican governments rewarded their governors when they proved they were responsible and effective, and this was true regardless of whether the legislature or the people did the electing.[2]

These varying practices at the state level, as well as the valuable lessons learned there, all became part of the experience the framers drew upon in Philadelphia in 1787. The diversity of these "models" doubtless shaped and perhaps prolonged discussions about executive term and tenure at the Federal Convention.

PRECONSTITUTION NATIONAL
"PRESIDENCIES," 1774–89

The United States had fourteen different "presidents" between the years 1774 and 1789. From the first Continental Congress through the end of the Articles of Confederation, a president was provided for, even if it was a position of markedly less prestige and authority than it would be once George Washington was inaugurated in 1789.

Congress assumed the executive power of the new, struggling nation throughout this period, and Congress exercised that power to instruct commanders in chief, diplomats, and ad hoc boards and commissions as the need arose. But the presiding officer in Congress—the president—also exercised certain executive functions, such as communicating on behalf of Congress with state governors, the commanders in chief, foreign heads of state, and others. "It was the President who was expected to receive official guests, such as foreign notables, and extend hospitality," Richard Morris has observed. "Their frequent dances, levees, and balls established the President as the ceremonial head of state, and indeed foreshadowed the high tone set by President Washington under the federal constitution."[3]

Even prior to the adoption of the Articles of Confederation, a principle of rotation was firmly established for presidents, no doubt reflecting once again the fear of executive power as a potential threat to liberty. From 1774 to 1781 the average length of "presidential service" was less than a year. The Articles of Confederation, which went into effect in 1781, stipulated that a president could serve no more than one year in any period of three years, an obvious protection against the perpetuation in office of the same individual. It was also an apparent attempt to guard against the abuse of what executive power was available to the presiding officer.

In many respects, of course, the Articles provided for no real executive. When Congress was in session, the body as a whole acted as the executive. When it was not in session, an executive committee of the states (one delegate from each state) presided over the government. Executive departments for foreign affairs and finance were gradually established, and these, too, further decentralized and diminished any power associated with the presiding office. Eventually the president under the Articles of Confederation became, for all practical purposes, a first among equals in Congress, a far-different position from what the framers designed in Philadelphia in 1787.

These early experiences with even a decidedly weak and primarily ceremonial presidency met with different evaluations. Men such as Patrick Henry, George Clinton, and Samuel Adams approved of the weak national federation and the absence of strong leadership because they reasoned the interests of their states were best served by this fragmented and decentralized set of arrangements. Others such as Alexander Hamilton, as early as 1780, despaired of the lack of an executive who had proper independence and tenure:

> Another defect in our system is want of method and energy in the administration. This has partly resulted from the other defect [the weakness of Congress]; but in a great degree from prejudice, and the want of a proper executive. Congress have [*sic*] kept the power too much in their own hands, and have meddled too much with details of every sort. Congress is properly a deliberative corps and it forgets itself when it attempts to play the executive. It is impossible such a body, numerous as it is, constantly fluctuating, can ever act with sufficient decision, or with system.[4]

DEBATES AT PHILADELPHIA
OVER TERM LENGTH AND TENURE

At the Constitutional Convention, at least sixty votes were taken on the issues of the proper length of term for the president, of who should do the electing, and of reeligibility. Governor Edmund Randolph's Virginia Plan called for a single executive to be chosen by the national legislature for an unspecified number of years and to be ineligible for a second term. Charles Pinckney of South Carolina proposed that the executive be reeligible to serve beyond the first term. Both plans were referred to the Committee of the Whole. Soon thereafter the delegates tentatively approved a single seven-year term. Even then there was decided division of opinion on both the questions of the length of term and reeligibility.

Considerable debate over presidential tenure ensued. There were almost as many different notions about the appropriate number of years a president should serve as there were state delegations. Delegates advocated at least the following: a term of two, three, six, seven, eight, ten, eleven, fifteen, or twenty years; a term of no more than six years in any twelve; and life tenure, or as long as the incumbent served with good behavior.

Attitudes on the length of the executive's term turned on the way the executive was to be elected, whether by the legislature, the people, or some other body. Those who wanted the legislature to elect the president urged longer terms and no reelection. Otherwise, the president, so this group held, would be dependent on the legislators' good will for reelection and therefore, in most instances, would be forced to curry their favor. Connecticut's Roger Sherman, for example, saw the proposed executive as nothing more than an institution for carrying out the will of the legislature and warned that the executive should and must be accountable to the legislature alone. Shorter terms, with the possibility of reelection when the job was well done, were advocated by those who wanted popular election and by those who wanted a president who would be more independent of the legislature.

The records of the convention suggest the flavor of these debates and differences. James Wilson favored a three-year term. Delegate Roger Sherman agreed with the idea of a three-year term, adding that he was against rotation in the office since it might throw out the very individuals who were best qualified for the job.

Charles Pinckney advocated a seven-year term. George Mason of Virginia declared in favor of at least seven years, and he wanted to prohibit reeligibility, which he thought would be the best means for preventing both a sense of false satisfaction by the national legislature in an unfit president and the temptation by presidents "to intrigue" with the legislature for their own reelection.

James Madison, the convention's principal note taker, recorded the strong opposition of Delaware's Gunning Bedford, Jr., to a term as long as seven years:

> Mr. Bedford was strongly opposed to so long a term as seven years. He begged the committee to consider what the situation of the Country would be, in case the first magistrate should be saddled on it for such period and it should be found on trial that he did not possess the qualifications ascribed to him, or should lose them after his appointment. An impeachment he said would be no cure for this evil, as an impeachment would reach misfeasance only, not incapacity. He was for a triennial [three-year term] election, and for an ineligibility after a period of nine years.[5]

On June 18, 1787, Alexander Hamilton of New York addressed the convention for five hours. He jolted his audience by saying the British government was the best in the world and he doubted whether anything much different from it would serve America's best interests. Although he recognized that monarchy was not acceptable to his fellow countrymen, he believed we should go as far in that direction as republican principles might then permit. Hence, Hamilton proposed a senate that would serve, in essence, for life; a second legislative assembly elected directly by the people; and a permanent president, or president for life, during good behavior. To his critics who might view this as monarchy, he replied that his proposed executive would be elected. Moreover, added Hamilton, by making the executive subject to impeachment, the term "monarchy" could not apply.

Hamilton's speech was praised by nearly all the delegates but was supported by none. If he saw their proposals of a three-, six-, or seven-year term as inadequate, his fellow delegates viewed his quasi-British model as too great a threat to liberty. Further, they viewed it as politically impractical. Such a scheme would never win ratification.

Hamilton later denied having endorsed such an imperial proposal, saying it was merely an experimental or speculative proposition; and he insisted that his final opinion at the convention favored a three- or four-year term allowing for reeligibility.

The vast majority of the delegates voted against proposals for a presidential term during "good behavior," because they feared it would prove too difficult to impeach and convict a president for misbehavior. One delegate said it would be impossible to define the misbehavior in such a manner as to subject a president to a proper trial, and perhaps still more impossible to compel so high an offender, holding his office for "life tenure," to submit to trial. Some feared this might also lead to a hereditary monarch. And if the system should fail, it might lead to another revolution. All this led some delegates, such as Gouverneur Morris of Pennsylvania, to favor a short term in order to avoid impeachments (and revolutions) that might otherwise be necessary.

By mid July the idea of a six-year term had won the favor of several delegates. If elections were too frequent, one delegate reasoned, the executive might not be firm or strong enough. Some of the executive responsibilities would make him unpopular. Doubtless, too, there would be *ins* as well as *outs,* and the executive would be misrepresented and attacked.

North Carolina's Hugh Williamson observed that if the elections were too frequent, the best men would not undertake the service, and those of inferior character would be likely to be corrupted.

By a vote of 9 to 1, the state delegations approved the six-year term. Yet this debate never really stopped.

Delegate Elbridge Gerry of Massachusetts soon urged a long term, saying the longer the duration of the appointment, the more the executive would have a proper independence of the legislature. Gerry favored a ten-, fifteen-, or even twenty-year term, with no reeligibility. Luther Martin of Maryland favored eleven years. Rufus King of Massachusetts proposed a twenty-year term, noting, perhaps sarcastically, "this is the medium life for princes." Another delegate advocated an eight-year term.

By late July, 1787, the idea of a seven-year term with no reelection was approved again. Still, confusion and uncertainties remained. The basic issues had yet to be resolved. The major difficulty stemmed from the means of election. That would have to be solved before the framers could reach a firm agreement on the issues of term length and reeligibility.

In early August, the Committee of Detail proposed that the executive power should be vested in a single person, to be called president of the

United States. He would be elected by a ballot of the legislature. He would be elected for the term of seven years, but could not be eligible for a second term. He could, in addition, be impeached by the House of Representatives and tried for conviction of impeachment by the Supreme Court.

Progress was being made. Yet once more the delegates were deeply divided on the matter of term length, and they postponed again this and related matters. But these could not be postponed much longer. The delegates were getting tired, and time was running out.

These much-postponed problems were finally referred to a Committee of Eleven. On September 4, this committee recommended that the term of the president should be for four years, with no restrictions on the reelection issue. The Committee of Eleven also recommended election of the executive by electors chosen by the states, but if no candidate received a majority or if two or more candidates tied, the United States Senate would choose the president. Later that week, because it was believed that the Senate was already too powerful and would be likely to be controlled by narrower interests, the convention modified the plan and made the House of Representatives responsible for choosing a president in case of a tie or when no candidate won a majority. In the event of a deadlock, this scheme would retain the familiar one-state, one-vote method of voting—the same method they were using at the convention in Philadelphia and under the Articles of Confederation.

The four-year term, with no statement as to reeligibility, won approval and became the provision in the Constitution. All of this won approval just eleven days before the adjournment of the convention.

As with most decisions, the provision for a four-year term with the possibility of reelection was a compromise. The sudden shift from seven years with ineligibility to the four-year term with possible indefinite reelection turned on the newly devised solution to how presidents would be elected. With the establishment of the electoral college, the controversy surrounding the four-year term seems almost suddenly to have disappeared without comment (at least at this secret conclave in Philadelphia).

The Committee of Eleven, which devised the solution and the final plan, left no notes about its deliberations. Students of their decisions are forced to theorize about the reasons underlying the framers' choices regarding this electoral structure.

Plainly, this was just one more of the several artful compromises among disparate views that were the hallmark of this convention. Virtually every group and view concerning the election, tenure, and reeligibility thus received something it wanted. For those who wanted a long term with ineligibility, to give the president independence from Congress, the president's election by a group of electors who could not hold federal positions, through the electoral college, would keep him independent.

Their fears about his scheming with Congress to ensure another term would be greatly lessened, allowing them to favor reeligibility, as permitted in the four-year term. His reeligibility would likewise satisfy those who opposed ineligibility for fear of losing an experienced and popular candidate, since it would not limit the options of the people. Besides, as Gouverneur Morris and some others believed, reeligibility was the main incentive for good performance and honest hard work.

Those who favored shorter terms with popular election obviously were satisfied because they won a populist or progressive means of keeping a president accountable at regular intervals. To be sure, four years would be a long term, yet it was only one year longer than the term for governor in New York. And many of the governors in the states, even when the term was merely for one year, averaged about four consecutive years in office.

George Washington's popularity and his possible service as first president probably softened the arguments of those who believed presidents would prove to be nothing less than kings for four years, and finally kings for life. Washington had already demonstrated, as a general, that he was not a power-seeking person.

The few delegates who ardently favored an elective monarchy or an executive to serve on "good behavior," along with those who desired a longer term of fifteen or even twenty years to ensure executive independence from the legislature, were also no doubt satisfied, for although they failed to win approval for a long term, they were given the chance of unlimited presidential reelection. As one delegate noted, indefinite reeligibility would allow a president a chance to truly be rewarded for good performance, because if a president is truly good, the people will return him to office.

Those delegates who wanted the president to be elected by the Congress and also wanted a long term were perhaps the most disappointed. Yet even they were given the electoral college, and many delegates, such as Madison, assumed that because of this new contrivance, the presidents after Washington would more than likely be selected by the House of Representatives.

Further, the impeachment provision, together with the fact that in the event of the failure of the electoral college to decide the president, the House would decide on the basis of one vote per state (a prospect clearly pleasing to the smaller states), also played a part in the relatively quick acceptance of this plan. The impeachment provision cut in two directions. A president could be impeached, and this might curb or restrain presidential power. On the other hand, several framers noted that a definition of impeachable offenses would be hard to write. In any case, as one delegate conjectured, impeachment would only throw a president out for criminality, not for incompetence. Thus the new plan gave protection against executive encroachment on the legislature's powers yet gave the president a certain degree of power and independence.

On balance, this plan appeared to fit in better with the overall constitutional scheme than did any other. The staggering of terms of offices—with two, four, and six years—also had something to do with the approval of the four-year plan. Obviously, the model of New York, with its respected three-year, reeligible, and popularly elected governor, definitely played a role in the thinking of the delegates. The availability and desirability of George Washington as the probable first president also heightened the plan's acceptance in Philadelphia.

THE REELIGIBILITY DEBATE IN PHILADELPHIA

While the framers ultimately accepted the principle of indefinite eligibility, some delegates and many Americans at the time continued to believe that rotation in the executive post was essential to liberty. It was pretty certain, a few delegates believed, that at some future time, Americans would have another king. But this should be postponed as long as possible.

As noted, most of the opponents of reeligibility based their criticism on the assumption that presidents would be elected by the national legislature. They yearned for an independent executive, yet they feared that if he was eligible for a second time, he would always be left under a temptation to court his own reappointment.

Fears of self-perpetuating kings and royal-appointed governors and judges were never far from their minds. Moreover, most states, after all, still had one-year terms for their chief executives.

At one point in late July, a South Carolina delegate suggested that no person be eligible for more than six years out of any twelve. This might have many of the benefits of a restriction yet avoid to some degree the inconvenience of an absolute ineligibility for a second term. This type of protective restriction was already present in several states, and it also applied to the president in the Continental Congress, then operating under the Articles of Confederation. Although a president would, under this plan, be ineligible after his first term, it opened the way for taking advantage of his future service.

The delegates went back and forth on the issue of reeligibility. Gouverneur Morris and James Wilson, both delegates from Pennsylvania, ultimately prevailed upon their colleagues to make the president independent of Congress. This would be accomplished through election by the people through the instrument of the states' chosen electors.

Morris championed also the virtues of reeligibility. He believed a major incentive or motive for good behavior rested on the hope of being rewarded by being reelected. Morris, in a blistering indictment, condemned the ineligibility provision that had been approved in July:

> What effect will this [ineligibility] have? In the first place it will destroy the great incitement to merit and public esteem by taking away the hope of being rewarded with a reappointment. It may give a dangerous turn to one of the strongest passions in the human breast. The love of fame is the great spring to noble and illustrious actions. Shut the Civil road to Glory and he may be compelled to seek it by the sword. In the second place it will tempt him to make the most of the short space of time allotted him, to accumulate wealth and provide for his friends. In the third place it will produce violations of the very constitution it is meant to secure. In moments of pressing danger the tried abilities and established character of a favorite Magistrate [president] will prevail over respect for the forms of the Constitution. . . . Let him be of short duration, that he may with propriety be re-eligible.[6]

A few days later, Morris continued his attack on the idea of a single, nonrenewable term:

> In order to get rid of the dependence of the Executive on the legislature, the expedient of making him ineligible a second time has been devised. This was as much as to say we should give him the benefit of experience, then deprive ourselves of the use of it. But make him ineligible a second time—and prolong his duration even to 15-years, will he by any wonderful interposition of providence at that period cease to be a man? No he will be unwilling to quit his exaltation, the road to his object through the Constitution will be shut; he will be in possession of the sword, a civil war will ensue, and the commander of the victorious army on which ever side, will be the despot of America. . . . Make him too weak: the legislature will usurp his powers: Make him too strong, he will usurp on the Legislature. He [Morris] preferred a short period, a re-eligibility, but a different mode of election. A long period [a long term for president] would prevent an adoption [ratification] of the plan [the proposed presidency in the Const.]: it ought to do so. He [Morris] should himself be afraid to trust it.[7]

In sum, Morris thought ineligibility would weaken if not destroy the proposed Constitution. Morris favored a strong presidency so it could defend itself against legislative encroachment. It could do this only if it was designed properly. Regular rotation in the office would, he believed, undermine the independence necessary for a vital executive. Moreover, Morris believed the forced retirement of a popular leader might sometimes lead to that leader's subsequent return to office or to his resisting departure through unconstitutional means. James Wilson, James Madison, and Alexander Hamilton generally agreed with Morris's position. So also, it appears, did George Washington.[8]

The keys to resolving the dilemma over whether to permit presidential reelection was the electoral college and, to a lesser extent, the provision for impeachment. Once it had been agreed that "the people," or at least a group of nonfederal leaders in the states, would do the electing, the fear of executive dependence on the legislature diminished. Once this new mode of election had been approved, the compromise of four-year terms with reeligibility was readily fashioned.

This would be agreed to by most, but not all delegates. And once again, the issue would not die. It would be raised and extended during the ratifying conventions in the states. Although in muted form, the debates about term, tenure, and reeligibility continue today.

THE ANTIFEDERALIST ATTACK

The Antifederalists, as the Constitution's critics were called, were especially upset by the absence of a bill of rights and by the fear that the states would become inferior to a strong, consolidated national government. Most of the Antifederalists conceded the need for some form of executive in a strengthened national government. Yet some of them would have preferred a plural executive or at least an executive with less power.

Various Antifederalists, especially in the key states of Massachusetts, Virginia, and New York, objected to virtually every power the president had been granted. Objections were posed to the four-year term and to the possibility of reelection; yet these were not as central as one might have expected.

> The relative lack of concern over the President's term is surprising, when there was so much criticism of the Senate on this score, and when the governments established by the Articles and the state constitutions were so different in this regard. Perhaps the reason lay in the popularity of Washington: most people agreed that he would be President, did not care how long he served, and could not see that it made any difference how he was chosen.[9]

A handful of critics of the Constitution, however, did aim their fire at the term and tenure of presidents. Populists said that the long terms of the senators and the four-year term with potential perpetual reelection for presidents invited an oligarchy. Governor Edmund Randolph of Virginia initially feared that either a monarchy or an aristocracy would result. Patrick Henry, the legendary patriot orator, viewed the overall scheme as the most fatal plan that could possibly be designed to enslave a free people. Critics up and down the Atlantic seaboard declared that the plan had critical defects, should be amended as soon as possible by a second federal (or constitutional) convention, called to vote upon amendments proposed by the states, and that finally this much-amended constitution should be resubmitted for ratification to the various state ratifying conventions.

The Antifederalists got a slow start. After all, the Constitutional Convention had met in secret at Philadelphia, and the exact details of their plan were slow to make their way through the states. The delegates who had attended the convention, moreover, were well versed in the subtleties and nuances of the proposed document. Moreover, many of the veterans of the Revolution—men and officers who had fought alongside George Washington—were known to support it. Still, confusion and uncertainties were great. And the average person was skeptical, if not outright opposed, to the proposed "great and mighty President" with "the powers of a king," to use Henry's words.

The influential and powerful governor of New York, George Clinton, condemned the length-of-term and the reeligibility provisions, saying that a president who was possessed of ambition would have "the power and time sufficient to ruin his country."[10] Thomas Jefferson, who was still representing American interests in Paris, wrote home disparagingly about the perpetual reeligibility of the president. It would cause, he said, cruel distress to the country even during his lifetime.

An Antifederalist, writing as "Federal Farmer," posed the fears this way:

When a man shall get the chair, who may be re-elected, from time to time, for life, his greatest object will be to keep it; to gain friends and votes, at any rate; to associate some favourite son with himself, to take the office after him: whenever he shall have any prospect of continuing the office in himself and family, he will spare no artifice, no address, and no Exertions, to increase the powers and importance of it; the servile supporters of his wishes will be placed in all offices, and tools constantly employed to aid his views and sound his praise. A man so situated will have no permanent interest in the government to lose, by contests and convulsions in the state, but always much to gain and frequently the seducing and flattering hope of succeeding. If we reason at all on the subject, we must irresistibly conclude, that this will be the case with nine-tenths of the presidents; we may have, for the first president, and, perhaps, one in a century or two afterwards (if the government should withstand the attacks of others) a great and good man, governed by superior motives; but these are not events to be calculated upon in the present state of human nature.[11]

Patrick Henry, holding forth at length at the Virginia convention called to ratify the Constitution, deplored its features as horribly frightful. "Among other deformities, it has an awful squinting; it squints toward monarchy." He feared this new American chief could make himself absolute. Who would stop him if he should violate the laws? asked the great orator. "We shall have a king; the army will salute him monarch: your militia will leave you, and assist in making him king and fight against you."[12]

James Monroe, a future president, also criticized the presidency provisions. He feared that once a clever president was elected, he would be elected forever. George Mason, another Virginian and one of the three delegates who remained to the bitter end of the convention yet refused to sign the completed draft of the Constitution, joined the chorus of Antifederalists at the ratifying convention in Richmond. He, too, attacked the reeligibility of presidents:

> Mr. Chairman, there is not a more important article in the Constitution than this. The great fundamental principle of responsibility in republicanism is here sapped. The President is elected without rotation. It may be said that a new election may remove him, and place another in his stead. If we judge from the experience of all other countries, and even in our own, we may conclude that, as the President of the United States may be reelected, so he will. How is it in every government where rotation is not required? Is there a single instance of a great man not being reelected? Our governor is obliged to return, after a given period, to a private station. It is so in most of the states. This President will be elected time after time: he will be continued in office for life. If we wish to change him, the great powers in Europe will not allow us.[13]

The Federalists, the defenders of the Constitution, counterattacked with at least as much intellectual force and with nearly as much overstatement as did their critics. George Washington, although he refrained from actively campaigning for adoption, let it be known that he believed there was no alternative between ratifying the Constitution and anarchy. Others argued, as they had in Philadelphia, that a strong, independent executive was needed because excessive legislative rule making might lead to failed policies and majoritarian tyranny, as it had in some of the states. The very success of the experiment in republican government was at stake.

Federalists such as James Madison, James Wilson, and Alexander Hamilton emphasized, too, that a president who misused his powers could be impeached. They stressed as well that a president was vastly different from a hereditary monarch and, indeed, had far more in common with the governor of New York State, who was elected for three years and was reeligible without exclusion. "If we consider how much less time would be requisite for establishing a dangerous influence in a single State, than for establishing a like influence throughout the United States," wrote Hamilton, "we must conclude that a duration of *four* years for the Chief Magistrate of the Union is a degree of permanency far less to be dreaded in that office, than a duration of *three* years for a corresponding officer in a single State."[14]

Alexander Hamilton devoted *Federalist* number 71 to defending the four-year term for the president. Duration in office, he said, was one of the requisites to the energy of executive leadership. An executive needs to be in office long enough to develop a strong interest in the government's goals and administrative needs. A four-year term is long enough, Hamilton seemed to be saying, to provide for a proper independence from the legislature, a firmness in authority, and continuity, yet "it is not enough to justify any alarm for the public liberty."[15]

In *Federalist* number 72, Hamilton debated the merits of presidential reeligibility. The best incentive to do an excellent job in the presidency, said Hamilton, is to have the possibility of being rewarded with another term of office. He worried, too, if reeligibility was not permitted, about the prospect of having several involuntarily retired presidents roam the countryside "like discontented ghosts, and sighing for a place which they were destined never more to possess." He also defended reeligibility on the grounds that it would provide for additional stability in the administration of the nation's laws.

Yet Hamilton's most compelling contention was that a prohibition against reelection would deprive the voters of the advantage of the experience a president would have gained in the performance of the office. "Can it be wise to put this desirable and essential quality [experience] under the ban of the constitution," wrote Hamilton, "and to declare that the moment it is acquired, its possessor shall be compelled to abandon the station in which it was acquired, and to which it is adapted?"

Further, why banish an experienced and wise executive on those occasions, four years into office, when a major war or emergency confronts the Republic?

There is no nation which has not, at one period or another, experienced an absolute necessity of the services of particular men in particular situations; perhaps it would not be too strong to say, to the preservation of its political existence. How unwise, therefore, must be every such self-denying ordinance as serves to prohibit a nation from making use of its own citizens in the manner best suited to its exigencies and circumstances! Without supposing the personal essentiality of the man, it is evident that a change of the chief magistrate, at the breaking out of a war, or at any similar crisis . . . would at all times be detrimental to the community; inasmuch as it would substitute inexperience to experience, and would tend to unhinge and set afloat the already settled train of the administration.[16]

Ultimately, the Federalists prevailed, and the Constitution had won ratification in eleven states by July, 1788—less than a year after it had been drafted and signed in Philadelphia. North Carolina held out for more than another year, and Rhode Island, for nearly one more.

Delegates to at least three of the state ratifying conventions proposed the immediate adoption of constitutional amendments to restrict presidential reeligibility. New York called for prohibiting a third term. North Carolina recommended that no president be permitted to serve for more than eight years during any fifteen-year period. Virginia approved the same recommendation, substituting sixteen years for fifteen.

Once the Constitution had been adopted, the Congress—which had assembled in New York, the temporary national capital—responded favorably to the call for a series of constitutional amendments to protect individual freedoms, but it ignored demands for revising the provisions for presidential tenure. In the First Congress, after the Constitution had gone into effect, a representative from South Carolina submitted to the House a measure that would have prohibited any president from serving more than eight out of any twelve years. Both it and a similar measure in the Senate failed. It is widely believed that Washington's election had "allayed doubts to permit the launching of the new government without alteration of any feature relating to the executive that had been agreed on in the Constitutional Convention."[17]

ESTABLISHING THE TWO-TERM AND ONE-TERM TRADITIONS

The founders expected George Washington to serve as the first president and to remain as long as he wished. Washington, however, was reluctant to serve at all, was reluctant to stand for reelection in 1792, and was happy to retire after two terms. The principle of unlimited eligibility for reelection, which Hamilton and others had fought to establish, was innocently yet clearly undermined by Washington's action. Washington, unlike Jefferson or the staunchest Antifederalists, saw no need of, or special merit in, the rotation principle. He in no way frowned upon the idea of a third term for presidents.

President Washington retired, not because he favored a two-term tradition, but because he was tired and wanted to return to private life. He believed he had served his nation long enough, and few could disagree. The two-term tradition may have been started by him, but he left the job because he no longer wanted it and its burdens, not because he was concerned about the fate of American democracy or was against a third or fourth or even more terms.

In the process of retiring voluntarily, he helped refute the critics who thought he or other presidents would harbor monarchical aspirations. "He was demonstrating the principle essential to a free government that succession should be determined as a matter of course by the people rather than by Father Time's scythe," wrote one of his biographers. "He had gone against the precedents of history, which made his act the more remarkable, the more endearing."[18]

Although the two-term tradition was started in 1796, Washington did not set the precedent for political reasons. Jefferson was the first executive to reject a third term primarily on political grounds. "Anyone who today endeavors to find substantial historical evidence for the hypothesis that a third presidential term will imperil such democracy as we may have," wrote Charles Stein in 1943, "must look beyond both the Founding Fathers and the Father of our Country; he must look instead, by one of the ironies of American history, to the founder of the Democratic Party— Thomas Jefferson."[19] Jefferson was unwilling to serve another term, even though several state legislatures urged him to do so. Jefferson stepped down, saying it was important to do so, for otherwise the presidency might degenerate into an inheritance.

In many respects, Jefferson can lay claim to having established the one-term tradition as well. For it was Jefferson, while serving as vice-president under John Adams, who fought successfully to oust Adams in 1800, at the end of just one term. Adams's defeat rests as much with the divisiveness in the ranks of the Federalists, especially in New York, as it does on Jefferson's cleverness or political astuteness. The Adams administration had been reasonably successful in terms of accomplishments, despite the personal deficiencies of Adams.

What is notable for our purposes about the one-term Adams presidency and the election of 1800 is that they began the one-term tradition—the dominant tradition in American presidential politics—and they marked the peaceful transfer of power from one political party to another. That this was accomplished "in a peaceful and orderly fashion demonstrated the majority of the nation's first system of political parties." It was also the first test of strength of the "two national parties that had been formed in the course of the 1790's, and, more than any Presidential election that had preceded or would follow for at least a generation, it was a *party* contest for control of the national administration and for determining the direction and the management of national policy."[20]

Only thirteen of our presidents have won reelection to a second consecutive term, and only Franklin D. Roosevelt won three such elections on the heels of his first term. For various reasons, Washington and Jefferson established the two-term tradition. Adams, aided by Jefferson, and Adams's son John Quincy Adams, aided by Andrew Jackson, began a familiar series of one-term presidencies. FDR broke the two term precedent, and the country retaliated by amending the Constitution and prohibiting a president from being elected for more than two terms. His unprecedented action and the adoption of the Twenty-second Amendment rekindled many of the old debates first waged in Philadelphia in 1787. Today the issues on this matter are posed in terms of the proposed six-year term, with no reeligibility and the occasional movement to repeal the Twenty-second Amendment.

A SINGLE SIX-YEAR TERM?
AN ENDURING DEBATE

The idea of a single six-year term has a long history, extending back to the Philadelphia debates of 1787. Thomas Jefferson revived the idea in 1809. Presidents Andrew Johnson, William Harrison, Rutherford B. Hayes, William Howard Taft, Lyndon B. Johnson, and Jimmy Carter have also advocated a single nonrenewable term. Further, at least two hundred constitutional amendments in favor of this idea have been proposed in Congress.

The basic argument in favor of the single nonrenewable term (and sometimes the term suggested is one of seven rather than six years) is that it would free a president from campaigning for reelection during the first term. Freed from that diversionary chore, presidents, or so the contention goes, could concentrate their time on performing the duties of being chief executive. Their motives might be purer, or at least not subject to as much suspicion. The intention is to create credible presidents who will talk directly to the people and take steps that need to be taken without putting off the tough decisions until after the next election.

There is also a legitimate concern that a presidential term of four years goes by very quickly and that four years is too short a time to get the job done. Federal budgets, for example have already been cast for about two years ahead when a president gets into office. Surely, too, there is a valid concern about whether a president in wartime can concentrate adequately on fighting and winning the war while waging an all-out campaign for reelection. Finally, say its advocates, the single term might lessen the role of narrow, partisan politics and negative campaigning and thereby lessen the likelihood of scandals such as Watergate.

All of this sounds strikingly familiar. Some delegates at Philadelphia emphasized that a president should not be left in a position to court reappointment. And a delegate in the South Carolina ratifying convention of 1788 strongly objected to the chief executive's being able to run again for an unlimited number of terms. The president's term is just for four years, James Lincoln reminded his fellow delegates, but "he may hold it for fourteen times four years: in short, he may hold it so long that it would be impossible, without another revolution, to displace him."[21]

The American people, when polled on the idea of a six-year nonrenewable term, have regularly rejected it, usually by at least a 60 to 40 percent vote. I believe the people are correct in this. By no means is the four-year term, with reelection allowed for a second term, perfect; but compared with the alternatives, it has served us well.

American voters have by and large made prudent decisions every four years. It is good for presidents, as well as for the general public, that after three and a half years, a president must get out of the White House and listen to real people and hear about *their* concerns, wants, and aspirations for the Republic. The controversial constitutional amendment for a lengthened presidential term would create more problems than it would solve, and it should be rejected. Here are at least six reasons.

First, a six-year nonrenewable term would give us either two more years of the "clunkers" or two years less of the truly outstanding presidents. Do we really want two years more of the Hardings, Pierces, and Buchanans and two years less of the Washingtons, Roosevelts, and Eisenhowers? A useful statistical analysis of the hypothetical impact of the six-year term has concluded that it would have reduced the tenure of relatively effective presidents and increased the tenure of ineffective presidents. "The nation's most highly regarded presidents through history and presidents who were relatively successful in dealing with Congress would have been the chief losers . . . lightly regarded presidents with limited success in congressional relations would have been the chief winners."[22]

Second, four years is long enough for the American voter to decide whether a president is doing the job and whether the incumbent deserves reelection or rejection. Supporters of the six-year term say presidents need more time to process their policies. Sweeping policy changes, to be sure, may take four years or even longer; however, four years provide enough time for a president to demonstrate initial success or to persuade the public of the merits of key policies. Lincoln, FDR, and Reagan, for example, were all able to make their cases before the fourth of November had rolled around. Voters do not demand instant results. But surely, near the end of the fourth year, major program initiatives of a first-term president should be able to stand the test of close voter evaluation. The six-year term would release presidents from the desirable test of submitting their records to the voters.

Third, a president can seek reelection and still be a creative, effective, full-time president. If Lincoln could run again in 1864 and Roosevelt in 1944, other presidents should also be able to face the voters. Frankly, the best way to campaign for reelection is to be a first-rate problem-solving president—doing the job, setting the directions, and shaping new policy strategies to the best of one's ability. American voters can usually detect the phony or the misfit in the White House. They can usually judge whom to keep and whom to turn out of office.

If a president is doing the job reasonably well and if there is no challenger on the scene who looks better, the American people will usually return the incumbent to office. If, however, the incumbent is failing to make the office work properly, people will question the performance and reject the incumbent. The important point is that a president does not have to campaign in every precinct. Presidents do not have to spend 20 or 30 percent of their precious time being candidates. That argument is spurious. An elective president, who is doing the right things, needs only to report to the nation and perhaps make a few swings around the major regions of the country. Television has helped tremendously to overcome the difficulty of communicating with the voters. Television has allowed a president to report directly to the citizens or "stockholders" of the nation.

Fourth, presidents *should be* guided by how the voters will judge them at the next election. Supporters of the six-year single term somehow think this is improper. In most instances, it is preferable to have a president who is guided by voters' appraisal at the end of four years than by what a president alone thinks is best or by what he or she alone thinks will look good in the history texts. The accountability of the four-year election cycle forces presidents to achieve their most salient campaign promises. In a sense, our current system is an action-forcing process. It is a midterm audit permitting the voters to judge whether a president has lived up to what he has said he would do. Under a six-year term, Lyndon Johnson might have continued to escalate the Vietnam War until 1970. Under a six-year term, Richard Nixon might have left troops in Vietnam until 1974 rather than 1972. In 1984 the nation witnessed the tempering effect that the desire for reelection had on President Reagan. He stopped his talk about the "evil empire," announced a serious interest in arms negotiations with the Soviets, and supported Social Security, among other moderate proposals. Under a six-year term, presidents might become removed from the public, just as many United States senators seem to forget whom they are representing.

Fifth, those who favor the six-year term do so in the vain hope that politics can be removed from the American presidency. Yet the presidency is a political position, and presidents at their best have to be shrewd politicians. Many of the supporters of the single term dislike the rough and tumble of contemporary American interest-group politics. They also seem to distrust the American voter. But politics in this country has always been a rough, demanding profession. Thus, presidents have to be politicians. To ask a president to rise above politics is like asking a bishop or a rabbi to rise above religion.

The idea of trying to elect a nonpartisan national "city manager" is an illusion, and it is not a very good idea anyway. A president has to be a party leader, has to be concerned with forming majorities, and should rightly be concerned with the possibilities of being reelected or turned out of office. Presidents must be mindful that this is a democratic republic, and ultimately they must be accountable to majority approval; this is precisely what the hope of reeligibility helps to achieve. Reelection or defeat is a principal tool for keeping elected executive officials in touch with the people.

Sixth, it is generally undesirable to limit the discretion of the voters as to whom they will choose to rule them or to represent them. Let the voters judge the ability of all of the available candidates for executive office, including the incumbent, at least for a second term. Imposing a restriction on the freedom to reelect a president is to violate an essential principle of democracy—namely, that voters have the right to exercise a free and uncensored ballot.

Finally, the Constitution should be amended only when there is compelling evidence that the Republic would be significantly improved by the proposed change. The notion that a six-year nonrenewable term for presidents would provide Americans with the leadership and governance they now lack is a suspect notion. The arms race, tension with the Soviets, trade imbalances, and soaring deficits are the product of deficiencies in political leadership or political theories. These conflicts are not deficiencies of governmental structure. If most of these problems would continue under a six-year term, the advocates of a lengthened presidential term may well be back a few years later advocating yet-another constitutional amendment for an eight- or a ten-year term.

The framers were right when they dismissed the idea of a single lengthy term. Four years is a long time. It was a good compromise.

THE TWENTY-SECOND AMENDMENT:
THE DEBATE CONTINUES

The idea inherent in the Twenty-second Amendment is also at least as old as the debates in Philadelphia. As I noted earlier, it was approved at the 1788 New York State ratifying convention as a proposed amendment to the newly drafted Constitution.

From 1789 to the 1940s the proposal was endorsed on countless occasions, yet it was never seriously considered until Franklin D. Roosevelt broke the two-term tradition. Early in 1940, New Jersey, New York, and Rhode Island passed resolutions in their state legislatures calling for a limit on presidential terms. In 1943, more states did the same. In 1940 and again in 1944, the Republican party platform called for a two-term limitation. Yet only after FDR had died did the motion win considerable support. In 1947 it passed Congress by substantial margins, and by early 1951 it had won final adoption by the requisite number of states. The Twenty-second Amendment states that "no person shall be elected to the office of President more than twice."

Presidents Truman, Eisenhower, and Reagan have all urged that this term limit be repealed. When President Reagan came to the White House, he supported the Twenty-second Amendment. Early in his second term, however, he changed his mind. Reagan then said he believed the Twenty-second Amendment violated the people's democratic rights: the people ought to have a right to decide who their leaders will be. Reagan also stated that if the people want to vote for someone, there should not be any rule telling them they can't.

Reagan believed the two-term tradition had wisely been established by George Washington because at the time citizens of the new republic were conscientiously watching to make sure that the United States would not become anything like a monarchy. Reagan thought FDR's reelection to third and fourth terms had proved that a multiterm presidency could happen without impairing the Republic. Reagan said, too, there were plenty of safeguards against the power of the presidency that would prevent him from becoming a lifetime monarch or the like.

Agreeing with Reagan, at least a third of Americans, according to a Gallup poll in October, 1986, said they would like to see this amendment repealed so that presidents could run for more than two terms. A 1986 *Wall Street Journal* poll found slightly stronger support for repeal. (Not surprisingly, twice as many Republicans as Democrats favored repeal.) Reagan and the "reforming public" are joined by a number of both conservative and liberal intellectuals. Some critics of the amendment say it is destructive to make a president a lame duck the day he is sworn in for the second term; the amendment eliminates much of his ability to insist upon respect and to instill fear, which form the basis of reasonable politics: the ability to reward and to punish.

By imposing a restriction on the freedom to reelect a president repeatedly, the essential principle of democracy is violated, say other proponents of repeal: people have a right to exercise a free ballot, even if they exercise it badly. The Twenty-second Amendment places a limitation upon the electorate, they add, the first change since the Constitution was adopted that has restricted rather than expanded the voter's suffrage.

The framers, historians note, considered and debated the idea of limiting the number of terms, but rejected it. Echoing Hamilton's reasoning in *Federalist* number 72, some historians have said nothing makes a president more attentive to popular needs and concerns than the desire for reelection. Again, reminiscent of Hamilton, they also claim that the country may desperately need an experienced veteran of public and world affairs during a time of crisis—for example, an FDR to run again in 1940 or a Lincoln in 1864.

Those who favor repeal raise some good points. Clearly, the amendment does diminish the choices of a voter, and it is valid to say that the voters in 2008 or 2088 will be in a better position than those who supported the Twenty-second Amendment in the post-FDR period to decide who should be their president.

Much of the rest of the case for repeal, however, appears either exaggerated or misleading. To be sure, it was indeed a "Republican revenge against Roosevelt." It is one of our less important amendments, yet its repeal could cause more harm than good, and it could send the wrong signals. It would, for example, be a positive affirmation of the virtues of multiterm presidencies. It might weaken our national party system. It might further strengthen the institution of the presidency in a century when this has already taken place in nearly every decade—usually at the expense of countervailing checks and balances. Until a more effective amendment can be devised to replace the Twenty-second, Americans would be better off retaining than repealing it.

Here are the chief reasons why two terms are enough. Eight years is long enough. Americans do not like the idea of a permanent president or to view the presidency as a career job. Such presidents as Jefferson, Jackson, and John F. Kennedy have praised the notion of rotation in office as desirable and healthy. Jefferson warned that history shows how easily unlimited tenure might degenerate into an inheritance. And as William F. Buckley, Jr., has written, "Against the proposition that a democratic people should have the right to continue whosoever is in power for whatever period they want is the republican tradition of the citizen leader, the Cincinnatus who lays down his plow to serve, and picks up his plow again, having served."[23]

The presidency is an awesome position for any person, however experienced and talented. Its powers and responsibilities have become enlarged during the last fifty years, and this will doubtless continue during the next fifty. The rise in the mechanisms and resources of power available to presidents, such as once-unimaginable nuclear weapons, covert operations, satellite intelligence systems, and a veritable "electronic throne," suggest new dangers even to those Americans who want a strong, effective presidency. The Twenty-second Amendment may not have been needed in 1947, but it will prove to be an invaluable additional check in the future, without taking away from the effectiveness of the good presidents. It is a check against the ultimate type of corruption—the arrogant view that a particular president is indispensable, the very inclination that motivated Ferdinand Marcos in the Philippines, General Anastasio Somoza in Nicaragua, the Duvaliers in Haiti, and countless others. The Twenty-second Amendment might, like impeachment, only be needed once in a century, yet it would be there to protect against our would-be savior who could in fact be our enslaver.

Eight years is ample time for a president and an administration to bring about major changes in policy. And if these changes have been valued and effective, they will be continued and honored by the succeeding presidents of whatever party. Further, an able and honest president need not become lame, although most presidents understandably witness a diminution of power in their last years because of normal fatigue and the reality that they have already advocated and fought for their best ideas during their first term and a half. Eisenhower's effectiveness was not impaired during his second term because of it. Nor was Reagan a lame duck because of this term limitation. "Reagan's experiences suggest that the 22nd Amendment is not bad," observed his ardent supporter the columnist George F. Will. "Eight years is almost always going to be long enough, and the limitation does not appreciably hasten the onset of lame-duck status. Even if Reagan were ten years younger, the amendment would not today be counted among the primary factors contributing to the anemia of his presidency."[24] Note too that a "lameness" set in on many a president before the amendment was adopted (Woodrow Wilson, Herbert C. Hoover, and Harry S. Truman, for example, saw their power and authority eroded during their last year or two in office). The two-term limitation is only one, and probably an exaggerated, cause of "lame-duck-ness."

The two-term limit is healthy for the two-party system. It helps prevent political stagnation. The two parties benefit and are rejuvenated by the challenge at least every eight years of nurturing, recruiting, and nominating a new team of national leaders. In this sense, the very existence of this amendment prevents the hardening of the political arteries. Change every eight years adds a degree of "freshness" and new energy—commodities our Madisonian system can always use.

Most Americans reject the idea that any political leader is indispensable. We have believed in citizen-leaders rather than career or long-tenured presidents. We are a nation of seventy times as many people as we were in 1789. There are plenty of talented leaders. Moreover, if a president of the stature and ability of a Washington, a Lincoln, or an FDR were available and if the nation were facing an exacting emergency, their services and leadership would not need to be thrown out and ignored merely because a successor president would come to office at the end of eight years. Common sense dictates that these exceptional public servants be retained as national counselors, roving ambassadors, or cabinet members without portfolio—precisely to take advantage of their experience and expertise.

Although the two-term limit does somewhat diminish the choice of the voter, this restriction is only likely to occur once every fifty years, if then. Most presidents do not even get a second term. Few leaders are likely to have the health, the intellectual energy, and the new ideas needed to perform the demanding responsibilities of the presidency after eight years in office. It might be noted also that the voters are not upset by this diminution of their voting privilege: at least 60 percent, according to several surveys, support the retention of the two-term limit. Moreover, the charge that it is undemocratic is somewhat irrelevant. Ours is not a pure democracy; it is a republican government under a federal system. Our republican government and constitutional forms purposely limit the majority of voters in a number of ways and protect the minority, however small. In a sense, the limits of the Twenty-second Amendment stand—together with judicial review, age and residency requirements to run for office, and the supermajorities needed for the ratification of treaties or the amending of the Constitution—as safeguards against undesirable or excessive majoritarianism.

A look at many of the big-city mayors who have stayed for a third or fourth four-year term provides additional skepticism about repealing this amendment. Of course there are exceptions. Yet in Boston, Chicago, Detroit, Newark, Kansas City, New York, Syracuse, and Washington, D.C., to suggest just a few, multiterm mayors and their associates during their later terms have often been less responsive, less accountable, and more tempted to engage in arrogance, deception, or even outright corruption than was the case during their first or second terms.

A president who stays on for twelve or sixteen years would very likely be able to stack, if not pack, the Supreme Court, and fundamentally to alter the partisan leanings of the *entire* federal judiciary. FDR appointed nine justices in twelve years. Nixon appointed four in just five years. Do we want presidents these days who could dominate and thereby control two branches of government?

Although the Twenty-second Amendment has its drawbacks, its virtues will be appreciated by future generations. Americans want an effective presidency, yet Americans fear the arbitrary abuse of power and the potential of presidents who someday may delude themselves into believing they are indispensable. The two-term limit allows a citizen to serve eight years in one of the world's most powerful positions, while it protects the country from the potential excesses of power that could come with prolonged tenure. It is an acceptable, if imperfect, compromise.

CONCLUSIONS

Plainly, the adoption of the constitution did not end the debates over constitutional structure and processes. That struggle was only beginning. When it comes to the questions of presidential term, tenure, and reeligibility, it often seems that the federal convention of 1787 is still in session. More than two hundred years later, Americans are still hearing the same debates and similar reasoning, and they are observing the familiar maneuvering aimed at enhancing or constraining presidential power.

Rarely are procedural reforms neutral in terms of their policy and power consequences. And so it is with these debates about presidential tenure. The post-Roosevelt crusade to enact the Twenty-second Amendment to the Constitution was clearly an exercise in retroactive partisan vengeance. A minor boomlet in 1972 and 1973 to repeal the two-term limit was an effort by Nixon's friends to pave the way for his possible reelection to a third term. A 1986 boomlet to banish the Twenty-second Amendment was another transparent partisan ploy to retain the White House for yet-another four years and to reap the political advantages of patronage, judicial nomination, and Reagan's once magical partisan fund-raising talents. These last two efforts died with the revelations of Watergate and the Iran-Contra affair. Predictably, however, there will be similar drives either to repeal the two-term limit or to enact a single six-year term.

The four-year presidential term with limited reeligibility has a long and complicated history. It can be defended more because of its practical working than by logic or by constitutional principles. Still, just as experience rather than grand theories was the chief guide for those at Philadelphia, so also experience necessarily and understandably shapes our constitutional outlook today. Term and tenure for presidents were the sources of prolonged dispute and deliberation in Philadelphia. The framers settled the matter temporarily. In 1951, Americans fundamentally altered the framers' decision. Most of the founders would have understood; many of them would have been pleased. And because of the ever-present American ambivalence toward executive power, we can almost assuredly say that Americans have not heard the last of this debate.

NOTES

1. Allan Nevins, *The American States during and after Their Revolution, 1775–1789* (New York: Macmillan, 1924), p. 166.
2. Jackson Turner Main, *The Sovereign States, 1775–1783* (New York: New Viewpoints, 1973), p. 190.
3. Richard B. Morris, "The Origins of the Presidency," *Presidential Studies Quarterly,* Fall, 1987, p. 674.
4. Alexander Hamilton, letter in 1780 to James Duane, reprinted in Harold C. Syrett and Jacob Cooke, eds., *The Papers of Alexander Hamilton,* 17 vols. (New York: Columbia University Press, 1961), 2:404.
5. Delegate Gunning Bedford, quoted in Madison's Notes, reprinted in Philip B. Kurland and Ralph Lerner, eds., *The Founders' Constitution,* 5 vols. (Chicago: University of Chicago Press, 1987), 3:492.
6. Madison's Notes, as edited by Wilbourne E. Benton, *1787: Drafting the U.S. Constitution* (College Station: Texas A & M University Press, 1986), 2:1133–34.
7. Ibid., pp. 1146–47.
8. See Donald L. Robinson, "Gouverneur Morris and the Design of the American Presidency," *Presidential Studies Quarterly,* Spring, 1987, pp. 322–23.
9. Jackson Turner Main, *The Antifederalists: Critics of the Constitution, 1781–1788* (Chicago: Quadrangle Books, 1961), p. 141.
10. George Clinton, "The Letters of Cato," reprinted in Harry A. Bailey, Jr., ed., *Classics of the American Presidency* (Oak Park, Ill.: Moore Publishing Co., 1980), p. 19.
11. Federal Farmer, letter no. 14 (Jan. 17, 1788), reprinted in Herbert J. Storing, ed., *The Complete Anti-Federalist,* 7 vols. (Chicago: University of Chicago Press, 1981), 2:179.
12. The Patrick Henry quotes are in Albert J. Beveridge, *The Life of John Marshall,* vol. 1 (Boston, Mass.: Houghton Mifflin, 1916), pp. 390, 391. See also Jonathan Elliot, ed. *The Debates in the Several State Conventions,* 2d ed., 5 vols. (New York: Burt Franklin, n.d.).
13. Mason, reprinted in Kurland and Lerner, *Founders' Constitution,* 3:514.
14. Alexander Hamilton, *Federalist* no. 69, in *Federalist,* ed. Jacob E. Cooke (Cleveland: Meridian Books, 1961), p. 483.
15. Hamilton, *Federalist* no. 71, ibid., p. 485.
16. Hamilton, *Federalist* no. 72, ibid., p. 490.
17. Joseph E. Kallenbach, *The American Chief Executive: The Presidency and the Governorship* (New York: Harper & Row, 1966), p. 67.
18. James Thomas Flexner, *George Washington: Anguish and Farewell (1793–1799)* (Boston, Mass.: Little, Brown, 1969), p. 304.
19. Charles W. Stein, *The Third Term Tradition: Its Rise and Collapse in American Politics* (New York: Columbia University Press, 1943), p. 30.
20. Noble E. Cunningham, Jr. "Election of 1800," in *The Coming To Power: Critical Presidential Elections in American History,* Arthur M. Schlesinger, Jr., ed. (New York: Chelsea House, 1971), p. 33.

21. Quoted in Stephen W. Stathis, *Presidential Tenure: A History and Analysis of The President's Term of Office* (Washington, D.C.: Congressional Research Service, Library of Congress, May, 1981), pp. 24–25.

22. David C. Nice, "In Retreat from Excellence: The Single Six-Year Presidential Term," *Congress and the Presidency,* Autumn, 1986, p. 218.

23. William F. Buckley, "Repeal 22?" *National Review,* Sept. 12, 1986, p. 61.

24. George F. Will, "Eight [Years] Is Enough," *Newsweek,* Nov. 23, 1987, p. 92.

4

PRESIDENTIAL IMPEACHMENT

JOHN R. LABOVITZ

The House of Representatives . . . shall have the sole Power of Impeachment.
—*Article I, section 2*

The Senate shall have the sole Power to try all Impeachments. When sitting for that Purpose, they shall be on Oath or Affirmation. When the President of the United States is tried, the Chief Justice shall preside: And no Person shall be convicted without the Concurrence of two thirds of the Members present.
—*Article I, section 3*

The President, Vice President and all civil Officers of the United States, shall be removed from Office on Impeachment for, and Conviction of, Treason, Bribery, or other High Crimes and Misdemeanors.
—*Article II, section 4*

The Constitution contains half a dozen provisions referring to impeachment. It provides that the president (as well as the vice-president and all civil officers of the United States) "shall be removed from Office on Impeachment for, and Conviction of, Treason, Bribery, or other High Crimes and Misdemeanors" (Art. II, sec. 4). It vests "the sole Power of Impeachment" in the House of Representatives (Art. I, sec. 2) and "the sole Power to try all Impeachments" in the Senate (Art. I, sec. 3). It requires that when sitting for the purpose of an impeachment trial, members of the Senate "shall be on Oath or Affirmation"; when the president is tried, the chief justice shall preside; "no Person shall be convicted without the concurrence of two thirds of the Members present"; and "Judgment in Cases of Impeachment shall not extend further than to removal from Office, and disqualification to hold and enjoy any Office of honor, Trust or Profit under the United States: but the Party convicted shall nevertheless be liable and subject to Indictment, Trial, Judgment and

Punishment, according to Law" (Art. I, sec. 3). The other references to impeachment are exceptions from provisions that would otherwise be applicable to offenses or crimes. Article II, section 2 provides that the president "shall have Power to grant Reprieves and Pardons for Offences against the United States, except in Cases of Impeachment"; Article III, section 2, provides that "the Trial of all Crimes, except in Cases of Impeachment, shall be by Jury; and such Trial shall be held in the State where the said Crimes shall have been committed."

THE DRAFTING OF THE IMPEACHMENT PROVISIONS OF THE CONSTITUTION

The constitutional provisions concerning impeachment were drafted with the removal of the president primarily in mind. The delegates to the Constitutional Convention wished to create an independent, but responsible, executive. They had difficulty, however, reconciling the concept of executive accountability with the principle of separation of powers, which was fundamental to their new scheme of government. To avoid the executive's usurpation of power, the delegates sought to provide checks upon his conduct, including a provision for removing him through impeachment. But to ensure the independence of the executive, they sought to avoid having him be subservient to the legislature. These general concerns were central to their deliberations on the related questions of the composition of the executive, the mode of selection, the length of term, reeligibility, and impeachment.

The Initial Deliberations of the Convention in the Committee of the Whole

The Constitutional Convention began its deliberations in the Committee of the Whole, considering the Virginia Plan for a national government—fifteen resolutions that had been drawn up by delegates from that state and proposed to the convention by Edmund Randolph on May 29, 1787. The resolutions called for a national legislature of two branches, a national executive, and a national judiciary. The seventh resolution proposed a national executive "to be chosen by the National Legislature for the term of _____ years, . . . and to be ineligible a second time; and that besides a general authority to execute the National laws, it ought to enjoy the Executive rights vested in Congress by the Confederation." The national judiciary, proposed in the ninth resolution, was to have jurisdiction over "impeachments of any National officers."[1]

After postponing the question of whether the executive should be a single person, the Committee of the Whole agreed that the executive should serve for a term of seven years and be elected by the national legislature.[2] One delegate, Gunning Bedford, Jr., of Delaware, opposed a seven-year term, arguing instead for a triennial election with ineligibility after nine years. Bedford thought a seven-year term too long and impeachment an insufficient remedy. "An impeachment would reach misfeasance only, not incapacity," he said, and it would provide no cure if it were found that the first magistrate "did not possess the qualifications ascribed to him, or should lose them after his appointment." Another delegate from Delaware, John Dickinson, moved that the executive be removable by the national legislature upon the request of a majority of the legislatures of the states. Dickinson agreed that it was necessary "to place the power of removing somewhere," but he did not like the plan of impeaching the great officers of the government, and he wished to preserve the role of the states. During the debate on Dickinson's motion, Roger Sherman of Connecticut suggested that the national legislature be empowered to remove the executive at pleasure. George Mason of Virginia replied that, although "some mode of displacing an unfit magistrate is rendered indispensable by the fallibility of those who choose, as well as by the corruptibility of the man chosen" to make the executive "the mere creature of the Legislature" would be a "violation of the fundamental principle of good Government." Dickinson's motion was opposed because it would have given the smaller states equal power with the more populous ones. James Madison of Virginia and James Wilson of Pennsylvania argued that it would "enable a minority of the people to prevent ye removal of an officer who had rendered himself justly criminal in the eyes of a majority," open a door to intrigues against the executive in states in which his administration was unpopular, and tempt him to pay court to particular states whose partisans he either feared or wished to engage in his behalf.[3] The motion was defeated, with only Delaware voting for it.[4]

The Committee of the Whole then agreed that the executive should be ineligible after a single seven-year term and, without debate, added a clause, proposed by Hugh Williamson of North Carolina, providing that the executive would "be removeable on impeachment & conviction of malpractice or neglect of duty."[5]

The delegates next considered whether there should be a single or plural executive. Randolph, who had previously said that he considered unity in the executive to be "the foetus of monarchy," declared "the permanent temper of the people was adverse to the very semblance of Monarchy." In support of a single executive, Wilson argued that this would give the "most energy dispatch and responsibility to the office," as well as provide tranquility to the government. He said that he could see no evidence of opposition on the part of the people; "[a]ll know that a single magistrate is not a King," and every state had a single executive. The Committee of the Whole agreed to a single executive, leading Mason to comment that the delegates were creating "a more dangerous monarchy" than the British, "an elective one."[6]

Initial Deliberations in the Convention

After it had completed the consideration and amendment of the Virginia Plan, the Committee of the Whole reported its resolutions to the convention,[7] which began its deliberations on them. The convention took up the resolution concerning the executive on July 17. After agreeing unanimously that the executive should consist of a single person, it turned to the method of his selection, his term, and his reeligibility. Gouverneur Morris of Pennsylvania proposed election by the people instead of by the legislature, arguing that if the legislature both appointed and could impeach the executive, he would be "the mere creature" of it. This proposal, as well as a proposal for selection by electors chosen by state legislatures, was rejected by the convention. Selection by the legislature and a seven-year term were unanimously retained. The delegates then struck the clause making the executive ineligible for reelection, with Morris contending that ineligibility "tended to destroy the great motive to good behavior, the hope of being rewarded by a re-appointment. It was saying to him, make hay while the sun shines."[8]

On July 19 the convention again considered the executive's reeligibility, a subject that reopened the question of the method of his selection and his term. The debate indicated the extent of the delegates' concern about executive dependence on the legislature. Morris, a proponent of reeligibility, argued:

> One great object of the Executive is to controul the Legislature. The Legislature will continually seek to aggrandize & perpetuate themselves; and will seize those critical moments produced by war, invasion or convulsion for that purpose. It is necessary then that the Executive Magistrate should be the guardian of the people, even of the lower classes, agst. Legislative tyranny.

He advocated a popularly elected executive with a two-year term, who would be eligible for reelection and would not be removable by impeachment. The impeachability of the executive was "a dangerous part of the plan," Morris said. "It will hold him in such dependence that he will be no check on the Legislature, will not be a firm guardian of the people and of the public interest. He will be the tool of a faction, of some leading demagogue in the Legislature." Morris did "not regard . . . as formidable" the danger from the executive's unimpeachability: "There must be certain great officers of State; a minister of finance, of war, of foreign affairs &c. These . . . will exercise their functions in subordination to the Executive, and will be amenable by impeachment to the public Justice. Without these ministers the Executive can do nothing of consequence."[9]

Morris was not the only delegate who emphasized the risk of executive dependence on the legislature. Wilson remarked that "the unanimous sense" seemed to be that the executive should not be appointed by the legislature unless he was ineligible for reappointment. The convention voted for selection by electors chosen by state legislatures, rejected ineligibility for a second term, and agreed to a six-year term.[10]

The July 20 Debate on Removal of the Executive by Impeachment

On July 20 the convention considered a motion to strike the provision making the executive removable on impeachment and conviction for malpractice or neglect of duty.[11] This was the major debate on impeachment during the Constitutional Convention. The delegates were concerned about the dependence of the executive on the legislature and had settled upon a method of election—electors chosen by state legislatures—intended to reduce that dependence. This provision was a temporary compromise, which was reconsidered (and discarded) the following week. The delegates had made no decision about the procedure that would be used to impeach and try the executive. The convention had struck the provision for trial by the judiciary and had not yet considered how impeachments would be originated, although impeachment by the popular branch of the legislature was the procedure followed in England and in several of the states. The delegates had also not determined whether impeachment would involve criminal sanctions. English impeachments could lead to criminal punishment, including execution; state constitutions varied on the point, with a few (such as New York's) expressly limiting judgment on impeachments to removal from office and disqualification from future office and with others (such as Virginia's) explicitly providing for the imposition of criminal sanctions.[12]

The motion to strike the impeachment clause was made by Charles Pinckney of South Carolina and Morris. Pinckney initiated the debate by suggesting that the executive "ought not to be impeachable whilst in office." (The Virginia and Delaware constitutions provided that the executive could be impeached only after he had left office.)[13] William Davie of North Carolina replied that if the executive were not impeachable while in office, "he will spare no efforts or means whatever to get himself re-elected." Davie considered impeachability to be "an essential security for the good behaviour of the Executive."

Morris repeated his point about the executive's subordinates, arguing that he "can do no criminal act without Coadjutors who may be punished. In case he should be re-elected, that will be sufficient proof of his innocence." Morris asked, "Who is to impeach?" and "Is the impeachment to suspend his functions?" If not, he suggested, "the mischief will go on"; if so, "the impeachment will be nearly equivalent to a displacement, and will render the executive dependent on those who are to impeach."

Mason, defending the impeachment clause, said: "No point is of more importance than that the right of impeachment should be continued. Shall any man be above Justice? Above all shall that man be above it, who can commit the most extensive injustice?" When great crimes were committed he was for punishing the principal as well as the Coadjutors. Mason noted that there had been "much debate & difficulty as to the mode of chusing the Executive." He preferred appointment by the legislature, in part because of the danger that the electors might be corrupted by the candidates. This, he said, "furnished a peculiar reason in favor of impeachments whilst in office. Shall the man who has practised corruption & by that means procured his appointment in the first instance, be suffered to escape punishment, by repeating his guilt?"

Benjamin Franklin argued that the clause was "favorable to the executive":

What was the practice before this in cases where the chief Magistrate rendered himself obnoxious? Why recourse was had to assassination in wch. he was not only deprived of his life but of the opportunity of vindicating his character. It wd. be the best way therefore to provide in the Constitution for the regular punishment of the Executive when his misconduct should deserve it, and for his honorable acquittal when he should be unjustly accused.

Franklin later mentioned the case of the Prince of Orange, who was suspected of having kept the Dutch fleet from uniting with the French in violation of an agreement between the two nations:

Yet as he could not be impeached and no regular examination took place, he remained in his office, and strengthe[n]ing his own party, as the party opposed to him became formidable, he gave birth to the most violent animosities & contentions. Had he been impeachable, a regular & peaceable inquiry would have taken place and he would if guilty have been duly punished, if innocent restored to the confidence of the public.

James Madison "thought it indispensable that some provision should be made for defending the Community agst the incapacity, negligence or perfidy of the chief Magistrate." A limited term was "not a sufficient security. He might lose his capacity after his appointment. He might pervert his administration into a scheme of peculation or oppression. He might betray his trust to foreign powers." The executive differed from the legislature or any other public body holding office for a limited period, Madison said; it could not be presumed that all or a majority of the members of an assembly would lose their capacity or be bribed to betray their trust, and "the difficulty of acting in concert for purposes of corruption was a security to the public." But he said, "In the case of the Executive Magistracy which was to be administered by a single man, loss of capacity or corruption was more within the compass of probable events, and either of them might be fatal to the Republic."

Pinckney, arguing in favor of his motion to strike the impeachment clause, asserted that he "did not see the necessity of impeachments," especially because the powers of the executive "would be so circumscribed." And he asserted, "they [impeachments] ought not to issue from the Legislature who would in that case hold them as a rod over the Executive and by that means effectually destroy his independence." The executive's revisionary (veto) power, in particular, "would be rendered altogether insignificant."

Elbridge Gerry of Massachusetts, disagreeing with Pinckney, urged "the necessity of impeachments. A good magistrate will not fear them. A bad one ought to be kept in fear of them." He hoped the maxim would never be adopted here that the chief Magistrate could do no wrong.

Rufus King of Massachusetts, who supported the motion to strike the impeachment clause, asked the delegates "to recur to the primitive axiom that the three great departments of Govts. should be separate & independent. . . . Would this be the case if the Executive should be impeachable?" Impeachment of the judiciary was appropriate, he said, because judges held their offices during good behavior and it was therefore necessary that "a forum should be established for trying misbehaviour." But the executive was to serve a six-year term, like members of the Senate; "he would periodically be tried for his behaviour by his electors, who would continue or discontinue him in trust according to the manner in which he had discharged it." (King later described "periodical responsibility to the electors" as "an equivalent security" to impeachments of those holding office for life, which "are proper to secure good behaviour.") Like members of the legislature, King asserted, the executive "ought to be subject to no intermediate trial, by impeachment." The executive should not be impeachable unless he were to hold his office during good behavior (a tenure, King said, that "would be most agreeable to him") and even then only if "an independent and effectual forum could be devised; . . . under no circumstances ought he to be impeachable by the Legislature. This would be destructive of his independence and of the principles of the Constitution."

Edmund Randolph commented that the "propriety of impeachments was a favorite principle with him":

> Guilt wherever found ought to be punished. The Executive will have great opportunitys of abusing his power; particularly in time of war when the military force, and in some respects the public money will be in his hands. Should no regular punishment be provided, it will be irregularly inflicted by tumults & insurrections.

Randolph noted "the necessity of proceeding with a cautious hand, and of excluding as much as possible the influence of the Legislature from the business." He suggested the consideration of a proposal made by Alexander Hamilton for a forum composed of state judges and "even of requiring some preliminary inquest whether just grounds of impeachment existed."

Morris, who had cosponsored the motion to strike the clause pertaining to impeachment, admitted during the debate that "corruption & some few other offences [were] such as ought to be impeachable"; but thought the cases ought to be enumerated & defined. As the debate ended, he acknowledged that his "opinion had been changed by the arguments used in the discussion" and that he was "now sensible of the necessity of impeachments, if the Executive was to continue for any time in office":

> Our Executive was not like a Magistrate having a life interest, much less like one having an hereditary interest in his office. He may be bribed by a greater interest to betray his trust; and no one would say that we ought to expose ourselves to the danger of seeing the first Magistrate in foreign pay without being able to guard agst it by displacing him.

Treachery, corrupting his electors, and incapacity were causes for impeachment, Morris said, although for incapacity "he should be punished not as a man, but as an officer, and punished only by degradation from his office." He concluded, "This Magistrate is not the King but the prime-Minister. The people are the King. When we make him amenable to Justice however we should take care to provide some mode that will not make him dependent on the Legislature."

The convention voted eight states to two to retain the clause making the executive removable on impeachment.

The Committee of Detail's Draft Constitution

Four days later the convention reconsidered the method of selecting the executive. Choice by electors was dropped, and the legislature again substituted. A motion to reinstate the one-term limitation led to a variety of proposals about the length of term, including eight, eleven, fifteen, and twenty years. The last was suggested as "the medium life of princes"; it was perhaps offered, according to Madison, "as a caricature of the previous motions." Wilson suggested election for six years by a small number of legislators selected by lot.[14] Debate on the question continued during the next two sessions, and finally the convention reinstated the provisions originally reported by the Committee on the Whole—a seven-year term, no reeligibility, appointment by the legislature.[15] The resolution on the executive was referred to the five-man Committee of Detail, which was charged with preparing a draft constitution.[16]

The Committee of Detail reported on August 6. Its draft provided that the House of Representatives "shall have the sole power of impeachment," a provision the convention unanimously adopted, without debate, on August 9.[17] The draft also provided that the president (the name it gave the executive) "shall be removed from his office on impeachment by the House of Representatives, and conviction in the supreme Court, of treason, bribery, or corruption."[18] The jurisdiction of the Supreme Court included "the trial of impeachments of Officers of the United States," but the legislature could "assign any part of the jurisdiction above mentioned (except the trial of the President of the United States) . . . to . . . Inferior Courts."[19] The draft included the provision, which was retained in the final version of the Constitution without debate by the convention, limiting judgment in impeachment cases to removal from office and disqualification from any office of honor, trust, or profit under the United States and stating that the convicted party is nevertheless liable and subject to indictment, trial, judgment, and punishment according to law.[20]

Article X of the Committee of Detail's draft, dealing with the president, was taken up by the convention on August 24.[21] Again the delegates were unable to agree upon the method of selecting the executive. On August 27 the impeachment provision was postponed at the instance of Morris, who contended that the Supreme Court was an improper forum for trying the president, especially if (as was then being considered) the chief justice would be a member of a privy council for the president.[22] On

August 31 the provisions of the draft constitution that had been postponed were referred to a committee that had one member from each state, the Committee of Eleven.[23]

The Committee of Eleven's Proposal on the Election of the President and Impeachment

On September 4 the Committee of Eleven reported to the convention; it recommended a four-year term for the president as well as for the vice-president, a new office which it proposed and which, Hugh Williamson later explained, "was not wanted," but "was introduced only for the sake of a valuable mode of election which required two to be chosen at the same time." Each state was to choose electors in the manner that its legislature directed. The electors (equal in number to the representatives and senators for the state) were to meet in the state and vote for two persons, one of whom could not be a resident of that state. The votes of the electors in all the states would be transmitted to the Senate, where they would be counted. If one person received a majority of the electoral vote, he would be elected president. If two persons were tied, each with a majority, the Senate would choose between them. If no person received a majority, the Senate would choose by ballot among the five receiving the most votes. The person receiving the second-greatest number of votes would be elected vice-president.

The committee also proposed that the Senate, rather than the Supreme Court, should try all impeachments, with a two-thirds vote required for conviction. The vice-president would be ex-officio president of the Senate "except when they sit to try the impeachment of the President, in which case the Chief Justice shall preside," and when he exercised the powers and duties of the president. The committee altered the impeachment clause so that it read, "[The President] shall be removed from his office on impeachment by the House of Representatives, and conviction by the Senate, for Treason, or bribery . . ."—dropping "corruption," which had been included in the Committee of Detail's draft, as well as substituting the Senate for the Supreme Court.[24]

The convention postponed its consideration of the proposal for trial of impeachments by the Senate "in order to decide previously on the mode of electing the President." Morris explained the reasons for the committee's recommendation:

> The 1st. was the danger of intrigue & faction if the appointmt. should be made by the Legislature. 2 the inconveniency of an ineligibility required by that mode in order to lessen its evils. 3 The difficulty of establishing a Court of Impeachments, other than the Senate which

would not be so proper for the trial nor the other branch for the impeachment of the President, if appointed by the Legislature, 4. No body had appeared to be satisifed with an appointment by the Legislature. 5. Many were anxious even for an immediate choice by the people—6— the indispensable necessity of making the Executive independent of the Legislature.

He said that "the great evil of cabal was avoided" because the electors would vote concurrently throughout the country at a great distance from each other; "it would be impossible also to corrupt them." He contended that a "conclusive reason" for having the Senate rather than the Supreme Court try impeachments was that the Court "was to try the President after the trial of the impeachment."[25]

The electoral plan encountered opposition, primarily on the ground that the Senate would almost always choose the president (nineteen times in twenty, George Mason argued) because no single candidate would receive a majority of the electoral votes. Pinckney asserted that the Committee of Eleven's proposal would make "the same body of men which will in fact elect the President his Judges in case of an impeachment." Wilson and Randolph proposed that the eventual selection be referred to the entire legislature, not just the Senate. Morris replied that the Senate was preferable "because fewer could then say to the President, you owe your appointment to us." He thought "the President would not depend so much on the Senate for his re-appointment as on his general good conduct." Wilson criticized the committee's report as "having a dangerous tendency to aristocracy; as throwing a dangerous power into the hands of the Senate," which would not only have, in fact, the power to appoint the president, but through his dependence upon it would also have the virtual power of appointment to other offices, and would make treaties and try all impeachments. "The Legislative, Executive & Judiciary powers are all blended in one branch of the Government," Wilson observed. The president "will not be the man of the people as he ought to be, but the Minion of the Senate."[26]

To meet this criticism, the convention, after considering a number of alternative proposals, agreed that the House, with one vote per state, should choose the president if no person received a majority of the electoral votes.[27]

The Addition of "Other High Crimes and Misdemeanors" to the Impeachment Clause

On September 8 the convention considered the Committe of Eleven's proposal that the Senate should try impeachment against the president for treason and bribery.[28] George Mason asked:

Why is the provision restrained to treason & bribery only? Treason as defined in the Constitution will not reach many great and dangerous offences. [Warren] Hastings is not guilty of Treason. Attempts to subvert the Constitution may not be Treason as above defined— As bills of attainder which have saved the British Constitution are forbidden, it is the more necessary to extend: the power of impeachments.[29]

Mason moved to add "or maladministration" after "bribery." James Madison said, "So vague a term will be equivalent to a tenure during pleasure of the Senate." Morris commented that "it will not be put in force & can do no harm— An election of every four years will prevent maladministration." Mason, however, withdrew "maladministration" and substituted "other high crimes & misdemeanors agst. the State," which the convention adopted by a vote of eight states to three. (The provision was later amended, by unanimous consent "in order to remove ambiguity," to read "against the United States," a phrase the Committee of Style and Arrangement deleted.)

The Adoption of Trial of Impeachments by the Senate

Madison then objected to a trial of the president by the Senate, "especially as he was to be impeached by the other branch of the Legislature, and for any act which might be called a misdemeanor. The President under these circumstances was made improperly dependent." Madison stated a preference for trial by the Supreme Court or by a tribunal of which it formed a part.

Morris replied that "no other tribunal than the Senate could be trusted. The Supreme Court were too few in number and might be warped or corrupted." He said he was against "a dependence of the Executive on the Legislature, considering the Legislative tyranny the great danger to be apprehended," but he contended that "there could be no danger that the Senate would say untruly on their oaths that the President was guilty of crimes or facts, especially as in four years he can be turned out."

Pinckney disapproved of trial by the Senate "as rendering the President too dependent on the Legislature. If he opposes a favorite law, the two Houses will combine agst him, and under the influence of heat and faction throw him out of office." Madison moved to strike the provision for trial by the Senate. His motion failed by a vote of two states to nine, and the impeachment clause was adopted, ten states to one.

The clause was amended to make the vice-president and other civil officers removable "on impeachment and conviction as aforesaid." Morris moved to add a provision that members of the Senate should be on oath when trying impeachments, and the amended clause was agreed to, nine states to two.[30]

A five-member committee was appointed "to revise the stile of and arrange the articles which had been agreed to by the House."[31] The committee reported on September 12. Among other stylistic changes, the committee shortened the impeachment clause.[32]

Rejection of Suspension upon Impeachment

On September 14 the last issue related to impeachment was brought before the convention. John Rutledge of South Carolina, along with Morris, moved that persons who were impeached be suspended from office pending the outcome of their trials. Madison objected, asserting that the president was already made too dependent on the legislature by the power of one branch to try him on an impeachment by the other. Suspension would "put him in the power of one branch only," which could at any moment, "in order to make way for the functions of another who will be more favorable to their views, vote a temporary removal of the existing magistrate." By a vote of three states to eight, the motion was rejected.[33]

THE ROLE OF IMPEACHMENT IN THE CONSTITUTIONAL SCHEME

Despite the attention the delegates to the Constitutional Convention had given to the provisions concerning presidential impeachment, supporters of the proposed constitution claimed that it was unlikely that a corrupt man would ever become president of the United States. The method of selecting the president, through electors chosen by the states for that specific purpose, "affords a moral certainty, that the office of President will never fall to the lot of any man who is not in an eminent degree endowed with the requisite qualifications," Alexander Hamilton wrote in *Federalist* number 68.

> Talents for low intrigue, and the little arts of popularity, may alone suffice to elevate a man to the first honors in a single State; but it will require other talents, and a different kind of merit, to establish him in the esteem and confidence of the whole Union, or of so considerable a portion of it as would be necessary to make him a successful candidate for the distinguished office of President of the United States.

Hamilton concluded that "there will be a constant probability of seeing the station filled by characters preëminent for ability and virtue."[34]

A "moral certainty" and a "constant probability," however, were not sufficient safeguards to assure that a president would faithfully execute his office, and the framers had also sought to make the president responsible for his conduct. The "two greatest securities" the people have for "the faithful exercise of any delegated power," Hamilton wrote in *Federalist* number 70, are "the restraints of public opinion" and "the opportunity of discovering with facility and clearness the misconduct of the persons they trust, in order either to their removal from office, or to their actual punishment in cases which admit of it." Censure was a more important safeguard than punishment, especially in an elective office, Hamilton explained. "Man, in public trust, will much oftener act in such a manner as to render him unworthy of being any longer trusted, than in such a manner as to make him obnoxious to legal punishment."[35]

The presidents eligibility for reelection every four years was therefore a major source of responsibility in the office. The framers envisioned that an incumbent president would seek reelection and that the outcome would be a test of his administration of the office. Madison referred to it as "an impeachment before the community, who will have the power of punishment, by refusing to re-elect him." The president, he said, "is impeachable before the community at large every four years, and liable to be displaced if his conduct shall have given umbrage during the time he has been in office."[36]

Unlimited eligibility for reelection was considered to be one of the major inducements to good behavior by the president, for, as Justice Joseph Story wrote in 1833, paraphrasing Hamilton, "A desire of reward is one of the strongest incentives of human conduct; and the best security for the fidelity of mankind is to make interest coincide with duty." If the president were excluded from reelection, he would be tempted "to sordid views, to peculation, to the corrupt gratification of favourites, and in some instances to usurpation," Story contended.[37] An avaricious president, excluded from reelection, might "have recourse to the most corrupt expedients to make the harvest as abundant as it was transitory," Hamilton wrote. If, on the other hand, the president were eligible for reelection, "his avarice might be a guard upon his avarice."[38] Ineligibility for reelection might be a temptation to usurpation, Story explained, "since the chance of impeachment would scarcely be worthy of thought; and the present power of serving friends might easily surround him with advocates for every stretch of authority, which would flatter his vanity, or administer to their necessities." Exclusion from eligibility for reelection, Story concluded, "would operate no check upon a man of irregular ambition, or corrupt principles, and against such men alone could the exclusion be important."[39]

The ultimate check on presidential conduct was, not denial of reelection, but impeachment and removal from office. "In addition to all the precautions . . . to prevent abuse of the executive trust in the mode of the President's appointment, his term of office, and the precise and definite limitations imposed upon the exercise of his power," Chancellor James Kent later wrote, "the constitution has also rendered him directly amenable by law for mal-administration":

> If . . . neither the sense of duty, the force of public opinion, nor the transitory nature of the seat, are sufficient to secure a faithful discharge of the executive trust, but the President will use the authority of his station to violate the constitution or law of the land, the House of Representatives can arrest him in his career, by resorting to the power of impeachment.[40]

Without any debate, the Constitutional Convention had vested the power of impeachment in the House of Representatives, as proposed by the Committee of Detail. Although question had been raised in the July 20 debate about who should have the powers to impeach, once the convention had decided that accusation and trial would be the procedure used to remove the executive, it was effectively settled that the proceeding would be initiated by the popular branch of the legislature. It was not disputed, Hamilton wrote in *Federalist* number 65, "that the power of originating the inquiry, or, in other words, of preferring the impeachment, ought to be lodged in the hands of one branch of the legislative body."[41] Impeachment, he explained, is a legislative remedy: "the powers relating to impeachments are . . . an essential check in the hands of that body [the legislature] upon the encroachments of the executive,"[42] "a bridle in the hands of the legislative body upon the executive servants of the government." Vesting the power to originate impeachments in a branch of the legislature was consistent with the English system of impeachment—"the model from which the idea of this institution has been borrowed," Hamilton wrote[43]— and with that of several of the states.

The House was the logical branch of the legislature to initiate removal proceedings, not only because of its resemblance to the House of Commons, which performed this function in English impeachments, but also because it was the branch of government most directly accountable to the people. In the original constitutional scheme, senators were to be elected by state representatives; the complicated mechanism for electing the president left it to each state to determine how to choose its electors, and in any case, the framers thought that the choice of a president would often be made by the House of Representatives, with each state casting one vote, because no candidate would win a majority of the votes of state electors.

One of the concerns of the convention, in fact, was that the House might be too ready to make complaints, and it was partly for that reason that the method of trying impeachments proved to be a thorny problem. The Senate was ultimately considered a more appropriate forum than the Supreme Court, because the Court might try the president on any criminal charge after his impeachment trial, the Court "were too few in number and might be warped or corrupted,"[44] and the issues in an impeachment proceeding did not resemble those in ordinary litigation. Impeachments, James Wilson said in *Lectures on Law,* "come not . . . within the sphere of ordinary jurisprudence. They are founded on different principles, are governed by different maxims, and are directed at different objects."[45] The considerations applicable to judging impeachments, Story reiterated forty years later, "do not properly belong to the judicial character in the ordinary administration of justice and are far removed from the reach of municipal jurisprudence."[46]

The primary reason for giving the Senate the power to try impeachments, however, was that it was considered to be the only body that would be unbiased by an accusation brought by the House. Any other tribunal, James Iredell of North Carolina said, might "be too much awed by so powerful an accuser."[47] Only the Senate was "sufficiently dignified" and "sufficiently independent," Hamilton asserted. It was likely "to feel confidence enough in its own situation, to preserve, unawed and uninfluenced, the necessary impartiality" between an accused official and the representatives of the people, his accusers. Members of the Supreme Court were not likely always to be "endowed with so eminent a portion of fortitude, as would be called for in the execution of so difficult a task"—a deficiency that "would be fatal to the accused." They were even less likely to "possess the degree of credit and authority, which might, on certain occasions, be indispensable towards reconciling the people to a decision that should happen to clash with an accusation brought by their immediate representatives"—a deficiency "dangerous to the public tranquillity."[48]

As Hamilton's arguments suggest, it was considered probable that the House, influenced by considerations of faction, would bring unjust or unwarranted accusations against the president. The safeguard for the impeached president was to be derived from the size of the Senate, its independence, the special oath senators would take to try impeachments, and the requirement of a two-thirds vote for conviction. "There could be no danger that the Senate would say untruly on their oaths that the President was guilty of crimes or facts, especially as in four years he can be turned out," Gouverneur Morris told the Constitutional Convention. Instead, Hugh Williamson suggested, there was "more danger of too much lenity . . . towards the President," considering the number of respects in which the Senate was associated with him.[49] This turned out to be the major criticism of the impeachment provision in the state ratifying conventions, particularly with reference to the possibility of removing the president for entering into treaties for corrupt or traitorous motives (and as Edmund Randolph said in discussing the impeachment provisions in the Virginia ratifying convention, treaties are the most common occasions of impeachments).[50] For example, James Monroe asked the Virginia convention: "To whom is he responsible? To the Senate, his own council. If he makes a treaty, bartering the interests of the country, by whom is he to be tried? By the very persons who advised him to perpetrate the act. Is this any security?"[51]

In the ratifying conventions almost no mention was made of the possibility that the House might be reluctant to impeach the president. One exception was an address by Luther Martin, who had been a delegate to the Constitutional Convention, explaining to the Maryland House of Delegates why he had refused to sign the Constitution and why he was opposed to its ratification. His lengthy explanation of the Constitution's defects included the arguments that it was "contrary to probability" that the House would ever impeach the president and that it was even less likely that he would be convicted by the Senate, his counsellors. According to Martin, there was

> little reason to believe that a majority will ever concur in impeaching the President, let his conduct be ever so reprehensible; especially, too, as the final event of that impeachment will depend upon a different body, and the members of the House of [Representatives] will be certain, should the decision be ultimately in favor of the President, to become thereby the objects of his displeasure, and to bar to themselves every avenue to the emoluments of government.[52]

Martin's argument was based on a cynical view of the motivations of those who would serve in the House. He contended that its members would be unduly under the influence of the president because the president alone could nominate them to lucrative offices of the government. Neither this misanthropic opinion nor other objections to vesting the power of impeachment in the House are repeated in the available proceedings of the state ratifying conventions.

In 1789, Fisher Ames, a member of the House in the First Congress, again referred to the duration of impeachments, arguing in favor of the power of the president to remove subordinate officers of the executive branch. He criticized "the slow formality of an impeachment," which made it ineffective as a method for preventing crimes. Without suspension pending the outcome of an impeachment trial, Ames said, "we shall find impeachments come too late; while we are preparing the process, the mischief will be perpetrated, and the offender will escape." He referred, as did other members of the House, to the English impeachment of Warren Hastings, then in its third year. The Hastings impeachment was "a transatlantic instance of [the] incompetency" of impeachment, said John Vining of Delaware: "With what difficulty was that prosecution carried on! What a length of time did it take to determine!" Impeachment "was attended with circumstances that would render it insufficient to secure the public safety, which was a primary object in every Government," Vining said. It was a "circuitous route":

> The dilatory and inefficient process by that mode, will not apply the remedy to the evil till it is too late to be of advantage. Experience has fixed an eternal stigma upon the system of impeachment . . . ; what delays and uncertainty with the forms of trial, details of evidence, arguments of counsel, and deliberate decision!

Impeachment was "tedious and uncertain at best" as a way of removing "bad or obnoxious officers," Vining asserted. Theodore Sedgwick of Massachusetts asked: "Must the tardy, tedious, desultory road, by way of impeachment, be travelled to overtake the man who, barely confining himself within the letter of the law, is employed in drawing off the vital principle of the Government?"[53]

There was a massive inconsistency in the argument that Ames, Vining, Sedgwick, and others (including James Madison) were making. On the one hand, they were contending that the president must have the power to remove executive officers partly because of the inadequacies of the impeachment process.[54] On the other, they argued that the president's amenability to impeachment—that "dilatory and inefficient process"—was a safeguard to ensure that he did not abuse his powers or fail to perform his duties. Vining, the most outspoken critic of impeachment for the removal of inferior executive officers, went on to say that the president would be responsible to the people if he did not effectually perform his duty to see the laws faithfully executed. "Have they the means of calling him to account, and punishing him for neglect?" Vining asked. "They have secured it in the Constitution, by impeachment, to be presented by their immediate representatives; if they fail here, they have another check when the time of election comes round."[55]

Whatever the rhetorical uses of the president's accountability through impeachment, it was recognized practically from the outset that it would be neither an easy nor an expeditious method of removal. The consolation, if there was one, was that the electorate could remove the president at the next election, and his misconduct would not have to be endured for any longer than four more years.

THE ENDURING DEBATE:
IMPLICATIONS FOR THE FUTURE

The basic issue in presidential impeachment remains the problem that most troubled the delegates to the Constitutional Convention in 1787: how to ensure that the president is legally accountable without making him subservient to Congress. The complicated solution the framers devised— selection of the president by electors specially chosen for the purpose, not by Congress; eligibility of the president for reelection; division of the procedure for removing him between the House and the Senate, with a two-thirds vote required in the Senate for conviction and removal—has been altered by both extraconstitutional developments (such as the rise of -political parties) and constitutional changes (most notably the two-term limitation of the Twenty-second Amendment). Nevertheless, the most important guarantee of presidential protection from partisan removal from office is still that the procedure requires formal accusation by a majority of the House, an adversary trial, and a vote of conviction by at least two-thirds of the Senate.

The Andrew Johnson impeachment demonstrated how formidable an obstacle the two-thirds requirement can be. Johnson had been elected vice-president on a national-unity ticket during the Civil War. That he might become president, especially during the critical period of postwar reconstruction, had simply not been contemplated. The Republican majority in Congress was inflated both because southern states were excluded from representation and because the Democratic party had been severely damaged elsewhere as a result of the war. Johnson was impeached by a House of Representatives that was overwhelmingly Republican (no Republican members of the House voted against his impeachment); he was tried by a Senate that consisted of forty-two Republicans and twelve Democrats. In partisan terms, his acquittal mathematically required defections from the Republican ranks. This highly political impeachment was eventually resolved in a manner that ran counter to the interests of the dominant political party. The recurrence of such a lopsided partisan majority in Congress in opposition to the president is highly improbable. The more typical situation is the one that caused President Nixon to resign rather than go through an impeachment trial. Although the Democratic party controlled both the House and the Senate in 1974, Nixon's removal from office would have required the votes of some senators who had been politically loyal to him. Their abandonment of him in the face of overwhelming evidence that he was guilty of serious wrongdoing precipitated his resignation.

Far from showing that the constitutional scheme is subject to partisan abuse, therefore, the Johnson trial ultimately demonstrated how strong the safeguard is against the successful use of presidential impeachment as a partisan weapon. Like the Nixon resignation more than a century later, it suggests that the outcome of a presidential removal proceeding will depend much more on whether guilt of serious wrongdoing is established than on partisanship. The two-thirds vote requirement makes it virtually inconceivable that a president could be removed from office through impeachment unless members of his own political party vote for his conviction—an outcome that is scarcely likely to be based on partisan considerations. "The security to innocence" from the two-thirds vote requirement is, as Hamilton wrote, "as complete as itself can desire."[56]

And that, it should be recalled, was the primary safeguard the framers of the Constitution adopted. The framers recognized that impeachment would be a political process; it is, after all, a proceeding involving a political issue of the most fundamental sort—the constitutional legitimacy of the chief executive's remaining in power. The purpose of a presidential impeachment and the issues in the proceeding differ from those in a criminal prosecution. A president is not removed from office to deter his successors from engaging in wrongdoing, to permit his rehabilitation, or as retributive punishment for his misdeeds. Deterrence and retribution may be among the effects of an impeachment (it is difficult to assign any role to rehabilitation), but they are incidental to the primary objective—to be rid of a chief executive whose past misconduct indicates that he ought to be replaced. And because presidential impeachment does not have the functions of a criminal prosecution, there is little reason to impose restrictions derived from analogies to the criminal law either in defining the grounds for impeachment or in establishing the procedures to be followed by the House and the Senate.

Away from the exigencies of a particular impeachment, it is hard to believe that anyone would seriously advocate that a president should be removable from office only if charged with and found guilty of a serious crime in a proceeding with all the procedural requisites of a criminal prosecution. If that had been what the framers intended, it would have been illogical for them to have entrusted the conduct of the proceeding to the House and the Senate, which have no particular competence in this regard. One good answer to the contention that impeachment is supposed to be a criminal prosecution for indictable offenses was given by John Randolph in the Chase trial. If that had been the intent, he asked, why did the Constitution provide for impeachment at all?

> Could it not have said, at once, that any civil officer of the United States convicted on an indictment, should *(ipso facto)* be removed from office? This would be coming at the thing by a short and obvious way. . . . Whence this idle parade, this wanton waste of time and

treasure, when the ready intervention of a court and jury alone was wanting to rectify the evil?[57]

Impeachment and removal are entrusted to the two branches of the legislature because the objectives and the questions to be resolved are political. Edmund Burke's opening argument in the Hastings impeachment trial, which was much quoted during the Nixon inquiry, makes the essential point. "It is by this tribunal," Burke told the House of Lords,

> that statesmen, who abuse their powers, are accused by statesmen, and tried by statesmen, not upon the niceties of a narrow jurisprudence, but upon the enlarged and solid principles of state morality. It is here, that those, who by abuse of power have violated the spirit of the law can never hope for protection from any of its forms:—it is here that those who have refused to conform themselves to its perfections can never hope to escape through any of its defects.[58]

Rhetoric aside, there has been substantial difficulty in the American system in conforming impeachment to this model. The limitations the framers imposed on impeachment in their written Constitution and the prohibition of the related devices (constructive treason and bills of attainder) that the English Parliament had used to establish its supremacy invited the argument that the framers also intended to restrict the causes for impeachment and the method by which it was conducted. Despite the express limitation on the purpose of impeachment—dismissal and disqualification from office—the argument could be made that the framers sought to create a purely adjudicative proceeding, a prosecution more criminallike than the English model from which they had borrowed. And as impeachment came to be a mechanism primarily for investigating and occasionally for trying judges who had misbehaved, its application to the basic purpose for which it was designed—the removal of the president—became more unfamiliar. A procedure invoked against only one president in the first 185 years of U.S. constitutional history obviously did little to solidify principles of state morality.

The Nixon impeachment inquiry, it is to be hoped, began to put presidential impeachment on a stronger footing. Although it involved the use of an unfamiliar procedure and was undertaken in the face of numerous obstacles, the Nixon inquiry succeeded in its immediate objective—a full and complete inquiry into allegations of misconduct against President Nixon and recommendations based on the results of that investigation—and in demonstrating that presidential impeachment and removal can be a workable, if difficult, constitutional remedy.

Two aspects of the Nixon inquiry may pose problems the next time presidential impeachment is considered. The first, which was probably inevitable under the circumstances, was that the Judiciary Committee may have overemphasized the adjudicative aspects of the function it was performing. The impeachment process and the committee's performance were themselves under intense scrutiny. The appearance of partisanship or one-sidedness might well have undermined an eventual recommendation to impeach, just as leaks to the press during the committee's evidentiary hearings resulted in attacks on the work of the committee. The committee reacted to the pressure it confronted by attempting to avoid any appearance of unfairness or partiality; this, in turn, created the risk that its eventual recommendations would be more judgmental than prosecutorial, in the nature more of a reasoned legal decision than of the strongest possible accusation for prosecution in the Senate. Had the proceeding continued, it was conceivable that members of the committee (and even other members of the House) might have had some difficulty adjusting to the accusatory role required of managers in an impeachment trial. In the circumstances of the Nixon case, the problem was not particularly serious. Neither the allegations against President Nixon nor the temper of the times were conducive to the declamatory flamboyance of the great impeachment trials of the past, and a low-key prosecutorial approach would probably have been most successful in the Senate and with the nation. On the other hand, an adjudicative approach to the conduct of an impeachment investigation and to the framing of articles of impeachment does postpone the consideration of trial strategy and may to some extent limit the options of those who must prosecute the case in the Senate.

The second problem, while exacerbated by the circumstances of the Nixon inquiry, is inherent in the impeachment process. Impeachment is a time-consuming way of getting an unfit president out of office, a point that has been recognized from the beginning. While the Johnson impeachment suggests that the House can act quickly (he issued his orders to remove Stanton and install Thomas on a Friday afternoon and was impeached the following Monday; articles of impeachment were adopted the next week), the Johnson trial was not completed for nearly three months. And the factual simplicity of the Johnson case is as unlikely to recur as are the evidentiary convolutions of the Nixon case, which helped make that impeachment inquiry as long and involved as it was. No future president is likely to be impeached three days later for what he does openly and in writing, just as no president is ever again likely to face impeachment and removal on the basis of such a complex and continuing series of events as were at issue in the Nixon inquiry.

Nevertheless, the length of time presidential impeachment takes is one of its major defects. The Nixon case suggested one method of shortening what Congressman Theodore Sedgwick described in 1789 as "the tardy, tedious, desultory road, by way of impeachment"—resignation by the president to avoid impeachment and conviction. President Nixon was not the first federal official facing impeachment who resigned. Resignation was not that uncommon in the heyday of impeachment investigations of judges, and it is still the usual result when judges or executive officials are charged with serious misconduct. Their resignations, however, hardly rival that of a president in importance. The Nixon case may eventually be regarded as precedent for forced resignation as an alternative to impeachment and trial, and the political pressure to resign on a future president who is accused of impeachable wrongdoing may be considerable. Added to that pressure will be personal considerations that may make resignation seem to be an appealing solution to a president facing impeachment and possible removal. Resignation would avoid the even more disgraceful fate of being the first president actually ousted from office, whose name might very well become, as one of Andrew Johnson's counsel put it, a word to frighten children with throughout the land. And it would permit the retention of the perquisites that are given to former presidents, including the retirement benefits granted (under current statute) to any former president who has not actually been removed by conviction in an impeachment trial. Resignation is not a bad proposition from the public's standpoint, either; it achieves the basic objective of impeachment while shortening the process and sparing the former president the vindictive consequences of an impeachment conviction. Of course, it cannot literally be forced on any president; the decision to resign is his alone.

One other choice is available to a president facing impeachment, which might also reduce the prolonged uncertainty and possible paralysis of the executive branch of the government resulting from presidential impeachment proceedings. Under the Twenty-fifth Amendment, adopted in 1967 for entirely different purposes, the president may declare himself "unable to discharge the powers and duties of the office," which are then temporarily discharged by the vice-president as acting president. As a temporary expedient, especially in a case in which a president thinks he is likely to prevail in an impeachment trial, this procedure—also voluntary with the president—may make some sense.[59]

The problem with impeachment, however, is not only that it is tedious and desultory, but that it may be tardy. No structural change can shorten the length of time it takes to set the impeachment process in motion in the House, although its replacement by a mechanism more akin to a vote of no confidence would presumably expedite decisions to remove or retain presidents. But a no-confidence system would create problems of its own, not the least of which is that it might invite manipulation by introducing elements of plebiscitary democracy, permitting a president and his supporters to seek a popular mandate for particular actions or policies.

The first two uses of the Twenty-fifth Amendment—to replace a vice-president who had resigned as part of a plea bargain in a criminal prosecution and to replace his successor, who became president after the incumbent had resigned to avoid impeachment and removal—are a recent reminder that constitutional mechanisms are likely to have unanticipated uses. Change should not be undertaken lightly.

There has been no clamor to reform the impeachment mechanism itself, despite a few suggestions to provide a more comprehensible listing of grounds for impeachment than the current constitutional catchall term "other high crimes and misdemeanors." The case for such an amendment is that it would prevent future claims that impeachment is directed at criminal rather than constitutional wrongdoing. But the likelihood of such claims, in the wake of the Nixon inquiry, seems slim. And the real difficulty in determining what presidential misconduct warrants impeachment is not in defining the misconduct—the constitutional duties of the president provide an appropriate, and an appropriately general, definition for purposes of impeachment proceedings—but in assessing whether the wrongdoing, taken together, is sufficiently serious to warrant removal from office. That is not a definitional problem; it is a judgmental one, and it can be as readily addressed under the existing constitutional clause as under a lengthier catalogue of impeachable misconduct—perhaps more readily. An effort to be explicit and comprehensive would invite an attempt to solve problems in the abstract that are better considered in the context of a particular case.

Obviously, if one were starting work on a new Constitution, "high crimes and misdemeanors" would be among the phrases that could stand to be replaced. Preferably, the substitute would be an even simpler and less explicit term—"for cause" or "for serious wrongdoing." But it hardly makes sense to consider a constitutional amendment to update the language of a provision that can be, and in practice has been, interpreted in just that way.

In short, there is little reason to meddle with the impeachment provisions, and there are some risks in trying to change them. More important, the prospect of amendment is practically nil. The next time a president is suspected of wrongdoing or is accused by his political opponents, the constitutional procedure for investigating his conduct and seeking his removal will almost certainly be the same as it is today. When the occasion again arises, it will be too late to consider structural change; whether the constitutional system works—and, indeed, how that is determined—will depend on the people who must use it.

The participants in that future proceeding will find it a harrowing enterprise, as anyone who endured the Nixon inquiry can attest. And they will discover that there is a paucity of precedent addressing their problems.

The rejection of an impeachment resolution by the House in 1867, an acquittal by the Senate in 1868, and a proceeding that was short-circuited by resignation in 1974 hardly provide an abundant body of case law. Perhaps the framers of the Constitution did not expect presidential impeachment to be so rare and therefore so awesome as it has turned out to be. For the people, through their representatives, to seek to remove the chief executive of their government does not seem an event that should lead to great constitutional hand wringing. Elected officials, after all, can turn out to be corrupt or maladroit; a procedure for removing them is an unexceptionable device; its use, while obviously not cause for jubilation, would not seem to be an occasion of grave crisis.

If past presidents had been worse or if past Congresses had been more assertive, presidential impeachment might have turned into a relatively routine proceeding. Yet one need not be a constitutional Pangloss, believing that all is for the best in the best of all governmental systems, to understand why presidential impeachment has been so seldom considered and, consequently, is a matter of such great moment when it is. Presidential incompetence usually does not manifest itself in the form of serious constitutional wrongdoing or, at least, as constitutional wrongdoing in which Congress and the public do not have a considerable degree of complicity. To remove a president is, in effect, to declare that the voters made a bad choice in electing him. That is not an easy message for other elected politicians to convey. Even a misbehaving and unpopular president, moreover, has means of dispelling pressures for his impeachment, including delay and conciliatory measures. For these reasons and others, presidential impeachment is difficult to get under way, much less to carry through to a conclusion. It has been, and it remains, a cumbersome and unwieldy weapon; its use is therefore an extraordinary constitutional event.

NOTES

This chapter is adapted, with permission of Yale University Press and the author, from John R. Labovitz, *Presidential Impeachment* (New Haven, Conn.: Yale University Press, 1978).

1. Max Farrand, ed., *The Records of the Federal Convention of 1787*, 4 vols. (New Haven, Conn.: Yale University Press, 1937), 1:21–22. Footnote numbers and brackets are omitted in all quotations from Farrand's work.

2. Ibid., pp. 64–77.

3. Ibid., pp. 69 (Bedford), 85 (Dickinson, Sherman), 86 (Mason, Madison, and Wilson).

4. Ibid., p. 87. The New Jersey Plan, later proposed to the convention on behalf of the small states by William Paterson of New Jersey, included a variant of

Dickinson's proposal. It provided that the executive (to be elected by Congress, to consist of an unspecified number of persons, and to serve a single term of unspecified length) would be "removable by Congs. on application by a majority of the Executives of the several States." The plan also gave the national judiciary jurisdiction over "all impeachments of federal officers" (1:244). Debate on the New Jersey Plan in Committee of the Whole concentrated on its preservation of the equality of state representation provided by the Articles of Confederation rather than specific provisions. The plan was rejected by the Committee of the Whole in favor of the Virginia Plan it had previously considered and amended (1:322).

5. Ibid., p. 88.
6. Ibid., pp. 66, 88 (Randolph), 65, 96 (Wilson), 97 (single executive), 101 (Mason).
7. Ibid., pp. 228–32.
8. Ibid., 2:29, 32 (selection by legislature), 33 (Morris).
9. Ibid., pp. 52–54.
10. Ibid., pp. 56–59.
11. This debate appears in ibid., pp. 64–69.
12. New York Constitution of 1777, art. 33, in Francis Thorpe, ed., *Colonial Charters, and Other Organic Laws, The Federal and State Constitutions,* 7 vols. (Washington, D.C.: Government Printing Office, 1909), 5:2635; the Virginia Constitution of 1776, ibid., 7:3818.
13. Virginia Constitution of 1776, ibid.; Delaware Constitution of 1776, art. 23, ibid., 1:566.
14. Farrand, *Records,* 2:64–68, 101–3.
15. Ibid., p. 120.
16. The committee consisted of John Rutledge of South Carolina, Randolph, Nathaniel Gorham of Massachusetts, Oliver Ellsworth of Connecticut, and Wilson: see ibid., p. 121.
17. Art. IV, sec. 6: see ibid., p. 231.
18. Art. X, sec. 2.
19. Art. XI, sec. 3.
20. Art. XI, sec. 5. The two other references to impeachment that are included in the Constitution—the limitation on the president's pardon power and the exception to the criminal trial provision—also first appeared in the draft of the Committee of Detail, although each was subsequently amended by the convention in minor respects. As reported by the committee, the pardon clause provided that the president's pardon "shall not be pleadable in bar of an impeachment" (Art. X, sec. 2, amended, Farrand, *Records,* 2:419–20). The criminal trial provision referred first to the place of trial and then to trial by jury, reading: "The trial of all criminal offences (except in cases of impeachments) shall be in the State where they shall be committed: and shall be by Jury" (Art. XI, sec. 4, amended, Farrand, *Records,* 2:434). One other provision of the draft should be mentioned because it used a term that was later to become part of the impeachment clause. The provision for rendition of criminal offenders from one state to another, patterned after a comparable provision in the Articles of Confederation, referred to "any person charged with treason, felony or high misdemeanor" (Art. XV). The convention substituted "other crime" for "high misdemeanor," "in order to comprehend all proper cases: it being doubtful whether 'high misdemeanor' had not a technical meaning too limited" (Farrand, *Records,* 2:443).
21. Farrand, *Records,* 2:401–4.

22. Ibid., p. 427. Morris and Pinckney had proposed a privy council consisting of the chief justice and the heads of executive departments (ibid., pp. 342–44). The proposal was referred to the Committee of Detail, which reported a revised version, with an expanded council that included the president of the Senate and the Speaker of the House (ibid., p. 367). The convention never voted on this proposal.

23. Its members, were Nicholas Gilman of New Hampshire, Rufus King of Massachusetts, Roger Sherman of Connecticut. David Brearley of New Jersey, Gouverneur Morris of Pennsylvania, John Dickinson of Delaware, Daniel Carroll of Maryland, James Madison of Virginia, Hugh Williamson of North Carolina, Pierce Butler of South Carolina, and Abraham Baldwin of Georgia (ibid., p. 473).

24. Ibid., pp. 537, 496–99.

25. Ibid., pp. 499, 500.

26. Ibid., pp. 500 (Mason), 501 (Pinckney), 502 (Morris), 522–23 (Wilson).

27. Ibid., pp. 527–28.

28. Ibid., p. 550.

29. The references in Mason's remarks were to the impeachment of Warren Hastings, the former governor-general of India, then pending in the English Parliament, and to two provisions the convention had previously adopted. The effort to impeach Hastings began in 1785; the House of Commons voted articles of impeachment against him in early 1787. The trial did not begin until 1788, and it dragged on until 1795, when Hastings was finally acquitted. On August 20 the convention had voted to limit treason against the United States to "levying war against them, or in adhering to their enemies, giving them aid and comfort" (ibid., pp. 345–50). Bills of attainder—legislation to punish an individual for past conduct without a judicial trial—had been prohibited by a provision adopted on August 23, as had ex post facto laws (ibid., p. 376).

30. Ibid., pp. 551–53.

31. Its members, were William Samuel Johnson of Connecticut, Alexander Hamilton of New York, Gouverneur Morris, James Madison, and Rufus King (ibid., p. 553).

32. Ibid., p. 600.

33. Ibid., pp. 612–13.

34. At p. 444 of the Modern Library edition.

35. At pp. 460–61, 459.

36. Annals of Congress, 1st Cong., 1st sess. (Gale and Seaton, eds., 1789; hereafter cited as Annals), pp. 498, 462.

37. Joseph Story, *Commentaries on the Constitution of the United States,* 3 vols. (New York: Da Capo Press, 1970, reprint of 1833 ed.), vol. 3., sec. 1437.

38. *Federalist* no. 72, at p. 471.

39. Story, *Commentaries,* vol. 3, secs. 1437, 1441. Story went on to say: "In truth, such men would easily find means to cover up their usurpations and dishonesty under fair pretensions, and mean subserviency to popular prejudices. They would easily delude the people into a belief, that their acts were constitutional, because they were in harmony with the public wishes, or held out some specious, but false projects for the public good." Story did not explain how, if this were true, eligibility for reelection would provide a check upon misconduct.

40. James Kent, *Commentaries on American Law,* 4 vols. 6th ed., (Boston, Mass.: Little, Brown, 1848), 1:289.

41. *Federalist* no. 65, at p. 424.

42. Ibid., no. 66, at p. 430.

43. Ibid., no. 65, at p. 425.

44. Farrand, *Records,* 2:551 (Gouverneur Morris).

45. Robert G. McCloskey, ed., *The Works of James Wilson* (Cambridge, Mass.: Harvard University Press, 1967), 1:324. Wilson was explaining why "the trial and punishment of an offense on impeachment, is no bar to a trial of the same offense at common law."

46. Story, *Commentaries,* vol. 2, sec. 764.

47. Jonathan Elliot, *The Debate in the Several State Conventions on the Adoption of the Federal Constitution,* 5 vols. (New York: Burt Franklin, 1974; reprint of 1836 ed.), 4:32.

48. *Federalist* no. 65, at p. 425 (emphasis omitted).

49. Farrand, *Records,* 2:551.

50. Elliot, *Debates,* 3:401.

51. Ibid., p. 489. George Mason, the author of the "high crimes and misdemeanor" language of the impeachment clause and an inveterate foe of a strong executive, made a similar argument. Mason also pointed to the danger of the president's continuance in office during the trial. "The President is tried by his counsellors," he told the ratifying convention, and because he is not suspended, "when he is arraigned for treason, he has the command of the army and navy, and may surround the Senate with thirty thousand troops" (ibid., 3:494).

52. Luther Martin's Letter and Address to the House of Delegates, Jan. 27, 1788, Elliott, *Debates,* 1:344, 379.

53. Annals, 1st Cong., 1st sess., pp. 475 (Ames), 373, 465, 571 (Vining), 460 (Sedgwick).

54. Madison suggested that impeachment was "a circuitous operation" for ousting executive officers for whom the president no longer wished to be responsible (Annals, p. 497); Elias Boudinot pointed out that if no officer could be removed except by impeachment, "we shall be in a deplorable situation indeed," both because of the difficulty of conducting a prosecution against an officer who resided far from the seat of government and because impeachment would not reach incapacity or disability (at p. 375). "If the necessity for dismission is pressing," Peter Sylvester asserted, "clearly the mode by impeachment is not likely to answer the purpose" (at p. 562). Thomas Hartley commented that the principle that impeachment was the only mode of removing an officer "would be attended with very inconvenient and mischievous consequences" (at p. 480).

55. Ibid., p. 572.

56. *Federalist* no. 66, at p. 430.

57. 2 Chase Trial 452.

58. *Works of Edmund Burke,* 8 vols. (London: G. Bell, 1883), 7:13–14.

59. The Twenty-fifth Amendment creates another procedure that is not voluntary with the president. It provides that the vice-president shall become acting president if he and a majority of the principal officers of the executive departments (or such other body as Congress may by law provide) declare that the president is unable to discharge the powers and duties of his office. If the president thereafter declares that no inability exists, he resumes the powers and duties of his office unless the vice-president and a majority of the cabinet (or other designated body) again declare him unable and each House affirms its declaration by a two-thirds vote. This complicated procedure, designed for instances of mental or physical incapacity, is ill adapted to the case of a president facing impeachment, although its terms do not preclude its use in that situation.

PART 2
POWERS

5
THE PRESIDENT'S
WAR-MAKING POWER

DAVID GRAY ADLER

The Congress shall have Power . . . To declare War, grant Letters of Marque and Reprisal, . . .

—*Article I, section 8*

The President shall be Commander in Chief of the Army and Navy of the United States, and of the Militia of the several States, when called into the actual Service of the United States.

—*Article II, section 2*

The executive power shall be vested in a President of the United States of America."

—*Article II, section 1*

Since World War II, a series of "presidential wars" from Korea and Vietnam to Cambodia and Grenada—has triggered an intense debate, within both the scholarly community and the corridors of power, on the question of whether Congress or the president is constitutionally empowered to commence war.[1] The issue of who has the power to decide to go to war is of surpassing importance for a nation faced with the specter of nuclear holocaust—the overwhelming, perhaps incomprehensible destruction from an all-out atomic war.

Before 1950, it had long been established that the Constitution vests in Congress the sole and exclusive authority to initiate total as well as limited war. But since then, that understanding has been subjected to a continual assault by revisionists who contend that the president holds that power.[2] In 1950, in an effort to justify President Harry S. Truman's unilateral decision to introduce United States troops into the Korean War, politicians and commentators, whom Edward S. Corwin has labeled "high-flying prerogative men," asserted that the president had broad executive powers to commence war.[3] Emboldened by Truman's claim, subsequent presidents have likewise unilaterally initiated acts of war, often with the acquiescence of Congress. These executive assertions, which have established a consistent pattern of behavior, have been based on the alleged authority that presidents derive from the executive-power and the commander-in-chief clauses of the Constitution, their constitutional authority to conduct foreign policy, and the inherent or prerogative power of the presidency. Finally, it is contended, each presidential war has constituted a "precedent" which, in turn, has legalized the next such action. If taken at face value, the revisionists' arguments would erase the Constitution's grant of power to Congress to embark upon war.

Since the Korean episode, then, there has been considerable tension between the theory of the Constitution and the practice of recent presidents. A shift of the war-making power from the legislative to the executive has given the president the dominant role. Of course, the substantive constitutional issues that the practice has raised are numerous and momentous; they cannot necessarily be answered by resorting to the text of the Constitution: What right, if any, does the executive have to commit troops to hostilities without Congress's authorization? What control of the war-making power did Congress retain once war had been declared? What authority might the president have in the face of invasion or the threat of imminent attack? The urgency of the circumstances induced scholars to search the historical records for discussion of these questions during the Constitutional Convention and during the early years of the Republic. Predictably, different interpretations of the sources emerged, and the questions lingered in confusion.

Because of the continuing debate over the war power and as a means of curbing unilateral war making by the executive and of ensuring a role for the legislative branch in the process, Congress passed the War Powers Resolution in 1973.[4] The resolution has yet to satisfy either purpose, and it has become a key part of the debate on the constitutional locus of the power to initiate military hostilities.

The critical nature of war making and the challenge raised by those who now contend that presidents are justified in making war compel a reexamination of the framers' understanding. In this chapter, I will examine the debates and proceedings that accompanied the framing and ratification of the war clause, the commander-in-chief clause, and the executive-power clause. I will also explore the late-eighteenth- and nineteenth-century understanding of the war-power design as manifested in the contemporary statements of legislators and other political actors, in the practice itself, and in judicial decisions. Further, I will consider the War Powers Resolution in terms of its content, aims, and impact. I will argue here that consistent with the understanding of the framers and under the Constitution, the authority to initiate hostilities, short of and including war, is vested in Congress. The president has only the constitutional power to repel invasions.

THE CONSTITUTION AND WARMAKING

The War Clause

The debate on the proper location of the authority to make war occurred at the outset of the Constitutional Convention. On May 29, 1787, Governor Edmund Randolph of Virginia proposed a constitution which included a provision "that a national Executive be instituted." The seventh paragraph stated that the executive "ought to enjoy the Executive rights vested in Congress of the Confederation."[5] The Randolph Plan was taken up by the convention on June 1. In considering the proposal to give to the national executive the executive powers of the Continental Congress, Charles Pinckney objected that "the Executive powers of [the existing] Congress might extend to peace and war which would render the Executive a Monarchy, of the worst kind, towit an elective one." His fellow South Carolinian, John Rutledge, said that "he was for vesting the Executive power in a single person, tho' he was not for giving him the power of war and peace."[6] James Wilson of Pennsylvania sought to reassure them: "Making peace and war are generally determined by writers on the Laws of Nations to be legislative powers." Wilson added: "The prerogatives of the British Monarchy [are not] a proper guide in defining the Executive powers. Some of the prerogatives were of a Legislative nature. Among others that of war & peace."[7] James Madison of Virginia agreed that the war power was legislative in character. Rufus King of Massachusetts noted: "Mad: agrees with Wilson in his definition of executive powers—executive powers ex vi termini, do not include the Rights of war & peace . . . but the powers should be confined and defined—if large we shall have the Evils of elective Monarchies."[8] There was no vote on Randolph's resolution, yet the discussion appears to reflect an understanding that the power of "war & peace"—the power to initiate war—belonged not to the executive but to the legislature.

On August 6 the Committee of Detail circulated a draft constitution which provided: "The legislature of the United States shall have the power . . . To make war."[9] This bore a sharp resemblance to the Articles of Confederation, which vested the "sole and exclusive right and power of determining on peace and war" to the Continental Congress.[10] When the "war clause" was considered in debate on August 17, Charles Pinckney opposed placing the power in Congress. "Its proceedings were too slow. . . . The Senate would be the best depository, being more acquainted with foreign affairs, and most capable of proper resolutions."[11] Pierce Butler of South Carolina "was for vesting the power in the President, who will have all the requisite qualities, and will not make war but when the nation will support it." Butler's opinion shocked Elbridge Gerry of Massachusetts, who said he "never expected to hear in a republic a motion to empower the Executive alone to declare war." Butler stood alone in the convention; there was no support for his opinion and no second to his motion.

The proposal of the Committee of Detail to vest the legislature with the power to "make war" proved unsatisfactory to Madison and Gerry. In a joint resolution, they moved to substitute "declare" for "make," "leaving to the Executive the power to repel sudden attacks."[12] The meaning of the motion is unmistakable: Congress was granted the power to make—that is, to initiate—war; the president, for obvious reasons, could act immediately to repel sudden attacks without authorization from Congress.[13] There was no quarrel whatever with respect to the sudden-attack provision, but there was some question as to whether the substitution of "declare" for "make" would effect the intention of Madison and Gerry. Roger Sherman of Connecticut thought the joint motion stood very well. The executive should be able to repel, but not to commence, war. " 'Make' better than 'declare' the latter narrowing the power [of the legislature] too much." Virginia's George Mason reportedly "was agst. giving the power of war to the Executive, because not [safely] to be trusted with it; or to the Senate, because not so constructed as to be entitled to it. He was for clogging rather than facilitating war; but for facilitating peace. He preferred 'declare' to 'make.' " The Madison-Gerry proposal was adopted by a vote of 7 to 2. When Rufus King explained that the word "make" might be understood to authorize Congress to initiate as well as conduct war, Connecticut changed its vote so that the word "declare" was approved, eight states to one."[14]

The debates and the vote on the war clause make it clear Congress alone possesses the authority to initiate war. The war-making power was specifically withheld from the president; a president was given only the authority to repel sudden attacks. Confirmation of this understanding was provided by remarks of ratifiers in various state conventions, as well as by the early practice and contemporaneous statements of political actors.

James Wilson, who was perhaps only slightly less influential than James Madison in the Constitutional Convention, told the Pennsylvania Ratifying Convention: "This system will not hurry us into war; it is calculated to guard against it. It will not be in the power of a single man, or a single body of men, to involve us in such distress; for the important power of declaring war is vested in the legislature at large: this declaration must be made with the concurrence of the House of Representatives: from this circumstance we may draw a certain conclusion that nothing but our national interest can draw us into a war."[15]

Similar assurance was provided in other state ratifying conventions. In North Carolina, James Iredell said, "The President has not the power of declaring war by his own authority. . . . Those powers are vested in other hands. The power of declaring war is expressly given to Congress." And Charles Pinckney, a delegate in Philadelphia, told the South Carolina Ratifying Convention that "the President's powers did not permit him to declare war." Likewise, in New York, Chancellor Robert R. Livingston responded to objections that the Continental Congress did not have "the same powers" as the proposed Congress: "They have the very same. . . . Congress have the power of making war and peace . . . they may involve us in a war at their pleasure."[16]

In spite of the illuminating debate and the vote on the war clause, the shift from "make" to "declare" has induced revisionists to find in the presidency a power to initiate war. Senator Barry Goldwater, for example, has said when the convention deleted from the working draft of the Constitution the authorization of Congress to make war, "the Framers intended to leave the 'making of war' with the President."[17] The scholar Leonard Ratner has explained that the "declare" clause recognized "the warmaking authority of the president, implied by his role as executive and commander-in-chief and by congressional power to declare, but not make, war."[18] John Norton Moore and others have suggested that acts of military force, short of war, might be committed by the president.[19]

For the moment I shall defer consideration of the executive-power and commander-in-chief clauses, but these views ignore that at the time of the framing, the word "declare" enjoyed a settled understanding and an established usage. Simply stated, as early as 1552, the verb "declare" had become synonymous with the verb "commence"; they both meant the initiation of hostilities.[20] This was the established usage of international law as well as in England, where the terms to declare war and to make war were used interchangeably.[21] This practice was familiar to the framers. Chancellor James Kent of New York, one of the leading jurists of the founding period, stated: "As war cannot lawfully be commenced on the part of the United States without an act of Congress, such an act is, of course, a formal official notice to all the world, and equivalent to the most solemn declaration." While Kent interpreted "declare" to mean "commence," he did not assert that the Constitution required a congressional declaration of war before hostilities could be lawfully commenced; he merely asserted that such a declaration is initiated by Congress.[22]

Given the equivalence of "commence" and "declare," it is clear that a congressional declaration of war would initiate military hostilities. According to commentators on international law a declaration of war was desirable because it announced the institution of a state of war, as well as the legal consequences that war entails, to the adversary, to neutral nations, and to citizens of the sovereign who initiated the war. Indeed, this is the essence of a declaration of war—notice by the proper authority of intent to convert a state of peace into a state of war.[23] But all that is required under American law is a joint resolution or an explicit congressional authorization of the use of military force against a named adversary. This can come in the form of a "declaration pure and simple" or in a "conditional declaration of war."[24] There are also two kinds of war, those that United States courts have termed "perfect," or general, and those that are labeled "imperfect," or limited, wars.

At the dawn of the Republic, in three important Supreme Court cases, it was decided that the power of determining perfect and imperfect war lay with Congress.[25] Thus, Chief Justice John Marshall, on behalf of the Court, held in 1801 in *Talbot* v. *Seeman,* that the power of Congress comprises the power to "declare a general war" and also to "wage a limited war."[26] The power of Congress to authorize limited war is, of course, a necessary concomitant of its power to declare general war. If, as John Bassett Moore has suggested, a president might authorize relatively minor acts of war, or perhaps covert military operations, in circumstances that did not demand a full-blown war, that power could be wielded in a way that would easily eviscerate the Constitution's placement of the war power in Congress. Moore, an eminent scholar of international law, has rebuked that proposition: "There can hardly be room for doubt that the framers of the Constitution, when they vested in Congress the power to declare war, they never imagined that they were leaving it to the executive to use the military and naval forces of the United States all over the world for the purpose of actually coercing other nations, occupying their territory, and killing their soldiers and citizens, all according to his own notion of the fitness of things, as long as he refrained from calling his action war or persisted in calling it peace."[27]

In fact, the framers withheld from the president the power to work such mischief. As we have observed, he was granted only the authority to respond defensively to the initiation of war through sudden attack upon the United States. In 1806, in *United States* v. *Smith,* Justice William Paterson of the Supreme Court, who had been a delegate to the convention, explained the rationale for a presidential response:

> If, indeed, a foreign nation should invade the territories of the United States, it would, I apprehend, be not only lawful for the president to resist such invasion, but also to carry hostilities into the enemy's own country; and for this plain reason, that a state of complete and absolute war exists between the two nations. In the case of invasive

hostilities, there cannot be war on the one side and peace on the other. . . . There is a manifest distinction between our going to war with a nation at peace, and a war being made against us by an actual invasion, or a formal declaration. In the former case, it is the exclusive province of Congress to change a state of peace into a state of war.[28]

As Justice Paterson observed, the reason for vesting the president with authority to repel sudden attacks was that an invasion instituted a state of war, thus rendering a declaration of war by Congress superfluous. In such an event, the president was authorized to initiate offensive action against the attacking enemy. But the president's power of self-defense does not extend to foreign lands. The framers did not give the president the right to intervene in foreign wars or to choose between war and peace or to identify and commence hostilities against an enemy of the American people. Nor did the framers empower a president to initiate force abroad on the basis of his own assessments of the security interests of the United States. These circumstances involve choices that belong to Congress. The president's power is defensive and is limited to attacks against the United States.

All of the offensive powers of the nation, then, were located in Congress. Consistent with this constitutional theory, the convention gave to Congress the power to issue "letters of marque and reprisal."[29] Dating back to the Middle Ages, when sovereigns employed private forces in retaliation for an injury caused by the sovereign of another state or his subjects, the practice of issuing reprisals gradually evolved into the use of public armies. By the time of the convention, the framers considered the power to issue letters of marque and reprisal sufficient to authorize a broad spectrum of armed hostilities short of declared war. In other words, it was regarded as a species of imperfect war. Thus, James Madison, Alexander Hamilton, and Thomas Jefferson, among others, agreed that the authorization of reprisals was an act of war that belonged to Congress.[30] As a direct reply to the revisionists' claim of a presidential power to order acts of war, we may consider what Jefferson said in 1793 about the authority necessary to issue a reprisal: "Congress must be called upon to take it; the right of reprisal being expressly lodged with them by the Constitution, and not with the executive."[31]

In short, it may be said that when the framers granted to Congress the power "to declare war," they were vesting in that body the sole and exclusive prerogative to initiate military hostilities on behalf of the American people. The record reveals that no member of the Philadelphia convention and no member of any state ratifying convention held a different understanding of the meaning of the war clause. Thus, if the revisionists are to find textual authority for a president's power to make war, it must derive from another source.

The Commander-in-Chief Clause

The commander-in-chief clause, in the words of Justice Robert H. Jackson, has been invoked for the "power to do anything, anywhere, that can be done with an army or navy."[32] While he said this in the context of reviewing President Truman's invocation of the clause to support his seizure of the steel mills, Justice Jackson's observations certainly foreshadowed the claims of recent executives who have seized the provision as justification for their military adventures.[33] Presidents Johnson, Nixon, Ford, Carter, and Reagan fall into this category.[34] The clause has also become the principal pillar for those who would vest in the president the constitutional power of war and peace.[35] As we shall see, however, the title of commander in chief conferred no war-making power whatever; it vested in the president only the authority to repel sudden attacks on the United States and to direct war, "when authorized or begun." In this capacity, presidents would direct the forces Congress placed at their command.

As Francis D. Wormuth has observed, the "office of commander in chief has never carried the power of war and peace, nor was it invented by the framers of the Constitution."[36] In fact, the office was introduced by King Charles I in 1639 when he named the earl of Arundel commander in chief of an army to battle the Scots in the First Bishops' War. In historical usage the title of commander in chief has been a generic term referring to the highest officer in a particular chain of command. The ranking commander in chief, purely a military post, always was under the command of a political superior.[37]

The government of England also transplanted the title to America in the eighteenth century by appointing a number of commanders in chief and by the practice of entitling governors of royal, proprietary, and chartered colonies as commanders in chief, or occasionally as vice-admirals or captains general. The appointment of General Thomas Gage as commander in chief from 1763 to 1776 caused grave concerns for the colonists, for he proceeded to interfere in civil affairs and to acquire considerable influence over Indian relations, trade, and transportation. The bitter memories of his decision to quarter troops in the homes of civilians spawned the Third Amendment to the Constitution. These activities, as well as others, prompted the colonists to complain in the Declaration of Independence that King George III had "affected to render the Military independent of and superior to the Civil Power."

But colonists had no reason to fear the governors as commanders in chief, even though they controlled the provincial forces. After all, the assemblies claimed and asserted the rights to vote funds for the militia and to call it into service. The historian Ernest May has correctly noted that "under one or the other of these principles, they neutralized whatever pernicious power the executive might have had."[38] In fact, the grievances came from the governors; like the duke of Wellington, they complained about the relative impotence of their positions.

The colonial assemblies (and, later, the states) asserted the power of the purse as a check on the commander in chief; this undoubtedly stemmed from the English practice, which extended at least as far back as the middle of the seventeenth century. By 1665, as a means of maintaining political control of the military establishment, Parliament had inaugurated the policy of making annual military appropriations with a lifetime of only one year. This practice, or strategy, sharply emphasized Parliament's power to determine the size of the army to be placed under the direction of the commander in chief.[39]

This practice had a long-term influence. Under the Constitution, the colonial and state assemblies' rights of voting funds for the armed forces were granted to Congress, under its powers to "raise and support armies" and to "provide and maintain a navy." Additionally, "no appropriation of money to that use shall be for a longer term than two years." With the framing of the Constitution, the requirement of legislative approval for the allocation of funds to raise troops—a requirement that had existed in England since the middle of the seventeenth century—underscored the principle of political superiority over military command. It also constitutes a sharp reminder that a commander in chief is dependent upon the legislature for an army to command.

Most of the early state constitutions followed the colonial practice of making the governor "commander in chief" under the authority of state legislatures. For example, Article VII of the Massachusetts Constitution of 1780 provided that the governor shall be "commander-in-chief of the army and navy." But it carefully circumscribed his power—the governor was to "repel, resist [and] expel" attempts to invade the Commonwealth—and it vested him "with all these and other powers incident to the offices of captain general . . . to be exercised agreeably to the rules and regulations of the Constitution and the laws of the land, and not otherwise."[40]

The Continental Congress continued to use the title when on June 15, 1775, it unanimously decided to appoint George Washington as "general." Dated June 17, his commission named him General and Commander in Chief, of the Army of the United Colonies. The instructions of the Congress, drafted by John Adams, Richard Henry Lee, and Edward Rutledge, kept Washington on a short leash. He was ordered "punctually to observe and follow such orders and directions, from time to time, as you shall receive from this, or a future Congress of these United Colonies, or Committee of Congress." Congress did not hesitate to instruct the commander in chief on military and policy matters.[41]

The practice of entitling the office at the apex of the military hierarchy as commander in chief and of subordinating him to a political superior, whether a king, parliament, or congress, had thus been firmly established for a century and a half and was thoroughly familiar to the framers when they met in Philadelphia. Perhaps this understanding, as well as the consequent absence of concerns about the nature of the post, was the reason there was no debate on the commander-in-chief clause at the convention.

The South Carolinian Charles Pinckney, in the plan he read to the convention on May 29, 1787, introduced the title of president and proposed: "He shall, by Virtue of his Office, be Commander in Chief of the Land Forces of U.S. and Admiral of their Navy."[42] Presumably, Pinckney had drawn on the traditional usage of the title, employed in the South Carolina Constitution of 1776, which provided for a "president and commander-in-chief," and that of 1778, which included a provision for a "governor and commander in chief."[43] There was no such provision in the Randolph, or Virginia, Plan, which was read to the convention on the same day. On June 15, William Paterson submitted the New Jersey Plan, which called for a plural executive and stipulated that the executives ought "to direct all military operations; provided that none of the persons composing the federal executive shall at any time take command of any troops, so as personally to conduct any enterprise as General, or in other capacity."[44] The qualifying clause was meant to discourage a military takeover of the government.[45] When Alexander Hamilton submitted a plan to the convention on June 18, he probably did not propose the title of commander in chief, but he undoubtedly had it in mind when he said the president was "to have the direction of war when authorized or begun."[46]

It was Hamilton's speech, then, that summarized the essence of the president's power as commander in chief: when war is "authorized or begun," the president is to command the military operations of American forces. There was no fear of the legal authority granted by the commander-in-chief clause, and in fact, the clause seemed to excite little dispute. The lone concern was that conveyed by the New Jersey Plan—namely, that a president who personally assumed command of army and naval forces might use them to institute a military coup. In the Virginia Ratifying Convention, George Mason, who had been a delegate to the Constitutional Convention, echoed the concerns of his fellow ratifiers when he said that although it was proper for a president to give overall orders, he thought it dangerous for a president to take command in person. The consent of Congress should be required before a president would be permitted to take command.[47]

But this concern was allayed in the North Carolina Ratifying Convention. Richard Dobbs Spaight, who also had been a delegate to the Constitutional Convention, said that the commander in chief could be controlled by Congress because it had the exclusive authority to raise and support armies, which, indeed, it has.[48] Similar assurance was offered by James Iredell, later an associate justice of the Supreme Court, who delineated the authority of the commander in chief and drew a sharp distinction between the powers of that post and those of the king of England:

> In almost every country, the executive has command of the military forces. From the nature of the thing, the command of armies ought to be delegated to one person only. The secrecy, dispatch, and decision, which are necessary in military operations, can only be expected from one person. The President, therefore, is to command the military forces of the United States, and this power I think a proper one; at the same time it will be found to be sufficiently guarded. A very material difference may be observed between this power, and the authority of the king of Great Britain under similar circumstances. The king of Great Britain is not only the commander-in-chief of the land and naval forces, but has power, in time of war, to raise fleets and armies. He also has the power to declare war. The President has not the power of declaring war by his own authority, nor that of raising fleets and armies. The powers are vested in other hands. The power of declaring war is expressly given to Congress, that is, to the two branches of the legislature. . . . They have also expressly delegated to them the powers of raising and supporting armies, and of providing and maintaining a navy.[49]

Iredell's speech reflected *Federalist* number 69, in which Hamilton sought to calm fears surrounding the commander-in-chief clause by noting that although the president's authority as commander in chief would be nominally the same as that of the English king, it would "in substance be much inferior to it." Hamilton added: "It would amount to nothing more than the supreme command and direction of the military and naval forces, as first general and admiral of the Confederacy; while that of the British king extends to the *declaring* of war and to the *raising* and *regulating* of fleets and armies,—all which, by the Constitution under consideration, would appertain to the legislature."[50]

In sum, the president, as commander in chief, was to be "first General and Admiral" in "the direction of war when authorized or begun." Political authority remained in Congress, as it had under the Articles of Confederation. The political scientist Louis Henkin has observed that "generals and admirals, even when they are 'first,' do not determine the political purposes for which troops are to be used; they command them in the execution of policy made by others."[51] The commander in chief, then, according to the tradition of a century and a half, was made subordinate to a political superior. The office carried with it no power to declare war. As Hamilton and Iredell explained, that power was the exclusive prerogative of Congress.

The Executive-Power Clause

In recent years, various presidents and commentators have sought to squeeze from the executive-power clause a presidential authority to make war. In 1966, for example, the State Department cited the president's role as "chief executive" to adduce constitutional support for Lyndon Johnson's entry into the Vietnam War.[52] Richard Nixon's legal advisors similarly invoked the clause to justify his wars in Southeast Asia.[53] In 1975, Gerald Ford found constitutional authority in the "President's Constitutional executive power" for the military activities he ordered in Cambodia.[54] On April 26, 1980, Jimmy Carter authorized an attempt to rescue American citizens who were being held hostage in Iran. He justified the attempt as being "pursuant to the President's powers under the Constitution as Chief Executive and as Commander in Chief."[55]

The very claim asserted by Presidents Johnson, Nixon, Ford, and Carter—that the grant of executive power includes the authority to initiate hostilities—was considered and rejected in the Constitutional Convention; indeed, it caused much alarm. As we have seen, the Randolph Plan provided for a "national executive," which would have "authority to execute the national laws . . . and enjoy the executive rights vested in Congress by the Confederation." In response to concerns that "executive rights" might include the power of war and peace, James Wilson pointed out that the prerogatives of the British monarchy were not a proper guide to defining executive powers in the United States. As Madison put it, executive powers "do not include the Rights of war and peace."[56]

No delegate to the convention ever suggested that "executive power" was a fountainhead of power to make war. For the framers, the phrase "executive power" was limited, as Wilson said, to "executing the laws, and appointing officers." Roger Sherman "considered the Executive magistracy as nothing more than an institution for carrying the will of the Legislature into effect." Madison, who agreed with Wilson's definition of executive power, thought it necessary "to fix the extent of Executive authority . . . as certain powers were in their nature Executive, and must be given to that department"; he added that "a definition of their extent would assist the judgment in determining how far they might be safely entrusted to a single officer." The definition of the executive's power should be precise, thought Madison; the executive power should "be confined and defined."[57] And so it was. In a draft reported by James Wilson, the phrase "The Executive

Power of the United States shall be vested in a single person" first appeared. His draft included an enumeration of the president's powers to grant reprieves and pardons and to serve as commander in chief; it also included the charge that "it shall be his duty to provide for the due and faithful execution of the Laws." The report of the Committee of Detail altered the "faithful execution" phrase to "he shall take care that the laws of the United States be duly and faithfully executed." This form was referred to the Committee of Style, which drafted the version that appears in the Constitution: "The executive power shall be vested in a president of the United States of America. . . . He shall take care that the laws be faithfully executed."[58]

The debate, to the extent that there was one, centered almost entirely on whether there should be a single or a plural presidency. The first sentence of Article II, section 2, "The Executive Power shall be vested in a President," depicts the conclusion reached.[59] Aside from this, there was no argument. There was no challenge to the definition of executive power held by Wilson and Madison; nor was an alternative understanding even advanced. And there was no argument about the scope of "executive power"; indeed, any latent fears were quickly arrested by assurances from Madison and Wilson that the power of "peace and war" was a legislative not an executive function. Given the framers' conception of the chief executive as little more than an institution to carry out the "will of the legislature"—that is, to execute the laws and to appoint officers—there was little about the office to fear. As legal historian Raoul Berger has observed "the 'executive power' was hardly a cornucopia from which could pour undreamed of powers."[60]

Of course, the widespread "aversion of the people to monarchy," the "unhappy memories of the royal prerogative; fear of tyranny, and distrust of any one man, kept the Framers from giving the President too much head."[61] That the framers did not vest the president with "too much" authority is evidenced by the relative calm with which the state ratifying conventions discussed the presidency. No doubt this is attributable to the careful and specific enumeration of the president's full powers. In South Carolina, Charles Pinckney reported that "we have defined his powers, and bound him to such limits, as will effectually prevent his usurping authority."[62] That view was echoed by James Iredell in North Carolina and by James Bowdoin in Massachusetts, who said the president's powers were "precisely those of the governors."[63]

And the powers of the governors were strictly limited. The Virginia Constitution of 1776, for example, stated that the governor shall "exercise the executive powers of government, according to the laws of the Commonwealth; and shall not, under any pretense, exercise any power or prerogative, by virtue of any law, statute, or custom of England."[64] Thomas

Jefferson, in his "Draft of a Fundamental Constitution for Virginia," written in 1783 and partially inspired by the excesses of the Virginia legislature, explained: "By Executive powers, we mean no reference to those powers exercised under our former government by the Crown as of its prerogatives. . . . We give to them these powers only, which are necessary to execute the laws (and administer the government)."[65] In short, as James Madison said, state executives across the land were "little more than Cyphers."[66]

It was in this context that the framers designed the office of the presidency. Executive powers amounted to little more than the duty to execute the laws and the right to appoint various officers. There is no intimation in the records of the Constitutional Convention or of the state ratifying conventions that executive power includes the right to make war.

A review of the proceedings in the Constitutional Convention and in the ratifying conventions leads to the conclusion that the war-making power, including the authority to initiate both limited and general war, was vested in Congress. The record establishes that neither the commander-in-chief clause nor the executive-power clause affords support for the claim that the president is empowered to commence hostilities. Indeed, such authority was specifically withheld from the president. That this was the settled understanding of the war power is suggested by the statements of the founding generation, by the views of eminent writers, by early judicial decisions, and by nineteenth-century practice.

THE EARLY UNDERSTANDING

Practice and Commentary

Early in 1793, war broke out between Great Britain and France. President Washington declared that the treaty of alliance of 1778 did not obligate the United States to defend French territory in America, and he issued a proclamation of neutrality. Whether this power belonged to the president or to Congress was debated by Alexander Hamilton and James Madison.[67] Hamilton sought to defend the proclamation: "If the Legislature have the right to make war on the one hand—it is on the other the duty of the Executive to preserve Peace till war is declared; and in fulfilling that duty, it must necessarily possess a right of judging what is the nature of the obligations which the treaties of the Country impose on the Government; and when in pursuance of that right it has concluded that there is nothing in them inconsistent with a state of neutrality, it becomes both its province and its duty to enforce the laws incident to that state of the Nation."[68]

In response, Madison contended that if the proclamation was valid, it meant the president had usurped Congress's power to decide between a state of peace and a state of war. Despite this difference, both agreed that the power to commence war is vested in Congress. Madison wrote: "Every just view that can be taken of this subject admonishes the public of the necessity of a rigid adherence to the simple, the received, and the fundamental doctrine of the constitution, that the power to declare war, including the power of judging of the causes of war, is *fully* and *exclusively* vested in the legislature; that the executive has no right, in any case, to decide the question, whether there is or is not cause for declaring war."[69] Throughout their lives, both Hamilton and Madison maintained that Congress alone had the authority to initiate hostilities; the president had only the power to repel invasions.[70]

In 1798, France repeatedly raided and seized American vessels. On April 27, 1798, Congress passed a law that increased the size of the navy.[71] Secretary of War James McHenry, who seemed to want war, asked Hamilton if the legislation authorized the president to initiate hostilities. Hamilton responded on May 17:

> Not having seen the law which provides the *naval armament,* I cannot tell whether it gives any new power to the President; that is, any power whatever with regard to the employment of the ships. If not, and he is left at the foot of the Constitution, as I understand to be the case, I am not ready to say that he has any other power than merely to employ the ships as convoys, with authority to *repel* force by *force* (but not to capture) and to repress hostilities within our waters, including a marine league from our coasts. Anything beyond this must fall under the idea of *reprisals,* and requires the sanctions of that department which is to delare *or make war.*[72]

During his first administration, Thomas Jefferson was confronted with attacks on American shipping in the Mediterranean by the pasha of Tripoli, who also demanded annual tribute from the United States. President Jefferson wrote the pasha on May 21, 1801, informing him that he, Jefferson, was ordering a "squadron of observation" to the Mediterranean to protect United States commerce. While the ships were forbidden to take offensive action, one U.S. vessel, the *Enterprise,* was attacked. Lieutenant Sterrett of the *Enterprise* rendered the attacking ship dead in the water and released it. On the occasion of his first annual message to Congress on December 8, 1801, Jefferson adopted the Hamiltonian position and explained:

> Unauthorized by the Constitution, without the sanction of Congress, to go beyond the line of defense, the [Tripolitan] vessel, being

disabled from committing further hostilities, was liberated with its crew. The Legislature will doubtless consider whether, by authorizing measures of offense also, they will place our force on an equal footing with that of its adversaries. I communicate all material information on this subject, that in the exercise of this important function confided by the Constitution to the Legislature exclusively their judgment may form itself on a knowledge and consideration of every circumstance of weight.[73]

But Jefferson's legal argument was met with harsh criticism from Alexander Hamilton. Hamilton thought the release of the Tripolitan vessel was contemptible, but he nonetheless maintained that the Constitution provided that

"the Congress shall have power to declare war"; the plain meaning of which is, that it is the peculiar and exclusive province of Congress, *when the nation is at peace,* to change that state into a state of war; whether from calculations of policy, or from provocations or injuries received; in other words, it belongs to Congress only *to go to war.* But when a foreign nation declares or openly and avowedly makes war upon the United States, they are then by the very fact *already at war,* and any declaration on the part of Congress is nugatory; it is at least unnecessary. . . .

Till the Congress should assemble and declare war, which would require time, our ships might, according to the hypothesis of the message, be sent by the President to fight those of the enemy as often as they should be attacked, but not to capture and detain them; if beaten, both vessels and crews would be lost to the United States; if successful, they could only disarm those they had overcome, and might suffer them to return to the place of common rendezvous, there to equip anew, for the purpose of resuming their depredations on our towns and on our trade.[74]

Hamilton probably attacked Jefferson for partisan reasons. The Tripolitan vessel had been rendered impotent; and Hamilton's hyperbole notwithstanding, there was no further threat to "our trade," let alone to "our towns." Thus it was proper for Jefferson to refer the matter to Congress, as the body that has the authority to change a state of peace into a state of war. At any rate, on February 6, 1802, Congress passed an act that met the concerns of Jefferson and Hamilton. The act empowered the president "fully to equip, officer, man and employ such of the armed vessels of the United States as may be judged requisite by the President of the United States, for protecting effectually the commerce and seamen thereof on the Atlantic Ocean, the Mediterranean and adjoining seas"; to direct the ships' commanders to "subdue, seize, and make prize of all vessels, goods and effects, belonging to the Bay of Tripoli, or to his subjects . . . and also to cause to be done all such other acts of precaution or hostility as the state of war will justify, and may, in his opinion, require."[75]

Jefferson's understanding of the war clause did not undergo any revision. On December 6, 1805, Jefferson informed Congress of the dispute with Spain over the boundaries of Louisiana and Florida. Jefferson said that Spain had indicated an

> intention to advance on our possessions until they shall be repressed by an opposing force. Considering that Congress alone is constitutionally invested with the power of changing our condition from peace to war, I have thought it my duty to await their authority for using force. . . . But the course to be pursued will require the command of means which it belongs to Congress exclusively to yield or to deny. To them I communicate every fact material for their information and the documents necessary to enable them to judge for themselves. To their wisdom, then, I look for the course I am to pursue, and will pursue with sincere zeal that which they shall approve.[76]

Like Jefferson, President James Madison was aggrieved by the punishment and harassment inflicted on United States vessels. On June 1, 1812, he expressed to Congress his extreme resentment of the British practice of seizing American ships and seamen and of inducing Indian tribes to attack the United States. Madison complained of this "state of war against the United States" and said, "Whether the United States shall remain passive under these progressive usurpations and these accumulating wrongs, or, opposing force, to force in defense of their national rights, is a solemn question which the constitution wisely confides to the legislative department of the Government."[77]

This exercise in presidential restraint speaks volumes for the intentions of the framers with respect to the initiation of hostilities. As the leading architect of the Constitution and as a principal actor in the debate on the war clause, Madison certainly knew that when the question arises of whether the United States should oppose force with force, it is a "solemn question which the Constitution wisely confides to the legislative department of the Government." This view is consistent with his earlier position. In 1793, Madison had written: "The power to declare war, including the power of judging the causes of war, is fully and exclusively vested in the legislature; that the executive has no right, in any case, to decide the question, whether there is or is not cause for declaring war."[78]

After his announcement of what has become known as the Monroe Doctrine on December 2, 1823, President James Monroe was confronted with international circumstances that seemed to invite the use of force, but Monroe repeatedly disclaimed any constitutional power to initiate hostilities.[79] In 1824, Colombia feared an attack by France. Citing the Monroe Doctrine, the Colombian government asked Secretary of State John Quincy Adams, "In what manner the Government of the United States intends to resist on its part any interference of the holy Alliance for the purpose of subjugating the new Republics or interfering in their political forms?" The question was considered in a cabinet meeting, which Adams summarized in his diary: "The Columbia republic to maintain its own independence. Hope that France and the Holy Allies will not resort to force against it. If they should, the power to determine our resistance is in Congress. The movements of the Executive will be as heretofore expressed. I am to draft an answer." While the matter was on the table, President Monroe wrote James Madison to explain the problem: "The subject will of course be weighed thoroughly in giving the answer. The Executive has no right to compromise the nation in any question of war." Adams informed Colombia that "by the Constitution of the United States, the ultimate decision of this question belongs to the Legislative Department of the Government."[80] The threat dissolved, and no force was used.

On December 7, 1824, President Monroe reported that American shipping off the coast of Florida was being plundered by pirates. While various measures might be employed to stop the pirates, Monroe referred the matter to Congress: "Whether those robbers should be pursued on the land . . . or any other measure be resorted to to suppress them, is submitted to the consideration of Congress." When the Senate asked for more information, Monroe responded with three proposals and asked that "a power commensurate with either resource be granted to the Executive."[81]

While President Andrew Jackson probably resented some congressional decisions regarding international affairs during his administration, he nonetheless agreed that Congress controlled the war-making power. On December 6, 1831, President Jackson delivered his third annual address, in which he said that an American ship had been seized "by a land acting, as they pretend, under the authority of the Government of Buenos Ayres." He augmented the naval squadron in the area, but he asked Congress to "clothe the Executive with such authority and means as they may deem necessary for providing a force adequate to the complete protection of our fellow citizens fishing and trading in those areas."[82] Congress did not act on his proposal.

In his annual message on December 1, 1834, President Jackson informed Congress that France had not honored an 1831 treaty by which the French government had agreed to meet claims for damages to American shipping between 1800 and 1817. He asked for legislation "authorizing reprisals upon French property, in case provision shall not be made for the payment of the debt at the approaching session of the French Chambers."[83] The Senate denied President Jackson's request. The denial was based on a report issued by the Senate Foreign Relations Committee, which was reported by Henry Clay on January 6, 1835:

> In the first place the authority to grant letters of marque and reprisal being specially delegated to Congress, Congress ought to retain to itself the right of judging of the expediency of granting them under all the circumstances existing at the time when they are proposed to be actually issued. The committee are not satisfied that Congress can, constitutionally, delegate this right. It is true that the President proposes to limit the exercise of it to one specified contingency. But if the law be passed as recommended, the President might, and probably would, feel himself bound to execute it in the event, no matter from what cause, of provision not being made for the fulfillment of the treaty by the French Chambers, now understood to be in session. . . . Congress ought to reserve to itself the Constitutional right, which it possesses, of judging of all the circumstances by which such refusal might be attended; of hearing France, and of deciding whether, in the actual posture of things as they may then exist, and looking to the condition of the United States, of France, and of Europe, the issuing letters of marque and reprisal ought to be authorized, or any measure adopted.[84]

As secretary of state, Daniel Webster echoed the views of his predecessors on the meaning of the war clause. In 1851, Webster denied a request for the United States to aid Hawaii in the latter's dispute with France. Webster stated:

> In the first place, I have to say that the war-making power in this Government rests entirely with Congress, and that the President can authorize belligerent operations only in the cases expressly provided for by the Constitution and the laws. By these no power is given to the Executive to oppose an attack by one independent nation on the possessions of another. We are bound to regard both France and Hawaii as independent states, and equally independent, and though the general policy of the Government might lead it to take part with either in a controversy with the other, still, if this interference be an

act of hostile force, it is not within the Constitutional power of the President; and still less is it within the power of any subordinate agent of government, civil or military.[85]

James Buchanan was insistent on the Constitution's placement of the war power. As secretary of state in 1848, he responded to a request from Hawaii for the United States to lend military aid to collect claims by stating: "The President could not employ the naval force of the United States to enforce its payment without the authority of an act of Congress. The war-making power alone can authorize such a measure." In 1860, President James Buchanan directed Secretary of State Lewis Cass to explain to a United States company in Nicaragua, which had asked the administration to use force to collect claims, that such a measure would constitute "an act of war," which "is a measure which Congress alone possesses the constitutional power to adopt."[86]

There was no departure from this understanding of the war clause throughout the nineteenth century; indeed, a search of the historical records for a claim that the president had the power to initiate hostilities is made in vain.[87] In fact, it was left to twentieth-century officeholders and commentators to claim that the president had the constitutional power to make war.

The Mexican War, 1846–48, deserves attention in this context. After the annexation of Texas, a dispute arose over the title to territory between the Nueces and the Rio Grande. President James Polk ordered an army into the area, and it defeated the Mexican forces. In a message to Congress, President Polk offered the rationale that "Mexico has passed the boundary of the United States, has invaded our territory and shed American blood on American soil." It was on the basis of this report that Congress declared, "By the act of the Republic of Mexico, a state of war exists between the Government and the United States."[88]

If President Polk's rationale was correct, this action could not be challenged on constitutional grounds, for it had been well established that the president possessed the authority to repel sudden attacks. If, however, he had been disingenuous, if he had in fact initiated hostilities, then he had clearly usurped the war-making power of Congress. Notice, too, that he made no claim of having the constitutional power to make war.

Polk's actions were resented, and in 1847 the two houses of Congress commenced an inquiry into the circumstances surrounding the outbreak of the war. On January 3, 1848, the House concluded, by a vote of 85 to 81, that the war had been "unnecessarily and unconstitutionally begun by the President of the United States."[89] Congressman Abraham Lincoln of Illinois voted with the majority. Lincoln's law partner, William H. Herndon, had written a letter in which he assumed that Polk had initiated the hostilities; but Herndon nevertheless defended the action as a legitimate means of preventing an invasion by Mexico. Lincoln answered his friend in a letter that has become legendary: "Allow the President to invade a neighboring nation whenever he shall deem it necessary to repel an invasion, and you . . . allow him to make war at his pleasure. . . . The provision of the Constitution giving the war-making power to Congress was dictated by the [fact that] . . . Kings had always been involving and impoverishing their people in wars . . . and they resolved to so frame the Constitution that no one man should hold the power of bringing oppression upon us."[90]

As president, Abraham Lincoln did not alter his view of the war power. This conclusion may be drawn from his first annual message on December 3, 1861, when he referred to prior congressional authorization for American ships to "defend themselves against and to capture pirates." It was his opinion that congressional authorization was necessary "to recapture any prizes which pirates may make of United States vessels and their cargoes." This was exactly the understanding of the war clause held by Madison, Hamilton, and Jefferson.[91] None of Lincoln's actions during the Civil War constitutes a precedent for presidential initiation of war. The attack on Fort Sumter represented a "sudden attack," which Lincoln, as president, had the constitutional power to repel.[92]

Constitutional experts during the nineteenth century were in agreement on the meaning of the war clause: War cannot lawfully be initiated by the president; it can be initiated only by Congress. James Kent, one of the Republic's eminent jurists, wrote in his *Commentaries* in 1829: "It is essential that some formal public act, proceeding directly from the competent source, should announce to the people at home their new relations and duties growing out of a state of war, and which should equally apprise neutral nations of the fact. . . . War cannot lawfully be commenced on the part of the United States without an Act of Congress."[93] In his *Commentaries* of 1833, Joseph Story, then an associate justice of the Supreme Court, observed: "[The] power of declaring war is . . . so critical and calamitous, that it requires the utmost deliberation, and the successive revise of all the councils of the nation. . . . The representatives of the people are to lay the taxes to support a war, and therefore have a right to be consulted as to its propriety and necessity."[94] In 1864, William Whiting wrote: "Congress has the sole power, under the Constitution, to sanction or authorize the commencement of offensive war. . . . But . . . when war is commenced against this country . . . , no declaration of war by the government is necessary. The fact that war is levied against the United States, makes it the duty of the President to call out the army or navy to subdue the enemy, whether foreign or domestic."[95] In his work on the Constitution in 1868, John Norton Pomeroy wrote: "It is sufficient to know that the people considered the act and state of war a matter of such transcendant importance and magnitude, involving such untold personal and material interests, hazarding the prosperity, and perhaps the very existence of the body politic, that they committed its formal inception to that department of the government which more immediately represents them,—the Congress."[96] Thomas M. Cooley, a legal scholar and chief justice of the Michigan Supreme Court, said in 1880 about the president as commander in chief: "The power to declare war being confided to the legislature, he has no power to originate it, but he may in advance of its declaration employ the army and navy to suppress insurrection or repel invasion."[97] In 1887, Hermann Eduard von Holst wrote: "The right to 'declare war' belongs to Congress alone. . . . Congress has the exclusive right of the initiative. If a foreign power brings war against the United States, then it is not only the right, but the duty, of the President to oppose the enemy with all the means placed at his disposal by the constitution and the laws."[98]

It is worth noting that in 1929, Westel W. Willoughby, an eminent political scientist, embraced the teaching and understanding of the nineteenth century in his commentary on the Constitution: "The right of making war belongs exclusively to the supreme or sovereign power of the State. This power in all civilized nations is regulated by the fundamental laws or municipal constitution of the country. By our own Constitution, the power is lodged in Congress."[99]

Judicial Precedents

The meaning of the war clause was put beyond doubt by several early judicial decisions. No court since has departed from this early view.

In 1800, in *Bas* v. *Tingy,* the Supreme Court considered for the first time whether Congress might declare an "imperfect," or limited, war, as well as a "perfect," or general, war. Decided in the context of a limited war between the United States and France, from 1798 to 1801, Justice Chase ruled that Congress is empowered either to declare a general war or to wage a limited war—limited in place, in object, in time.[100] Justices Washington and Paterson wrote separate opinions, but each agreed that Congress possesses the exclusive right to decide for war.[101]

Chief Justice John Marshall was not on the Court when it decided *Tingy,* but he embraced the decision in an opinion for the Court in 1801 in *Talbot* v. *Seeman:* "The whole powers of war being, by the Constitution . . . vested in Congress, . . . Congress may authorize general hostilities . . . or partial war."[102] In 1804, in *Little* v. *Barreme,* Marshall also held that President John Adams's instructions to seize ships were in conflict with an act of Congress, and were therefore illegal.[103]

In 1806, in *United States* v. *Smith,* the question of whether the president may initiate hostilities was addressed by Justice Paterson, who wrote: "Does he [the president] possess the power of making war? That power is exclusively vested in Congress. . . . There is a manifest distinction between our going to war with a nation at peace, and a war made against us by an actual invasion, or a formal declaration. In the former case, it is the exclusive province of Congress to change a state of peace into a state of war."[104]

In the *Prize Cases,* 1863, the Supreme Court considered for the first time the power of the president to respond to sudden attacks. Justice Robert C. Grier delivered the opinion of the court: "By the Constitution, Congress alone has the power to declare a national or foreign war. . . . If a war be made by invasion by a foreign nation, the President is not only authorized but bound to resist force, by force. He does not initiate the war, but is bound to accept the challenge without waiting for any special legislative authority. And whether the hostile party be a foreign invader, or States organized in rebellion, it is none the less a war, although the declaration of it be "unilateral."[105]

These judicial decisions established that Congress alone has the power to initiate hostilities, whether in the form of a general or a limited war; the president is granted only the power to repel sudden attacks against the United States.

Moreover, the Supreme Court has never held that the commander-in-chief clause confers the power to initiate a war. In 1895, in *United States* v. *Sweeny,* Justice Henry B. Brown wrote for the Court that the object of the clause was to give the president "such supreme and undivided command as would be necessary to the prosecution of a successful war."[106] In 1919, Senator George Sutherland, who later became an associate justice of the Supreme Court, wrote: "Generally speaking, the war powers of the President under the Constitution are simply those that belong to any commander-in-chief of the military forces of a nation at war. The Constitution confers no war powers upon the President as such."[107] In 1942, in *Ex parte Quirin,* Chief Justice Harlan F. Stone said of the commander in chief's power: "The Constitution thus invests the President with power to wage war which Congress has declared, and to carry into effect all laws passed by Congress for the conduct of war and for the government and regulation of the Armed Forces, and all laws defining and punishing offenses against the law of nations, including those which pertain to the conduct of war."[108]

It is thus against the intentions of the framers, against their debate and vote on the war clause, and against a wealth of executive, legislative, and judicial precedents of the nineteenth century that recent executives have invoked the president's power to initiate military hostilities. The evidence against their case is compelling. Their claims ignore the Constitution, and they find no authority in American legal history.

THE ENDURING DEBATE

Public concern over the legitimacy of United States military involvement in Indochina sparked considerable interest in the constitutional power to make war. Congressional efforts to provide for a legislative role in the decision-making process to commit forces abroad culminated with the passage, over President Nixon's veto, of the War Powers Resolution in 1973. The resolution has been shadowed by controversy since its birth. It has been attacked as an unconstitutional and ill-conceived effort to legislate a division of the war powers.[109] The controversy surrounding its validity has been renewed by a Supreme Court decision in 1983, which seemingly invalidated a critical provision of the legislation. To date, the law has yet to receive presidential compliance and enforcement.

The War Powers Resolution consists of three main procedures: (1) the president must consult with Congress; (2) the president must report to Congress; and (3) Congress must terminate any military action. The purpose of the resolution, according to section 2(a), is "to fulfill the intent of the framers of the Constitution . . . and insure that collective judgment of both Congress and the President" will apply to the introduction of American troops into hostilities. The act, however, has failed to accomplish either purpose.

Section 2(c) seems to restrict the president's exercise of his powers as commander in chief to three situations: a declaration of war, specific authorization, or a national emergency created by an attack on the United States, its territories, or its possessions. However, this apparent delimitation of presidential discretion is eviscerated by the fact that the conference report reveals that the provisions regarding consultation, reporting, and congressional action are not dependent on the language of section 2(c).[110]

Apparently, the president is free to determine when and where to commit military forces to battle. This is confirmed by section 3, which provides that the president is to "consult" with Congress "in every possible instance . . . before introducing" troops. Obviously, this clause contemplates situations in which a president will commit troops to military hostilities without consulting Congress. This grant of considerable discretion to the president, which history reveals has been frequently and easily exploited, is the principal vice of the resolution; it deserves close consideration.

By permitting a president to introduce forces abroad without congressional authorization, section 3 not only repudiates the resolution's stated aim of ensuring the "collective judgment" of both branches; it also actually attempts to give to the presidency a power greater than that it derives from the Constitution. To state it bluntly, the resolution has given presidents the power to initiate war.[111]

Such an attempt, properly undertaken, would require a constitutional amendment since it involves a fundamental transfer of power from the legislative branch to the executive. It is of no moment that the shift may be only of a temporary nature—60 to 90 days—for it is the transfer of the authority to go to war, the power to determine war and peace, that is so critical.

In the convention the suggestion of giving the president that power shocked the delegates and was therefore rejected. In 1834, a Congress mindful of the constitutional dimensions of the use of force properly rejected President Jackson's request for a legislative grant of authority to order reprisals against France in the event that it did not pay its debt to the United States. Henry Clay reported the view of the Senate Foreign Relations Committee that Congress could not "constitutionally delegate this right," that having been vested by the Constitution with this authority, "Congress ought to retain to itself the right of judging of the expediency of granting them [war powers] under all the circumstances existing at the time when they are proposed to be actually issued."[112]

The denial of Jackson's request clearly reflected the desire of the framers for Congress to judge the expediency of committing troops abroad. By virtue of the War Powers Resolution, however, Congress has surrendered that prerogative to the president.

Ironically, the single clause of the act that might have retained for Congress some genuine measure of "collective judgment" with respect to the continuation of the use of troops abroad—if not the initiation—has perhaps been gutted by the Supreme Court's ruling in *INS* v. *Chadha,* which struck down the legislative veto.[113] Section 5(c), the "legislative veto" provision, empowered Congress to order the removal of troops involved in hostilities "at any time" by concurrent resolution. At least in theory, Congress might order the withdrawal of forces that had been committed by the executive without having consulted the legislative branch. However, once engaged in battle, it might be politically impossible to halt the operation.

Flawed in design, the War Powers Resolution has failed to restrain unilateral war making by the executive. Since its passage, no president yet has been willing to comply fully with the reporting provision, which requires a president, after introducing troops into hostilities, to report to Congress within forty-eight hours. But if no report is filed under the terms of the act, then the restrictions contained in the act, as well as congressional means of control, including the sixty-day limitation on military action, do not apply. Hence, presidents since Gerald Ford typically have filed reports of their military actions well beyond the forty-eight-hour requirement. They have done this, not on their statutory authority "under" the resolution, but on their alleged constitutional authority as chief executive and commander in chief. Thus, President Reagan justified his military initiatives in Lebanon in 1982 and 1983, as well as his invasion of Grenada on October 25, 1983, on grounds of his "constitutional authority with respect to the conduct of foreign relations and as Commander-in-Chief of the United States Armed Forces."[114]

Other Arguments

It has been justly observed that until 1950, "no judge, no President, no legislator, no commentator ever suggested that the President had legal authority to initiate war."[115] Since then, however, a steady pattern of presidential war making has developed, and its legality has been defended on a number of grounds. Yet claims based on textual grants of authority are without merit. In fact, there is little or no evidence to support these claims. So, defenders have contrived additional arguments which, for the sake of completeness, require consideration.

First is the contention that the president derives a war-making authority from his "prime responsibility for the conduct of foreign relations."[116] It is difficult to locate the source of this broad grant of power. As Article II indicates, the president shares with the Senate the treaty-making power and the power to appoint ambassadors. In fact, the framers assumed that the treaty power would constitute the primary mechanism by which American foreign relations would be conducted. Alexander Hamilton echoed the sentiment of the convention when he assured the delegates to the New York State Ratifying Convention that the Senate "together with the President are to manage all our concerns with foreign nations."[117] Moreover, Congress has complete power over foreign commerce, and it alone is the repository of the power to declare war. Only two powers in foreign relations are assigned exclusively to the president. A president is commander in chief; but he acts in this capacity by and under the authority of Congress. And a president has the power to receive foreign ambassadors. Hamilton, Madison, and Jefferson agreed that this clerklike function was purely ceremonial. While it has come to entail the recognition of states in international law, which carries with it certain legal implications, the framers declined to make it a discretionary policy-making instrument. As Hamilton explained, the duty of recognizing states was more conveniently placed in the hands of the executive than in the legislature.[118] This exhausts the textual grant of authority which confers jurisdiction over foreign affairs. Plainly, the framers granted the bulk of foreign-relations powers to Congress. The president's constitutional authority pales by comparison.

Extollers of a unilateral war-making authority for the executive also have invoked the shopworn argument about the allegedly "inherent" or prerogative powers of the president. Drawing on John Locke's defense of an executive's right to act for the common good, even if it should require breaking the law, defenders have adduced a similar claim for the president.[119] This contention is frankly unfit for constitutional analysis. There is no evidence whatsoever that the framers intended to incorporate the "Lockean Prerogative" in the Constitution. And lacking a textual statement or grant of power to that effect, such an intent is indispensable to the claim of a constitutional power. In fact, the evidence runs in the other direction. Fears of executive power led the framers to enumerate presidential powers, to "define and confine" the scope of authority. And clearly, an undefined reservoir of discretionary power, in the form of Locke's prerogative, would have unraveled the carefully crafted design of Article II and thus would have repudiated the founders' stated aim of corralling executive power.

The absence of such authority means that by definition, any presidential assertion of a prerogative power to violate the law is an extraconstitutional claim; an action based on such an assertion is, by definition, unconstitutional. This claim, then, does not afford a president any constitutional or legal authority to initiate war. The issue is merely whether a president could commence war in violation of the supreme law of the land and then attempt to justify it on the grounds of necessity. Of course, presidents cannot be the judge of their own actions. They must seek immunity and exoneration from Congress in the way of retroactive authorization, a practice that is deeply embedded in our legal tradition.[120] Whether or not congressional approval of the claimed prerogative is granted, the review itself is an admission of presidential usurpation.

Finally, the extollers have fashioned the argument that executive war making, if it has been repeated often enough, acquires legal validity. This is the contention, as expounded by Henry P. Monaghan, that "history has legitimated the practice of presidential war-making."[121] Their argument rests on the premise that the president has frequently exercised the war power without Congress's authorization. The actual number of these episodes varies among the several compilations, but defenders usually list between one and two hundred unilateral sets, each of which constitutes a legitimizing "precedent" for future executive wars.[122]

In detail and in conception, the argument is flawed. First, the revisionist's lists are inaccurately compiled.[123] Space does not permit a critical analysis of each alleged assertion of executive precedents. Consider, however, an error common on these lists: the claim that unilateral war making was initiated by the "undeclared" war with France in 1798.[124] That claim, as Francis D. Wormuth has observed, "is altogether false. The fact is that President Adams took absolutely no independent action. Congress passed a series of acts which amounted, so the Supreme Court said, to a declaration of imperfect war; and Adams complied with these statutes."[125] Many of the episodes involved the initiation of hostilities by a military commander, not by the authorization of the president. If practice establishes law, then the inescapable conclusion is that every commander of every military unit has the power to initiate war. What is perhaps most revealing about a president's understanding of the constitutional locus of the war power is that in the one or two dozen instances in which presidents have personally made the decision, unconstitutionally, to initiate acts of war, they have *not* purported to rely on their authority as commander in chief or chief executive. In "all of these cases the Presidents have made false claims of authorization, either by statute or by treaty or by international law."[126]

Further, it cannot be maintained that constitutional power—in this case the war power—can be acquired through practice. In *Powell* v. *McCormack,* Chief Justice Earl Warren wrote: "That an unconstitutional action has been taken before surely does not render that action any less unconstitutional at a later date." Earlier, Justice Felix Frankfurter, writing for a unanimous Court, echoed a centuries-old principle of Anglo-American jurisprudence: "Illegality cannot attain legitimacy through practice."[127] The Court has repeatedly denied claims that the president can acquire power by a series of usurpations. If it were otherwise, the president might aggrandize all governmental power. Neither Congress nor the judiciary could lawfully restrain the exercise of his accumulated "constitutional" powers. Clearly, this practice would destroy our entire constitutional jurisprudence. Thus, the most recent act of usurpation stands no better than the first.

Finally, it is unwarranted to conclude that presidential usurpation, indulged by congressional acquiescence or passivity, attains a legal status. Congress cannot divest itself of those powers conferred upon it by the Constitution, a necessary predicate of the doctrine of separation of powers.[128] Neither congressional abdication nor acquiescence can accomplish a transfer of its power to the executive. The Court has held, harking back to an old axiom of English law, that once powers are "granted, they are not lost by being allowed to lie dormant, any more than non-existent powers can be prescripted by an unchallenged exercise."[129]

CONCLUSION

In recent years, Congress's power to decide for war or peace has been usurped by the executive. In this regard there is a fundamental conflict between the theory of the Constitution and the practice of the government. It has sometimes been observed that the intentions of the framers are outdated and irrelevant. But before we too readily acquiesce in this verdict, we might consider the policy reasons underlying their decision to vest the war power in Congress, not in the president. Painfully aware of the horror and destructive consequences of warfare, the founders decided that before the fate of the nation would be put to risk, there ought to be some discussion, some deliberation by Congress, the people's representatives.

NOTES

Research for this chapter was made possible by a grant from the Idaho State University Research Committee. I am indebted to Tom Cronin for his helpful criticism and encouragement. A version of this chapter was published as "The Constitution and Presidential Warmaking: The Enduring Debate," *Political Science Quarterly* 103 (Spring 1988): 1.

1. I have borrowed the phrase "presidential wars" from Francis D. Wormuth, "Presidential Wars: The Convenience of 'Precedent,'" *Nation*, Oct. 9, 1972, p. 301. A body of literature has examined this question of whether Congress or the president is constitutionally empowered to start wars. See, e.g., Francis D. Wormuth, "The Nixon Theory of the War Powers: A Critique," *California Law Review* 60 (1972): 623; his earlier monograph, *The Vietnam War: The President versus the Constitution* (Santa Barbara, Calif.: Center for the Study of Democratic Institutions, 1968), and the book that he coauthored with Edwin Firmage, *To Chain the Dog of War: The War Power of Congress in History and Law* (Dallas: Southern Methodist University Press, 1986). See also Leonard Ratner, "The Co-ordinated Warmaking Power: Legislative, Executive and Judicial Roles," *Southern California Law Review* 50 (1970): 19; Eugene Rostow, "Great Cases Make Bad Law: The War Powers Act," *Texas Law Review* 50 (1972): 833; Raoul Berger, "War-Making by the President," *Pennsylvania Law Review* 121 (1972): 29; William Rogers, "Congress, the President, and War Powers," *California Law Review* 59 (1971): 1194; Charles Lofgren, "War-Making under the Constitution: The Original Understanding," *Yale Law Journal* 81(1972): 672.

2. See, e.g., the articles by Ratner and Rostow, cited in note 1 above.

3. Edward S. Corwin denounced Arthur M. Schlesinger, Jr., and Henry Steele Commager for their support of Truman's action. See *The President: Office and Powers, 1787–1957*, 4th rev. ed. (New York: New York University Press, 1957), p. 14. By the late 1960s, both Schlesinger and Commager had altered their views and favored a more powerful congressional role in the conduct of foreign policy (cited by Louis Fisher in *Constitutional Conflicts between Congress and the President* [Princeton, N.J.: Princeton University Press, 1985], p. 291).

4. 87 Stat. 555, Public Law 93–148 (1973). For a discussion of the act see text accompanying notes 110–15, below.

5. Max Farrand, ed., *The Records of the Federal Convention of 1787*, 4 vols. (New Haven, Conn.: Yale University Press, 1911), 1:21.

6. Ibid., p. 65.

7. Ibid., pp. 73–74, 65–66.

8. Ibid., pp. 70, 66.

9. Ibid., 2:182.

10. Henry Steele Commager, *Documents of American History,* 7th ed. (New York: Appleton-Century-Crofts, 1963), p. 133. Charles Warren has observed that this power, as well as others, came "bodily from the old Articles of Confederation" (*The Making of the Constitution* [Cambridge, Mass: Harvard University Press, 1947], p. 389).

11. Farrand, *Records,* 2:318. Hamilton also believed that "the Senate [should] have the sole power of declaring war" (ibid., 1:292). He added that the president was to direct the war when "authorized or begun."

12. Ibid., 2:318.

13. If the United States were attacked, it would automatically be involved in war, and a congressional declaration of war would not be necessary. See the opinion of Supreme Court Justice Paterson on this point, text accompanying note 49, below.

14. Farrand, *Records,* 2:318, 319.

15. Jonathan Elliot, ed., *Debates in the Several State Conventions on the Adoption of the Federal Constitution,* 2d ed., 4 vols. (Washington, D.C.: By the Editor, 1836), 2:528. Robert McCloskey has written that Wilson was the "most learned and profound legal scholar of his generation" (*The Works of James Wilson,* ed. Robert G. McCloskey, 2 vols. [Cambridge, Mass.: Harvard University Press, 1967], 1:2).

16. Elliot, *Debates,* 4:107, 108, 287, 2:278.

17. *Congressional Record,* 119 (daily ed., July 19, 1973), p. 514141.

18. Ratner, "Co-ordinated Warmaking Power," p. 467.

19. John Norton Moore, "The National Executive and the Use of Armed Forces Abroad," in *The Vietnam War and International Law,* ed. R. Falk, 4 vols. (Princeton, N.J.: Princeton University Press, 1969), 2:814. Senator Paul Douglas defended President Truman's unauthorized venture in Korea on this ground; see *Congressional Record* 96 (1950): 9648.

20. Huloet's dictionary provided this definition: "Declare warres. Arma Canere, Bellum indicere." We have here two meanings: to summon to arms; to announce war (quoted by Wormuth and Firmage, *To Chain the Dog of War,* p. 20).

21. In 1744, *Comyn's Digest,* an authoritative treatise on English law, stated: "To the king alone it belongs to make peace and war," as well as "the king has the sole authority to declare war and peace" (ibid.). For a discussion of the understanding of international law see Lofgren, "War-making under the Constitution," pp. 685–95.

22. James Kent, *Commentaries on American Law,* 2d. ed., 4 vols. (Boston: Little, Brown, 1896), 1:55.

23. Lofgren, "War-Making under the Constitution," pp. 685–95.

24. According to Emmerich de Vattel, the leading international-law publicist, a conditional declaration of war, an ultimatum demanding satisfaction of grievances, ought properly to precede a declaration of general war (*The Law of Nations,* trans. C. Fenwick [Washington, D.C.: Carnegie Institution, 1916], pp. 254–57).

25. See text accompanying notes 100–105, below.

26. 5 U.S. (1 Cranch) 1, 28 (1801).

27. J. B. Moore, *The Collected Papers of John Bassett Moore,* 7 vols. (New Haven, Conn.: Yale University Press, 1944), 5:195–96.

28. *United States* v. *Smith,* 27 F. Cas. 1192,1230 (C.C.D.N.Y. 1806).

29. For a discussion of the origins and development of the use of letters of marque and reprisal, with an application to contemporary covert war, see Jules Lobel, "Covert War and Congressional Authority: Hidden War and Forgotten Power," *Pennsylvania Law Review* 134 (1986): 1035.

30.. Ibid., pp. 1045–47.

31. Quoted by J. B. Moore in *A Digest of International Law*, 8 vols. (Washington, D.C.: Government Printing Office, 1906), 7:123.

32. *Youngstown Sheet and Tube Co.* v. *Sawyer*, 343 U.S. 579,642 (1952) (concurring opinion).

33. In 1793, in opposition to a novel construction of presidential power which, to him, seemed foreign to the framers' conception of the office, James Madison lamented: "We are to regard it as morally certain, that in proportion as doctrines make their way into the creed of the government, and the acquiescence of the public, every power that can be deduced from them, will be deduced, and exercised sooner or later by those who have an interest in so doing" (quoted by Richard Loss, ed., *The Letters of Pacificus and Helvidius* [Delmar, N.Y.: Scholars Facsimiles, 1976], p. 87).

34. E.g., the State Department justified Lyndon Johnson's involvement in Vietnam on the basis of his power as commander in chief (*Department of State Bulletin* 54 [1966]: 474, 484). The same justification was used by Ronald Reagan with respect to his actions in Lebanon and Grenada.

35. Senator Barry Goldwater, e.g., has said that the commander-in-chief clause gives the president "the power of war and peace" (*Congressional Record* 117 [daily ed., Apr. 26, 1971], p. 55640).

36. Wormuth, "Nixon Theory," p. 630.

37. Quoted ibid.; see also Ernest May, ed., *The Ultimate Decision: The President as Commander in Chief* (New York: George Braziller, 1960), pp. 3–19.

38. Quoted by May, *Ultimate Decision*, pp. 9–10.

39. Abraham D. Sofaer, *War, Foreign Affairs and Constitutional Power: The Origins* (Cambridge, Mass.: Ballinger, 1976), pp. 9, 382, 383.

40. Benjamin Perley Poore, comp., *The Federal and State Constitutions, Colonial Charters*, 2 vols., (Washington, D.C.: Government Printing Office, 1877), pp. 965–66.

41. E.g., the Continental Congress ordered Washington to Massachusetts to take command of the United Colonies (*Journals of the Continental Congress*, 34 vols. [1904–37], 2:101). Washington was directed to intercept two British vessels on Oct. 5, 1775 (ibid., 3:278).

42. Farrand, *Records*, 3:606.

43. Francis Thorpe, ed., *The Federal and State Constitutions, Colonial Charters, and Other Organic Laws*, 7 vols. (Washington, D.C.: Government Printing Office, 1909), 3:3243, 3249.

44. Farrand, *Records*, 1:20, 244.

45. See below, text accompanying notes 49–52.

46. Farrand, *Records*, 1:292. Madison's version does not include the commander-in-chief title. Nor do the reports made by Robert Yates of New York and David Brearley of New Jersey, each of which states: "To have the entire direction of war when authorized or begun" (Elliot, *Debates*, 1:179). But the version in the Hamilton papers states: "The Governor . . . is to be the Commander-in-Chief of the land and naval forces of the United States—to have the entire direction of War when authorized or begun" (*The Papers of Alexander Hamilton*, ed. Harold C. Syrett

and Jacob Cooke, 17 vols. [New York: Columbia University Press, 1962], 4:208; hereinafter cited as *Hamilton Papers*). Presumably, the inclusion of the title of commander in chief in the *Papers* was a subsequent addition.

47. Elliot, *Debates*, 3:496. For similar concerns see ibid., pp. 220, 59; 1:378.

48. Ibid., 4:114.

49. Ibid., 4:107–8. As a member of the Supreme Court, Justice Paterson held that Congress alone had the power to declare war (*United States* v. *Smith*, 27 F. Cas. 1192, 1196–97 [no. 16342] [C.C.D.N.Y. 1806]).

50. In *The Federalist*, ed. Isaac Kramnick (New York: Penguin Books, 1987), p. 398.

51. Louis Henkin, *Foreign Affairs and the Constitution* (Mineola, N.Y.: Foundation Press, 1972), pp. 50–51.

52. Leonard Meeker, "The Legality of the United States Participation in the Defense of Vietnam," *Department of State Bulletin* 54 (1966): 474.

53. Ibid., pp. 1194, 1207–12.

54. On May 13, 1975, President Ford ordered a military assault to rescue an American merchant vessel, the *Mayaguez*, which had been seized by Cambodian patrol boats. He said of his action: "The operation was ordered and conducted pursuant to the President's constitutional executive power and his authority as Commander-in-Chief of the U.S. Armed Forces" (communication from Gerald R. Ford to the Speaker of the House of Representatives and the President Pro Tempore of the Senate, May 15, 1975, in *Weekly Compilation of Presidential Documents* 11 [1975], p. 514).

55. President Carter justified his attempted rescue of the hostages on April 24, 1980, on the basis of his powers as chief executive and commander in chief (*Congressional Record* 126 [daily ed. April 28, 1980], p. H2991).

56. Farrand, *Records,* 1:66. For discussion of these points see the text accompanying notes 5–8, above.

57. Ibid., pp. 65–70.

58. Ibid., 2:171, 185, 572, 574, 597, 600.

59. Edward Corwin has remarked: "The Records of the Constitutional Convention make it clear that the purposes of this clause were simply to settle the question whether the executive branch should be plural or single and to give the executive a title" ("The Steel Seizure Case: A Judicial Brick without Straw," *Columbia Law Review* 53 [1953]: 53).

60. Raoul Berger, *Executve Privilege: A Constitutional Myth* (Cambridge, Mass.: Harvard University Press, 1974), p. 52.

61. Hamilton, in *Federalist* no. 67, p. 436; Henkin, *Foreign Affairs*, p. 33.

62. Elliot, *Debates*, 4:329; see also 2:540, 3:201.

63. Ibid., 4:107, 2:128.

64. Poore, *Federal and State Constitutions*, 2:1910–11.

65. Quoted in Warren, *Makings of the Constitution*, p. 177.

66. Farrand, *Records*, 2:35.

67. Hamilton wrote under the pseudonym Pacificus; Madison used the pen name Helvidius. The debate is reprinted in Loss, *Letters*.

68. "Pacificus, No. 1," in *Hamilton Papers*, 15:40. Hamilton noted specifically "the right of the Legislature to declare war and grant letters of marque and reprisal" (ibid., p. 39).

69. "Helvidius, No. 1," in *Writings of James Madison*, ed. G. Hunt, 9 vols. (New York: G. P. Putnam's, 1900–1910), 6:174, hereinafter cited as *Madison Writings*.

70. See above, text accompanying notes 71–78.

71. 1 Stat. 552 (Apr. 27, 1798).

72. *The Works of Alexander Hamilton,* ed. Henry C. Lodge, 2d. ed., 12 vols. (New York: G. P. Putnam's, 1904), 10:281–82, hereinafter cited as *Hamilton Works.*

73. Quoted by James D. Richardson, comp., in *Compilation of the Messages and Papers of the Presidents, 1787–1897,* 10 vols. (Washington, D.C.: Government Printing Office, 1897), 1:326–27, hereinafter cited as *Messages and Papers.*

74. "Letters of Lucius Crassus, No. 1," quoted in *Hamilton Works,* 8:249–50.

75. 2 Stat. 129.

76. *Messages and Papers,* 1:389–90.

77. Ibid., 2:489–90.

78. *Madison Writings,* 6:174, 148.

79. *Messages and Papers,* 2:218.

80. Moore, *Digest of International Law,* 6:446; see also W. S. Robertson, "South America and the Monroe Doctrine, 1824–1828," *Political Science Quarterly* 30 (1915): 89.

81. *Messages and Papers,* 3:258, 279.

82. Ibid., 1:1116.

83. Ibid., 2:1325.

84. Moore, *Digest of International Law,* 7:126–28.

85. Ibid., p. 163.

86. Ibid., pp. 165–66. In 1857, Secretary of State Cass informed Great Britain that "under the Constitution of the United States, the executive branch of the government is not the war-making power" (ibid., p. 164).

87. Albert Putney, "Executive Assumptions of the War-Making Power," *National University Law Review* 7 (1927): 1.

88. 9 Stat. 9 (May 13, 1846); *Messages and Papers,* 3:2292.

89. *Congressional Globe,* 30th Cong. 1st sess., p. 95.

90. Quoted in Wormuth, *Vietnam War,* p. 11.

91. *Messages and Papers,* 6:47; see also the text accompanying notes 30–31, 68–79, above.

92. Arthur M. Schlesinger, Jr., has written: "There is no suggestion that Lincoln supposed he would use this power in foreign wars without congressional approval." ("Congress and the Making of American Foreign Policy," *Foreign Affairs* 51 [1972]: 78, 89). For a contrary view see Clinton Rossiter, *The Supreme Court and the Commander in Chief* (Ithaca, N.Y.: Cornell University Press, 1951), pp. 75–77. For a discussion of Lincoln's action in the context of the Prize Cases see note 106, below.

93. Kent, *Commentaries,* p. 55.

94. Joseph Story, *Commentaries on the Constitution of the United States,* 4th ed., 2 vols. (Boston, Mass.: Little, Brown, 1873), 2:87.

95. William Whiting, *The Government's War Powers under the Constitution of the United States,* 10th ed. (Boston, Mass.: Little, Brown, 1864), pp. 38–40.

96. John Norton Pomeroy, *Introduction to the Constitutional Law of the United States,* 10th ed. (Boston, Mass.: Houghton Mifflin, 1888), p. 373.

97. Thomas Cooley, *The General Principles of Constitutional Law in the United States of America,* 3d. ed. (Boston, Mass.: Little, Brown, 1898), p. 316.

98. Hermann von Holst, *The Constitutional Law of the United States of America,* 8 vols. (Chicago: Callaghan, 1887), pp. 164–65.

99. Westel W. Willoughby, *The Constitutional Law of the United States,* 3 vols. (New York: Baker, Voorhis and Co., 1929), p. 1560.

100. 4 Dall. 37 (1800). The Federal Court of Appeals, established by the

Continental Congress, had reached the same conclusion in 1782; see *Miller* v. *The Ship Resolution*, 2 Dall. 19, 21 (1782).

101. 4 Dall. 45–46.

102. 1 Cranch, 1, 28 (1801).

103. 2 Cranch 170, 177–78.

104. 27 F. Cas. 1192, 1230 (No. 16342) (C.C.D.N.Y. 1806).

105. 2 Black 635, 668 (1863).

106. 157 U.S. 281, 284 (1895). In *Fleming* v. *Page*, Chief Justice Taney held that the president's "duty and his power are purely military. . . . The power of the President . . . [is] simply that of a military commander prosecuting a war waged against a public enemy by authority of his government" (9 How. 603, 615 [1850]).

107. George Sutherland, *The Constitution and World Affairs* (New York: Columbia University Press, 1919), p. 73.

108. 317 U.S. 1, 26 (1942).

109. Pub. L. No. 93–148, 87 Stat. 555 (codified at 50 U.S.C. sec. 1541–48 (1976)). The constitutionality of the act has been debated since President Nixon vetoed it as an unconstitutional encroachment on the power of the commander in chief (*Public Papers of the Presidents*, 1973, p. 893). Eugene Rostow has sided with Nixon on the grounds that the resolution upsets the original balance of power between the executive and legislative branches. Indeed, it "repudiates that history root and branch, and seeks to substitute parliamentary government for the tripartite constitution we have so painfully forged" (Rostow, "Great Cases," p. 843). Others defend it; see, e.g., Stephen Carter, "The Constitutionality of the War Powers Resolution," *Virginia Law Review* 70 (1984): 101.

110. H. Rept. no. 547, 93d Cong., 1st sess. 8 (1973). See the close textual analysis of William Spong, Jr., "The War Powers Resolution Revisited: Historical Accomplishment or Surrender?" *William and Mary Law Review* 16 (1975): 823, 837–41.

111. Senator Thomas Eagleton contended that the act was "an open-ended, blank check for 90 days of warmaking, anywhere in the world," (Congressional Record 119 [1973], p. 33556).

112. Moore, *Digest of International Law*, 7:126–28.

113. 103 S. Ct. 2764 (1983).

114. *Weekly Compilation of Presidential Documents* 18 (Sept. 29, 1982), p. 1232, 19 (Aug. 30, 1983), p. 1186. With respect to Grenada see ibid., 19 (Oct. 25, 1983), p. 1494. For a good discussion of this practice see Fisher, *Constitutional Conflicts*, pp. 314–18; see also the article by Michael Rubner, "The Reagan Administration, the 1973 War Powers Resolution, and the Invasion of Grenada," *Political Science Quarterly* 100 (Winter 1985/86): 627.

115. Wormuth and Firmage, *To Chain the Dog of War*, p. 28.

116. The State Department's legal advisor adduced this power on behalf of President Johnson in 1966; see Meeker, "Legality," pp. 474–85. More recently, President Reagan claimed this role to justify his war against Grenada; see *Weekly Compilation of Presidential Documents* 19 (Oct. 25, 1983): 1494.

117. Elliot, *Debates*, 2:305. Rufus King, who, as a member of the Committee of Detail, had helped to draft the final provision for the presidential role in treaty making, observed in 1819 that except for receiving ambassadors, "the validity of all other definitive proceedings in the management of foreign affairs, the constitutional advice and consent of the Senate are indispensable" (*Annals of Congress* 31 [1818], pp. 106–7).

118. Hamilton, *Federalist* no. 69, p. 451.

119. See, e.g., Kenneth M. Holland, "The War Powers Resolution: An Infringement on the President's Constitutional and Prerogative Powers," in *The Presidency and National Security Policy,* ed. R. Gordon Hoxie (New York: Center for the Study of the Presidency, 1984), p. 378.

120. For discussion see Wormuth and Firmage, *To Chain the Dog of War,* pp. 12–15; Fisher, *Constitutional Conflicts,* pp. 287–92.

121. Henry P. Monaghan, "Presidential War-Making," *Boston University Law Review* 50 (Spring 1970), p. 19.

122. E.g., in 1967 the State Department published a study that listed 137 cases of unilateral presidential action; see Department of State, Historical Studies Division, *Armed Actions Taken by the United States without a Declaration of War, 1789–1967* (Washington, D.C.: Government Printing Office, 1967). J. Terry Emerson, legal assistant to Senator Barry Goldwater, published a list in 1973 which ran to 199 incidents of presidential acts of war without congressional authorization; see *Congressional Record* 119 (daily ed., July 20, 1973), p. S14174.

123. Berger, *Executive Privilege,* p. 76. See Wormuth, "Nixon Theory," pp. 652–64; Wormuth and Firmage, *To Chain the Dog of War,* pp. 133–49.

124. "Since the Constitution was adopted," said the State Department's report, "there have been at least 125 instances in which the President has ordered the armed forces to take action or maintain positions abroad without obtaining prior Congressional authorization, starting with the 'undeclared' war with France (1799–1800)"; Office of the Legal Adviser, U.S. Department of State, "The Legality of the United States Participation in the Defense of Vietnam," reprinted in *Yale Law Journal* 75 (1966): 1085, 1101.

125. Wormuth, *Vietnam War,* p. 718.

126. Wormuth and Firmage, *To Chain the Dog of War,* p. 149.

127. *Powell* v. *McCormack,* 395 U.S. 486, 546 (1969); *Inland Waterways Corp.* v. *Young,* 309 U.S. 517, 524 (1940).

128. Edward S. Corwin has observed that "none of the departments may abdicate its powers to either of the others" (*President,* p. 9); see also *Panama Refining Co.* v. *Ryan,* 293 U.S. 388, 421 (1935).

129. *United States* v. *Morton Salt Co.,* 338 U.S. 632, 647 (1950). Sir Edward Coke stated that no "act of Parliament by non-user can be antiquated or lose [its] force" (quoted by Berger in *Executive Privilege,* p. 87).

6

THE PRESIDENT'S VETO POWER

ROBERT J. SPITZER

> Every bill which shall have passed the House of Representatives and the Senate, shall, before it become a Law, be presented to the President of the United States; If he approve he shall sign it, but if not he shall return it, with his Objections to that House in which it shall have originated. . . . If after such Reconsideration two thirds of that House shall agree to pass the Bill, it shall be sent, together with the Objections, to the other House, . . . and if approved by two thirds of that House, it shall become a Law.
>
> —*Article I, section 7*

An understanding and appreciation of the antecedents and construction of the presidential veto is important for two related reasons. First, the executive veto has (at least in the British and American cases) been a kind of barometer of executive power and authority, as seen in whether or not the power was made available to executives and, if so, to what degree— qualified or absolute, advisory or obligatory.

Second, and more specific to the American presidency, the struggle over the nature and extent of the veto power has been symptomatic of the central question of how the power of the American presidency should be defined. Both in the federal convention and afterward, the veto was at the center of disputes over the degree and scope of presidential power, especially as it helped shape the relationship between the executive and legislative branches. Although the resolution of this struggle during the nineteenth and twentieth centuries lies beyond the scope of this chapter, the beginnings of the struggle coincide with those of the presidency.[1]

ANTECEDENTS OF THE VETO

The veto is a power that transcends the American experience. It is thus important to understand its antecedents, not only because the American founders were influenced by this history, but also because the very nature of the veto power as it can be traced through history may reveal itself to us in ways useful to the study of the presidential veto.

Ancient Rome

The *Oxford English Dictionary* identifies the word "veto" as deriving from Latin meaning "I forbid." Early in the Roman Republic, the veto (called *intercessio*) was adopted as a device by the Roman tribunes, starting in the sixth century B.C., to protect the interests of the plebeians (citizens whose interests the tribunes represented) against the encroachments of the patricians. A tribune's *intercessio* was an absolute veto that could block any magisterial act—that is, one that had been passed by the patrician-dominated senate (where tribunes also served) and accepted by the consuls and other magistrates—as long as it affected plebeians. The veto could also preclude bringing a bill before the plebeian assembly. A bill that had been vetoed in the senate could still pass through, but it lacked the force of law and served only as an expression of opinion.[2]

As the Roman Republic evolved, the plebeians' struggle with the patricians for political and economic equality was greatly facilitated by the veto power, although the use of the veto contributed importantly to a certain degree of institutional paralysis and anarchy.[3] Veto power was not limited to the tribunes, however. Patrician representatives possessed similar power, as did the two consuls—the highest elective offices of the Roman Republic. The consuls' powers were kingly, extending to all matters except religion. They operated on the principle of "colleagueship," meaning, quite simply, that mutual cooperation was necessary for decision making in most matters. When the two consuls could not agree, either could invoke the *intercessio,* vetoing the action of the other, thus leaving matters as they were. In the Roman magistracy, power was seen as twofold: 1) the affirmative management of state affairs and (2) the power of restraint against the actions of magistrates of equivalent or inferior rank. While the highest leaders possessed both types of power, the tribunes were limited mostly to the veto. Yet, the plebeians gained important concessions through its use, and it was instrumental "as a means of checking the arbitrary exercise of political power."[4] As Rome evolved, the significance of the politics of *intercessio* was overshadowed by the return of the monarchy and by the increasingly autocratic control by the caesars.[5]

The Veto in Europe

It might reasonably be presumed that the veto was but one of many Roman vestiges left to subsequent civilizations. In 1652, the Imperial Diet of the kingdom of Poland allowed for the right of a deputy to block a decision approved of by the other members through the utterance of the phrase "Nie pozwalam," or "I do not permit it." In 1789, the French king was given a "suspensory veto" by the National Assembly—that is, one subject to override "if the Assembly persisted in its resolution." The French Revolution came the same year; it brought an end, not only to the veto, but to the king as well. The Spanish Constitution of 1812 adopted a similar qualified veto, saying that the king might return a bill twice that had been presented to him by two sessions of the Cortes. If the same bill were presented a third time, however, he could not then refuse his assent. This procedure was also adopted for the Norwegian monarch in that country's Constitution of 1814.[6]

THE ENGLISH TRADITION

The centrality of the English monarchs to the lawmaking process was related directly to their use of the veto. More to the point, its use was symptomatic of the monarch's relations with Parliament.

To appreciate this assertion more fully, one must begin with two important observations. First, the English king was initially the supreme lawmaking authority, even though his/her authority was usually exercised through noblemen.[7] Second, the Parliament, which today holds this authority, was a creation of the monarch.[8] Even though the monarch has played no important role in lawmaking during the last two centuries, he or she has been considered a member of Parliament, because it "is in theory his Great Council."[9]

During and after the time of the Norman Conquest of England in the eleventh century, kingly powers were enhanced. The Parliament of the time maintained formalistic power over lawmaking, but substantively, the legislative agenda was controlled by the king. Formalisms were sometimes swept aside when the king issued proclamations. More often, however, the king would present matters to the Parliament; yet even then, the king's final approval was necessary.[10]

Parliament increasingly resented the king's creation of laws, however; and as its power and the democratic urge grew, so, too, did its hand in lawmaking, beginning about the fourteenth century. The House of Commons began petitioning the monarch to make a law on a particular subject. The monarch could exceed parliamentary requests, however, and often issued laws that bore no relation to the petitions presented. Commons's petitions then became more precise, and pressure on monarchs to conform increased, so that, by the sixteenth century, the Crown was reduced to either accepting or rejecting what had become an Act of Parliament. Thus,

"The veto is a remnant of the more extensive legislative power formerly held by the English kings."[11]

Even after Parliament acquired the right of lawmaking, the Crown still maintained parallel power through "royal legislation," also called "ordinances" and "proclamations."[12] The initial purpose of proclamations was to enforce laws, yet they were soon adapted by monarchs to create law.[13] In 1539, Henry VIII formally granted to the British monarch this authority in the Act 31, which said that such monarchical declarations "shall be observed as though they were made by Act of Parliament"—a definition remarkably similar to that of presidential executive orders.[14] Yet clearly, such monarchical discretion was at odds with the rule of law and democratic values, and the law was repealed during the reign of Henry's successor, Edward VI. Monarchs continued to issue proclamations, however, until Parliament prohibited this in 1766.[15]

The atrophy of kingly lawmaking left only the veto as a weapon against Parliament. What was once an integral aspect of lawmaking became simply a power to prevent. The use of the veto was invoked with the phrase *Le Roi s'avisera* ("the king will consider it"); approval of a bill was *Le Roi le vult* ("the king wishes it").[16] Both phrases were remnants of the time when French was the language of the court.

The veto continued to be employed, but being absolute in nature, it also aroused progressively greater passions as time wore on. Queen Elizabeth I was not reluctant to use the veto; in 1597, for example, she approved forty-three bills but vetoed forty-seven. Her successor, James I, was more parsimonious. At the end of the 1606 session, he observed that his restraint in vetoing no bills that year was explainable "as a special token of grace and favour, being a matter unusual to pass all acts without exception."[17] Charles I provoked considerable ire with his veto of a militia bill and other measures, which by at least one account was a direct cause of the 1643 revolution.[18] Parliament subsequently enacted the militia bill despite the veto.[19]

The veto continued to be used, even after the English Revolution of 1688, although with even greater circumspection. William III invoked the veto at least six times, "always exciting thereby some indignation on the part of parliament," even though the vetoes involved bills that "infringed upon some part of the prerogative or seemed to him of doubtful expedience."[20] His successor, Queen Anne, was the last monarch to employ the veto, on March 11, 1707. The bill in question was a measure to arm the Scottish militia. The bill aroused little interest until, on the day it was to be signed, news arrived that the French were sailing toward Scotland. Anne quickly had broad support for the veto, as the loyalty of the Scots was questionable, and a veto was the most expeditious way to kill the bill.[21]

As the veto became a relic of a bygone era, so too did a companion power—impeachment. As the king could "bash" the Parliament with the veto, so too could Parliament "bash" the king with impeachment—that is, accuse royal officials, including the monarch, of misconduct, and then try them on such charges. According to one expert on the British constitution, these two powers represented a "conflict of the old sort between executive and legislature."[22] As if to verify the symmetry between the veto and impeachment, impeachment was also abandoned in the eighteenth century.

The typical explanation for the fact that British monarchs ceased to apply the veto is simply that its absolute nature discouraged its use.[23] Still, closer scrutiny reveals that the veto issue was not by any means a dead letter after 1707.

First, as is well known, the veto power continued to be used with regularity over acts of American colonial legislatures, either through colonial governors, Parliament, or the monarch through his/her ministers. The first two complaints lodged against George III in the Declaration of Independence—that "He has refused his Assent to Laws, the most wholesome and necessary for the public Good" and "He has forbidden his Governors to pass Laws of immediate and pressing Importance"—are complaints against the use of the veto. As Ronald Moe has noted, however, the colonists' resentment was directed, not at the idea of the kingly negative, but at "the arbitrary and detailed nature of the negative in practice."[24] Despite the adverse effect this had on British-American relations, monarchical vetoes over measures enacted in other British colonies continued into the twentieth century, although the exercise of the veto was more parsimonious by then.[25]

Second, as is not so well known, the fact that the royal veto fell into disuse was not explainable solely, or even principally, by the fear that it was too great a power; rather, it was clear, at least in the eighteenth century, that royal influence (exercised through the king or his ministers) could alter or defeat a bill before it was passed, obviating the need to use the veto. In fact, concern that the king's influence was excessive prompted various measures to limit it—in particular, in a Bill for Economic Reform, pushed by Edmund Burke, which was designed to eliminate various lucrative sinecures used by the king to buy votes.[26] Even during the Stuart era of the seventeenth century, the monarchs were able to avoid the broader use of the veto because, according to one British historian, they "lightly assented to bills that they never intended to observe."[27]

Moreover, many have argued that the royal veto or the threat of a royal veto has continued to play a role in British politics.[28] In 1852, Benjamin Disraeli said that he thought the right of the Crown to refuse assent to legislation "was still outstanding."[29] During a fierce political battle over the Home Rule Bill in the period from 1912 to 1914, some argued that

George V could refuse his assent.[30] "It was assumed by the King throughout that he had not only the legal power but the constitutional right to refuse assent."[31] At the same time, the king was acutely aware that to do so would result in the resignation of ministers, the dissolution of Parliament, and wide-ranging debate over the power of the Crown. A veto could only be palatable politically if used on direct advice from political leaders.[32] Still, the specter of the veto was part of the public debate, as was the ability of monarchs to avoid a possible veto confrontation by applying political pressure.[33]

In 1913, during the controversy over home rule, the British constitutional expert Albert V. Dicey wrote a letter to the *Times* in which he argued that the veto had become obsolete simply because any circumstances that might give rise to it could be more cleanly dealt with by dissolution of Parliament.[34] Dicey went on to quote with approval Edmund Burke, who wrote 150 years earlier: "The King's negative to Bills is one of the most undisputed of the Royal prerogatives, and it extends to all cases whatsoever. . . . But it is not the propriety of the exercise which is in question. Its repose may be the preservation of its existence, and its existence may be the means of saving the Constitution itself on an occasion worthy of bringing it forth."[35]

One other trait of the British monarchical veto warrants mention. For a time, its use was encouraged for a reason remarkably similar to that heard today about the presidential veto. During the latter part of the seventeenth century, the House of Commons resorted to a practice referred to by the British as "tacking." Based on the rule that the House of Lords could not amend a money bill, the Commons would include in such bills what we refer to as "riders"—nongermane amendments—that would not otherwise be acceptable to the Lords, so that the Lords would be obliged to accept or reject such a bill *in toto*. This tacking first occurred in 1667. In 1668, Charles II announced that he would veto any such bill. Still, tacking was used successfully in 1692, 1698, and 1701. The practice fell into disuse during the eighteenth century, as there was a "wide sense of [its] being a misuse of technicalities for the purpose of evading a recognised constitutional principle."[36]

Although this examination of the British veto takes us past the time of the writing of the United States Constitution, it is important for at least two reasons. First, British practice was much on the minds of the Founding Fathers in constructing our Constitution, as can be seen in the public debate and documents of the time (see subsequent section). Second, the veto as a political tool as used in Britain—despite the fact that its user was a hereditary monarch—is very similar in political consequences to those of the American veto. The use of the veto in Britain was considered a politically extreme and controversial act; it was viewed as a weapon of last resort; it was understood to be a legislative power; it intertwined with the issue of "tacking"; finally, and perhaps most importantly, it was symptomatic of the political jockeying between the executive and the legislative branches.

THE VETO IN THE UNITED STATES

The establishment of colonies in America occurred primarily through the prerogative of the British Crown, which sanctioned early colonial constitutions. As mentioned, colonial governors were appointed by the king, except for those of Connecticut and Rhode Island, which elected their governors to one-year terms. All governors possessed absolute veto powers over colonial legislation, either through charter, royal instruction, or proprietary grant, although in Maryland, the burgesses refused to recognize the gubernatorial veto. The king's absolute veto could be applied to colonial acts in any of the colonies except Connecticut and Rhode Island (charter colonies) and Maryland (a proprietary colony). Yet even in these states, royal disapproval could be transmitted through Crown-appointed officials.[37]

The king not only had the veto, but he also used it with relative frequency, as the veto was considered a vital tool for protecting British interests, as seen, for example, in the Crown's veto of Virginia's attempt to limit the slave trade.[38] Gubernatorial vetoes were similarly odious. For example, in a 1722 bill designed to amend the constitution of the Corporation of Harvard College, Governor Samuel Shute vetoed the bill, but he conditioned his subsequent approval on the reinstatement of three corporation fellows who would otherwise have been removed. The Massachusetts House balked, but it ultimately gave in to Shute's demand.[39] During the deliberations of the federal Constitutional Convention, Benjamin Franklin described how the colonial governor extracted private perquisites in exchange for assent: "The negative of the Governor was constantly made use of to extort money. No good law whatsoever could be passed without a private bargain with him."[40]

The State Experience

Once the colonies had broken free of British control, their initial response to the onerous veto was to make it unavailable to their own executives. In fact, with the exception of New York, most state constitutions were careful to subordinate the executive to the legislature; some states abandoned the governor altogether in favor of a commission.[41] That New York allowed its executive a veto and greater independence is explained by the larger fact that, unlike the other states, it established a strong governor in its constitution of 1777, because of the state's relative conservatism, the influence of such leaders as John Jay, Robert Livingston, and Gouverneur Morris, and the fact that New York delayed in finalizing its constitution (it was the last state to ratify the Declaration of Independence), which gave it the chance to observe the adverse consequences of weak executives in other states.[42] According to the New York Constitution, the governor would join with judges of the state's Supreme Court and the chancellor of the court of chancery to form a council of revision to assess all bills passed by the state legislature: "All bills which have passed the senate or assembly shall before they become laws be presented to the said council for their revisal and consideration."[43] If a majority of the council shared reservations, the bill was to be returned to the chamber of origin, with the inclusion of written objections, for reconsideration. A two-thirds vote in both chambers would override the veto. If the council did not return the bill to the legislature within ten days, the bill automatically became law, unless the legislature had adjourned for more than ten days, in which case the bill would be returned on the first day of the new session. Within its first three years, the council of revision vetoed ten bills; during its first ten years, it vetoed fifty-eight bills.[44]

Two observations warrant special mention here—that these provisions bear remarkable resemblance to the veto in the federal constitution and that the emphasis of the veto power was on reconsideration and revision of legislation, not simply on blocking its passage. We will return to both of these themes later.

Later in 1777, the Vermont Constitution incorporated what was, in effect, a nonbinding veto.[45] It said that "all bills of a public nature shall be first laid before the governor and council for their perusal and proposals of amendment."[46]

In 1780 the Massachusetts Constitution gave to the governor, for the first time, sole "power of revision" over legislation. The provisions of the constitution pertaining to the veto, adopted in Massachusetts with little debate, were nearly identical in wording and concept to the New York Constitution, with the exception that the governor had only five days to consider the bill, and he could act alone.

The previously proposed Massachusetts Constitution, which had been defeated in a state referendum in 1778, had made no provision for the veto.[47] It was clear that the utility and the desirability of "revisionary power" had been demonstrated by New York. Alexander Hamilton observed in 1780 that the council of revision's "utility has become so apparent that persons who in compiling the constitution were violent opposers of it, have from experience become its declared admirers."[48] In the Massachusetts convention, the rationale for adopting the veto was "to preserve the laws from being unsystematical and inaccurate" and so that "due balance may be preserved in the three capital powers of government."[49] In the succeeding ten years, the Massachusetts governor returned a total of one bill and two resolves to the legislature.[50]

The Articles of Confederation

Antipathy not only to the veto power but also to the very idea of a single, autonomous executive found its most naked expression in the country's first constitution, the Articles of Confederation. They made no provision for an executive. The paralytic nature of decision making under the Articles was amply demonstrated by the fact that most of the important measures considered by the national congress required a majority vote of nine out of thirteen states for passage; proposals to amend the Articles required a unanimous vote. Thus, a single state or a group of five could "veto" important measures.[51] In addition, the combination of executive and legislative powers in the hands of Congress heightened interest in the concept of separation of powers. The resultant stalemates and inefficiency did much to prompt the call for major changes in the governing document.

AT THE FEDERAL CONVENTION

When the founders convened in Philadelphia in May 1787, they faced countless problems, not the least of which was the matter of executive power. Was there to be an executive? If so, would the executive power be held in the hands of an individual or a group? And what would be the scope of the executive's power? Central to all of these questions was the matter of the veto power.

The initial resolution of these issues was embodied in the Virginia Plan, offered by Edmund Randolph but authored mostly by James Madison. It called for a single president, to be elected by Congress for a single term (the length of which was not initially set). The president was to have a qualified veto—that is, subject to override (the percentage was not specified)—but it was to be exercised in concert with a council of revision, composed of "a convenient number of the National Judiciary" (1:21).

The Virginia Plan gave the convention a fresh starting point, although the plan was changed substantially during the hot Philadelphia summer. In relation to the veto power, the options considered ran the full range from having no veto, as proposed in the New Jersey Plan (it also proposed a plural executive elected by Congress) to granting an absolute veto (1:244). Also, was the veto to be exercised with a council or alone? If the veto was to be subject to override, what percentage was appropriate? Should veto powers be held by anyone else in the national government? And finally, what were the founders' perceptions of the nature of this power? The resolution of these questions was central to determining whether the president would be strong or weak, dependent or independent, assertive or compliant. In this way, the story of the veto is also the story of the presidency.

The Veto: Absolute or Qualified?

Despite the stigma surrounding the veto power, based on its use by the British, there was surprisingly little objection to incorporating the veto in some form.[52] The arguments against granting any veto to the president included the sense that the president was not likely to have any greater wisdom or insight than a given congressman; that the veto resembled too closely a monarchical power; that ultimate sovereignty rested, not with the president, but with the legislature; that his single voice ought not to supersede two houses of Congress; and that the president would play a role in the legislative process anyway, obviating the need for a veto (1:106–10, 3:202–3). Although these individual arguments cropped up periodically throughout the proceedings, they did little to sway the convention as a whole against some kind of veto power.

Arguments were made at various junctures to grant an absolute veto, based on the sense that the president would need such a tool to maintain his independence and strength. Foremost among those pressing this argument was Hamilton. By virtue of his advocacy of an absolute veto as the keystone of a strong executive, he was unjustly accused later of promoting monarchy.[53] Wilson argued for the necessity of an absolute veto. "Without such a self-defence the Legislature can at any moment sink it [the executive] into non-existence" (1:98). George Read of Delaware said that the absolute negative was "essential to the Constitution, to the preservation of liberty, and to the public welfare" (2:200). Hamilton pointed out that little danger of overuse of the veto existed, as even the British monarch had not used it in many years. Yet the reference to the British king backfired. Roger Sherman of Connecticut argued against one man's having the power to stop the will of Congress as too antimajoritarian (1:99).[54] Mason observed, with what must have been some sarcasm: "We are not indeed constituting a British Government, but a more dangerous monarchy, an elective" (1:101). To him, the absolute veto meant, in effect, the popular surrender of the rights of the people to a single leader. Pierce Butler of South Carolina observed, with some presentiment, that "in all countries the Executive power is in a constant course of increase"; there was, thus, legitimate concern that even a nonmonarchical executive, such as England's Cromwell, could become too powerful (1:100).

Franklin also spoke against an absolute veto, citing the tendency of the Pennsylvania colonial governor to extort money and other perquisites (1:98–99). Madison spoke in favor of the efficacy of a qualified veto, arguing that the president would rarely use a veto unless he already had at least some political support in Congress (1:99–100). Later, Hamilton adopted a similar tack in *Federalist* number 73, when he wrote that the qualified veto "would be less apt to offend" and "more apt to be exercised" and therefore "more effectual." Despite the fact that the vote on the Wilson-Hamilton proposal was decisively against it (0 to 10), the proposal was reintroduced several times and was decisively defeated on each occasion.[55]

The convention was less decisive on the admittedly more arbitrary question of the fraction needed to override. Early in the convention's deliberations (June 4), a two-thirds veto override was agreed on (by a vote of 8 to 2 without debate). In August, however, Hugh Williamson of North Carolina proposed that the fraction be changed to three-fourths. Carroll argued that when two-thirds had been agreed to, no quorum had yet been set for the new Congress. But now that it had, he perceived the need to set a higher override threshold to establish "greater impediments to improper laws" (2:300). This, combined with a sense that presidential self-protection would be enhanced, resulted in a 6 to 4 to 1 vote for the change (2:299–301). A month later, however, the convention changed its mind, reverting back to two-thirds, again on Williamson's motion. Madison observed that when three-fourths had been adopted the president was to be elected by Congress for a single seven-year term; but since that time, the presidential election had been changed to four years and by the people. There was a sense at this juncture, on the part of Wilson and others, that three-fourths gave too much to the president. Charles Pinckney of South Carolina in particular observed that three-fourths would put too much power in the hands of the president and a handful of senators who would be capable of blocking an override attempt (2:586). The vote on the motion to revert to two-thirds was 6 to 4 to 1. One other fine-tuning amendment was made on August 15, when the length of time allotted for the president to sign or return a bill was increased from seven to ten days, Sundays excepted, by a vote of 9 to 2, apparently with no significant debate (2:295).

The Proposal for a Council of Revision

Provisions for executive power were drawn heavily from the state constitutions of New York and Massachusetts.[56] Clearly, the successful operation of a council of revision in New York inspired the same proposal in the Randolph Plan.[57] Yet it was challenged from the start, primarily on the grounds that it violated the principle of separation of powers.[58] Elbridge Gerry of Massachusetts argued that it was "quite foreign from the nature of ye. office to make them [court justices] judges of the policy of public measures" (1:97–98). Rufus King of Massachusetts argued that "the Judges ought to be able to expound the law as it should come before them, free from the bias of having participated in its formation" (1:98). Nathaniel Gorham of Massachusetts pointed out that English judges possessed no similar power and that judges "are not to be presumed to possess any peculiar knowledge of the mere policy of public measures" (2:73). In general, there was a strong sense among opponents of this plan that the involvement of judges in the legislative process at this or any other point would give the court, in essence, two chances to rule on a law.[59]

Despite these arguments, several persisted on behalf of a council of revision to share the veto power. Wilson argued that a council was needed to shore up executive power, so that both branches, and the people, might be better protected from congressional encroachments (1:138). He also observed that while judges would have the opportunity for subsequent review of legislation, they might be confronted with laws that were unjust, unwise, dangerous, and destructive but still not unconstitutional (and thus beyond the court's power to change) (1:138, 2:73). Madison concurred, adding that the veto would be too weak if it rested in the hands of the president alone. To Madison, the genius of the scheme of government was "to collect the wisdom of its several parts in aid of each other whenever it was necessary" (1:110, 144). The persistence of this debate was evidenced by the fact that four attempts (all unsuccessful) were made by Madison and Wilson to join the president and the Supreme Court in the exercise of the veto. The idea of constituting a council of revision, composed of the president and members of his cabinet, was also floated, but this notion found little support (2:135). Mason said, "We can hardly find worse materials out of which to create a council of revision" (1:111).

A Veto over State Laws

The original Virginia Plan included provision for Congress "to negative all laws passed by the several States, contravening in the opinion of the National Legislature the articles of Union" (1:21). This veto was viewed initially as instrumental to assuring that state powers be kept subordinate to federal authority, especially given recent experience under the Articles which revealed a tendency for states to encroach on federal authority (1:164–69). By July, however, sentiment had shifted. Sherman argued that the power was unnecessary, especially given the likelihood that state courts would not uphold state laws that contravened national law. Morris concurred, citing the courts generally as a check, as well as the option of federal legislation against states should the need arise. He also considered such a congressional veto to be unnecessarily harsh on the states. Madison strongly defended the proposal as necessary to the integrity of the federal system. By one account, in fact, this veto "occupied a central place in his [Madison's] plan for extending the sphere of republican government."[60] Nevertheless, the provision was excised by a vote of 3 to 7 (2:27–28).

A proposal was also floated to grant the president the power to veto state laws. Reportedly, it was moved by Madison, seconded by Pinckney, and probably supported by Hamilton (3:399). It was not, however, an idea that garnered much support or serious attention.

A Power of Suspension

One effort to resolve the dispute over the veto power was proposed by Butler on June 4. Seconded by Franklin, it proposed that "the National Executive have a power to suspend any legislative act for the term of _____" (1:103). Presumably, such a power would have simply held a given bill in abeyance for a given period of time, without requiring an override vote but allowing for subsequent (re)consideration by Congress. Mason argued that such a power would simply be insufficient, and Gerry said that "a power of suspending might do all the mischief dreaded from the negative of useful laws; without answering the salutary purpose of checking unjust or unwise ones (1:102, 104). The vote to grant suspending power was unanimous against (0 to 10).

The Purpose of the Veto

Again and again during the convention's consideration of the veto power, one central theme persistently surfaced—namely, the veto was instrumental as a device of executive self-protection against encroachments of the legislature. This had indisputably been the lesson gleaned from state experiences. As Charles C. Thach has observed, state experiences "demonstrated the necessity for the veto as a protective measure."[61] In addition, it also showed the utility of the veto "as a means of preventing unwise legislation" and "revealed the desirability of bringing legislative business into a single whole by the executive department."[62] In the convention, Gerry stated that the purpose of "the Revisionary power was to secure the Executive department agst. legislative encroachment" (2:74–75). Reflecting on state experiences, Madison observed: "Experience had proved a tendency in our governments to throw all power into the legislative vortex. The Executives of the States are in general little more than cyphers; the legislatures omnipotent" (2:35). Wilson and Hamilton justified their proposal for granting an absolute veto by saying that "the natural operation of the Legislature will be to swallow up the Executive" (1:107).[63] This precise theme of tying the veto to presidential defense from legislative usurpation appears in three of the four *Federalist* papers that mention the veto (nos. 51, 66, 73), and later.[64] This narrow focus on self-defense is understood, of course, to be part of the larger concern with separation of powers and checks and balances, as the executive's successful participation in the government is predicated on the ability to interact and compete successfully with the other branches of government.

The concept of executive self-defense also arises with the pocket-veto power. As mentioned, federal provisions for the veto bore a close resemblance to those of Massachusetts and, especially, New York. Yet the one major difference between the New York and federal provisions for the veto was that bills vetoed within ten days of legislative adjournment in New York were held over until the legislature reconvened. A comparable presidential veto, however, is in effect an absolute veto, as the bill is not returned. The reason for this change was again executive self-protection. It was feared that Congress might decide to adjourn, as a means of preventing the president from returning bills—ergo no veto, and the bills would become law without the president's signature.[65] There is no indication that the founders realized the full consequences of this de facto absolute veto. This is reflected also in the storm of protest that arose later when the pocket veto was used in the nineteenth century.[66]

The Functions of the Veto

Based on the debates and discussion in the convention, it is clear that the functional application of the veto was conceived to be wide-ranging. Madison summarized several purposes, including the protection of other branches of government from legislative aggression, the protection of the rights of the people, the prevention of laws "unwise in their principle" as well as laws "incorrect in their form," and the prevention of "popular or factious injustice" (1:139).[67] Hamilton made similar arguments in *Federalist* number 73.

Luther Martin of Maryland talked of the veto as being used to block measures "*hastily* or *rashly* adopted" (3:203). Mason similarly considered it a shield against "unjust and pernicious" laws (2:78). The use of the veto to block laws that were deemed unconstitutional was a motive traced back to the veto in New York.[68] This precedent became part of the rationale during the federal convention as well (2:78).[69] Writing to Jefferson in 1788, Madison said, "A revisionary power is meant as a check to precipitate, to unjust, and to unconstitutional laws" (4:81). This wide array of functions becomes especially significant when examining how the veto was initially applied by early presidents, and the fierce political debate throughout the nineteenth century over the appropriate and inappropriate uses of the veto.[70]

The Nature of the Veto Power

Three observations about the nature of the veto power as conceived by the founders merit particular attention. First, as with the exercise of many varieties of governmental power, the founders felt a certain ambivalence toward the veto power. One indication of this is seen in the very use—or more properly, nonuse—of the word itself. Nowhere in the Constitution does the word "veto" appear, even though the paragraph that describes it is the second-longest in the document. In Farrand's *Records of the Federal Convention,* the word appears in the text no more than once or twice. During actual debates, the terms "negative," "qualified negative," "revisionary power," and "restraining power" are all used as synonyms. In the four *Federalist* papers in which this power is mentioned (nos. 51, 66, 69, 73), the word veto appears but once (in no. 73). It is well understood that this semantic ploy was no accident; it reflected a keen awareness of the monarchical roots of this power and the resentment that its use by the king and his colonial governors had engendered in America. The use of the word was considered impolitic, and the founders certainly wanted to avoid an adverse reaction from the country to a power considered essential for the president.[71]

Second, the veto power that the president was to possess was also understood by the founders to be a legislative power. The very fact of its inclusion in Article I of the Constitution (the article that deals with legislative powers) instead of Article II (which deals with presidential powers) reflects this understanding. As mentioned previously, the British monarch's exercise of the veto over parliamentary acts was considered a legislative power, and this view was accepted by the founders as well (e.g., 3:203). More recent analysts have offered the same observation. "The exercise of the veto power is patently a legislative act . . . , being associated with the Legislature for the special purpose of arresting its action by his disapproval."[73]

Third, both the founders' conception of the circumstances under which the veto could be applied and the quality of the power itself were substantially broader than is typically realized or acknowledged. This is important, partly because of the subsequent conflicts over the circumstances of using the veto, which in the minds of the founders were extremely broad. Essentially, the president was free, in constitutional terms, to veto any bill that crossed his desk, as long as he stated his reasons for doing so and then returned the bill to the legislative chamber of origin. In a Draft of the Constitution written by the Committee of Detail during the federal convention in July, the application of the veto was summarized by saying that a bill might be returned if "it shall appear to him [the president] improper for being passed into a Law" (2:167). No other circumstances were specified. It is difficult to conceive of any given piece of legislation that would not be covered by this language.

Moreover, no limitation on the frequency of using the veto was prescribed. Here also, the words of the framers are often misunderstood. *Federalist* number 73 is often cited as evidence to support the proposition that the founders *intended* the veto to be used rarely, because of its extraordinary nature. Yet Alexander Hamilton was making a different point in this essay. He first defended the necessity of the veto as "a shield to the executive," a check against improper laws, and a check against the legislature as a whole. He then countered the objection to the veto that it imposes the president's will by virtue of his "superior wisdom" by arguing, instead, that the veto is justifiable because of "the supposition that the legislature will not be infallible." Although the veto might be used to block good laws as well as bad, the power is eminently defensible because it ensures more hands and more consideration in the legislative process. Hamilton then offered the political observation that the singular nature of the veto power is such that it "would generally be employed with great caution." Even the British king, Hamilton noted, showed care and restraint toward the use of the veto. Such consideration would be even greater for an elective executive who shares governing authority. In fact, Hamilton suggested, the principal concern would likely be that the veto would be used too rarely, not too often. The president would be constrained in his use of the veto by its effects on "the power of his office" and "the sanction of his constituents." Hamilton's defense of the veto power represents a prediction *of* its likely use, not a prescription *for* its use. As recently as the last decade, President Ford was criticized for his frequent and wide-ranging use of the veto.[74]

In terms of the quality of the veto power itself, the typical consideration of it today is that it is simply a power to block—a power of refusal, purely negative in nature. Although the founders spoke of "the negative," the federal debates emphasized not so much its negative nature as its revisionary nature—that is, as a tool for the reconsideration and/or revision of legislation.[75] This is seen both in the ability of Congress to override the veto (unlike the absolute veto) and in the constitutional requirement that the president must state his objections in writing.[76] These two stipulations underscore a role for the president in actively shaping legislation by using the veto, although this is not the only presidential entree into the lawmaking process described in the Constitution. To state the matter another way, why should the president be required to state reasons for vetoes if the veto exists merely as a blocking device? This "revisionary," constructive component has been mostly lost during two hundred years of acrimonious political squabbling over the veto.

Up until the final draft of the Constitution (as late as September 10; the convention concluded on September 17), the veto paragraph was worded this way:

> Every bill . . . shall, before it become a law, be presented to the President of the United States, *for his revision;* if, *upon such revision,* he approve of it he shall signify his approbation by signing it: But if upon such revision it shall appear to him improper, for being passed into a law, he shall return it, together with his objections against it, to that House in which it shall have originated. (2:568–69, emphasis added).

The language does not say, as it might have, that the president may, at his discretion, employ the negative. The final changes in the wording of this paragraph involved grammatical weeding and paring. No debate on dropping the revisionary wording appears in the *Records.*

In a letter written to Jefferson, who had been in Europe during the convention, Madison talked of the veto power in this way:

> . . . some contended for an absolute negative, as the only possible means of reducing to practice the theory of a free Government which forbids a mixture of the Legislative & Executive powers. Others would be content with a revisionary power, to be overruled by three fourths of both Houses. It was warmly urged that the judiciary department should be associated in the revision. The idea of some was that a separate revision should be given to the two departments—that if either objected two thirds, if both, three fourths, should be necessary to override. (3:133)

From this excerpt, one gets a sense of the more creative capacity of the qualified negative, as compared to the absolute negative, including the mention of the possible involvement of the judiciary in the revision process.

The Antifederalists

The views expressed to explain and defend the newly constructed Constitution to the country were summarized in *The Federalist* papers. Needless to say, however, many took issue with the new Constitution and the veto power. These arguments were summarized in the Antifederalist papers. In point of fact, most Antifederalists accepted the veto power as a way of "securing executive independence."[77] This was, therefore, a further indication of the widespread sense that the president needed the veto power to defend himself from congressional aggrandizement.

Complaints about the veto power did arise, nevertheless. One participant in the federal convention who refused to sign the document, Luther Martin, registered reservations about the veto in an address to the Maryland General Assembly. In particular, he took issue with the antimajoritarian aspects of the veto, insofar as a voting block of one-third plus one in one house supportive of the president could uphold any veto, thereby depriving the congressional voting majority "of even the faintest shadow of liberty."[78] The British monarchical antecedents of this power also raised doubts; "We were eternally troubled with arguments and precedents from the British government."[79]

The Antifederalist Philadelphiensis (many antifederalists used pseudonyms) was relatively sanguine about the veto power. His reasons bear repeating:

> Among the substantial objections to the great powers of the president, that of his *negative* upon the laws, is one of the most inconsiderable, indeed it is more a sound than any thing else; For, if he be a bold enterprising fellow, there is little fear of his ever having to exercise it . . . if, however, I say, he should not be a man of an enterprising spirit, in that case he will be a *minion* of the aristocratics, doing according to their will and pleasure, and confirming every law they may think proper to make.[80]

This prediction of how the veto would be used by future presidents comes closer to approximating the actual course of events than most predictions that appear during this time.

An Antifederalist writing under the name William Penn raised the separation-of-powers question, pointing out that six state constitutions contained language that specified that the three branches of government should be "forever separate and distinct from each other."[81] As a legislative power given to the executive, the veto was seen as contradicting the maxim, derived from Montesquieu, that the best way to avoid the abuse of power is to divide it. Penn also noted that even the British king refrained from using the veto, being sensitive to such intrusion into the legislative realm.[82]

The Albany (N.Y.) Antifederal Committee took the veto power as symptomatic of the president's vast executive powers, which were perceived as superior to those of many European monarchs. Here again, the veto was seen as a power that even kings were reluctant to use.[83] Finally, the Impartial Examiner took strong exception to the veto, both as a misapplication of a power from the British system and as a power liable to upset the political balance. As to the former, the Examiner implored "let this collateral jurisdiction, which constitutes the *royal negative,* be held by kings alone, since with kings it first originated."[84] As to the latter complaint, the Examiner speculated that the veto would be rarely overridden in practice. Thus armed with the veto, the president "cannot be the object of any laws; he will be above all law: as none can be enacted without his consent—he will be elevated to the height of supremacy."[85]

THE FIRST VETOES

As with so many facets of the presidency, institutional precedent was set by the first chief executive. President Washington was keenly aware of the precedent-setting nature of his actions, and as the presiding officer at the Constitutional Convention, he had been a party to the debates, including consideration of the veto power.

At the start of his first term, Washington considered withholding his signature from a tonnage bill as an expression of displeasure. Although not a veto, it aroused enough concern that members of the Senate promised to accommodate the president's objections in a subsequent bill in exchange for his signature. A few days after this, Washington indicated in a letter to James Madison (then a member of the House of Representatives) that he was considering a veto of a pay bill for the members of Congress. The bill set equal salaries for members of both chambers, but Washington was of the opinion that senators should receive higher pay. He asked Madison his opinion of such a veto in correspondence marked "Confidential." Madison's response is not known, but Washington signed the bill in question on September 22, 1789. He may have felt the bill too trivial to warrant the first presidential veto, or he may have decided to refrain from interfering with an essentially internal matter of congressional pay.[86]

In February 1791, Washington seriously considered a veto of the Hamilton-inspired bill to establish a national bank. This major bill was, in the view of many, an unconstitutional intrusion by Congress into fiscal affairs. The president solicited advisory opinions from Attorney General Edmund Randolph, Secretary of State Thomas Jefferson, and Madison, all of whom recommended a veto. Washington even asked Madison to draft a possible veto message. Finally, the president solicited an opinion from Hamilton, who presented a memo to Washington (on the ninth day after the passage of the bill) that made the case for the bank based on the doctrine of implied powers. Hamilton's arguments were so compelling and important that they eventually made their way into Justice Marshall's opinion in the landmark Supreme Court case of *McCulloch* v. *Maryland* (1819). On the last day of the ten-day period, Washington signed the bill.

The first actual veto occurred on April 5, 1792. The bill in question dealt with congressional reapportionment. The Constitution called for an apportionment in the House based on one representative for every thirty thousand people. Yet the bill passed gave more representation than this to some of the larger states in an effort to compensate for the remainder of these states' populations over the thirty-thousand multiple (so that the total number of representatives in the House would equal the total population of the country divided by thirty thousand). Jefferson expressed his strenuous objection to this bill to Washington, as it seemed plainly unconstitutional; Jefferson added his concern that after Washington's four years in office, his "non-use of his negative begins already to excite a belief that no President will ever venture to use it."[87] Washington was sympathetic to Jefferson's arguments, and on the tenth day after passage, the president met with Jefferson to discuss the bill. The men discussed the bill's primary political problem—that the reapportionment scheme would benefit primarily northern states and that a veto might appear to be a sop to the South—but they also noted that it had passed by a bare majority in both houses, indicating that a veto would probably not be overridden. At the conclusion of the meeting, Washington sent for Randolph and Madison, who, with Jefferson, drew up a veto message, which was sent immediately to the House. The underlying rationale for the veto was clearly a constitutional question; the bill was, in Jefferson's words, "contrary to the common understanding of that instrument [the Constitution]."[88] Jefferson was also highly pleased that the veto had at last been used: ". . . it gave pleasure to have at length an instance of the negative being exercised."[89] The House considered a motion to override, but it fell far short of the necessary two-thirds. Congress soon thereafter passed a substitute bill, with a new apportionment scheme, that was passed and signed without problem.

Washington's second and final veto occurred four days before the end of his presidency; it involved a bill that included a provision to reduce the size of the already-small army by disbanding two dragoon companies. Acting essentially on his own this time, Washington argued in his veto message that the dragoons were needed and that the move to disband the companies was unfair to the men involved. This time, the justification for the veto had nothing to do with the Constitution; it was purely and simply a disagreement over policy. The House failed in its attempt to override the veto. It then proceeded immediately to pass the same bill, this time with the offending provision excised. Washington signed the new bill on March 3, 1797, his last day in office. Interestingly, Washington's second veto had an item-veto effect, insofar as Congress removed the provision in question in response to the veto and to the veto message identifying the objectionable portion. Ironically, Washington had addressed this very issue four years previously, in a letter to Edmund Pendleton. Washington also summarized a broader view of his philosophy about the veto:

> You do me no more than Justice when you suppose that from motives of respect to the Legislature (and I might add from my interpretation of the Constitution) I give my Signature to many Bills with which my Judgment is at variance. In declaring this, however, I allude to no particular Act. From the nature of the Constitution, I must approve all the parts of a Bill, or reject it in toto. To do the latter can only be Justified upon the clear and obvious ground of propriety; and I never had such confidence in my own faculty of judging as to be over tenacious of the opinions I may have imbibed in doubtful cases.[90]

Here we see in Washington's assessment of the veto a reflection of his restrained view of the presidency as a whole. He was not inclined to veto any given bill simply because he disagreed with it, in part or in whole. Nor did he consider his wisdom and judgment to be inherently above that of Congress. Yet the functional constraints he observed on the veto were not of a constitutional nature; rather, they were those that emphasized his own values of parsimony and restraint. As Washington's second veto shows, he considered the president's policy judgment to be an acceptable rationale for use of the veto.

Already, the first presidential administration had exemplified many of the accepted features of the veto. Its two applications provided cases of both constitutional- and policy-justified vetoes. The legitimacy of the president's mature judgment in deciding whether to veto was accepted. The use of the veto as a positive tool for shaping policy was also demonstrated, and there was even a glint of the item-veto controversy yet to come. Finally, the "real importance of these vetoes was not what they were about or what they said," historian Carlton Jackson has observed, "but simply that they occurred."[91]

Neither of Washington's two immediate successors, John Adams and Thomas Jefferson, applied the veto in their collective twelve years in office.[92] In the case of Adams, this is somewhat ironic, as he had been a proponent of absolute veto powers for the president.[93] Jefferson, despite his eagerness to have Washington use the veto, seemed to share the first president's sense of parsimony and gravity when it came to the actual use of the veto. Jefferson summarized his view of the veto in this way:

> Unless the president's mind on a view of everything which is urged for and against a bill is tolerably clear that it is unauthorized by the

Constitution, if the pro and con hang so even as to balance his judgment, a just respect for the wisdom of Legislature would naturally decide in favor of their opinion. It is chiefly for cases where they are clearly misled by error, ambition or interest that the Constitution has placed a check in the negative of the President.[94]

The question of constitutionality evidently played a key role in Jefferson's thinking, yet so did consideration of "error, ambition or interest" as reflected in congressional enactments.

CONCLUSION

Since its first chronicled use, the veto has been inextricably connected with the lawmaking process, especially as the crucial connecting link between the executive and the legislature. For obvious reasons, the British experience provides the most pertinent history for the American veto. Like whittling down a stick, the veto was finally all that was left of the British monarchs' once-supreme lawmaking authority. Yet even when the king's only recourse was the veto, the power served as a useful prompter of political bargaining. The veto issue even became intertwined with the issue of legislative riders.

The colonial experience illustrated from the start that a strong executive also meant a strong (in the case of royal colonial governors, an absolute) veto. The initial American reaction embodied governing by legislative supremacy and executive subordination—ergo, the elimination of veto powers. The unsatisfactory governing consequences of weak executives led first in New York and later at the federal convention to a reinvigorated executive, which meant also the bestowal of the veto power, this time in qualified form. Yet the veto was not viewed as simply a checking or blocking device. It was a "revisionary power," seen as part of the larger process whereby the president could play an active role in improving legislation. The veto was also a block against having a dominating legislature try to impinge on the executive and against irredeemably bad legislation, but later political squabbling was what caused the former aspect to be lost.

In the years to come, the veto would appear at the center of numerous political disputes. During the nineteenth century, in particular, controversy over the veto power would arise in ways that, although they were revealing of the changing role of the presidency, the founders would have found surprising.[95] Indeed, as with virtually every power enumerated in the Constitution, the veto power evolved over time as experimentation, circumstance, and cumulative precedent combined to give the power its actual shape.

NOTES

The research for this chapter was supported by a summer stipend grant from the National Endowment for the Humanities and by a SUNY Cortland Faculty Research Program Grant.

1. For more on the evolution and modern applications of the veto see Robert J. Spitzer, *The Presidential Veto* (Albany, N.Y.: State University of New York Press, 1988).

2. W. W. Buckland, *A Manual of Roman Private Law* (Cambridge: Cambridge University Press, 1925), pp. 1–2; and Herbert F. Jolowicz, *Historical Introduction to the Study of Roman Law* (Cambridge: Cambridge University Press, 1967), pp. 10–13.

3. Jolowicz, *Historical Introduction,* pp. 12–13.

4. *Encyclopaedia Britannica,* 1910/11 ed., p. 14; and Richard Watson, "Origins and Early Development of the Veto Power," *Presidential Studies Quarterly* 17 (Spring 1987): 402.

5. Jolowicz, *Historical Introduction,* pp. 43–45.

6. *Encyclopaedia Britannica,* 1910/11 ed., p. 14.

7. Edward C. Mason, *The Veto Power* (Boston, Mass.: Ginn & Co., 1890), p. 12; Charles A. Beard, "Veto Power," *Cyclopaedia of American Government,* vol. 3 (New York: Appleton & Co., 1914), p. 613; and Albert V. Dicey, *Introduction to the Study of the Law of the Constitution* (London: Macmillan, 1927), p. 48.

8. S. B. Chrimes, *English Constitutional History* (London: Oxford University Press, 1965), p. 13.

9. James Bryce, *The American Commonwealth* (New York: Macmillan, 1891), 1:52–53.

10. Mason, *Veto Power,* pp. 12–13.

11. Ibid., pp. 14–15; and Beard, "Veto Power," p. 613.

12. Dicey, *Introduction,* pp. 48–49.

13. Mason, *Veto Power,* p. 13.

14. Dicey, *Introduction,* p. 49.

15. Mason, *Veto Power,* p. 13.

16. Chrimes, *English Constitutional History,* p.13.

17. William E. Hearn, *The Government of England* (Melbourne: George Robertson, 1867), p. 60.

18. Mason, *Veto Power,* p. 16.

19. In 1890, Mason speculated that this may have inspired the authors of the Massachusetts Constitution to insert a "suspensive veto"—i.e., one capable of being overridden—into the document, an idea that later became part of the federal Constitution.

20. Mason, *Veto Power,* p. 16 n.6; George Burton Adams, *Constitutional History of England* (New York: Henry Holt & Co., 1934), p. 373; and Hearn, *Government of England,* p. 60.

21. Hearn, *Government of England,* p. 61.

22. Adams, *Constitutional History of England,* p. 373.

23. George T. Curtis, *Constitutional History of the United States,* vol. 2 (New York: Harper & Bros., 1859), p. 266; Charles J. Zinn, "The Veto Power of the President," U.S. Congress, House of Representatives, Committees on the Judiciary, 82d Congress, 1st sess. (Washington, D.C.: Government Printing Office,

1951), p. 3; *Federalist* no. 73; and William A. Clineburg, "The Presidential Veto Power," *South Carolina Law Review* 18 (1966): 734.

24. Ronald C. Moe, "The Founders and Their Experience with the Executive Veto," *Presidential Studies Quarterly* 17 (Spring 1987): 413–32.

25. Dicey, *Introduction,* pp. 111–15.

26. Thomas Pitt Taswell-Langmead, *English Constitutional History* (Boston, Mass.: Houghton Mifflin, 1946), p. 717.

27. Hearn, *Government of England,* p. 60.

28. For arguments that the veto is not dead (despite Walter Bagehot's oft-quoted axiom that if Parliament passed the queen's death certificate, she would be obliged to sign it) and discussion of circumstances under which it might reemerge see ibid., pp. 62–63; Chrimes, *English Constitutional History,* p. 14; and William I. Jennings, *Cabinet Government* (Cambridge: Cambridge University Press, 1959), p. 545.

29. Jennings, *Cabinet Government,* p. 395.

30. Ibid., p. 395.

31. Ibid., p. 400.

32. Ibid., p. 300.

33. David K. Watson, *The Constitution of the United States,* 2 vols. (Chicago: Callaghan & Co., 1910), p. 363 n.32.

34. *Times* (London), Sept. 15, 1913.

35. Jennings, *Cabinet Government,* p. 545.

36. Taswell-Langmead, *English Constitutional History,* pp. 613–14.

37. Mason, *Veto Power,* p. 17; and Zinn, "Veto Power," p. 3.

38. Mason, *Veto Power,* pp. 17–18.

39. Ibid., p. 18 n.3.

40. Max Farrand, *The Records of the Federal Convention of 1787,* 4 vols. (New Haven, Conn.: Yale University Press, 1966), 1:98–99. Subsequent references to this work will be given parenthetically in the text by volume and page number.

41. Charles C. Thach, Jr., *The Creation of the Presidency, 1775–1789: A Study in Constitutional History* (Baltimore, Md.: Johns Hopkins Press, 1923), p. 28.

42. Ibid., pp. 34–35.

43. Josiah H. Benton, *The Veto Power in the United States: What Is It?* (Boston, Mass.: Addison C. Getchell, 1888), p. 37.

44. Ibid., pp. 40, 42. The New York Council of Revision operated until 1821, when veto powers were consolidated in the hands of the governor alone. During that time, 169 bills had been vetoed out of 6,590 presented; 51 vetoes had been overridden (ibid., p. 61). For an exhaustive history of the gubernatorial veto in New York see Frank W. Prescott and Joseph F. Zimmerman, *The Politics of the Veto of Legislation in New York State* (Washington, D.C.: University Press of America, 1980).

45. Vermont drew up a constitution in 1777, after having driven the British out. But Vermont did not become a state until 1791, when it became the fourteenth one.

46. Benton, *Veto Power,* p. 38.

47. Ibid., pp. 39, 40.

48. Ibid., p. 40.

49. Ibid., p. 41.

50. Ibid., p. 59.

51. The term "veto" is sometimes applied in ways that seem to take it far from a

more precise political meaning. For purposes of this study, the concept of veto applies to the ability of one actor to block, or "veto," the completed actions of another actor, as when the president blocks a bill that has been approved by Congress, or when the British king blocks an act of Parliament. The first extended definition of "veto" in the *Oxford English Dictionary* refers to veto as "the word by which the Roman tribunes of the people opposed measures of the Senate or actions of the magistrates." Even though many actors in the Roman Republic could veto, this definition clearly alludes to blocking the action of one actor or institution by another. Thus, to say that a member of Congress could "veto" a bill during the time of the Articles of Confederation is, according to this definition, an overly broad use of the term.

52. Mason, *Veto Power,* p. 20.

53. Max Farrand, *The Framing of the Constitution of the United States* (New Haven, Conn.: Yale University Press, 1913), p. 88.

54. One recent observer has argued that the founding fathers "had inserted the veto to thwart rather than represent the 'popular will'" (Edward Pessen, "The Arrogant Veto," *Nation,* Aug. 30, 1975, p. 135). Aside from the underlying elitist attitudes of many of the framers, there is no particular evidence to suggest that this was a motivation. If anything, a few in the convention thought that the president could represent the popular will through his veto, in circumstances when the legislature failed to do so.

55. Balloting at the convention was conducted by state.

56. Mason, *Veto Power,* pp. 20–21; Farrand, *Framers,* pp. 145–46; and Henry Jones Ford, *The Rise and Growth of American Politics* (New York: Da Capo Press, 1967), p. 176.

57. Prescott and Zimmerman, *Politics of the Veto,* pp. 49–52; and Thach, *Creation,* p. 88.

58. Alexander Hamilton, *Federalist* no. 73.

59. Farrand, *Framers,* pp. 119–20.

60. Charles F. Hobson, "The Negative on State Laws: James Madison and the Crisis of Republican Government," *William and Mary Quarterly* 36 (Apr. 1979): 216.

61. Thach, *Creation,* p. 53.

62. Ibid.

63. See also ibid., pp. 45–46.

64. Joseph Story, *Commentaries on the Constitution of the United States* (Boston, Mass.: Hillard and Gray, 1833), 2:347; Alexis de Tocqueville, *Democracy in America* (New York: Vintage, 1945), 1:126; Bryce, *American Commonwealth,* 1:219–20; and Zinn, "Veto Power," p. 5.

65. Story, *Commentaries,* 2:355; and Debates in Congress, Dec. 5, 1833, p. 18.

66. See Spitzer, *Presidential Veto,* chap. 4.

67. Farrand, *Framers,* p. 184.

68. Thach, *Creation,* pp. 40, 41.

69. Story, *Commentaries,* 2:348; and Farrand, *Framers,* pp. 119–20.

70. See Spitzer, *Presidential Veto,* chap. 2.

71. Vernon L. Wilkinson, "The Item Veto in the American Constitutional System," *Georgetown Law Journal* 25 (Nov. 1936): 108 n.

72. E.g., Bryce, *American Commonwealth,* 1:220.

73. Zinn, "Veto Power," p. 6, also p. 37.

74. Christopher H. Pyle and Richard M. Pious, *The President, Congress, and the Constitution* (New York: Free Press, 1984), p. 220.

75. Some may consider this to be semantic nit-picking; but as the careful avoidance of the word "veto" illustrates, the founders were sensitive to such word usage; see, e.g., Farrand, *Records,* 2:73–79, 161, 568–69, 3:133, 385.

76. See Benton, *Veto Power,* pp. 35–36.

77. Herbert J. Storing, ed., *The Complete Anti-Federalist,* 7 vols. (Chicago: University of Chicago Press, 1981), 1:61.

78. Ibid., 2:31.

79. Ibid., 2:54, also 5:195.

80. Ibid. 3:129.

81. Ibid., p. 173.

82. Ibid., pp. 173–74.

83. Ibid., 6:124.

84. Ibid., 5:196.

85. Ibid.

86. Harry C. Thomson, "The First Presidential Vetoes," *Presidential Studies Quarterly* 8 (Winter 1978): 28.

87. Ibid., p. 30.

88. Watson, *Constitution of the United States,* 1:373.

89. Thomson, "First Presidential Vetoes," p. 30.

90. Zinn, "Veto Power," p. 22.

91. Carleton Jackson, *Presidential Vetoes: 1792–1945* (Athens: University of Georgia Press, 1967), p. 4.

92. For more on the evolution and modern applications of the veto see Spitzer, *Presidential Veto,* passim.

93. Thomson, "First Presidential Vetoes," p. 28.

94. Watson, *Constitution of the United States,* 1:373.

95. As Zinn ("Veto Power," p. 22) has observed, the historic exercise of the veto "has not followed the course set for it in the Constitution but has worked out a path different in direction and extent from that prophesied." See also Mason, *Veto Power,* p. 139.

7

THE PRESIDENT'S
EXECUTIVE POWER

THOMAS E. CRONIN

The executive power shall be vested in a President of the United States of America.
—*Article II, section 1*

The President . . . he may require the Opinion, in writing, of the principal Officer in each of the executive Departments, . . . he shall nominate, and by and with the Advice and Consent of the Senate, shall appoint Ambassadors, other public Ministers and Consuls, Judges of the supreme Court, and all other Officers of the United States.
—*Article II, section 2*

He shall from time to time give to the Congress Information of the State of the Union, and recommend to their Consideration such Measures as he shall judge necessary and expedient; . . . he shall receive Ambassadors and other public Ministers; he shall take care that the Laws be faithfully executed.
—*Article II, section 3*

The Constitutional Convention of 1787 successfully invented the American presidency, yet its outline of executive powers in Article II was loosely drawn. The framers were unsure of how much authority should be vested in the executive, and in nearly every instance, they created a presidency that had to share its executive authority with Congress. If the office was broadly defined as well as vaguely outlined, this may have been because many of the framers believed they had to leave considerable leeway for the future play of political forces.

American presidents have taken advantage of these ambiguities. While executive power in 1787 was almost always subject to the control of, or at least shared with, Congress, executive authority nowadays has become very broad. Cumulative precedents for more than two hundred years have increased and redefined the scope of executive power.

Congress and the courts can still, if they become determined about it, rein in and restrict the exercise of presidential executive power, and they occasionally do. However, much of the time, Congress delegates, the courts defer, and our conceptions of presidents as administrators and executives grow.

A good part of the confusion surrounding the executive power of the president stems from three clauses in Article II that need to be read together. And it depends on how they are read and on how we read the intentions of the framers in connection with them. These clauses are the opening sentence about "executive power," the "faithful execution" clause, and the clause specifying the oath of presidential office. A longstanding debate exists over whether the vesting of executive power in the president is a grant of broad and general executive power or just a declaratory expression that summarizes the specific grants which follow—such as commander in chief, veto, appointment, and pardon powers. Scholars such as Raoul Berger and David Gray Adler contend that these clauses should be narrowly construed, while scholars such as Harvey Mansfield, Jr., and Robert Scigliano hold that the "executive power" clause, together with the oath and other specified powers, confer general and necessary authorities for presidents to act as more forceful and independent chief executives.[1] This debate is important. How one interprets the Constitution and the framers' views shapes any discussion and explication of executive power. To compound the confusion, many of the framers did not regard their debates and early writings as the final word on the meaning of the Constitution.

A modern-day president is expected to be the national government's chief executive and administrative chief, as well as an entrepreneurial leader and manager of at least two thousand public programs. The nation's basic charter, the Constitution, confers certain executive functions, such as nominating top officials, and it specifies the responsibility of a president to see that the laws are implemented. However, the Constitution does not exactly empower presidents to act as the chief executive. Many of their plausibly administrative powers, such as those dealing with personnel and budgets, are shared with Congress. Moreover, although the Constitution says "executive power" shall be vested in a president, it does not explain that now much-debated phrase, nor does it suggest more than a few vague means that a president would have in order to exercise executive power.

In this chapter, I examine the nature of executive functions under the Articles of Confederation. I describe the debates over executive and administrative powers at the Constitutional Convention of 1787 and in some of the ratifying conventions during the following year. I treat the precedent setting in this area by early presidents, and finally, I note the enduring debates surrounding the president's administrative powers.

THE EXECUTIVE FUNCTION
UNDER THE ARTICLES OF CONFEDERATION

The Articles made no specific mention of an executive branch, and they provided for no executive as we now use the term. Congress did elect a president, but this person served primarily as a presiding officer and had little administrative or executive responsibilities. When Congress was in session, it assumed what we often now consider executive functions: determining matters of war and peace, sending and receiving ambassadors, entering into alliances and treaties, resolving disputes between states, and appointing committees and temporary administrators or boards to handle its affairs when it was not in session.

When Congress was not in session, the Articles specified, an executive committee, composed of one delegate from each state, would preside over the affairs of state. Administrative operations generally were left to congressional committees, supplemented by ad hoc boards that reported to committees. By 1781, the Continental Congress had created War, Foreign Affairs, and Treasury "departments," yet these were viewed, not as an executive branch, but as subordinate appendages of the national legislature.

In its early days, Congress entrusted the implementation of its policies and programs to whatever agency or level of government seemed most convenient at the moment. Thus, sometimes it delegated matters to a committee of its own members, sometimes to a state convention or council; and at other times, it commissioned private individuals to undertake a specific mission.

Out of necessity Congress was forced to establish semipermanent organizations and to provide for various duties and a means for controlling delegated activities. The creation of the commander-in-chief position, which was filled first by General George Washington, was illustrative.

Congress was, Charles C. Thach has written, conspicuously uninterested in and unwilling to divest itself of power. Thus, it made its various boards, commissions, and departments report to it despite the inefficiency and waste this entailed. "It is common knowledge this system failed, and failed lamentably. Inefficiency and waste, if not downright peculation and corruption, were as sure to follow as the night the day. In the wake of inefficiency came discontent, a discontent which seized on the features of the system as causes of a general administrative debacle, and demanded reform."[2]

Critics, at the time, said Congress needed to set up more permanent agencies to do the business of government. Hire good people, pay them, and fix them with independent tasks. Alexander Hamilton, in 1780, urged Congress to vest the great executive departments in the hands of single individuals.

Hamilton, George Washington, Gouverneur Morris—all proponents of getting Congress out of the business of day-to-day management—argued their case against the obvious cultural and historical fears of centralized government. Plainly, many state leaders and veterans of the Revolution feared government, feared an independent executive, and looked favorably upon a weak national legislature that would lack efficient and effective executive competence. They believed, too, that this weak national set of arrangements served the interests of the states, or at least the short-term interest of many of the states. And defenders of liberty found solace, no doubt, in keeping the national government limited and weak.

EXECUTIVE AUTHORITY
DEBATED AT PHILADELPHIA

Most of the framers came to Philadelphia recognizing the need for some kind of national executive to supervise the day-to-day operations of the small yet growing national government. Still, if the experience under the Articles of Confederation had proven that Congress was unable to provide continuous direction and effective coordination of the administrative agencies, the framers were not wholly agreed as to how this might best be provided for in an overhauled new government.

"The conception of the President as an officer vested with powers and responsibilities of such scope as to make him a potent force in the governmental scheme evolved slowly in the minds of the Convention delegates," Joseph Kallenbach has written. "In the beginning the prevailing view seemed to be that the head of the executive branch should be little more than a national administrative manager—an instrument for efficient administration of polities determined by the legislature."[3] Eventually, however, many of the delegates came to accept the veto power, the appointment power, and other functions or roles that led to the creation of a stronger, if not wholly independent, administrative chief executive.

As they did on so many other matters, the delegates got many of their ideas from state constitutions, notably those of New York and Massachusetts. The delegates who feared a too-powerful national executive proposed annexing an executive council to the executive as a means of diminishing the dangers of tyranny. James Madison, ever fearful of a concentration of powers, proposed a council to advise the president and to record the council's sentiments. Certain delegates suggested that the heads of the executive departments be members of this council. Oliver Ellsworth of Connecticut favored adding the chief justice and the president of the Senate to the council. Another delegate favored the inclusion of representatives from the various regions of the new nation.

James Wilson defended a single executive because it would encourage provision of the most energy and responsibility to the office. Unlike the British monarch, however, Wilson's proposed executive would not have powers of war and peace. Wilson agreed that those prerogatives were legislative in nature. However, he did consider strictly executive in nature the powers of executing the laws and appointing top governmental officials.

Wilson's proposal came early in June, and it aroused strenuous opposition. Governor Edmund Randolph of Virginia, for example, regarded the notion of a single executive as "the fetus of monarchy." He characterized Wilson's proposal as too similar to the British model, and he declared that the American people desired and required a different form of government. Why couldn't, he asked, vigor, dispatch, and responsibility just as easily be found in three men?

Wilson disagreed, saying a single executive, rather than leading to monarchy, would prove to be the best safeguard against tyranny. He would eventually win his case, but not until the framers had more fully settled the scope of authority that would be given to the president and not until executive powers were created in such a way that they would be shared with Congress, especially the Senate.

When it came to specifying the powers a president would exercise, one of the most important was that of the veto power. After considerable debate, the framers granted presidents the crucial role of being part of the legislative process, for the person who has the ultimate power to veto a measure also has the additional opportunity to bargain for what that person wants in a given piece of legislation.

In addition to the veto power—even if it is a qualified veto as opposed to an absolute veto (it could be overridden by a two-thirds vote in each house of Congress)—the framers also provided that presidents shall, from time to time, give to Congress information about the state of the Union and recommend to Congress any measure they judged necessary. This provision ensured that presidents would be more than national clerks or national city managers, solely attending to the enforcement of laws passed by the legislature. No, presidents were expected to help set the agenda, to clarify priorities, and to provide leadership in an emergency. And our best presidents have capitalized on this constitutional proviso.

Plainly, too, when the framers made the president the commander in chief of the army, navy, and the state militia when called into service (presumably by Congress), they conferred an enormously important power on future presidents. This is especially true today when we maintain large standing armies and when nuclear war is an ever-present danger.

In providing that presidents shall have the power to grant pardons and reprieves for all offenses against the nation, except in cases of impeachment, the framers again expanded the role of the president. Note, too, that this power, unlike most of the so-called executive powers, could be exercised alone by a president; it did not require the advice and consent of Congress. It is one of the few exclusive powers available to a president; some have even called it the only "imperial" power a president can exercise.

The other major executive powers decided upon at Philadelphia were: the appointment power, the right to require written opinions from each of the department heads, the obligation to take care that the laws be faithfully executed, and the duty of receiving ambassadors and other public ministers. Each deserves discussion.

The Appointment Power

"And he shall nominate, and by and with the Advice and Consent of the Senate, shall appoint Ambassadors, other public Ministers and Consuls, Judges of the supreme Court, and all other Officers of the United States, whose Appointments are not herein otherwise provided for, and which shall be established by Law: but the Congress may by Law vest the Appointment of such inferior Officers, as they think proper, in the President alone, in the Courts of Law, or in the Heads of Departments" (Art. II, sec. 2).

The framers at Philadelphia were reluctant to grant unrestricted authority to the new executive position they were creating. Thus, they would never, as had been true in England, have granted to the president the right to create offices as well as to appoint people to them. That type of royal prerogative was never even considered. The questions before them in Philadelphia centered around whom a president could appoint and how this appointing power would be shared with Congress.

Some of the framers thought top officers and judges should be appointed by Congress, especially by the Senate. After all, the Senate represented the states, and it was not clear whom the new president would represent. Also, the power to appoint administrative officers, both in the states and under the Articles of Confederation, had been a legislative responsibility.

James Wilson, the convention's most propresidency delegate, said presidents should have the power to appoint judges and top officials. John Rutledge of South Carolina disagreed; he disliked granting so great a power to any single person. The people would think the delegates were leaning, he said, too much toward monarchy. James Madison, however, worried about the danger of intrigue and favoritism if the election of judges were left to the whole of Congress. Further, he noted, legislative talents are very different from judicial talents; hence, legislators might not be the best judges of the requisite qualifications. Still, Madison was uneasy about granting this power solely to the president. Perhaps, Madison said, it should be a power given not to Congress but only to the Senate.

Connecticut's Roger Sherman favored the election of judges by the Senate, saying it would on the whole have more wisdom than the executive. It would be less easy for a candidate for a judicial position to intrigue with the senators than with the national executive.

Nathaniel Gorham of Massachusetts urged his fellow delegates to consider the procedure long tested in his home state. He proposed that judges be appointed by the executive, with the advice and consent of the Senate. Other delegates favored the exact reverse of the Massachusetts plan: namely, let the Senate nominate and the president veto, with a provision that two-thirds of the Senate could override the executive's negative.

In the end, most of the delegates agreed to permit executives to have the nominating power yet also provided a role for the Senate to reject the presidential nomination. They did so with reluctance, in large part because of the evident shortcomings of the familiar legislative appointment system—petty deal making, cabal, and intrigue.

It was only during the closing weeks of the Philadelphia convention that the framers placed the nominating power for judges and diplomatic positions in the executive's hands. It was only then, too, that they struck a clause that reserved to Congress the sole power to appoint the national treasurer, the position we now know as the secretary of the Treasury.

Thus, the appointment power would not be the prerogative of one branch but of two. As they did so often, the framers tried to arrange it so that one branch could do little without the concurrence of at least one other branch.

Alexander Hamilton devoted an entire *Federalist* essay to the virtues of this shared power of appointment. Doubtless, in this instance his reasoning reflected the general mood of most of his fellow delegates in Philadelphia:

> It will readily be comprehended, that a man who had himself the sole disposition of offices, would be governed much more by his private inclinations and interests, than when he was bound to submit the propriety of his choice to the discussion and determination of a different and independent body; and that body an entire branch of the legislature. The possibility of rejection would be a strong motive to care in proposing. The danger to his own reputation, and, in the case of an elective magistrate, to his political existence, from betraying a spirit of favoritism, or an unbecoming pursuit of popularity, to the observation of a body whose opinion would have great weight in forming that of the public, could not fail to operate as a barrier to the one and to the other.[4]

Nowadays, presidents nominate several thousands to top executive and diplomatic positions and several hundred to the federal judiciary.[5] It is a major source of their influence in American politics. Yet if a president can decide in most instances whom to appoint, it is up to Congress to decide whether an agency or a court should exist and what its functions are. Additionally, Congress has found a number of ways to limit a president's nominating authority, such as stipulating the qualifications for an office or insisting, as the Senate regularly does, on "senatorial courtesy" in the appointment of federal district judges, United States attorneys, and United States marshals. Moreover, a new president comes into office with 99 percent of the civilian, military, and judicial positions already filled, most of them with career tenure of one sort or another. Thus, as one scholar has noted, "The chief executive may be the captain of the Ship of State; but he must function with a crew that is not entirely of his own choosing." And that's an understatement these days.[6]

Reports from Department Heads

The president "may require the Opinion, in writing, of the principal Officer in each of the executive Departments, upon any Subject relating to the Duties of their respective Offices" (Art. II, sec. 2).

Certain framers would have liked to have had the Constitution speak in considerable detail about the various departments, their names, and their functions. Others, as noted earlier, wanted to mandate various types of executive councils with whom presidents would share their executive powers. Late in the convention, Gouverneur Morris of Pennsylvania and Charles Pinckney of South Carolina submitted a detailed organizational plan for five departments, at the head of which there would be a secretary of domestic affairs, a secretary of commerce and finance, a secretary of foreign affairs, a secretary of war, and a secretary of marine (navy). All of these officials would be appointed by the president and would serve at the president's pleasure. Each would be subordinate and would serve as an advisor to the president.

The Morris-Pinckney plan provided that the president should also appoint a secretary of state, who would serve as secretary to a council of state and as a public secretary to the president. This official would prepare all public dispatches and would countersign all such messages from the president. Morris and Pinckney proposed that the chief justice of the Supreme Court would also serve on this council of state, together with the five department heads and the secretary of state. In the absence of the president, moreover, the chief justice would serve as president of the council.

The intent of this scheme was to force on the president a collegial body with which to confer. The president could, from time to time, submit any policy or executive question to be discussed by this council. A president could also, the Morris proposal said, require the written opinions of any one or more of the members. "But he shall in all cases exercise his own judgment, and either conform to such opinions or not as he may think proper; and every officer abovementioned shall be responsible for his opinion on the affairs relating to his particular department."[7]

Theirs was a bold plan, yet it was left out of the Constitution. It was left out no doubt because it provided too much detail, more than most framers thought was necessary in a basic constitutional charter. And this omission "does not necessarily signify opposition to the basic idea, but rather a belief that the matter was properly one for legislative determination."[8]

Even though it was rejected, this plan suggests some of the thinking the framers had about the role of department heads in relation to the chief executive. The plan clearly posited presidential supremacy with respect to the heads of the departments. Implicit, too, was that the business of the various departments was to be conducted under the general leadership of the president.

Even though the creation of departments was left to be dealt with by legislative act and the specification of an executive cabinet or council of state was dropped altogether, it is noteworthy that the framers did place in the Constitution the clause authorizing the president to require the written opinion of the heads of these departments. Here was a clear indication that the president was the chief executive and that department heads would not only serve as advisors to the president but also be subject to presidential directives.

Yet it is also important to note that, as Edward S. Corwin has suggested, the consultative relationship indicated here is an entirely one-sided affair, conducted in writing and in an individual or separate way. Moreover, the relationship was to relate only to the duties of their respective offices. If an executive council was intended, perhaps some of the framers hoped and believed the Senate would perform this role.[9]

Take Care that the Laws Be Faithfully Executed

The president "shall take Care that the Laws be faithfully executed" (Art. II, sec. 3).

The framers agreed both that a president was needed and that the implementation of the laws and law enforcement were to constitute a, if not the, major responsibility for presidents. The "take care" clause, as it is now often called, is reasonably straightforward, and it was not discussed in detail at the convention. Presumably, there was little to debate. State governors were similarly charged with faithfully executing the law, and the framers were convinced that Congress could no longer both make and administer the laws. A clearly defined division of labor was necessary. Continuity, energy, and efficiency would all be gained.

The "take care" clause may be short and sweet, yet it has triggered scholarly and constitutional debate in later periods. Those who believe in a broad interpretation of this and the "vesting" clauses ("the executive power shall be vested in a President") often claim extensive discretionary powers for a president. These scholars suggest that the framers intended there to be some inherent power for presidents to do what was necessary to protect the country and to defend the Constitution. These scholars also believe that these clauses convey additional power above and beyond the enumerated or specified powers, such as the veto, pardon, or commander-in-chief responsibilities.

Complicating the meaning of the "take care" clause is the clause in Article I, section 8, that delineates as a legislative responsibility the authority "to make all Laws which shall be necessary and proper for carrying into Execution the foregoing Powers, and all other Powers vested by this Constitution in the Government of the United States, or in any Department or Officer thereof." This, Kallenbach has said, "appears to be a clear reservation of authority to Congress to regulate by law the manner in which the President should go about discharging duties placed in his hands by the Constitution." Thus, Congress may pass laws that control how presidents and their administrative subordinates carry out their administrative functions.

> The constitutional language concerning control over the administrative establishment and its operation is thus quite ambiguous. Whether the framers intended to invest the President with an independent authority beyond the range of congressional control or intended him to function in this regard merely as an agent of Congress, was, and remains, one of the enigmas of the Constitution. Do the laws he must execute include congressional enactments that in his judgment violate the oath required of him to "faithfully enact the office of President of the United States" and to "preserve, protect and defend the Constitution of the United States"? Do they include laws that in his judgment invade his own constitutional prerogatives as chief executive? The Constitution gives no answer to this riddle. Its arrangements seem rather to set the conditions for a never-ending tug-of-war between the President and Congress in the area of administration.[10]

At the very least, however, the "take care" clause does make the president the nation's primary administrator and, together with the appointment power, has paved the way for presidents to become the nation's central agent in the administrative, regulatory, welfare, and warfare domains.

Receiving Ambassadors

The president "shall receive Ambassadors and other public Ministers" (Art. II, sec. 3).

Here, again, another brief phrase in the Constitution may not have meant much to the framers, and it was little discussed at their constitutional convention, yet it has come to play a critically important role in the enlargement of presidential power. Alexander Hamilton dismissed the importance of this phrase in *Federalist* number 69, saying that it would, of course, be inconvenient for Congress to gather every time a new ambassador or minister was sent here. Hamilton was clever in his argument, but he was wrong:

> The President is also to be authorized to receive ambassadors and other public ministers. This, though it has been a rich theme of declamation, is more a matter of dignity than of authority. It is a circumstance which will be without consequence in the administration of the government; and it was far more convenient that it should be arranged in this manner, than that there should be a necessity of convening the legislature, or one of its branches, upon every arrival of a foreign minister, though it were merely to take the place of a departed predecessor.[11]

This clause about receiving ambassadors may have been understood by many of the framers as a routine, mechanical function, yet it has come to confer far more power than the framers intended. From this clause is inferred the presidential power to recognize countries and to make major decisions about our relations with foreign nations. Although the framers left little evidence about what they intended in connection with this clause, some scholars think they meant for presidents to exercise a narrow diplomatic function as opposed to having a broad discretionary power. Still, the reception of an ambassador from a foreign nation involves, among other things, according to international law, the recognition of the nation represented by the ambassador. Thus the "receiving clause" also becomes a "recognition clause."

Is this responsibility a merely administrative and ceremonial function, devoid of major policy-making consequence, or does it confer upon presidents the extensive power to make foreign policy?[12] The framers probably meant it to be a limited function rather than the spacious "power" it has turned out to be. Throughout our nation's history, presidents have performed scores of acts of recognition and some acts of nonrecognition as well. These are usually performed without consulting or seeking the advice and consent of Congress. Thus, the receiving or recognition clause, in practice if not in theory, has proved to be a potent instrument of foreign policy, and in the twentieth century, it has served to enhance the role of the president enormously.

EXECUTIVE POWER AND THE RATIFYING DEBATES

Those who objected to the proposed Constitution, who are usually called Antifederalists, thought the proposed new president had been given too many powers and too much power. Their chief worry was for their personal liberty and for the future of their states. They feared, understandably enough, big government and centralized institutions of leadership. Some Antifederalist writers emphasized the dangers of permitting presidents to be reelected without limit. They bewailed the vast appointment and treaty-making powers assigned to the president. Others denounced the vice-presidency, saying it was a dangerous office that would surely be the source of contests over power or usurpations of authority.

Critics at the various ratifying conventions spoke in favor of providing for an executive council. They hoped such a council would help to prevent the danger of monarchy or the dominance by any one sector of the country. In essence, these notions reiterated the concerns raised by Morris, Mason, Randolph, and Charles Pinckney at the Philadelphia convention. New York delegates proposed a council to assist presidents in making appointments; a Pennsylvania delegate called for a council; and the idea was also put forth in North Carolina.

James Iredell, speaking at the North Carolina ratifying convention on July 28, 1788, gave several reasons why the absence of an executive council in the Constitution was not a cause for alarm. Unlike the king in England, Iredell noted, presidents could be removed from office should they commit any misdemeanor. Moreover, a president would always have the advice of his principal officers, "which he can at all times command." Iredell added:

> He can at no time want [for] advice, if he desires it, as the principal officers will always be on the spot. Those officers, from their abilities and experience, will probably be able to give as good, if not better, advice than any counsellors would do; and the solemnity of the advice in writing, which must be preserved, would be a great check upon them.[13]

Iredell also suggested it would be difficult to establish a council that would adequately reflect the interests of all the regions. Too much regional jealousy would undermine the council.

Most important, Iredell added, a council might make it hard to hold a president properly accountable. A president could, in essence, hide behind the council and its advice, making it difficult to know whether the president or his counsellors were most to blame.

> But the method proposed in the Constitution creates no such embarrassment. It is plain and open. And the President will personally have the credit of good, or the censure of bad measures; since, though he may ask advice, he is to use his judgment in following or rejecting it. For all these reasons, I am clearly of the opinion that the clause is better as it stands than if the President were to have a council. I think every good that can be derived from the institution of a council may be expected from the advice of these officers, without its being liable to the disadvantages to which it appears to me, the institution of a council would be.[14]

North Carolina ratified the Constitution, as did, eventually, all the remaining states. Antifederalists still worried about a president's being vested with too much power, but even most of these critics appreciated the need for a unitary executive and for the improved administration of the laws. Some Antifederalists wanted this new executive to be at least strong enough to resist the aristocratic tendencies of the legislature, especially the Senate.[15]

On balance, the Antifederalists apparently were prepared to accept a stronger executive than had been provided in the Articles of Confederation. They would have preferred a weaker executive; yet except for the notion of an executive council, they failed to devise an alternative set of arrangements for executive power.

In the end, many Antifederalists voted against the Constitution, yet less because they objected to any part of it—such as the executive-powers clause—than because they still remembered life under the king and royal governors. Historian Jackson Turner Main put it this way:

> Many Antifederalists contemplated the possibility of a union of interest between the Senate and the President, concluding that if it should occur the result would be despotism: a king and a House of Lords equaled an oligarchy. The House of Representatives was nothing but a "pretended concession to democracy," and would be unable to contend with such vast superiority of power. Perhaps taken

singly, individual parts might be justified, but as a whole it could lead only to tyranny.[16]

Surprisingly, however, the Antifederalists as a group did not raise as extensive an attack on the executive-powers section of the Constitution as might have been expected. Many of them apparently hoped that proposed new amendments, urging the adoption of an executive council, tenure limits for presidents, or the protection of a bill of rights—all of which were much discussed at several of the ratifying conventions—would, when acted upon, allay the Antifederalists' misgivings. Antifederalists agreed that there was a need for political change. If the Constitution was too radical a departure from the Confederation, it was nonetheless a step in the right direction. This fact, plus their hope that the Constitution might soon be corrected through amendments, persuaded enough Antifederalists in crucial states to switch over and support the new Constitution despite its shortcomings. "Thus a few Antifederalists—just enough—felt that the Constitution was better than 'anarchy and confusion,' and the promise of amendments was enough to quiet their fears."[17]

PRECEDENTS FROM EARLY PRESIDENCIES

As noted, the framers designed a presidency with several executive powers and with various responsibilities, yet the brevity and vagueness of Article II left many matters unclear. The Constitution, it turns out, was silent on much that would later become important. Much was left for future presidents to interpret and for Congress and the judiciary to debate and define. Could a president remove people from office as well as appoint them? Could a president form a cabinet? Could a president reorganize the executive department? Could a president terminate treaties as well as negotiate them? Could a president withhold documents and information from Congress and, if so, under what conditions? Could a president, by executive order, buy large new territories to be added to the United States? Could a president negotiate informal or executive agreements with other nations that would not have to be ratified with the Senate's approval? On these and other important matters the Constitution was either silent or ambiguous.

The framers doubtless were less specific than they may have wanted to be because they yearned for a Constitution that would win ratification. Their dilemma was that they needed a stronger executive institution, yet they absolutely had to avoid stirring up the still-widespread popular fear of monarchy. Then, too, the expectation that George Washington would serve as the first president apparently made many of the framers and many of those at the ratifying conventions less concerned about the precise job description of the proposed executive. When citizens of that day spoke of a national hero or the guardian of the people, they almost always were thinking of General Washington: "Entre nous, I do [not] believe they [the executive powers] would have been so great had not many of the members [of the Constitutional Convention] cast their eyes toward George Washington as President; and shaped their Ideas of the Powers to be given a President, by their opinions of his Virtue."[18]

In the end, most of the delegates to the convention in Philadelphia had agreed to create an independent and potentially powerful presidency. The office, as we now know, had the potential to acquire even greater power than most of the delegates imagined.

George Washington appreciated the critical significance of his presidential actions. He realized that nearly all his initial interpretations of the presidential job would serve as precedents for future presidents.

On the one hand, Washington respected the separate powers allocated to each branch. Yet, several of his major decisions were efforts to circumvent the barriers of separation in the name of energy, efficiency, and unity. He forcefully guarded presidential prerogatives, yet at the same time he creatively worked for cooperation between the president and Congress. His general tone was one of cooperation with Congress. He keenly appreciated the lawmaking supremacy of the Congress, and he construed his own veto power narrowly. He refused to exercise the power in order to express policy differences with Congress; he held that the presidential veto should be used only if a legislative act was demonstrably unconstitutional as it affected the president's power.

Despite his deferential relations with Congress, President Washington assertively exercised his clearly executive powers. He did, for example, select the heads of the major departments, subject of course to the Senate's confirmation, and these department heads were responsible directly to him. On matters of top personnel, he believed he needed the Senate's consent yet not necessarily its advice, because they would be his lieutenants, and he wanted loyal as well as competent administrators to assist him.

Washington was not a constitutional clause-bound literalist. He had, after all, been a delegate to the Constitutional Convention. He knew well the many implicit understandings, as well as the many areas that would need to be settled by experiment and experience. His military command and staff experience served him well as he appointed and made use of his departmental heads. He wanted to be kept informed of their suggestions and problems. He consulted with them regularly, and after a while, he began to meet with his departmental heads collectively. It was then that they became known as the "president's cabinet."

He worked with the cabinet much as he had with his senior officers during the Revolutionary War, often changing his own plan in the face of adverse opinion from his advisers. In the early years, the president encouraged opposing views and he got them in abundance in bitter clashes between Secretary of State Thomas Jefferson and Treasury Secretary Alexander Hamilton. By 1793 as the burdens of the presidency increased, Washington concluded that henceforth he would avoid advisers "whose political tenets are adverse to the measures which the general government is pushing."[19]

Washington won the confirmation of all his cabinet appointees. Indeed, no cabinet-level appointee of the first six presidents was rejected by the United States Senate.

In general, Washington recruited highly qualified people to serve in government, and Congress respected his personnel decisions. Washington welcomed personnel suggestions from members of Congress, yet he refused to be badgered by legislators when he believed he had a better choice for an office. On occasion, however, the Senate did exercise its prerogative of negating his choice.

His [Washington's] prestige was so enormous that only on rare occasions were his nominations turned down. The first was the rejection of Benjamin Fishbourne as naval officer in the Port of Savannah. Fishbourne had been one of about a hundred nominations that the President had submitted for posts as collectors, naval officers and surveyors. Washington quickly proposed a different candidate after Colonel Fishbourne's rejection, but he took the occasion to remind the Senate in detail of the rejected nominee's high qualifications for the office, and tartly suggested that in the future, if the Senate was disposed to question the propriety of a nomination, it would be expedient "to communciate that circumstance to me, and thereby avail yourself of the information which led me to make them [appointments], and which I would with pleasure lay before you."[20]

Despite this plea, the Senate later rejected other nominees, including his nomination of John Rutledge of South Carolina as chief justice of the United States. The Constitution plainly made the appointment power a shared power, and if presidents sometimes ignore the advice of the Senate, they find that at least several times a term the Senate will withhold its consent on a few nominees. Subsequent presidents have, as Washington did, lamented the Senate's unwillingness to accept the president's exclusive judgment on top personnel matters, but clearly the intention of the framers has been realized in practice.

PRESIDENTS, CONGRESS, AND THE REMOVAL POWER

The Constitution nowhere explicitly indicates whether the president or Congress or both possess the power to remove top executive-branch officials; and this was bitterly debated during Washington's first year in office. Although this 1789 debate was almost entirely held among competing points of view in Congress, it has come in time to be a critical point of dispute between presidents and Congress.

The Constitution explicitly provides for one—and only one—means to remove an individual from public office: impeachment. But impeachment is a cumbersome process, and it is not usually the appropriate instrument for ousting an ineffective, irresponsible, or simply incapable administrator.

Who should have the right to dismiss senior officials in the executive department? Should the power belong exclusively to the president? Presidents, after all, appoint these top aides. Shouldn't presidents, as chief executive officers, be empowered to fire them as well? Yet what about the Senate? If senators are involved in the confirmation process, shouldn't they also enjoy or at least share in the process of removal?

At the most fundamental level, this constitutional debate between the two branches is a classic argument, pitting separation of powers against checks and balances.

Proponents of an exclusive removal power for the executive contended that dividing the removal task between the branches would abolish the compelling principle of unity and responsibility in the executive department, which was intended for the security of liberty and the public good. James Madison and others pointed out that a shared removal process would clearly devitalize the executive branch if there were no way to dismiss appointed officials for acts less egregious than those that would qualify for their impeachment.

James Madison saw the removal power as an implied power stemming from the executive's responsibility to fulfill the constitutional obligation that the laws be faithfully executed. Madison held that displacing officers who are incapable of performing their duties makes presidents responsible to the public for the conduct of the people they have nominated and appointed to aid them. Plainly, said Madison and others, presidents must have the power to dismiss officials when they find that the qualifications that induced the initial appointment have ceased to exist.

Allies of the Madisonian view relied on what is called the "executive grant theory." This theory essentially holds that because the Constitution vests executive power in the president and because the authority to remove is an executive power, the removal or dismissal authority clearly belongs to no one but the chief executive; the legislature has no right to diminish, modify, or undermine the integrity of a president's executive authority.

The case for the Senate's participation in the removal of executive officers was posed by a vocal minority in 1789. It is only fair, they reasoned, that if both the president and the Senate share in the process of appointment, they should also share in the power of removal. That minority also emphasized the need for balance between the branches of government. The equal and jealous operation of the three branches of government allows for a free government. If these powers are unduly assimilated in one branch, they argued, it is easy to see the evil or tyranny that may result.

Supporters of the Senate's role in the removal process criticized Madison and his friends for exaggerating the separation-of-powers principle. They agreed with Hamilton's view, suggested in one of the *Federalist* essays, that the consent of the Senate would be necessary to displace as well as to appoint. Just because the legislature and the executive would be sharing authority on this matter did not mean it would lead to a weakening of the executive. Moreover, these supporters reiterated, if Congress creates an office, it should also be able to attach to it any conditions it decides are appropriate, including tenure and grounds for dismissal.

This controversy over the removal power arose when a bill before Congress provided that departmental heads (now known as cabinet secretaries) should be "removable by the president." This posed several questions, because there was no such language in the Constitution. Was this, then, a legislative delegation of power—a grant by Congress of its power to the executive? Or was it merely a legislative interpretation of the United States Constitution? Congress reworded the phrase, yet it adopted the clear position that presidents would indeed have this power. Madison's general view prevailed. His view, as noted, held that if presidents did the nominating and appointing with merely a check by the Senate (the need for their consent), then the appointing power was essentially executive in nature. Therefore the displacing of an executive official would also be an executive responsibility. In his view, both the appointing and the dismissing powers are presidential. "The legislature," Madison noted, "creates the office, defines the powers, limits its duration, and annexes a compensation. This done, the legislative power ceases."[21]

Yes, Madison and his friends acknowledged, the Senate did participate in the process of appointment; yet this did not make the Senate an executive body. It must give its consent to an appointment, but nomination and appointment were executive functions, whereas the role of the Senate was advisory, external, and nonexecutive.

Congressman Fisher Ames expressed the prevailing position:

The executive powers are delegated to the President, with a view to have a responsible officer to superintend, control, inspect, and check the officers necessarily employed in administering the laws. The only bond between him and those he employs, is the confidence he has in their integrity and talents; when that confidence ceases, the principal ought to have power to remove those whom he can no longer trust with safety.[22]

And on the precise role of the Senate, Ames added:

It is doubted whether the Senate do actually appoint or not. It is admitted that they may check and regulate the appointment by the President, but they can do nothing more; they are merely an advisory body, and do not secure any degree of responsibility, which is one great object of the present constitution. . . . The President, I contend, has expressly the power of nominating and appointing, though he must obtain the consent of the Senate. He is the agent; the Senate may prevent his acting, but cannot act themselves.[23]

President Washington was undoubtedly pleased by the outcome, for he believed that an efficient and effective executive who was capable of executing the laws must also be capable of demanding extensive accountability from his subordinates. Even Hamilton came to agree with and support the position of Madison and Washington.

This debate about the role of Congress in influencing the termination of service for executive-branch officials is an enduring one. Congress on several occasions has tried to limit the presidential removal power. With such a debatable and constitutionally sensitive issue, it is no wonder the Supreme Court avoided ruling on the removal question for over a century. Congress's assertion of the power to limit the president's removal of executive-branch officers was reintroduced in the Tenure of Office Act of 1867, which forbade the president to remove designated cabinet members without the consent of the Senate. That act, even though it was repealed twenty years later, and related legislation were declared unconstitutional by the Supreme Court in 1926. *Myers* v. *U.S.* (1926) evolved from a presidential order to dismiss a postmaster. The Court struck down as unconstitutional a congressional provision that certain postmasters, appointed by the president with the consent of the Senate, could not be dismissed by a president without the approval of the Senate.

Chief Justice William Howard Taft, himself a former president, wrote the majority opinion in *Myers.* Echoing the 1789 views of Madison and Fisher Ames, Taft declared that the power of removal of executive officers is essentially inherent in the power of appointment and therefore that a president has the exclusive power of removing executive officers whom he has appointed by and with the advice and consent of the Senate. Taft said, too, that the removal power had to be the peculiar province of the president because the Constitution charges the chief executive with ensuring that the nation's laws be faithfully executed.[24]

Taft's capaciously propresidency interpretation has been criticized both for going far beyond what was necessary to dispose of the case before the Court and for trivializing the role of Congress in ensuring that the laws are faithfully executed. What, for example, is Congress to do if a president turns his or her head while top officials break the law? Taft "did not admit that the presidents might be *unwilling* to execute the laws."[25]

Three of Taft's associate justices dissented, noting that Congress creates offices, abolishes them, and may set conditions on the duration of the office. Surely, the justices suggested, Congress ought to be able to pass a law that involves its members in the removal process.

Taft's decision would be modified in later decisions, notably *Humphrey's Executor* v. *U.S.* (1935), both because it was much too drastic an interpretation and because Congress, given its responsibilities in legislation and program oversight, could and would never make matters of suspension, removal, demotion, and reassignment the exclusive preserve of the chief executive. Edward Corwin has highlighted the problems about Taft's sweeping decision in this way:

> That the President ought to be able to remove at will all subordinates whose discretion he is entitled by the Constitution or by the laws of Congress to control, and for whose conduct he is hence responsible, must be granted. . . . But the Chief Justice's [Taft's] conclusion that this fact "must control interpretation of the Constitution as to be appointed by him" was much too drastic and resulted in the paradox that, while the Constitution permitted Congress to vest duties in the executive officers in the performance of which they were to exercise their own independent judgment, it at the same time permitted the President to guillotine such officers from exercising the very discretion which Congress had the right to require.[26]

In the 1935 *Humphrey* ruling, the Court held that Congress had established the Federal Trade Commission (FTC) as a quasi-legislative and quasi-judicial regulatory agency precisely in order to ensure that the commission would be independent of executive control. It was clear, the Court said, that one who holds office only during the pleasure of another cannot be depended upon to maintain an attitude of independence against the latter's will.

In short, the Supreme Court invalidated the president's exclusive power of removal for two reasons. First, Congress had specified the grounds for removal, should it be necessary, when it had created the FTC. Second, because the FTC was an independent regulatory commission, it was imperative that it be isolated from White House influence.

In general, nowadays a president may use the removal power over those whose powers are purely ministerial and over those who exercise the president's own powers. However, various civil service reforms, dating back to the Civil Service Act of 1883, impose restrictions on the presidential removal power, limiting such decisions to specific malfeasances or violations of official duties. Also, many members of Congress even today maintain that Congress, too, has to have a say in the suspension and removal of federal employees. Thus, political scientist Louis Fisher has pointed out that Congress can still abolish offices through reorganization and program cutbacks, and it can apply enormous pressure on federal employees through its investigative power and the passage of resolution. It also can design an office as adjudicatory and nonpartisan, thus placing it clearly outside the control of the White House. "There will always be circumstances requiring the active intervention of Congress in questions of suspension, removal, demotion, and reassignment," Fisher has written; "given the responsibilities of Congress in legislation and program oversight, these matters can never remain the monopoly or exclusive preserve of the president."[27]

Here again, then, while presidents plainly have considerable executive authority to conduct most of what they have to do, their ultimate authority is in many ways rooted in shared power with Congress.

WASHINGTON AND THE WHISKY REBELLION

A president's power to take care that the laws be faithfully executed is only as clear as what presidents actually do to enforce the laws of the land. President Washington established numerous precedents in the area of executive leadership, yet perhaps none is as famous as his forceful display of executive and national governmental power in suppressing the whisky rebels in the westernmost counties of Pennsylvania. Washington acted to secure recognition of the idea of supremacy of the law and the power of the federal government to levy taxes.

The insurrection of hundreds of westerners against a federal excise tax on whisky angered Alexander Hamilton, Washington's chief deputy and secretary of the Treasury. Hamilton was especially upset when federal tax collectors were terrorized and when a small unit of troops guarding the home of a General John Neville, the excise inspector for western Pennsylvania, was forced to surrender to a much larger force of antiwhisky tax rebels. Lives were lost, and the rebels were threatening to march on Pittsburgh and the federal arsenal there. To Hamilton it was a matter of law versus anarchy and of whether the nation should rule or be ruled. Shall the general will prevail, or the will of a faction?

The real story of the Whisky Rebellion is more complicated, of course.[28] But the interest here is that Washington acted, in accord with provisions spelled out in legislation. Washington and Hamilton, even if they resorted to too much display of federal force in this particular instance, believed that a government that cannot enforce its laws is at best a vulnerable government. They believed, as well, that it is the responsibility of the president to see to it that the laws are obeyed.

Congress had passed a law authorizing the president to call state militia into national service to help in the execution of federal laws. A standing national army did not really exist at the time. The 1792 law also stipulated that the chief executive had to be formally notified by a federal district court that the execution of the federal laws was being obstructed by unusual forces too powerful to be suppressed by routine judicial proceedings or by federal marshals in the district. Further, the president had to issue a proclamation, warning the resisters of the lawlessness of their actions and notifying them that there would be a military response if they persisted.

Washington tried negotiations. Then he tried proclamations—indeed, three of them—but all were in vain. So he went ahead and secured from a federal judge certification that the situation was well beyond the control of judicial proceedings or federal marshals. The president then requested the governors of Virginia, Maryland, New Jersey, and Pennsylvania to supply a militia army to proceed westward and to put down the Whisky Rebellion. Within a few weeks, nearly thirteen thousand militiamen had assembled in Harrisburg, Pennsylvania.

President Washington came out from the then-seat of the national government, Philadelphia, helped to organize them, and even accompanied them for a few days as they moved into central Pennsylvania—the only time in American history when a president, as commander in chief of the armed forces, actually took to the field with the troops. Secretary of the Treasury Hamilton, capitalizing on Secretary of War Henry Knox's absence from the seat of office, had himself made acting secretary of war and similarly took to the field; but unlike Washington, Hamilton actually stayed with the troops until they met the rebels.

Washington's highly publicized involvement and his presence with the army as it mobilized, trained, and moved through Pennsylvania helped "to generate support for his policy among the populace and also with the militiamen, many of whom had been highly unenthusiastic about the enterprise at the beginning."[29]

Washington's and Hamilton's show of strength proved effective. Leaders of the tax resistance fled to Ohio. An armed revolt failed to materialize. Only a score or so of the rebels were arrested, and most of these were released or pardoned a short while later. Ironically, the suppression of the whisky rebels marked the beginning of the decline in popularity of the Federalist party, even as it demonstrated the extent to which a president and a cabinet member could go to win compliance with federal laws.

Hamilton plainly felt vindicated, and he would later boast that whenever the government appears in arms, it ought to inspire respect by the display of its strength. The consideration of expense is, he said, of no moment compared with the advantages of energy. The American voters did not necessarily agree. Jeffersonian followers may have been energized by this confrontational lesson in constitutional government. Even a strong Federalist such as Fisher Ames was prompted to observe that "a regular government, by overcoming an unsuccessful insurrection, becomes stronger; but elective rulers can scarcely ever employ the physical force of a democracy without turning the moral force, or the power of public opinion, against the government."[30]

THOMAS JEFFERSON AND THE LOUISIANA PURCHASE

Jefferson came to the presidency at fifty-seven years of age with impressive credentials. He had drafted revolutionary state papers, first in Virginia and then in the Continental Congress, where he was the chief author of the Declaration of Independence. He had served as a diplomat, a governor, a secretary of state, and, under John Adams, as vice-president. Jefferson had also, with Madison, founded the Republic's first political party.

Jefferson had warned in earlier years about the presidency's becoming so strong as to threaten republican virtues. His Republican or Whig theories called for deference to Congress and for suspicion of executive power. But if these were his theories, as president he appears to have believed that the Republic, at a crucial stage of growth, demanded strong executive leadership.

Jefferson often acted as chief legislator as well as chief executive. More than his two predecessors, he initiated and personally pressed for legislative measures. Nor was he timid in his relations with the Court or in his use of military authority to protect or promote United States interests. Jefferson is remembered most for negotiating the Louisiana Purchase in 1803. Credit for this vast "gift" is due to Napoleon's vain ambitions and military adventures in Europe, yet Jefferson shrewdly capitalized on the situation. Although no one fully understood the exact boundaries, this purchase instantly doubled the land area of the United States, all for less than $15 million.

These negotiations and the purchase itself posed some constitutional questions. The authority to buy territory from foreign countries and simply to incorporate it into the new Republic is nowhere to be found among the enumerated powers either of the president or of Congress. Certain New England Federalists viewed this purchase as threatening their influence, and they argued that Jefferson's purchase violated the Constitution.

Even Jefferson expressed concerns about the constitutionality of the Louisiana Purchase. For a time he tried to design a constitutional amendment that might legitimize his action, but friends persuaded him to drop that idea. In the end, he convinced himself that he was clearly acting in the nation's best interests. Still, he wanted Congress to endorse what he had done, and, pointedly, he made no claims to find explicit constitutional authority for his action. In these actions, Jefferson in effect authorized what had come to be called a "loose construction," or even a rationalization, of the Constitution; he had earlier criticized Hamilton and the Federalists for a similar loose construction of the Constitution in the case of the establishment of a national bank.

Jefferson's advisors convinced him to play down his constitutional qualms about the purchase for fear that it might hinder negotiations with Napoleon or even encourage the French leader to change his mind. And as both Jefferson's advisors and his supporters in Congress argued, the Constitution nowhere specifies any boundaries on the country's frontiers; thus the government could not be limited by boundaries that were not clearly defined at the time the United States came into being. Jefferson doubtless acted on pragmatic grounds, justifying his action by saying that the larger our landmass in that area, the less it would be disrupted by local passions. Further, Jefferson said it was better that American citizens settle the opposite bank of the Mississippi than that strangers from foreign nations do so.

Jefferson's Louisiana Purchase suggests that the presidency and the American constitutional system have the flexibility to respond quickly to a challenge that was not spelled out by the framers. William Goldsmith has commented: "It is ironic that Jefferson was a protesting, and at least ideologically unwilling, participant in this act which had a lasting effect upon the growth of presidential power. Perhaps this irony can be explained by noting that Jefferson's instinct for political leadership usually triumphed when it came in conflict with his ideology."[31]

OTHER PRECEDENTS, OTHER CONTROVERSIES

Several presidencies later, Abraham Lincoln became president. His election gave him anything but a mandate to lead. He won less than 40 percent of the popular vote. And the votes were barely in when South Carolina seceded from the Union.

Lincoln had subscribed in general to the notions of limited presidential powers and to a presidency that was mainly responsive and subordinate to Congress. But when he was thrust into an unprecedented emergency, President Abraham Lincoln exercised decisive power. He stretched his executive power to save the Union.

If Lincoln in his younger days had been ambivalent about the scope of presidential executive power, his words in his First Inaugural Address suggested a broader approach: "The chief magistrate derives all his authority from the people. . . . His duty is to administer the present government, as it comes to his hands, and to transmit it, unimpaired by him, to his successor."[32]

Note how Lincoln looked at least as much to the people for legitimacy as he did to the Constitution or to Congress. Lincoln proclaimed a blockage of southern ports, called out thousands of troops, and suspended the right of habeas corpus—all of which probably violated the express intent of the Constitution. In each case Congress is usually supposed to act first on such matters.

Lincoln believed he was compelled to take whatever measures were needed to subdue the secessionists. On several occasions when he had to stretch, or go beyond, the Constitution, Lincoln thought measures that were otherwise unconstitutional might become lawful because they were indispensable to the preservation of the Union. Usually, however, Lincoln insisted that the Constitution did provide the necessary authority for his actions.

Invariably, if Lincoln acted before Congress could act, he later asked for its approval, and he usually received it. He never won the blessing of Chief Justice Roger B. Taney, however. Taney thought Lincoln's actions were illegal. Lincoln's response was: Are all the laws but one to go unexecuted and the government itself to go to pieces lest that one be violated?

Plainly, Lincoln stretched the emergency powers of the office, and many future presidents would point to his example for historical support to evade constitutional restraints on the presidency. Few presidents, however, would serve in such tumultuous times or enjoy the seeming popular acquiescence that sustained Lincoln's memorable and celebrated executive leadership.

Later presidents have withheld information from Congress, have sent military troops into other nations without having declared war, and have claimed the authority to terminate treaties with other nations. Congress has sometimes protested, yet time and again, the Supreme Court has either sided with the president's claims or refused to decide the issue. Occasionally, the Court or Congress has narrowed the scope of presidential power, but for almost 150 years, the executive power of the presidency has steadily expanded.

By the 1960s the federal bureaucracy had become so sprawling and entrenched in its relations with Congress and friendly clientele groups that the very bureaucracies that Woodrow Wilson, Franklin D. Roosevelt, and more recent presidents had fought to create often resisted direction from the White House.

In one of the paradoxical twists of American politics, the federal bureaucracy in several ways has become a force separate from and sometimes in competition with White House priorities. This is why FDR proposed and, with the approval of Congress, established the Executive Office of the President. At first an advisory agency of a few dozen assistants and budget analysts, it has grown to have a staff of more than two thousand, including the White House staff of at least five hundred.

Presidential decisions that are sent to the federal agencies and departments often have a way of getting watered down or ignored. The routines of governmental bureaucracies are geared to preserving the status quo. That's fine if a president merely wishes to maintain the status quo, but most presidents want to change at least some policies.

A president and his staff have to be extraordinarily clear in their policy directives. An aide to FDR once emphasized how even cabinet members sometimes ignore a president's request.

> Half of a President's suggestions, which theoretically carry the weight of orders, can be safely forgotten by a cabinet member. And if the President asks about a suggestion a second time, he can be told that it is being investigated. If he asks a third time a wise cabinet officer will give him at least part of what he suggests. But only occasionally, except about the most important matters, do Presidents even get around to asking three times.[33]

If that is what cabinet members do, what do you imagine remote career bureaucrats do? That's why presidents such as Nixon and Reagan have made efforts both to centralize decision making in the White House and to establish additional coordinating and clearance mechanisms—all to enable them to gain better control over their own administrative branch. Reagan, for example, in his first year in office, issued an executive order requiring that all regulations issued by executive departments and agencies be reviewed first by the Office of Management and Budget, in order to determine whether they conformed to White House priorities, as well as to consider, to the extent possible, whether their social costs would exceed their social benefits. This and related White House processes of clearance and approval, put into effect during the 1970s and the 1980s, have the effect of encouraging an even more highly institutionalized presidency.

The vast growth of the federal bureaucracy has had profound effects on our system of government. More people are now employed in our federal executive branch than existed in all the thirteen original states at the birth of the Republic.

Bureaucratization and the rise and expansion of the "Administrative State" have several, sometimes contradictory consequences. First, along with other social and economic forces, the administrative state necessitates an assertive, activist, and power-conscious presidency. Second, the sheer size, complexity, and organizationally diverse claims and priorities of the sprawling bureaucracy pose one of the most exacting burdens on a president. To control the bureaucracy and give it proper direction requires more energy and time than any president will ever have. This necessitates the expansion of the White House staff and related Executive Office "coordinating" teams. In effect, our presidents have created a vast personal bureaucracy to try to enable them to win the cooperation of the "permanent bureaucracy." Congress has acted in a similar manner; it has enlarged its staff fourfold during the past twenty-five years.

The job of the president of the United States as chief executive is different now from what it was two hundred years ago. The dynamics of American democracy increasingly revolve around the presidency in ways the framers could not have foreseen. But neither were political parties, nuclear wars, deficit spending, the welfare state, the warfare state, and countless other realities of modern American life anticipated by the framers of the Constitution.

While it can be said that the role of presidential leadership and the executive powers of the president in recent years differ from certain of the early expectations of the framers as to what the role ought to be in the governmental system, in fact the differences between the two are to some extent more in kind than degree. For despite certain opposing views and fears about the character and extent of presidential executive power, in general the framers agreed upon the need for a strong, independent executive. Much of what they created remains intact, and the executive powers of the president, even as they have become enlarged by usage and precedent, have stood the test of time. The Hamiltonian model of executive energy and broad interpretation of its powers, although modified on occasion, endures even as we approach the twenty-first century.

The enduring challenge for us today is to encourage the appropriate presidential leadership we need and simultaneously to strengthen the constitutional checks and balances necessary to ensure that our presidential form of government always remains accountable. We need to affirm our desire for a government by rule of law and not by self-proclaimed indispensable individuals.

NOTES

1. See, e.g., Raoul Berger, *Executive Privilege: A Constitutional Myth* (Cambridge, Mass.: Harvard University Press, 1974); David Gray Adler, "The President's War-Making Powers," above; Harvey Mansfield, Jr., "The Modern Doctrine of Executive Power," *Presidential Studies Quarterly* 17 (Spring 1987): 237–52; and Robert Scigliano, "The President's 'Prerogative Power,'" below.

2. Charles C. Thach, Jr., *The Creation of the Presidency, 1775–1789: A Study in Constitutional History* (Baltimore, Md.: Johns Hopkins Press, 1923), p. 62.

3. Joseph E. Kallenbach, *The American Chief Executive: The Presidency and the Governorship* (New York: Harper & Row, 1966), p. 56.

4. Alexander Hamilton, *Federalist* no. 76.

5. See Calvin MacKenzie et al., *The In and Outers: Presidential Appointees and the Problems of Transient Government in Washington* (Baltimore, Md.: Johns Hopkins University Press, 1987); Henry Abraham, *Justices and Presidents,* 2d ed. (New York: Oxford University Press, 1985); and Neil D. McFeeley, *Appointment of Judges: The Johnson Presidency* (Austin: University of Texas Press, 1987).

6. Kallenbach, *American Chief Executive,* p. 387; see also Louis Fisher, *The Politics of Shared Power: Congress and the Executive* (Washington, D.C.: Congressional Quarterly Press, 1981), pp. 5–6.

7. Gouverneur Morris, Constitutional Convention, Aug. 20, 1787, quoted by Wilbourne E. Benton, ed., in *1787: Drafting the U.S. Constitution,* vol. 2 (College Station: Texas A & M University Press, 1986), p. 1249.

8. Thach, *Creation of the Presidency,* p. 123.

9. Edward S. Corwin, *The President: Office and Powers, 1787–1957,* 4th rev. ed. (New York: New York University Press, 1957), p. 82.

10. Kallenbach, *American Chief Executive,* pp. 376–77.

11. Alexander Hamilton, *Federalist* no. 69.

12. This dilemma is well posed by David Gray Adler in "The President's Recognition Power," an unpublished paper, and by Louis Henkin, *Foreign Affairs and the Constitution* (Mineola, N.Y.: Foundation Press, 1972).

13. James Iredell, July 28, 1788, quoted by Philip B. Kurland and Ralph Lerner, eds., in *The Founders' Constitution,* 5 vols. (Chicago: University of Chicago Press, 1987), 4:12.

14. Ibid., p. 13.

15. Herbert Storing, *What the Anti-Federalists Were For* (Chicago: University of Chicago Press, 1981), p. 49.

16. Jackson Turner Main, *The Antifederalists: Critics of the Constitution, 1781–1788* (Chicago: Quadrangle Books, 1961), p. 142.

17. Ibid., p. 256.

18. Pierce Butler, delegate from South Carolina, in a letter to W. Butler, May 5, 1788, quoted by Thach in *Creation of the Presidency,* p. 169.

19. Richard Allan Baker, "The 'Great Departments': The Origins of the Federal Government's Executive Branch," *This Constitution,* no. 17 (Winter 1987): 11.

20. William M. Goldsmith, *The Growth of Presidential Power,* 3 vols. (New York: Chelsea House Publishers, 1974), 1:161.

21. Quoted by Thach in *Creation of the Presidency,* p. 152.

22. Ibid., p. 147.

23. Ibid., p. 153.

24. Taft opinion, *Myers* v. *U.S.,* 272 U.S. 52 (1926).

25. Louis Fisher, "Congress and the Removal Powers," *Congress and the Presidency* 10 (Spring 1983): 64. See also, for criticism of Taft's broad decision, Edward S. Corwin, "Tenure of Office and the Removal Power under the Constitution," *Columbia Law Review* 29 (Apr. 1927): 353–99.

26. Edward S. Corwin, "The President as Administrative Chief," in *Presidential Power and the Constitution: Essays by Edward S. Corwin,* ed. Richard Loss (Ithaca, N.Y.: Cornell University Press, 1976), p. 102.

27. Fisher, "Congress and the Removal Power," p. 76.

28. See, e.g., Thomas P. Slaughter, *The Whiskey Rebellion* (New York: Oxford University Press, 1986); see also Forrest McDonald, *The Presidency of George Washington* (Lawrence: University Press of Kansas, 1974), pp. 145–47.

29. Kallenbach, *American Chief Executive,* p. 453.

30. Quoted by Richard B. Morris, in *Great Presidential Decisions* (New York: Perennial Library, 1973), p. 24.

31. Goldsmith, *Growth of Presidential Power,* p. 447.

32. Lincoln, First Inaugural Address, from Carl Sandburg, *Abraham Lincoln: The War Years,* vol. 3 (New York: Charles Scribners', 1946), p. 133.

33. Jonathan Daniels, *Frontiers on the Potomac* (New York: Macmillan, 1946), pp. 31–32.

8

THE PRESIDENT'S PARDON POWER

DAVID GRAY ADLER

> The President . . . shall have Power to grant Reprieves and Pardons for Offences against the United States, except in Cases of Impeachment.
>
> —*Article II, section 2*

The authority to grant pardons, the roots of which are traced to the royal prerogative of the king of England, is perhaps the most imperial and probably the most delicate of a president's powers. A presidential pardon prevents the punishment of a person who has committed an offense against the United States. Mindful of the fact that the impeachment exception is the only explicit textual limitation on the exercise of the power, commentators have described the authority as "unqualified," "unfettered," and immune to the doctrine of checks and balances. The Supreme Court, in dictum, has called this power "unlimited" in scope.[1] The apparently untrammeled power always has carried with it a great potential for abuse. The framers of the Constitution were steeped in English history; the king frequently used pardons as partisan indulgences for friends and supporters. In spite of their familiarity with absolutist Stuart claims and their fear of a power-hungry executive with a proclivity for usurpation, the framers opted, by the pardon clause, to vest the president with a broad discretion to correct miscarriages of justice and to restore tranquillity in the wake of rebellion. The decision to create a pardon power thus recognized the possibility of judicial errors and made it possible to temper justice.

While considerable in scope and virtually unfettered in its exercise, the pardon authority, nevertheless, is subject to some restraints. The framers' decision to make the presidency the repository of this discretion reflected their confidence in the availability of the impeachment power as a means of preventing the executive from abusing the pardon power. Consistent with this reasoning the Supreme Court has held that the excessive abuse of the pardon authority would be an impeachable offense, and the Court has declared its willingness to invoke judicial review to restrain the administration of the power.[2] Further, there are strong practical considerations that would urge against viewing the power as unlimited. The claim of an illimitable, unchecked power is alien to a nation committed to the rule of law and to a Constitution that was designed to corral all governmental authority and to prevent the exercise of arbitrary power. The specter of a president who would open the jailhouse doors, pardon political cronies for illegal covert operations, cut deals to aggrandize his own power—in short, rampage at will because he is the final judge of the boundaries of his powers—is a nightmare sufficient in itself to justify institutional restraints. Finally, the court of public opinion carries its own sanction, a fact that former President Gerald Ford became painfully aware of. His generic pardon of Richard Nixon "for all offenses against the United States which he . . . has committed or may have committed or taken part in" during the course of his presidency riveted the attention of the nation on the breadth of the pardon power in a way that surpassed the intensity of public interest in other pardons, before or since, and possibly cost Ford the 1976 presidential election.[3] Indeed, Ford's controversial act seemed to invite Justice John McLean's condemnation in 1855 of an uncurbed pardon power: "Who can forsee the excitements and convulsions which may arise in our future history. The struggle may be between a usurping Executive and an incensed people."[4]

The constitutional grant of power to issue pardons has, then, occasionally engendered controversy. The exercise of the authority during and after the Civil War, President Warren G. Harding's pardon of Eugene Debs, Ford's pardon of Nixon, and the speculation in 1988 of a pardon for those who had been indicted on charges stemming from their involvement in the Iran-Contra affair—all have excited discussion and drawn scholarly inquiry. Important questions remain: What is the scope of the pardon power? Is a pardon restricted to postconviction acts? May a preconviction pardon be granted? Are there institutional checks on the power, and, if so, how practical and extensive are they? In order to better understand the place of the pardon power in the constitutional scheme and its potential for the future, these and other questions deserve close scrutiny.

DEFINING THE TERMS

By Article II, section 2, the Constitution confers upon the president the power "to grant reprieves and pardons." The English common-law meaning and compass of these terms was adopted by the Constitutional Convention, and the Supreme Court has stated on numerous occasions that its interpretation of the pardon clause is guided by that understanding. A reprieve is a temporary postponement of the execution of a court's sentence. Generally speaking, the purpose of a presidential reprieve is to allow time for the executive branch to investigate and consider a request for a pardon.[5] The essential characteristic of a full pardon is its preclusion of the punishment that has been imposed or that might be imposed on those persons who have been convicted or who might be convicted of a crime. In 1866, in *Ex parte Garland,* the Supreme Court, drawing from the deep well of English legal history, described a pardon as making a "new man" of the offender: "A pardon reaches both the punishment prescribed for the offense and the guilt of the offender; . . . it releases the punishment and blots out of existence guilt, so that in the eye of the law the offender is as innocent as if he had never committed the offense. . . . It removes the penalties and disabilities, and restores him to all his civil rights; it makes him, as it were, a new man, and gives him a new credit and capacity."[6] While the grant of a pardon may "blot out" guilt, it does not mean that the recipient is innocent of the charges against him; indeed, it is generally held that the acceptance of a "pardon" is an admission of guilt. There are, of course, numerous reasons for granting a pardon, but two broad rationales have dominated our jurisprudence. In 1833, Chief Justice John Marshall emphasized the English view when he stated that "a pardon is an act of grace." But Justice Oliver Wendell Holmes, in 1927, rejected that characterization; he regarded it as "the determination of the ultimate authority that the public welfare will be better served by inflicting less than what the judgment fixed."[7] But these rationales are not mutually exclusive; President Ford invoked both in the explanation of his pardon to former President Nixon. Regardless of whether a pardon is granted on grounds of mercy or public interest, it has been established that it may be "conditioned" by particular requirements or duties, so long as the conditions themselves are not unconstitutional.

The pardon clause also encompasses amnesties and commutations. Amnesties are general pardons that are either full or conditional in character; they may be granted either by the president or by Congress to exempt from prosecution or punishment an entire class of citizens. For example, on December 8, 1863, President Abraham Lincoln issued a pardon "to all persons who have, directly or by implication, participated in the existing rebellion."[8] A commutation is a reduction of judicial sentence, which means that a president will substitute a less severe punishment for the one imposed by the court. Thus, a president might commute a death-penalty sentence for one of life imprisonment.

The president's power to grant pardons extends to "Offences against the United States, except in Cases of Impeachment." The impeachment exception is discussed below, but its purpose was evidently twofold: (1) to prevent a presidential pardon from interfering with impeachment proceedings and (2) to ensure that an impeached official could not be restored to his position by presidential pardon. Presumably, "offences," which were virtually synonymous with crimes in English law, must have been committed before a pardon could be granted. Otherwise, the issuance of a pardon in the anticipation of an offense would amount to a power to dispense with the law, a claim made by King James II that led to his forced abdication. The "offences" phrase seems implicitly to limit the pardon authority to federal, as opposed to state, crimes. Moreover, consistent with English law, the phrase, according to the Court, includes criminal but not civil contempts of court, as well as rebellions or insurrections.[9]

THE PARDON PROCESS

The administration of the pardon authority is housed in the Department of Justice. The president looks to the attorney general for advice on all matters concerning executive clemency. The latter officer, in turn, depends upon the Office of the Pardon Attorney, which was established by an act of Congress on March 3, 1891, to prepare cases for the president to consider.[10] In effect, the pardon attorney supervises the five stages involved in the process: application, investigation, preparation, consideration and action, and notification. In brief, the pardon attorney receives and reviews all petitions for executive clemency, including applications for full and unconditional pardons, conditional pardons, and commutations of sentences, among others. An inquiry is then initiated which involves consultation with a number of people, including the sentencing judge, the prosecuting attorney, probation personnel, employers and friends, and an examination of all pertinent documents, records, and other materials. The pardon attorney's recommendation is then made to the attorney general, who considers the case and makes his own recommendation to the president. The attorney general's opinion carries great weight with the president, although some presidents, such as Andrew Johnson, have often insisted on reviewing the requests themselves.[11] In any event, a number of factors, including political considerations, will be weighed in the evaluation process.

ENGLISH ORIGINS

Executive mercy is to be found in ancient Mosaic, Greek, and Roman law; it was introduced into English jurisprudence in the seventh century. According to Sir William Blackstone, the king's first assertion of his grand role as the "fountain of justice" was made by King Ine of Wessex (A.D. 688–726) with the statutory provision that "if anyone fights in the king's house, let him be liable in all his property, and be it in the king's doom whether he shall or shall not have life." Given the king's role as "general conservator of the peace of the kingdom" and the fact that all "offenses are either against the king's peace or his crown and dignity," it is the king who is injured in the eyes of the law by fighting in his house. As Blackstone observed, "It is reasonable that he only who is injured should have the power of forgiving."[12]

The historical record suggests, however, that the grant of a pardon was not so much an act of grace or charitable mercy as it was the tool of pecuniary and political aggrandizement. From the outset, the pardon power was abused for personal gain. A pardon, for example, frequently required the payment of a fee. Those unable to afford a pardon were forced to flee the kingdom and as a consequence became "outlaws." Occasionally, kings were more generous and offered deferred-payment plans. Under Edward I, it became customary, upon a declaration of war, to exercise the pardon power as an instrument of conscription. In return for a year's service, general pardons were granted to those who had committed felonies and homicides. Evidently, pardons were so easily obtainable for persons who had committed such crimes as homicide, larceny, and robbery that law-abiding subjects who had "accused them do not dare remain in their country for fear of those robbers, and many refrain from bringing accusations for this reason."[13] On the whole, pardons were issued for rather arbitrary and irrelevant reasons, and rarely were the benefits of the power made available to persons who had erroneously been condemned to death.

The systematic abuse of the pardon power, upon the flimsiest of pretexts, provoked several formal complaints from Parliament, which feared for its statutes and petitioned the king to exercise the power with more restraint. Parliament also attempted to curtail by statute the abuses of the pardoning power, but to no avail. While its record was littered with defeats, Parliament could, nevertheless, lay claim to at least one important accomplishment. In 1389, under Richard II, Parliament enacted a statute that forbade the issue of pardons in the case of serious crimes unless the pardon specified the nature of the crime and contained the name of the culprit. While this principle was frequently violated, it has remained a part of the law of pardons. With this exception, then, the king's authority to pardon, like most of his powers, remained virtually absolute. Limitations on it would require the legal and political convulsions of the seventeenth century.[14]

The bold attempt by Charles II to use the pardon power as a means to preempt the impeachment in 1678 of Thomas Osborne, the earl of Danby, lord high treasurer of England from 1673 to 1679, triggered a constitutional crisis. The House of Commons had resolved to impeach Danby of high treason and other crimes and misdemeanors for having empowered the English minister at the Court of Versailles to make an offer of neutrality between France and Holland. Just five days before, Parliament had passed an act to raise supplies for carrying on the war with France. On the day Danby was called to answer the charges in the House of Commons, he pleaded for a royal pardon from Charles that dismissed all offenses against him. In a century replete with constitutional crises between the Commons and the Crown, here, suddenly, was yet another: May a royal pardon prevent an impeachment? On numerous occasions during the preceding centuries, Parliament had attempted to restrain the prerogative, but it had always failed. But for members of the Commons who viewed the impeachment power as a means of bringing corrupt ministers to heel and, more importantly, as "the chief institution for the preservation of the government," the act of executive clemency could not be tolerated. As one member stated: "It was for the safety of the King and the nation, that a minister be afraid of this House."[15] Concerns were voiced, moreover, that a pardon before trial would stifle testimony and therefore bury the facts surrounding the plot. "When a man comes to be tried, then is his proper time to plead his Pardon. This man must come to be tried, to show the world how ill a minister he has been to the King." At all events, it was assumed that a thorough investigation would serve the people. Ultimately, a committee of Commons decided to rest on the absence of precedent for a pardon to bar impeachment, and it resolved "that the pardon pleaded by the Earl of Danby is illegal and void, and ought not to be allowed in bar of impeachment of the Commons of England."[16]

The constitutional question of the scope of the pardon power was not resolved by the crisis, for Charles prorogued Parliament, and the impeachment effort was not revived. The king did not want to lose his trusted aide, but "Danby was not worth another civil war." Therefore, in spite of the pardon, Danby spent five years in the Tower of London, without trial. But in the wake of the Danby affair, it became clear that the institution of an impeachment could not be impeded by a pardon. Had Danby's pardon been accepted, the pretended accountability of the ministers would have ceased, for the king would have been free to exercise the prerogative to screen them from inquiry by Parliament. The question of whether a royal pardon may bar impeachment was finally settled in 1700 by the Act of Settlement, which declared "that no pardon under the great seal of England [shall] be pleadable to an impeachment by the Commons in Parliament."[17] The right of the Crown to grant reprieves or pardons after sentencing was left intact. The act, then, effectuated the arguments and sentiments of the Commons as expressed during the impeachment of Danby. Both the act and those arguments, moreover, had a direct influence on the framers' design of the pardon clause.

PARDONING POWER IN THE UNITED STATES

The English practice was constantly before the eyes of those who drafted the state constitutions during the Revolutionary War period. For most states, it was the norm: a pardon may not be pleaded to bar impeachment. Exceptions to this practice were more restrictive of the governor's pardoning authority. According to the Georgia Constitution of 1777, the governor was strictly forbidden from issuing pardons. The Massachusetts Constitution of 1780 permitted pardons only after convictions and put impeachments beyond their reach. The Pennsylvania Constitution of 1776 likewise denied authority to grant pardons for impeachment and, like the New York Constitution of 1777, also precluded pardons for treason and murder, for which the governor could grant reprieves until the legislature should convene. The New Hampshire Constitution of 1784 vested the pardoning power exclusively in the legislature.[18]

The pervasive suspicion of executive power during the founding period, as well as the abuse of the pardon authority in England, understandably led the states to place sharp limitations on the scope of executive clemency. The states employed different methods, of course, and it was to be expected that these various prescriptions would be debated in the Constitutional Convention.

The Virginia Plan and the New Jersey Plan, the initial draft documents that served as the foundation for the debates at the convention, omitted any reference to the pardon power. On May 29, 1787, Charles Pinckney of South Carolina submitted a proposal that the executive "shall have power to grant pardons and reprieves except in impeachments," thus duplicating the English practice. Pinckney's plan framed the context for the debate on the pardon authority, one that focused primarily on the scope of the president's power to pardon. Once introduced into discussion, the impeachment exception was virtually taken for granted and thereafter all but ignored. On August 6, John Rutledge of South Carolina read to the convention the report of the Committee of Detail: "He shall have power to grant reprieves and pardons; but his pardon shall not be pleadable in bar of impeachment." The report, of course, echoed Pinckney's proposal, and it was not opposed. In fact, there was no further discussion about the impeachment exception for the remainder of the convention. But the framers' silence on this matter is not at all surprising. Their high regard for and their confidence in the impeachment power as an instrument for preserving republican government and restraining ambitious executives were bolstered by their familiarity with King Charles II's use of the pardon to thwart the impeachment of Danby. There was no desire among the framers to vest the president with a power that had been denied to the king. Moreover, the state constitutions, with which the delegates were familiar, had consistently embraced the English practice. In short, it was from the outset virtually self-evident that the pardon power would not apply to cases of impeachment. Given the framers' understanding of impeachment as the Grand Inquest of the Nation, "it is of great consequence," wrote Justice Joseph Story, "that the president should not have the power of preventing a thorough investigation of their [public officials'] conduct, or of securing them against the disgrace of a public conviction by impeachment, if they should deserve it."[19]

The question of whether the president should be empowered to grant pardons for treason was particularly troublesome for the framers, and it provoked an impassioned debate on the scope of the pardon authority that was not resolved until the last days of the convention. On June 17, 1787, in a lengthy address to his fellow delegates, Alexander Hamilton of New York said the executive should "have the power of pardoning all offenses except treason; which he shall not pardon without the approbation of the Senate." On September 10, Edmund Randolph of Virginia reiterated Hamilton's concern about excluding pardons for treason. Randolph had grave reservations about "the unqualified power of the president to pardon treasons." He believed if this and other defects remained uncorrected, the proposed system would end in tyranny. Five days later, Randolph moved to amend the pardon power to exclude cases of treason. In rhetoric that stirred images of a presidential coup, he warned: "The prerogative of pardon in these cases was too great a Trust. The President may himself be guilty. The Traytors may be his own instruments." Randolph's motion was supported by George Mason of Virginia, who had earlier recorded his objections to the inclusion of treasonous acts in words that sharply echoed the concerns of the Commons a century before: "[It] may be sometimes exercised to screen from punishment those whom he had secretly instigated to commit the crime, and thereby prevent a discovery of his own guilt."

Against this nightmare, the subversion of the Republic by pardons, James Wilson of Pennsylvania, who was second in importance to Madison as an architect of the Constitution, adduced the necessity of the availability of pardons for acts of treason and said this power ought to be vested in the president. If the president were involved in the treason, he could be "impeached and prosecuted."[20] Apparently, this rationale, which Madison embraced in the Virginia ratifying convention as a means of assuaging Mason's fears, turned the tide; Randolph's motion to exempt treason from the scope of the power was defeated. Wilson had alleviated the convention's concerns by offering impeachment as a remedy for the abuse of the pardon power in cases of treason. In speaking of treason, he was undoubtedly referring to presidential involvement in a rebellion against the United States, that is, the act of levying war against the country, which is the embodiment of treason. In *Federalist* number 74, Hamilton elaborated on this theme and said the principal reason for vesting the pardon authority in the president was to enable him to grant pardons in order to halt rebellions: "In seasons of insurrection or rebellion, there are often critical moments, when a well-timed offer of pardon to the insurgents or rebels may restore the tranquillity of the commonwealth; and which, if suffered to pass unimproved, it may never be possible afterwards to recall." From history and firsthand experience in the form of Shays's Rebellion in Massachusetts, the framers had learned the value of a well-aimed and well-timed pardon. They knew that men might be seduced by a rebellion but after a period of reflection might be willing to lay down their arms in exchange for executive clemency. The availability of the power and the timing of its exercise were critical. It might be possible, thought Justice James Iredell, to "prevent a Civil War" by using the power. Without the authority, however, the insurgents might just "as well die in the field as at the gallows."[21]

In the end, in spite of their grave concerns, the framers could not bring themselves to fashion an exception for treason. Their failure to exempt treason as well as impeachment makes a powerful argument that the president was vested with a virtually untrammeled power to pardon. The upshot of their deliberations was that they chose to follow the English practice.

What, then, persuaded the founders—a generation that lived in dread of an expansive, undefined executive power—to vest in one man a seemingly unbridled authority with potentially disastrous implications for the nation? From the framers' perspective, the exercise of the power itself provided sufficient restraints on the president. In *Federalist* number 74, Hamilton stated: "As the sense of responsibility is always strongest, in proportion as it is undivided, it may be inferred that a single man would be most ready to attend to the force of those motives which might plead for a mitigation of the rigor of the law, and least apt to yield to considerations which were calculated to shelter a fit object of its vengeance. The reflection that the fate of a fellow-creature depended on his *sole fiat,* would naturally inspire scrupulousness and caution; the dread of being accused of weakness or connivance, would beget equal circumspection, though of a different kind."

There are three other factors that must be considered. First, as Hamilton explained, a timely pardon might be issued as a means to quell rebellion and help restore domestic tranquillity. Second, there was a centuries-old understanding of the pardon power as an instrument to overcome the failings of the criminal-justice system. It may occasionally occur that the judicial process works an injustice, as it does, for example, in cases in which peculiar or mitigating circumstances are ignored. In cases in which it is necessary to mitigate miscarriages of justice, executive clemency is available. As Hamilton explained in *Federalist* number 74: "The criminal code of every country partakes so much of necessary severity, that without an easy access to exceptions in favor of unfortunate guilt, justice would wear a countenance too sanguinary and cruel." Finally, every warning that a president might use the pardon power to exonerate accomplices, to forestall investigations, and generally to subvert law and government was met with assurances that the threat of impeachment—"the terror of punishment"—would prevent such misconduct. The threat of impeachment, then, was viewed as an important security, the ultimate safeguard against the abuse of the pardon power. What Iredell said generally about the impact of the instrument has particular application to the framers' concerns about the pardon authority: "If this power were not provided, the consequences might be fatal. It will be not only the means of punishing misconduct, but it will prevent misconduct."[22]

PRACTICE

Presidents have granted pardons for various offenses since the dawn of the Republic. George Washington initiated the use of the pardon authority in 1795 when he issued a proclamation of amnesty to participants in the Whisky Rebellion. Since then, pirates who have assisted United States military causes, participants in insurrections, deserters, federal officials, and polygamists, among others, have received clemency. An occasional pardon—to Jefferson Davis and the confederate soldiers or to Richard Nixon, for example—has excited intense controversy and heightened public interest in the power; but a great many pardons have been issued without fanfare to federal prisoners who have reached the late stages of their lives and are near death.[23] The frequency and volume of pardons granted, moreover, are perhaps greater than most Americans would suppose. During the Civil War and its aftermath, some 200,000 persons benefited from amnesties issued by Presidents Abraham Lincoln and Andrew Johnson. Johnson granted an additional 13,500 pardons to those who were not embraced by the amnesty programs. In 1933, President Franklin D. Roosevelt exercised the power to restore the civil rights of about 1,500 persons who had completed prison terms for violating the draft and the Espionage Acts during World War I, and in 1945 he restored citizenship rights to several thousand former convicts who had served at least one year in the military and subsequently had earned an honorable discharge. In 1946, President Harry Truman granted pardons to more than 1,500 people who had been sentenced to prison for violating the Selective Service Act, and on Christmas Day, 1952, he restored civil rights to 9,000 people who had been convicted of desertion during peacetime. In addition to the more than 10,000 beneficiaries of the Vietnam clemency and amnesty programs of Presidents Gerald Ford and Jimmy Carter, some 4,600 pardons and 500 commutations were granted between 1953 and 1984 by presidents from Dwight D. Eisenhower to Ronald Reagan.[24] President Reagan issued about 380 pardons during his eight years in the White House.

Until the Civil War, the exercise of the pardoning authority had not provoked controversy or question. But the stresses of that war, the vindictive mood of many Northerners, and the desire for retribution among some in Congress collided with the rather "lenient" clemency programs of Lincoln and Johnson. There were other grounds for concern about the use of the power. Some members of Congress objected to the inconsistent consideration of requests for pardons and to the preferential treatment accorded to Kentuckians; the influence peddling of pardon brokers; and the insincerity of the recipients, who were required to take a loyalty oath to the Union. Congress even undertook an examination of Johnson's bank account pursuant to allegations that he had been bribed to issue pardons. To some Americans, it seemed that the administration of the pardon power was as arbitrary as it had been in England. As a consequence of these and other factors, Congress launched a challenge to the "president's" pardon authority and attempted to limit it through legislation. In 1862, Congress passed a statute that "authorized" the president to issue amnesties. But since Lincoln and Johnson believed the Constitution empowered the president to issue amnesties, they regarded the act as meaningless and made no reference to it in granting clemency. In 1867, Congress responded by enacting legislation that annulled the political benefits of the pardons already extended by denying recipients the rights to vote, hold office, and own property. The conflict hinged on the severity of punishment to be inflicted on the confederates, and it required the intervention of the Supreme Court on two occasions. In both *Ex parte Garland* and *Klein* v. *United States,* the Court ruled that the president's pardon power could not be restricted by legislation.[25]

President Warren G. Harding's commutation on December 23, 1921, of the sentences of the famed labor organizer and Socialist Eugene V. Debs and twenty-three other political prisoners provided a happy conclusion to the widespread efforts of those who had campaigned for Debs's release for more than two years. In a speech on June 15, 1918, in Canton, Ohio, Debs had attacked the draft for World War I, condemned capitalist exploitation in general and war profiteers in particular, and supported the Bolshevik Revolution. For this speech he was indicted for violating the Espionage Act of 1917 on grounds that he was trying to obstruct the draft. Although he claimed he was only exercising his First Amendment right to free speech, the Supreme Court in 1919, in an opinion by Justice Oliver Wendell

Holmes, upheld Debs's conviction and sentence to ten years in prison. A campaign for clemency, which consisted of a group of prowar former Socialists, including some supporters of President Woodrow Wilson, petitioned Attorney General A. Mitchell Palmer for a pardon. One might have supposed that the progressive president would warm to the request. But Wilson, who was fighting the war to "make the world safe for democracy," would not abide the leftist assault from Debs. Wilson refused the request, saying: "While the flower of American youth was pouring out its blood to vindicate the cause of civilization, this man, Debs, stood behind the lines, sniping, attacking, and denouncing them. . . . This man was a traitor to his country and he will never be pardoned during my administration."[26]

It remains one of the rich ironies in the history of the pardon power that while a liberal Democratic president refused clemency for Debs, a deeply conservative Republican president granted it. In his campaign for the presidency in 1920, Harding supported amnesty for political prisoners on a case-by-case basis. He pursued this platform plank when, in a highly unusual act in March 1921, his attorney general, Harry M. Daugherty, instructed the warden of the prison in Atlanta, where Debs was being held, to place Debs on a train and send him to Washington, D.C. Debs rode alone and unguarded; then he spent a day with Daugherty and other administration officials, whom he deeply impressed. By the fall, the campaign for clemency had amassed about three hundred thousand signatures and the endorsement of seven hundred organizations. When Harding commuted Debs's sentence, he attached a condition: Debs was to travel to Washington to see Harding. The president wanted to meet the famous dissident.

The exercise of the pardon power and the consideration of its use in more recent times have perhaps excited more public dissatisfaction with and curiosity in the scope of the power and its political and legal dimensions than at any other point in our history. In particular, Americans have witnessed the possibility that President Nixon might pardon himself and more than thirty aides involved in Watergate offenses, the unconditional pardon that President Ford granted to Nixon, and in the late 1980s, the prospect that Ronald Reagan or George Bush might pardon Lt. Col. Oliver North and his codefendants for charges stemming from their role in the Iran-Contra debacle. These episodes have revealed the darker ways in which a power to temper justice with mercy might be transformed into a political tool to be exploited and abused for partisan causes.

As the Nixon White House began to collapse under the crushing weight of Watergate, the president and those involved in the various criminal offenses related to the break-in and cover-up feared for their futures, which likely included prison terms, and they looked to the pardon authority as the solution to their problems. As early as January 1973, Nixon began discussions with advisors about using executive clemency to buy the silence of the Watergate defendants. H. R. Haldeman, Nixon's one-time chief of staff, persistently sought a pardon, first for himself and then for others involved in Watergate. Finally, he advocated a general amnesty for the Watergate defendants and those who had violated the Vietnam War selective-service laws. In a formal proposal to Nixon, Haldeman explained the political advantages of his plan in terms both self-serving and cynical:

> On a personal basis, better to close the chapter now than to have to sit by helplessly for the next several years and watch trials and appeals.
>
> Historically—would be far better to grant the pardon and close the door to such process than to let it run and have the trials become a surrogate impeachment. Also, history will look kindly on loyalty and compassion to subordinates caught in the web.
>
> Solves problem of potential prosecutor access to files and tapes by eliminating basis for further prosecution—also solves problem of defense forcing access to files.
>
> The only way to wipe the slate clean is to shut down the prosecution totally. As long as it is there, there is a possibility of other new things.
>
> To avoid trauma of country, injustice to defendants, personal problems to RN, adverse historical effects—all point to necessity of overall pardon.[27]

Haldeman's invocation of the pardon power "to shut down the prosecution" certainly gives credence to the fears, expressed two centuries earlier by several framers and ratifiers, that the power would be abused precisely for this reason. Such a cynical exercise of the power, George Mason had warned, would "screen from punishment those whom he [the president] had secretly instigated to commit the crime, and thereby prevent a discovery of his own guilt." To Alexander M. Haig, Jr., who had succeeded Haldeman as chief of staff, Haldeman's letter seemed to threaten Nixon with prison if Nixon did not pardon Haldeman. Haig characterized the request as "blackmail"; nevertheless, he asked the White House lawyers if all the Watergate defendants could be pardoned. Leonard Garment, a member of the legal team, described the possibility as "grotesque. . . . Pardons would be outside the system. It would be saying to hell with the system, with justice. . . . [Moreover] If the President grants this pardon, he will be insuring his own trial. He will be forcing it. The public has to have a head, and if the President takes the heads away the public will have his."[28] Garment added that while the president might technically have the legal authority to provide blanket clemency, he doubted that Nixon retained the political power necessary to pardon his old friends and aides. While the subject of limitations on the pardon power is discussed below, it is worth noticing that Garment seemed to imply the existence of certain limits by virtue of his allusion to an impeachment trial should Nixon grant the group pardon. Then, too, if there are no legal limitations on the pardon power, why should Garment have been concerned that Nixon lacked the political strength to pardon his cronies?

In the end, President Nixon did not issue any pardons to those involved in Watergate, not even to himself. But on September 8, 1974, President Gerald Ford granted "a full, free and absolute pardon unto Richard Nixon for all offenses against the United States which he, Richard Nixon, has committed or may have committed or taken part in during the period from January 20, 1969 through August 9, 1974."[29]

The American people had not expected this bombshell. At his confirmation hearings after his nomination to the vice-presidency, Ford had said that a pardon for Nixon probably would not be tolerated by the public. Moreover, after his elevation to the presidency, Ford stated in a press conference on August 28, 1974, that the question of a pardon, while still open, was premature: "I've asked for prayers for guidance on this very important point. In this situation I am the final authority. There have been no changes made. There has been no action by the court. There's been no action by any jury, and until any legal process has been undertaken, I think it's unwise and untimely for me to make any commitment." For many, the pardon was difficult to reconcile with Ford's earlier deference both to public opinion and to the judicial system. On what grounds, therefore, was the pardon explicable? Congress wanted answers, and Ford appeared before the House Judiciary Committee. Congresswoman Elizabeth Holtzman (D, N.Y.) posed the question that the nation wanted answered: Had a deal been struck? Ford reassured the committee: "There was no deal, period. . . . There never was at any time any agreement whatsoever concerning a pardon to Mr. Nixon if he were to resign and I were to become President."[30]

With a stroke of his pen, President Ford placed Nixon beyond the reach of the criminal-justice system. He had granted the pardon, he explained, as an act of mercy to Nixon, a man who had spent most of his adult life in public service and whose health was then threatened by the "common knowledge that serious allegations and accusations hang like a sword over our former president's head"; and for the broader purpose of restoring domestic tranquillity by putting Watergate behind the nation. Ford was convinced of the propriety of his act, but he knew the political costs would be high, both for himself and for his party. Opposition ran high. Within one week of the pardon, Ford's standing in public-opinion polls had plummeted from 71 to 49 percent. By a vote of 55 to 24, the Senate passed a resolution opposing any more pardons for Watergate defendants until all appeals had been exhausted. To make matters worse, the resolution was supported by the minority leader, Hugh Scott, and the assistant minority leader, Robert P. Griffin, both of whom were close friends of Ford's. Moreover, Ford's press secretary resigned in disgust. And during his travels, Ford frequently was met by an irate public that believed a conspiracy had been mounted by Ford and Nixon. All of this led the new president to wonder "whether, instead of healing wounds, my decision had only rubbed salt in them."[31] The pardon haunted Ford throughout the remainder of his presidency and, in all likelihood, doomed his chances for election to that office. Perhaps, as he said, Ford pardoned Nixon to end the nation's long nightmare. But as Philip Kurland, a professor of law at the University of Chicago, has justly concluded, Ford "had salvaged not the country, but the Watergate President."[32]

In the wake of the indictments on March 16, 1988, of Lt. Col. Oliver North, Rear Adm. John M. Poindexter, retired Gen. Richard V. Secord, and Albert Hakim, a businessman, on charges of conspiring to defraud the United States by illegally providing Nicaraguan rebels with profits from the sale of United States weapons to Iran, speculation by the press and public was running high that the codefendants would be pardoned by President Reagan, if not before their trial, then surely afterward. A pretrial pardon seemed unlikely if only because it would hand the Democratic party a red-hot weapon to use against the Republicans in the November elections. Moreover, a *New York Times*–CBS poll, conducted between March 19 and 22, revealed that 64 percent of the public was firmly opposed to a pretrial pardon, with only 27 percent in support of it. But when asked whether the codefendants should be pardoned if found guilty, those who were polled were equally divided, 43 to 43 percent. Proponents of a pardon said North and company were good men who had served the president faithfully and honorably and who believed they were implementing the president's foreign-policy wishes. Moreover, the codefendants had been serving the national interest when they defied the congressional ban on military assistance to the Nicaraguan rebels and then deceived Congress about their "enterprise." As such, they were patriots, and patriots should not be imprisoned. Opponents contended that North and Poindexter had shown utter contempt for the American people, the political system, and the rule of law. They had subverted the Constitution by establishing a shadow government to conduct an unlawful foreign policy that they knew not only circumvented the doctrine of checks and balances but was also anathema to the Congress that had banned military aid to the contras. When the story broke in November 1986, North had shredded critical National Security Council documents, altered others, and continued his pattern of deceit. He had thus willfully obstructed justice.[33]

For reasons that only Reagan will be able to explain, he decided not to pardon Oliver North. Perhaps it was because Reagan hoped North would be acquitted and no pardon would be needed. But North was convicted in mid 1989, and again this triggered speculation about a pardon from President Bush. Once more the country was divided on the question.

LIMITATIONS

Befitting its royal heritage, the presidential pardoning power is subject to few constitutional restraints, and only then in rare and unlikely circumstances. In theory, judicial review and impeachment are available to restrain the pardon power, but in practice they are not apt to be invoked unless the president abuses the power excessively or otherwise administers it in a grossly arbitrary manner. Contrary, therefore, to Supreme Court dictum and scholarly assertions of an illimitable power to pardon, there are boundaries that fence about the exercise of executive clemency. Nevertheless, it is easier to speak of abuses, as opposed to illegal uses, of the pardon authority. The principal restriction on the power remains political, to be exercised by Americans on election day.

Role of the Judiciary

It has been assumed that the president's power to pardon is beyond the reach of the judiciary. This assumption has been fed by Supreme Court dictum in 1866 in *Ex parte Garland,* in which Justice Stephen J. Field stated: "The power thus conferred is unlimited, with the exception stated [impeachment]. It extends to every offense known to the law, and may be exercised at any time after its commission, either before legal proceedings are taken, or during their pendency, or after conviction and judgment."[34]

This sweeping language had nothing to do with the issue in *Garland.* In 1860, Augustus H. Garland had been admitted to practice before the Supreme Court. Subsequently, he joined the confederate cause during the Civil War, for which he was granted a pardon in July 1865 from President Johnson that allowed him to resume practice before the Court. But there was an obstacle in his path: Congress had passed the Test Oath Act on January 24, 1865, which required attorneys who practiced before the Court to take a loyalty oath. Garland contended that Congress lacked the authority to restrict the pardon he had been granted by the president. In addressing the sole issue of the case, Justice Field held for the Court: "This power of the President is not subject to legislative control. Congress can neither limit the effect of his pardon, nor exclude from its exercise any class of offenders. The benign prerogative of mercy reposed in him cannot be fettered by any legislative restrictions."[35]

While the Court said the presidential power cannot be shackled by the statutory authority of Congress, it said nothing about immunity from judicial review. Moreover, subsequent cases have mitigated the opinion by ruling that Congress shares with the president the power to grant amnesties.[36] Most important, the *Garland* dictum about illimitability has been swept away by Supreme Court rulings that have asserted that the pardon power is subject to judicial review.

In 1925, in *Ex parte Grossman,* Chief Justice Taft allowed for the possibility that excessive abuses of the pardoning power might provoke a test of its validity in federal court, but he noted that sufficient abuses had not yet occurred.[37] In 1974, in *Shick* v. *Reed,* Chief Justice Warren E. Burger stated that under the "right" circumstances, at least, conditions to pardons could be declared invalid.[38]

Grossman and *Shick* established a foundation, however slim, for judicial review of the pardon power, a function pursuant to the Court's duty to police constitutional boundaries. As Chief Justice Warren wrote in *Powell* v. *McCormack:* "It is the province and duty of the judicial department to determine . . . whether the powers of any branch of the government . . . have been exercised in conformity to the Constitution; and if they have not to treat their acts as null and void."[39] But the judicial role is a narrow one, restricted to a review of the constitutionality of the pardon in the light of considerations of due process and separation of powers. The imaginable lawsuits that might develop in reaction to a presidential pardon probably are few in number, but they could occasion judicial limitations on the exercise of executive clemency. For example, suppose both the president and Congress grant amnesties to a group of citizens, with the former's being conditional and the latter's being absolute. Such a case could arise since the Court has held that each branch has the authority to issue amnesties. In this case of conflicting grants, it would be difficult to see how a court could avoid resolving the dispute if a defendant were pleading the absolute amnesty issued by Congress. Consider another case. It has been contended that the president may not grant a pardon to persons found in contempt of Congress, since this would interfere with the fundamental need of the legislature to use the contempt power to preserve its independence and effectiveness in conducting its lawmaking and investigative functions.[40] A judicial ruling that upheld the pardon would afford the president the power to foil congressional investigations and, ultimately, would render Congress dependent upon the president during inquiries of the executive branch. Apparently, such a situation has never actually arisen, but it would present the Court with a dramatic separation-of-powers issue badly in need of resolution.[41] A third case might arise if a president were to pardon himself. This was perhaps thought unlikely until the Nixon presidency. Congress might challenge the validity of the pardon on grounds that it impeded the impeachment process and violated the maxim that a man may not be the judge of his own actions.[42]

The presidential power to grant pardons includes the authority to attach conditions to commutations or reductions of the penalties imposed, but as Chief Justice Burger stated in *Shick,* this power is subject to restrictions. Burger made it clear that the Court would strike down a condition under any of three circumstances: if the condition "offends the Constitution," if it "aggravates punishments," and if it is not properly "accepted."[43] Thus the threshold question with regard to a conditional pardon is whether the condition enlarges rather than mitigates the punishment. If so, it constitutes a usurpation of the legislative power to fix punishment, and Congress could attack the validity of the pardon on the demonstrable ground that the president may not make law.[44]

President Richard Nixon's pardon of former Teamsters' president Jimmy Hoffa, in 1971, provoked the recipient to challenge the conditions attached to his pardon along lines that I have discussed here. While Hoffa's sentence was commuted, it was also enlarged, because it included banishment from all labor-union activity. The banishment, which was upheld by a lower court for the reason that it would preserve the integrity of the labor union, still constituted a violation of the congressional power to regulate interstate commerce, which includes the authority to regulate labor activity. The ruling of the lower court seemed to suggest that the pardon power is superior to legislative power and is not restrained by the doctrine of the separation of powers.[45] Hoffa's disappearance in 1975 precluded an appeal and therefore an ultimate determination by the Supreme Court of the balance between executive and legislative power and the rights of recipients of clemency. At bottom, the commutation seemed to violate the Constitution on both separation-of-powers and due-process grounds, because President Nixon had made a law that deprived Hoffa of his liberty without due process of law, as required by the Fifth Amendment.[46]

It is unlikely that many pardons would provoke lawsuits. But it is critical that citizens have some avenue of appeal from the arbitrary exercise of power. It was for this reason that the framers empowered the Supreme Court to enforce constitutional boundaries. As John Marshall said in the Virginia ratifying convention: "To what quarter will you look for protection from infringement on the Constitution, if . . . not . . . to the judiciary? There is no other body that can afford such protection."[47]

Impeachment

The framers adopted impeachment as the ultimate means of preserving republican government. When other measures and institutions failed, it was available to restrain an errant or oppressive president. Viewed in that light, can it be supposed that the pardon power would be beyond the reach of the impeachment power? What constitutes an impeachable offense? Article II, section 4, of the Constitution provides that "the President . . . shall be removed from Office on Impeachment for, and Conviction of, Treason, Bribery, or other high Crimes and Misdemeanors." In Article III, section 3, "treason" is narrowly defined as "levying war against" the United States or in adhering to its "Enemies, giving them Aid and Comfort." The constitutional meanings of "bribery" and "high crimes and misdemeanors" are derived from English law. Although not as sharply defined as treason or bribery, they are reducible to comprehensible categories. Those that seem pertinent to our purposes include the abuse of official power, bribery, the betrayal of trust, perfidy, subversion, and the introduction of arbitrary power.[48]

Since the degree to which a pardon is legitimate is a question of whether it is prohibited by the Constitution, let us consider whether the administration of executive clemency might fall within one or more of these categories of impeachable offenses. First, if a president were to grant a pardon to an official who is the subject of impeachment proceedings, it is all but certain that the president would be impeached, probably on several grounds, for his action would plainly violate the provision in the pardon clause that prohibits clemency "in cases of impeachment." Indeed, a refusal by the House to impeach and the Senate to convict would amount to the surrender of the impeachment power.[49] Second, it seems clear that a president would be subject to impeachment if he accepted a bribe in exchange for a pardon, because the Constitution makes "bribery" an impeachable offense. Bribery involves the offer or acceptance of payment to influence behavior; it is an attempt to corrupt the administration of the state. It is an especially loathsome act of corruption, a rank betrayal of the trust placed in the president by the Constitution and the people. For the framers, bribery of the president was a frightful possibility. Madison warned that the president "might betray his trust to a foreign power." Gouverneur Morris added that the president might "be bribed . . . to betray his trust," and he reminded the convention that in the course of the impeachment of Danby, it was learned that "Charles II was bribed by Louis XIV."[50]

The framers' familiarity with the details of the Danby affair meant that the possibility of bribing the president for a pardon involved no idle musing. Indeed, English history nurtured the suspicion; under King Edward II, as we have seen, not only were pardons frequently sold, but they were largely beyond the grasp of those too poor to purchase them. To some members of the Reconstruction Congress, it appeared that Madison's warnings had become reality, as they suspected that President Johnson had been accepting payment for pardons. Because an examination of his bank account revealed no evidence of bribery, the allegations did not become part of the indictment against the president, but it is worth noting that the prostitution of the pardon power was considered an impeachable offense.[51] Again, in 1974, as we have seen, some members of Congress were wondering whether President Ford's pardon to Nixon had been fraudulently awarded. On the authority of Blackstone, a pardon is invalid if it is fraudulently obtained. In England, according to Blackstone, it was a general rule that if the king had been deceived, the pardon would be void. While in agreement with Blackstone, Philip Kurland has suggested that "if the fraud is not perpetrated on the person exercising the prerogative of pardon, but with his connivance, so that it cannot be said that he was deceived, the rule might be otherwise."[52] Whether such fraud or "connivance" would vitiate the validity of the pardon probably would require resolution by the judiciary. But the fate of a president who had connived or otherwise engaged in fraud would seem clear, since on definitional grounds alone, the sale of a pardon obviously constitutes an impeachable offense. His fate would also appear to be encompassed by certain offenses within the category of "high crimes and misdemeanors," for example, subversion of the law, betrayal of trust, and perfidy.[53]

In addition to these textually impeachable exercises of the pardon power, there is the weighty opinion of Chief Justice William Howard Taft in *Ex parte Grossman* that the excessive abuse of the power would be grounds for impeachment. In *Grossman,* the Court held that a president may pardon those who are guilty of criminal contempts of court, even though contempt citations were important means of preserving the dignity, integrity, and effectiveness of the court. Taft said the president must have "full discretion to exercise" the pardon power, which, he said, had been conferred with "confidence that he will not abuse it." Taft then considered the effects of an abuse of the power: "An abuse in pardoning contempts would certainly embarrass courts, but it is questionable how much more it would lessen their effectiveness than a wholesale pardon of other offenses. If we could conjure up in our minds a President willing to paralyze courts by pardoning all criminal contempts, why not a President ordering a general jail delivery. . . . The detrimental effect of excessive pardons of completed contempts . . . is of the same character as that of excessive pardons of other offenses. . . . Exceptional cases like this if to be imagined at all would suggest a resort to impeachment."[54] To be sure, Taft was speaking only of the availability of impeachment for "excessive" abuses of the pardon power. This emphasis reflected the concern of the framers to restrict the application of the impeachment power to "great offenses," injuries that could convulse the nation. Nevertheless, whether the pardon power has been excessively abused has been left by the Constitution to Congress, from which there is no appeal. The flagrant and frequent abuse of the authority, such as a general jail delivery, would constitute a gross subversion of law, a betrayal of trust, and perfidy, all impeachable offenses under the Constitution.[55]

It must be acknowledged, of course, that impeachment is an unlikely response to the executive abuse of the pardon power. That it has been invoked sparingly across two centuries and never with respect to the administration of the pardon power at the federal level is not, however, an argument against its use under the proper circumstances. The framers intended that impeachment would be employed only with respect to great political injuries to the political community. Should circumstances arise in which the president has grossly abused the pardon power—the acceptance of a bribe, for example—its availability should not be ignored.

Finally, it remains to be considered whether the president may lawfully issue a preconviction pardon. The issue was brought center stage by Ford's controversial pardon of Nixon, and although Ford's action was criticized, there is no real issue as to its validity.[56] In England, the pardon power could be employed before a conviction. In the Constitutional Convention, James Wilson spoke of the need for preconviction pardons with respect to obtaining testimony from accomplices. In *Federalist* number 74, Hamilton defended the usefulness of preconviction pardons to quell rebellions. These instances may have been illustrative rather than exhaustive of circumstances in which preconviction pardons might be granted. Finally, several Supreme Court opinions have at least implicitly approved preconviction pardons.[57]

In spite of the lack of evidence in the historical record of a legal prohibition on preconviction pardons, they ought to be discouraged as a matter of public policy. A preconviction pardon bypasses the judicial process and sows the seeds of doubt and cynicism among Americans toward the political system. Citizens begin to question the vitality of such revered concepts as the rule of law and equal justice under the law. Are some people—former presidents, for example—above the law? In short, the credibility and legitimacy of the system are called into question. Moreover, the grant of a pardon prior to conviction is likely to bury forever the facts surrounding the offense. That ill serves a system such as ours which is based on the premise that the disclosure of facts and truth best promotes the interests of the Republic.

With the exception of cases of rebellion, it is difficult to conceive of interests sufficiently compelling to justify a preconviction pardon. In a nation committed to the rule of law, the judicial process should be allowed to run its course. In the event of a miscarriage of justice, then, and only then, should the pardon power be administered.

CONCLUSION

At its best, the pardon power is a tool of mercy, an instrument to correct abuses of power and miscarriages of justice. At its worst, this semi-imperial power can be employed as a corrupt tool to suppress great political offenses and crimes. Although it may not have been Ford's intention, that was the effect of his pardon of Richard Nixon. On the whole, perhaps, the pardon power has been judiciously administered, and so the country has been well served. Yet its questionable use by President Ford, the consideration given to its employment by the Nixon White House, and the possibility that it will again be abused to shelter high-ranking officials are reasons compelling enough to induce the nation to rethink the constitutional structure governing the pardon power.

Perhaps the time has come to amend the Constitution, and the change might take the form of a proposal introduced in 1974 by Senator Walter F. Mondale: "No pardon granted to an individual by the President under Section 2 Article II shall be effective if Congress by resolution, two-thirds of the members of each House concurring therein, disapproves the granting of the pardon within 180 days of its issuance."[58]

There is merit in Mondale's proposal. Above all, it would place the pardon power in the mainstream of the political system by rendering it subject to the doctrine of checks and balances. A busy Congress would not be apt to intervene, and only then in controversial cases. Thus the vast number of pardons, noncontroversial in character, would be issued in the same way they always have been—on the basis of the independent judgment of the executive branch. The Mondale proposal, however, would afford Congress an opportunity to carefully review particular acts of executive clemency. And if it were indicated, Congress could check the presidential abuse of the pardon power. The nation would have nothing to lose by such a constitutional amendment, and it would have much to gain. At the very least, the amendment would make it more difficult for high-ranking officials to escape justice.

NOTES

I am indebted to Raoul Berger and Tom Cronin for support, encouragement, and advice, even though I have not always taken it. I am grateful to the Idaho State University Research Committee for its assistance.

1. Edward S. Corwin, *The President: Office and Powers, 1787–1984: A History and Analysis of Practice and Opinion,* 5th rev. ed. (New York: New York University Press, 1984), p. 189; William Duker, "The President's Power to Pardon: A Constitutional History," *William and Mary Law Review* 18 (1977): 475, 525, 535; *Ex parte*

Garland, 4 Wall. 333, 380 (1866). It also has been described as "free from control by other branches of government"; see Leonard B. Boudin, "The Presidential Pardons of James R. Hoffa and Richard M. Nixon: Have the Limitations on the Pardon Power Been Exceeded?" *Colorado Law Review* 48 (1976): 39.

2. *Ex parte Grossman,* 267 U.S. 87 (1925); *Shick* v. *Reed,* 419 U.S. 256 (1974); Boudin, "Presidential Pardons," pp. 6–7. For a discussion of the founders' fear of power see, generally, Bernard Bailyn, *The Ideological Origins of the American Revolution* (Cambridge, Mass.: Harvard University Press, 1967).

3. President Gerald R. Ford knew the pardon "could easily cost me the next election if I run again"; see *A Time to Heal: The Autobiography of Gerald R. Ford* (New York: Harper & Row, 1979), p. 162. Public opinion polls immediately after the pardon indicated a dramatic (20 percent or more) drop in Ford's popularity.

4. *Ex parte William Wells,* 18 How. 421, 427 (1855) (dissenting opinion).

5. For the Court's reliance on English law see, e.g., *United States* v. *Wilson,* 7 Pet. 150 (1833); *Ex parte William Wells,* 18 How. 307 (1855); *Ex parte Grossman,* 267 U.S. 87 (1925); *Shick* v. *Reed,* 419 U.S. 256 (1974). For an explanation of reprieves see United States Department of Justice, *The Attorney General's Survey of Release Procedures* (Washington, D.C.: Government Printing Office, 1939), 3:221–26; see also the standard work on the pardon power, W. H. Humbert, *The Pardoning Power of the President* (Washington, D.C.: American Council on Public Affairs, 1941), p. 26.

6. 71 U.S. 333, 380–81. The "new man" theory was apparently created by Bracton, a thirteenth-century English legal scholar; see Samuel Williston, "Does a Pardon Blot out Guilt?" *Harvard Law Review* 28 (1915): 647, 649.

7. *United States* v. *Wilson,* 7 Pet. 150, 161 (1833) (C. J. Marshall); *Biddle* v. *Perovich,* 274 U.S. 480, 486 (1927) (Holmes, J.). For the view that acceptance of a pardon is an admission of guilt see *Burdick* v. *United States,* 236 U.S. 79, 80 (1915); Humbert, *Pardoning Power,* p. 77. Of course, when a pardon is granted because of the innocence of the party, its acceptance does not connote guilt: see Williston, "Does a Pardon Blot out Guilt?" p. 653.

8. Quoted in Duker, "President's Power to Pardon," p. 511. Congress's power to issue amnesties was upheld in *Brown* v. *Walker,* 161 U.S. 591, 601 (1895), in which the Court sustained a congressional act that granted immunity from prosecution for testimony as state's witness. For the view that Congress has the exclusive authority to issue amnesties see Max Radin, "Legislative Pardons: Another View," *California Law Review* 27 (1939): 387. Of course, there never has been any doubt about the president's authority to grant amnesties; see Alexander Hamilton, *Federalist* no. 74 (New York: Modern Library, 1937), pp. 481–84. For discussion of conditional pardons see *Shick* v. *Reed,* 419 U.S. 256, 266 (1974); and the text accompanying notes 39–47 above. In England, kings frequently made pardons conditional. See also *Ex parte William Wells,* 59 U.S. 307, 311 (1855).

9. See J. W. Ehrlich, *Ehrlich's Blackstone,* 2 vols. (New York: Capricorn Books, 1959), 2:283–84; F. W. Maitland, *Constitutional History* (Cambridge: Cambridge University Press, 1931), pp. 302–6; Boudin, "Presidential Pardons," p. 5; *Ex parte Grossman,* 267 U.S. 87 (1925); *Ex parte Garland,* 71 U.S. 333 (1866).

10. 26 Stat. 946 (1891). My discussion here draws heavily upon the detailed explanation of the pardon process found in Humbert, *Pardoning Power,* pp. 82–94; 28 C.F.R., sec. o.35-o.36, 1.1–1.9 (1976).

11. In Johnson's case this involved the consideration of perhaps 15,000 to 20,000 personal requests. He granted about 13,500 pardons in addition to those within classes of persons granted amnesties; see Jonathan T. Dorris, *Pardon and*

Amnesty under Lincoln and Johnson (Chapel Hill, N.C.: University of North Carolina Press, 1953), p. 141.

12. Ehrlich, *Ehrlich's Blackstone,* pp. 68–69; Duker, "President's Power," p. 476.

13. Duker, "President's Power," pp. 477–79; William S. Holdsworth, *A History of English Law,* 12 vols. (London: Methuen, 1923), 2:448–76.

14. A. B. White, *The Making of the English Constitution* (New York: AMS Press, 1970); Duker, "President's Power," pp. 482–85.

15. Raoul Berger, *Impeachment: The Constitutional Problems* (Cambridge, Mass.: Harvard University Press, 1973), p. 1; Duker, "President's Power," p. 489.

16. Duker, "President's Power," p. 490; T. F. T. Plucknett, ed., *Taswell-Langmead's English Constitutional History,* 11th ed. (Boston, Mass.: Houghton Mifflin Co., 1960), p. 533.

17. Quoted by Plucknett in *Constitutional History,* p. 534. "The Commons," as the English historian Henry Hallam has observed, "in impeaching Lord Danby, went a great way towards establishing the principle (recognised by the modern theory of the Constitution) that no minister can shelter himself behind the throne by pleading obedience to the orders of his sovereign," but is answerable "for the justice, the honesty, the utility of all measures emanating from the crown, as well as for their legality," thus rendering the executive administration "subordinate," in all great matters of policy, to the . . . virtual control of the Two Houses of Parliament" (ibid., p. 533).

18. Citations to state constitutions are found in Francis Thorpe, ed., *The Federal and State Constitutions, Colonial Charters, and Other Organic Laws,* 7 vols. (Washington, D.C.: Government Printing Office, 1909).

19. Max Farrand, ed., *The Records of the Federal Convention of 1787,* 4 vols. (New Haven, Conn.: Yale University Press, 1937), 3:599, 185; Joseph Story, *Commentaries on the Constitution of the United States,* 3 vols. (New York: Da Capo Press, 1970), 3:352. The two Houses of Parliament—Lords and Commons—viewed impeachment as a grand inquiry; see Berger, *Impeachment,* p. 26.

20. Farrand, *Records,* 1:292, 419, 426, 564, 2:626.

21. Hamilton, *Federalist* no. 74, p. 483; Jonathan Elliot, ed., *Debates in the Several State Conventions on the Adoption of the Federal Constitution,* 5 vols. (Washington, D.C.: J. Elliot, 1836), 4:112.

22. Hamilton, *Federalist* no. 74, pp. 481–84; Elliot, *Debates,* 4:32.

23. For a discussion of the unpublicized acts of executive clemency see Humbert, *Pardoning Power,* pp. 82–94. For a discussion of the controversy surrounding the pardon on Christmas Day of 1868 for Jefferson Davis, president of the confederacy, who was indicted for treason, see Dorris, *Pardon and Amnesty,* pp. 278–312. The Nixon pardon is discussed above, in the text accompanying notes 27–32.

24. See, generally, Morris Sherman, *Amnesty in America* (Passaic: New Jersey Library Association, 1974); Lawrence M. Baskir and William Strauss, *Reconciliation after Vietnam: A Program of Relief for Vietnam Era Draft and Military Offenders* (Notre Dame, Ind.: University of Notre Dame Press, 1977), pp. 111–13; Timothy Flanagan and Edmund F. McGarrell, eds., *Sourcebook of Criminal Justice Statistics–1985,* U.S. Department of Justice Statistics (Washington, D.C.: Government Printing Office, 1986), p. 488, table 5.29; Dorris, *Pardon and Amnesty,* p. 141. The end of the Vietnam War brought renewed calls for amnesty for draft-law violators. On Sept. 16, 1974, President Ford issued a conditional amnesty to those draft evaders of the war who would be willing to work for up to two years in public-service jobs; see Executive Order 11803, *Weekly Compilation of Presidential Docu-*

ments, Sept. 23, 1974, pp. 1149–54. On Jan. 21, 1977, one day after his Inaugural Address, President Jimmy Carter granted an unconditional pardon to draft evaders. However, Vietnam deserters were not affected by the grant and were to be considered on a case-by-case basis; see Executive Order 11967, *Weekly Compilation of Presidential Documents,* Jan. 24, 1977, pp. 90–91.

25. 71 U.S. 333 (1866); 80 U.S. 128 (1872). My discussion here draws upon Dorris, *Pardon and Amnesty,* pp. 34–35, 64, 80–85, 111–15, 144–52, 238–39, 316–48.

26. Quoted by Harold W. Currie in *Eugene V. Debs* (Boston, Mass.: Twayne Publishers, 1976), p. 48. In this discussion I have drawn from the excellent biography by Nick Salvatore, *Eugene V. Debs: Citizen and Socialist* (Urbana: University of Illinois Press, 1982), pp. 294–328.

27. Quoted by Bob Woodward and Carl Bernstein in *The Final Days* (New York: Simon & Schuster, 1976), pp. 407–8.

28. Farrand, *Records,* 2:639; Woodward and Bernstein, *Final Days,* pp. 410–11. For discussions about using the pardon power in exchange for the silence of Watergate defendants see Woodward and Bernstein, *Final Days,* pp. 407–34; J. Anthony Lukas, *Nightmare: The Underside of the Nixon Years* (New York: Viking Press, 1976), p. 263.

29. 39 Fed. Reg. 32601–2 (1974). Nixon has since expressed regret that he did not pardon the Watergate defendants; see "Talking Pardons, Unforgivably Early,'' *New York Times,* Apr. 12, 1988, p. 26, col. 1.

30. *New York Times,* Aug. 29, 1974, p. 1, col. 8; *Pardon of Richard Nixon, and Related Matters,* Hearings before the Subcommittee on Criminal Justice of the Committee on the Judiciary, House of Representatives, 93d Cong., 2d sess., Sept. 24, Oct. 1 and 17, 1974, pp. 96, 97.

31. *New York Times,* Sept. 9, 1974, p. 24, col. 1; Ford, *A Time to Heal,* pp. 172–81; Clark R. Mollenhoff, *The Man Who Pardoned Nixon* (New York: St. Martin's Press, 1976), pp. 93–123.

32. Philip Kurland, *Watergate and the Constitution* (Chicago: University of Chicago Press, 1978), p. 138.

33. *New York Times,* Mar. 24, 1988, p. 1, col. 2. For support of a pardon see Patrick J. Buchanan, "This Time the Liberals Blew the Coup," *Washington Post,* Aug. 3, 1987, p. 23. For an opposition view see "No Pardon," in the *New Republic,* Dec. 28, 1987, pp. 7–9; and the *New York Times* editorials "The Case against the President," Mar. 18, 1988, p. 24, col. 1, and "Talking Pardons, Unforgivably Early," Apr. 12, 1988, p. 26, col. 1.

34. 71 U.S. 333, 380 (1866). For assertions of illimitability see Duker, "President's Power," pp. 525, 535.

35. 71 U.S. at 380; see also *United States* v. *Klein,* 80 U.S. 128 (1871).

36. See *Brown* v. *Walker,* 161 U.S. 591, 601 (1895); *The Laura,* 114 U.S. 411 (1885).

37. "The pardoning by the President of criminal contempts has been practiced more than three-quarters of a century, and no abuses during all that time developed sufficiently to invoke a test in the federal courts of its validity"; see 267 U.S. 107, 122 (1925).

38. 419 U.S. 256–66 (1974).

39. 395 U.S. 486, 506 (1969); *Marbury* v. *Madison,* 5 U.S. 137 (1803).

40. William Rawle, *A View of the Constitution of the United States of America* (New York: Da Capo Press, 1970), pp. 165–66.

41. Historically, the Court has acted "as umpire between the Congress and the

president"; see Nathaniel L. Nathanson, "The Supreme Court as a Unit of National Government: Herein of Separation of Powers and Political Questions," *Journal of Public Law* 6 (1957): 331, 332. See, e.g., *Myers* v. *United States*, 272 U.S. 52 (1926); *United States* v. *Lovett*, 328 U.S. 303, 312 (1946).

42. Hugh McGill, "Nixon Pardon, Limits on the Benign Prerogative," *Connecticut Law Review* 7 (1974): 57; Boudin, "Presidential Pardons," p. 36. James Madison stated that neither the executive nor the legislative "can pretend to an exclusive or superior right of settling the boundaries between their respective powers"; see *Federalist* no. 49, at p. 328.

43. 419 U.S. at 265.

44. The Court has consistently denied any lawmaking authority to the president; see, e.g., *Youngstown Sheet and Tube Co.* v. *Sawyer*, 343 U.S. 579 (1952); *New York Times Co.* v. *United States*, 403 U.S. 713 (1971).

45. *Hoffa* v. *Saxbe*, 378 F. Supp. 1221 (D.D.C. 1974). Moreover, the commutation violated congressional jurisdiction over membership in labor unions; see Boudin, "Presidential Pardons," pp. 21–34.

46. The Fifth Amendment provides that "no person" shall "be deprived of life, liberty, or property, without due process of law." "Due process" has been epitomized by the Court as the "protection of the individual against arbitrary action"; see *Ohio Bell Telephone Co.* v. *Public Service Commission*, 301 U.S. 292, 302 (1937).

47. Elliot, *Debates*, 3:554.

48. Justice Story stated: "What are and are not high crimes and misdemeanors is to be ascertained by a recurrence" to English law; see *Commentaries*, vol. 1, sec. 800. Raoul Berger has reduced impeachable offenses to intelligible categories; see *Impeachment*, pp. 67–69, 70–71.

49. It may be objected that this example is too pat; but unlikely as it may be, it does illustrate the pardon power's vulnerability to impeachment. It "will not do to say that the argument is drawn from extremes. Constitutional provisions are based on the possibilities of extremes"; see *General Oil Co.* v. *Crain*, 209 U.S. 211, 226–27 (1908).

50. Farrand, *Records*, 2:68–69; see also Berger, *Impeachment*, p. 176 n. 243; Ehrlich, *Ehrlich's Blackstone*, p. 62.

51. See remarks by Senators Chandler and Johnson in the *Congressional Globe*, 39th Cong., 2d sess., pp. 8–15 (1866). The specter of bribery played a role in the impeachment in 1936 of District Judge Halsted Ritter. The Senate convicted him on the grounds that he had brought his court "into scandal and disrepute," in part because he had accepted expensive gifts from affluent members of his district, even though they had no business before his court; see Berger, *Impeachment*, pp. 92–93. It seems clear that the constitutional definition of "high crimes and misdemeanors" applies to judges and presidents alike; see ibid.

52. Ehrlich, *Ehrlich's Blackstone*, p. 519; Kurland, *Watergate*, p. 143.

53. See the remarks of Madison and Morris, above, in the text accompanying note 50. In North Carolina, James Iredell said that the president would be liable to impeachment where he "had acted from some corrupt motive or other"; see Elliot, *Debates*, 4:126. In South Carolina, Gen. C. C. Pinckney said that those are impeachable "who behave amiss or betray their public trust." In that same state convention, Edward Rutledge said that an abuse of trust was impeachable; see ibid., at pp. 281, 276; see also Berger, *Impeachment*, pp. 67–71.

54. 267 U.S. 121 (1925).

55. In 1923 the governor of Oklahoma was impeached for having abused the pardon power; see *Attorney General's Survey,* 3:150–53.

56. For criticism see *New York Times,* Sept. 11, 1974, p. 1, col. 2; I. F. Stone, "On Pardons and Testimony," *New York Times,* Oct. 9, 1974, p. 43, col. 2; McGill, "Nixon Pardon"; Kurland, *Watergate,* pp. 131–52.

57. See, e.g., *Burdick* v. *United States,* 236 U.S. 79 (1915); *Ex parte Garland,* 71 U.S. 333, 380 (1866) (dictum).

58. Senate Joint Resolution 240, 93d Cong., 2d sess. (1974). See Mondale's defense of the proposal, "Harnessing the President's Pardon Power," *American Bar Association Journal,* Jan. 1975, pp. 108–10.

9
THE PRESIDENT'S "PREROGATIVE POWER"

ROBERT SCIGLIANO

> The executive Power shall be vested in a President of the United States of America.
>
> —*Article II, section 1*

> Before he enter on the Execution of his Office, he shall take the following Oath or Affirmation:—"I do solemnly swear (or affirm) that I will faithfully execute the Office of President of the United States, and will to the best of my Ability, preserve, protect and defend the Constitution of the United States."
>
> —*Article II, section 1*

> He shall take Care that the Laws be faithfully executed, and shall Commission all the Officers of the United States.
>
> —*Article II, section 3*

What is executive "prerogative"? Does the Constitution provide for it? If so, how? And what is the relation of executive prerogative to presidential power?

Modern writers on the presidency often trace prerogative to the English philosopher John Locke, who discussed it in the second of his *Two Treatises of Government,* published in 1690. I too shall go to Locke and then to the Constitution and those who framed and (often the same persons) those who conducted the new government the Constitution created. In considering both Locke and the Constitution, I shall be interested in the connection between prerogative and the ordinary powers of government.[1]

MODERN SCHOLARS

The first person to connect Locke's discussion of prerogative to the presidency seems to have been Edward S. Corwin, a leading scholar on the Constitution, in his influential work, *The President: Office and Powers,* which was published in 1940 and has gone through several editions. It has since then been customary for scholars on the presidency to make that connection. Not only that, but Corwin set an example for other writers by depicting Locke as having an expansive view of prerogative and by regarding prerogative (most of the time, at least) as identical to executive power. Thus Corwin stated that Locke, along with the French philosopher Montesquieu and the English jurist William Blackstone, conceived executive power as "a broadly discretionary, residual power which is available when other governmental powers fail," and he found that "the framers had in mind [their] idea of a divided initiative in the matter of legislation and a broad range of autonomous executive power or 'prerogative.'" Corwin found "especially illuminating" Locke's chapter "Of Prerogative" in the *Second Treatise of Government,* from which he quoted a long passage, including Locke's statement that prerogative was the "Power to act according to discretion, for the publick good, without the prescription of the Law and sometimes even against it." Later in *The President,* Corwin stated that Locke claimed for the executive "a broad discretion capable even of setting aside the ordinary law in the meeting of special exigencies for which the legislative power had not provided."[2]

It is unclear in Corwin's account how prerogative, as "broad discretion," passed from the framers' "mind" into the Constitution. For example, did it enter through Article II's "vesting clause," which states that "the executive Power shall be vested in a President" and which has sometimes been construed to grant to the president a general executive power? Corwin seemed to think so when he declared that the clause "carries the implication that the sum total of executive power which is known to or recognized by the Constitution belongs to the President." Or did prerogative enter the Constitution (perhaps also) through certain of the president's enumerated powers—for example, the commander-in-chief clause, through which, Corwin stated in a separate writing, the framers conferred "all the prerogatives of monarchy in connection with war-making except only the power to declare war and the power to create armed forces"?[3]

Or did Locke's prerogative, as understood by Corwin, pass into the Constitution at all? Elsewhere in *The President,* Corwin disparaged the tendency to regard "the 'executive power' as an always available peg on which to hang any and all unassigned powers in respect to foreign intercourse," and he questioned whether the Constitution conveyed any residual power through this clause. Indeed, he tended in his study to speak of "prerogatives"—to pardon, veto, and make treaties—and not of "residual prerogative"; and he stated at one place that the commander-in-chief power originally meant no more than "the simple power of military command." And at another place, he stated that in imposing on the president the duty to execute the laws faithfully, most of the framers "unquestionably thought" they had provided against a president's acting contrary to the laws.[4]

In this second, contradictory view, Corwin thought that prerogative, as broad or residual power, had not been put into the Constitution at all by its framers but rather had been grafted on the presidency after the government had been launched, by such statesmen as Alexander Hamilton, Abraham Lincoln, Theodore Roosevelt, and Franklin Roosevelt. The framers' contribution was merely to make Article II "the most loosely drawn" part of the Constitution, thereby leaving "considerable leeway for the future play of political forces." It was Corwin's judgment that "taken by and large, the history of the Presidency is a history of aggrandizement."[5]

Corwin concluded *The President* with the observation that the Constitution embraced two conceptions of executive power: one makes the president subordinate to Congress, whereas the other allows him to be autonomous and self-directing within broad limits. Whatever the truth of the observation, it expresses Corwin's own equivocation regarding presidential power. In any event, his discussion of prerogative and, in particular, his discovery of "broad discretion" in it, especially in "special exigencies," seem to have had a remarkable influence on succeeding scholarship, as the following citations from well-known studies of the presidency are intended to show. It will be noticed that scholars who have followed Corwin have not agreed as to how, or even whether, prerogative, understood as the power to act without or in violation of law, entered the Constitution, but that they have all discerned its presence in the conduct of the presidency and have traced it to Locke.[6]

In *The American Chief Executive*, Joseph E. Kallenbach cited the vesting clause of Article II as furnishing the basis for the later claim of presidents to "constitutional prerogative," that is, to the claim that the president's authority includes all executive powers. Kallenbach found "respectable authority" for this view in Locke's chapter on prerogative, and he discovered "the most striking application of Locke's concept" in the measures (unspecified by Kallenbach) that Lincoln took "beyond his statutory powers" during the Civil War. Louis W. Koenig, in *The Chief Executive*, did not find prerogative in the Constitution, but he averred that presidents throughout history "have drawn upon Locke's doctrines of executive power and, particularly, prerogative" to justify their claims to power. Koenig treated prerogative as a power to be used in emergencies. Arthur M. Schlesinger, Jr., in *The Imperial Presidency*, agreed with Koenig that the Constitution did not make prerogative a part of presidential power, and yet he thought "the idea was in the minds of the founders," who were "steeped" in Locke. For Schlesinger, "only major threat" justified the use of "emergency prerogative"; in the history of the nation "only the Civil War, the Second World War, possibly the Cuban missile crisis" qualified. Richard M. Pious, in *The American Presidency,* is harder to pin down. He referred to "constitutional prerogative" and to "what the framers knew as 'Lockean Prerogative,'" apparently different things but not clearly distinguished. "Constitutional prerogative" is the authority of the president "to resolve crises or important issues facing the nation," and "Lockean prerogative" is a doctrine of "emergency powers," the president's going "beyond the limits of the constitution or laws to preserve the nation." Anyway, Pious held that the Constitution was "ambiguous, incomplete, underdefined, or silent"—an unusual choice of defects—regarding "prerogative powers" and that it did not include "emergency powers"; but he added that the framers did not foreclose the exercise of Lockean prerogative and that Hamilton "smuggled" prerogative into the presidency through his discussion of executive power in *The Federalist.*[7]

To my knowledge, no earlier writer had talked about the presidency in these ways. Neither James Kent, in his *Commentaries on the Laws,* nor Joseph Story, in his *Commentaries on the Constitution,* both written in the early part of the nineteenth century, discerned "a broad range of autonomous executive power or prerogative" in the office, let alone power that was "capable even of setting aside the ordinary laws." Nor did William Whiting, in *The Government's War Powers under the Constitution,* invoke prerogative, in name or substance, in his study of the legal powers of the president and Congress during the Civil War. Looking back on that war from the 1920s, James G. Randall, in his *Constitutional Problems under Lincoln,* was likewise silent on the question of prerogative. And Clarence A. Berdahl's *War Powers of the Executive in the United States* makes no mention of Locke or executive prerogative.[8]

Surely something has happened since the 1940s in the way the American presidency is understood. The question is important enough to warrant a fresh look as to how Locke and the founders regarded prerogative and its relationship to executive power. I intend my study to have relevance for subsequent times, including the time in which we live, but I shall venture beyond the early nineteenth century only for an occasional glance at Lincoln's actions during the Civil War.

LOCKE

As I have already quoted Locke in my discussion of Corwin, prerogative is defined as a power "to act according to discretion, for the publick good, without the prescription of the Law, and sometimes even against it." Locke says this power is "left" to the person who has the "executive power" in governments "where the Legislative and Executive power are in distinct hands" (that is, in "moderated Monarchies and well-framed Governments"). Echoing Aristotle's discussion of "equity," Locke states that prerogative is needed because legislators cannot foresee and provide for all that might arise in society, nor can law itself provide for everything. The people may judge whether prerogative has in fact been used for their good, and they may limit or define it by law when it has not.[9]

Locke gives two examples in which the executive may act "without the prescription of Law" (or, as he also says, "where the Law [is] silent"). One relates to the law's inability to foresee and provide for everything and the other relates to the inability of the legislators. The executive has the prerogative to call the legislature into session (and fix the place and duration of its meetings) because "the uncertainty, and variableness of humane affairs could not bear a steady fixed rule." And he has the prerogative to restore the original basis of representation when the passage of time has led to inequalities in it because the people in constituting the legislature—Locke is evidently thinking of England—gave it no power to reapportion itself, apparently through a lack of foresight. Everybody agrees that something ought to be done about the situation, Locke says, but "most" think there is no remedy.[10]

Locke's treatment of the prerogative to act "against" the law is more intricate. I begin with his single example of it, in his own words.

> 'Tis fit that the Laws themselves should in some Cases give way to the Executive Power. . . . For since many accidents may happen, wherein a strict and rigid observation of the Laws may do harm; (as not to pull down an innocent's Man's House to stop the Fire, when the next to it is burning) and a Man may come sometimes within the reach of the Law, which makes no distinction of Persons, by an action, that may deserve reward and pardon; 'tis fit, the Ruler should have a Power, in many Cases, to mitigate the severity of the Law, and pardon some Offenders.

It is in this passage evidently that Corwin discerned a prerogative "capable even of setting aside the ordinary law in the meeting of special exigencies." Other scholars, as I have noted, have followed his lead. But those who understand Locke in this way can be right only if the exercise of prerogative in the example consists in having pulled down a house during a fire and if it is the executive who has done or authorized the act. Such an interpretation makes no sense for, as Locke says, the executive ("Ruler") should have the prerogative ("power") to pardon some persons who violate the laws—in his example, the man who has pulled down the house.[11]

Right after the discussion of making laws "give way to the Executive Power," Locke restates the need for prerogative. He observes that "harm" will be done if laws "are executed with an inflexible rigour, on all occasions, and upon all Persons, that may come in their way" and concludes "therefore" that "there is a latitude left to the Executive power, to do many things of choice, which the Laws do not prescribe." He makes no reference here to doing things "against" what the laws prescribe.[12]

Later in his chapter on prerogative, Locke substitutes acting "against the direct Letter of the Law" and acting "contrary to the Letter of the Law" for acting "against" the law. It is not very clear what he intends by these new definitions. They suggest that the executive, in departing from the law's letter, will be obedient to its "spirit" or "reason." In this sense, Locke's prerogative corresponds to the equity that English judges were said to exercise in their interpretation of the laws. For example, Blackstone says that equity "arises" from the judicial practice of considering the "reason and spirit" of laws when the words themselves are dubious as a way of discovering their "true meaning," and he defines equity (quoting Grotius) pretty much as Aristotle did, as "the correction" of laws made necessary by the fact that all cases to which they might apply "cannot be foreseen or expressed." What the judges do then is to define the circumstances that the legislator himself would have defined when he enacted the law. Blackstone's example of equity concerns the sick passenger who was unable to abandon ship along with everyone else in a storm and who, when the ship by accident came safely into port, claimed the vessel and its cargo according to the terms of law. It was decided that the sick person did not come within "the reason of the law," whose purpose it was to encourage those at sea to risk their lives to save a ship in distress.[13]

Both prerogative and equity, it seems, consider the spirit and reason of the law when the letter of the law varies from them, and both, I should add, involve the exercise of "discretion." It should be emphasized that, like prerogative, equity is needed because "all cases cannot be foreseen or, if foreseen, cannot be expressed" in general laws. The fact that the executive exercises the one power and judges exercise the other power does not seem to mark an important difference, from either the standpoint of Locke or English tradition. Locke's executive power includes the activities of judges (there is no distinct judicial power in his doctrine of government powers), and equity was traditionally regarded as originating in the monarch's prerogative as the fountain of English justice.[14]

According to Blackstone, judges are bound by "the true intent of the legislature" in interpreting laws by their spirit. Is Locke's executive similarly restrained in executing them? He may use his pardon against what the law prescribes, or against the letter of the law. How much further he may go is uncertain, but surely his authority stops considerably short of

Corwin's "broad range of executive power" and Pious's power "to resolve crises or important issues facing the nation."[15]

In Locke's time the prerogative to act against the laws (other than by pardoning) went under the name of the suspending and dispensing powers: the Crown's authority to suspend or repeal the laws and its authority to permit persons to disobey them. (Sometimes both actions were placed under the dispensing power.) Like the royal pardon, alongside which they grew in the Middle Ages, the suspending and dispensing powers were employed to make laws "give way," but they differed from the pardon in that they made legal what otherwise would have been illegal, whereas the pardon freed a person from the legal consequences of an illegal action—for example, for having pulled down an innocent man's house to prevent the spread of fire. The suspending and dispensing powers had been recognized by Parliament and the courts over the years, but they were subjected to increasing criticism during the seventeenth century, especially as to the use that James II made of the dispensing power after he had mounted the throne in 1685, in exempting Catholics from the test, established by law, designed to keep them from holding military and other public offices. James's challenge to Parliament and, as it was thought, to the people's liberties resulted in his being chased from the throne into exile in 1688. Parliament in that year, in the Bill of Rights that marked the event, condemned the suspending and dispensing powers.[16]

Is it likely that Locke favored the suspending and dispensing powers? How could he have, when he declared in the Preface to his *Two Treatises of Government* that his work would justify what the English people had done to save their nation from "Slavery and Ruine"? If prerogative may set aside the laws, in the sense that Corwin and others have in mind, why should Locke remark toward the end of the *Second Treatise* that "the exceeding the Bounds of Authority is no more a Right in a great, than a petty Officer; no more justifiable in a King, than in a Constable"? Why say that "against the Laws there can be no Authority"? And how can the people declare "limitations of Prerogative," if prerogative may set aside those limits?[17]

In his chapter on prerogative, Locke refers to "God-like Princes," whom the people allowed to "inlarge their Prerogative as they pleased." He proceeds to reveal that the reigns of such princes were dangerous to the liberties of the people, for the precedents that these rulers established were certain to be abused by those who came after them. Locke's true "God-like" prince, apparently, is the one mentioned early in the *Second Treatise*, whom he credits with "establishing laws of liberty to secure protection and incouragement to the honest industry of Mankind." And though Locke indicates in his chapter on prerogative that prerogative is not an arbitrary power, capable of hurting the people (inasmuch as what is arbitrary cannot be prerogative), he remarks parenthetically toward the end of the *Second*

Treatise that prerogative is "an Arbitrary Power in some things left in the Prince's hand." Still elsewhere he observes that no one naturally has an arbitrary power over another and that the power of government "ought not to be Arbitrary and at Pleasure."[18]

If Locke meant to confine the prerogative of acting against the laws to pardoning offenders and sometimes to following the spirit rather than the letter of the law, why didn't he say so? Why did he use intricate syntax in discussing the power of pardon, so that a reader might be misled into a broader conception of prerogative? Why refer to laws "giving way" and to actions "against" the laws? I can only suggest that Locke wished to disguise his meaning regarding prerogative in order to protect himself. Until nearly the time when he published his *Two Treatises* in 1690, and surely while he was writing them, it was dangerous to question the royal prerogative. In 1688, the final year of James II's reign, for example, several bishops were prosecuted for seditious libel for having questioned the king's right to dispense with the laws (and although they were acquitted by the jury, two of the four judges in the case favored conviction). Ever cautious in matters respecting his safety, Locke could not be sure that the toleration introduced into English life by James's forced abdication would last. Indeed, his caution led him to publish his work anonymously and to keep no record suggesting his authorship.[19]

What does the Lockean executive do when circumstances seem to require him to suspend, dispense with, or otherwise violate the law? He acts but not, apparently, as a matter of prerogative, or right. The following episode from eighteenth-century English history will make my meaning clear. Mainly, however, I present the episode because it casts light on how Locke's doctrine of prerogative was understood nearly a century after the appearance of his *Two Treatises of Government*.

In the summer of 1766, George III, acting through his ministers, ordered an embargo on the exportation of wheat and flour—"corn"—because of a shortage at home and strong demand abroad. The business was laid before the Lords and the Commons for their "advice" when they came into session that fall, leading to a sharp debate in both houses as to the government's authority to take the action. The ministry seemed at first unsure of its ground, for early in the session it brought in a bill to indemnify—protect—those who had enforced the embargo from civil and criminal liability, conceding thereby that the action rested on doubtful legal ground. It was reluctant, however, to yield to demands that those who had advised the embargo—the ministers themselves—should be included in the bill, and some ministers and their parliamentary supporters undertook to argue that the Crown had a power to suspend or dispense with the laws. "Citing the opinion of Mr. Locke," according to a report made at the time, they "asserted, that it was ridiculous to suppose any state without a power of providing for the public safety in cases of emergency." The king's leading minister, Lord Chatham (William Pitt the elder), himself made use of Locke in the House of Lords in order to show that "although not strictly speaking legal, the measure was right in the opinion of that great friend of liberty." The opposition replied that Locke was "misunderstood, when brought as an authority on the other side . . . for surely there was not a man in England a greater enemy of the dispensing power than himself," and that "when Mr. Locke speaks of the prerogative as acting sometimes against law, or of the laws themselves yielding to the executive," he means the power of "pardoning offenders where the law condemns, which is certainly undoubted prerogative. There the law yields, not in its force or subsistence but only in its consequences, and in a particular instance." The balance of parliamentary opinions is indicated by the reaction in the House of Commons to the views expressed by one Alderman Beckford, a friend of the ministry. Beckford declared there that "whenever the public is in danger, the King has a dispensing power." On being required to explain himself, he stated he had meant to add "with the advice of council, whenever the *salus populi* required it." Required again to explain himself, he stated he only meant to say, "That on great and urgent occasions, where the safety of the people called for an exertion of a power contrary to the written law of these kingdoms, such exertion of power is excusable only by necessity, and justifiable by act of Parliament." The House of Commons was then satisfied.[20]

"When the point was brought home to him," Chatham's biographer informs us, "the minister yielded to Parliament's demand for a bill of indemnity that would cover the ministers who advised as well as the subordinates who carried out the embargo."[21]

Blackstone seems to have understood Locke in the same way as the majority of Parliament in the corn-embargo debate. In his *Commentaries on the Laws of England,* written about the time of the debate, he mentioned the power of pardon among the specific prerogatives of the Crown and then, referring generally to prerogative, he declared that it was, "as Mr. Locke well defined it," the power to act "where the positive laws are silent." He was silent at this point as to a power (independent of the pardon) to act "against" the laws. Elsewhere in the *Commentaries,* Blackstone stated that an act of Parliament "cannot be altered, dispensed with, suspended, or repealed" except by Parliament.[22]

Locke helped greatly to transform prerogative. In past English history, it had been a privilege attached to the person of the monarch, "something real and durable . . . with the sanction of religion," as David Hume described it in the reign of James I, in the early seventeenth century. As an English court declared in the time of Charles I, James's successor, the monarch could "charge his subjects for the safety and defense of the kingdom, notwithstanding any act of Parliament." And as another court declared in James II's reign, the monarch had an "inseparable prerogative to dispense with penal laws in particular cases and upon particular necessary reasons of which the king himself is the sole judge." Locke converted prerogative into a power "left" with the "executive" by "the people," to be used for their good; and he made them the judge as to "when this Power is made a right use of."[23]

Also, Locke brought prerogative into harmony with the doctrine of separation of powers, which is his own invention. The legislative power, which "direct[s] how the Force of the Commonwealth shall be imploy'd," cannot, as we have learned, "foresee and provide by Laws for all," and so it needs assistance. The executive power in itself cannot give it, for it "see[s] to the Execution of the Laws that are made, and remain in force," that is, to "the Execution of the Municipal Laws of the Society within itself"; nor can the federative power, for it concerns itself with "the management of the security and interest of the publick without." Prerogative lends needed discretion to the execution of the laws.[24]

The legislative power seems to resemble prerogative: both entail the use of discretion, and the more there is of one, the less there is of the other. "In the Infancy of Governments," Locke observes, when "a few establish'd Laws served the turn . . . the Government was almost all Prerogative." It is tempting to say that prerogative is legislative power in the hands of the executive; however, prerogative acts without a rule whereas the legislative power acts by rules. In a brief "History of England," Locke shows that the people have replaced prerogative by laws as they have experienced its bad effects, and he seems to suggest in his examples of prerogative that it can be further curtailed. The people might, he indicates, set "certain appointed Seasons" for legislative elections in their constitution of government, instead of leaving the matter to the executive. Also, they might require the executive to convoke the legislature at "certain intervals" or combine "settled periods" of convening with "a liberty left to the Prince." And he implicitly dissociates himself from those ("most") persons who think the legislature is without authority to reapportion itself. As reformed by Locke, prerogative is the irreducible discretionary power left with the executive after the rest of prerogative has been transferred to the legislature.[25]

We might say that Blackstone placed the traditional prerogatives of the English Crown on a Lockean foundation. He followed tradition in naming as prerogatives such powers as vetoing bills and making war, peace, and treaties, instead of putting the veto under the legislative power and the others under the federative power, as Locke did. Yet he followed Locke in the decisive respect of tracing government back to an "original contract" that individuals made in leaving the state of nature to enter civil society. This contract, or "Constitution," he observed, secured the people by "the limitation of the king's prerogative, so that it is impossible he should exceed its bounds without the consent of the people." And, like Locke, Blackstone found the source of the power of war and peace in "the right of making war" that every person had in "the natural state."[26]

THE FOUNDERS

The Constitution combines prerogative with executive power. Conforming to Locke's definition of executive power, which I have cited, Article II provides that the president "shall take care that the laws be faithfully executed" and empowers him, with the consent of the Senate, to appoint those who will be engaged in the task. The article does not mention how such officers shall be removed from office, and Madison argued in 1789 that the president possessed that power solely, either as implied in his duty to see to the faithful execution of the laws or as implied in a general grant of executive power that was conveyed to the president in the article's declaration that "the executive power shall be vested in a President of the United States." Madison's view of executive power is of great practical importance for the president's control of the executive branch of government, but it does not expand the president's executive power beyond the duty of carrying out the laws.[27]

Article II also grants to the president powers that are not executive, strictly speaking. Both Publius in *The Federalist* and Joseph Story in his *Commentaries on the Constitution of the United States* treated the powers to pardon and make treaties as prerogatives, and Story also named the power to adjourn Congress as a prerogative. Story mentioned that the framers gave Congress some executive prerogatives, such as the powers to declare war, coin money, and regulate weights and measures. All of these prerogatives, Story said, were derived from the British Crown, and, I note, the framers, in the spirit of Locke, limited the exercise of some of them. The Senate must approve treaties and the president may convene Congress only on "extraordinary occasions" and may adjourn it only when its two houses cannot agree on a time. Rather quickly Americans came to refer to the Constitution's prerogatives simply as "powers," except when they wished to be precise or sound eloquent. Thus did these prerogatives exchange their royal titles for the republican names "executive" or "legislative" power, assigned to them by the Constitution's doctrine, derived from Locke, of the separation of powers. These prerogatives differ from executive power, however, in the discretionary authority they bring to the president.[28]

Treaties and war also figure in Locke's doctrine of separation of powers, as part of the federative power, although Locke did not care by what name the power was called. In *The Federalist,* Hamilton seemed to regard the treaty power as Locke had, suggesting that it was neither executive nor legislative but formed a "distinct" power of government. In the Constitutional Convention, some delegates thought that war and treaties and the like might be considered part of the executive power. Perhaps they took their cue from the eighteenth-century French philosopher Montesquieu, who, in elaborating Locke's doctrine of separation of powers, made Locke's federative power into a second executive power, relating to external affairs. By 1793, Hamilton had come to regard foreign affairs (including war) as executive in nature, and he argued that Article II's vesting clause granted those matters generally to the president, with certain exceptions: Congress possessed the executive power of declaring war and the Senate shared the executive power of making treaties. In this view, the president could suspend treaties (the Senate participates only in making them), fight a war once declared or begun by another power (for what is there then for Congress to declare?), conduct hostilities below the threshold of war, and speak for the nation in its relations with other nations. Madison rejected this expanded understanding of executive power and accused Hamilton of having borrowed it from the prerogatives of the British Crown—an opinion that Corwin, incidentally, shared. This is not the place to settle the dispute between Hamilton and Madison over the scope of the executive power—whether it relates to the execution of the laws (including the control over executive personnel) or whether it relates also to foreign affairs. I merely observe that Hamilton's conception has largely won out in the practice of American government, and what I wish to emphasize is that this conception gives a considerable amount of discretionary authority to the president. Perhaps some scholars have had foreign affairs in mind when they have treated prerogative as identical with executive power; for example, Corwin attributed to the framers the idea of "a broad range of autonomous executive power or 'prerogative.'"[29]

What did early Americans think of what Locke called prerogative to act "without" law and "against law"? I begin with a preliminary observation. Early statesmen seldom cited Locke in their political writings, for all the influence that he seems to have had on their thinking; indeed, they cited him much less often than they did Blackstone or Montesquieu. Only once, to my knowledge, was Locke cited for his view on prerogative, in Madison's remark, in 1793, that Locke's chapter on that subject "shows how much the reason of the philosopher was clouded by the royalism of the Englishman." We should not, however, conclude from this remark that Madison understood Locke to include within prerogative the power of the executive to suspend or dispense with the laws for, in a report he prepared for the Virginia House of Delegates about six years later, he said that prerogative consisted of enlarged discretion granted to the executive to "suit" general legislative provisions "to the diversity of particular situations." He feared that a "disproportionate increase" in the president's "prerogative and patronage" would enable him to lead the country into monarchy. Madison would have found sufficient evidence of Locke's "royalism" in the latter's definition of prerogative as the power to act without law or contrary to its letter.[30]

In what follows, as the occasion offers, I shall relate the views of early Americans on prerogative to those of Locke, without insisting that Americans necessarily got their views from him.

The first thing to notice is that Americans only rarely used the word "prerogative" in connection with the laws and then always, it appears, in a pejorative way. To be specific, the term was used by Republicans when they wanted to taint their Federalist adversaries with monarchism. Recall Madison's assertions that Hamilton got his ideas about executive power from British prerogatives and that too much prerogative and patronage held by the president might lead to monarchy. Madison based the second assertion on rather complicated reasoning: the Federalists' interpretation of the "general welfare" clause would expand congressional power; in exercising its expanded power, Congress would have to delegate more "prerogative" to the president; and this would help bring about the feared result. Otherwise, Republicans as well as Federalists spoke of executive "discretion," not of executive "prerogative." Locke helped to prepare the way for the change, for he had made the word "prerogative," with its monarchic attachments, ill suited to describe the activities of a republican executive. Indeed, as we have seen, he used the word "discretion" as a definition of prerogative. Those modern scholars on the American presidency who have written about "residual prerogative," "emergency prerogative," and "constitutional prerogative" that embrace all executive powers have not been using the language of American constitutionalism.[31]

Further, American statesmen never, to my knowledge, claimed for the executive a right—what our modern scholars call a "prerogative"—to engage in an illegal or unconstitutional act. Even when, as subjects of the Crown, they spoke in the old manner, they insisted, as James Wilson said, that "prerogative can operate only when the law is silent." Several of the early state constitutions repudiated the power of state governors to suspend laws or their execution without the consent of the people's representatives. The English ministry's "error" in the episode of the corn embargo was evoked in an early Congress as a reminder that illegal acts cannot be cloaked with legal authority.[32]

Thus legal discretion was to be exercised to aid the laws, not to set them aside. Federalists were more favorably disposed to its exercise than were Republicans, just as they favored an interpretation of the Constitution that allowed more discretionary authority to the national government in exercising its powers than did the Republicans, with their doctrine of strict construction. And yet rarely did anybody in the founding period speak of a right of executive officers to act "without" law or where the law was "silent," that is, a right to act in the absence of authority. For example, Washington believed that he could not appoint Indian agents because Congress had not voted funds specifically for the purpose in authorizing him to carry on trade with the Indians. Hamilton once remarked to one of his customs collectors, when he was secretary of the Treasury, that "my maxims are not favorable to much discretion," and, after he had left office, he advised the secretary of the navy that "without the authority of law," all the president might do in the face of French seizures of American merchant ships was "to repel force by force (but not to capture), and to repress hostilities within our own waters. . . . In so delicate a case, in one which involves so important a consequence as that of war—my opinion is that no doubtful authority ought to be exercised by the President."[33]

When President John Adams went beyond the express terms of the Non-Intercourse Act of 1799, the Supreme Court ruled his action invalid. The act had authorized the capture of American ships traveling to French ports, and Adams instructed navy commanders to capture such ships when traveling to or from such ports, apparently in order to make the law more effective. Chief Justice John Marshall, speaking for the Court, said that the president might have been able to order such captures "without any special authority for that purpose," in his capacity as commander in chief and under his duty to see to the execution of the laws, if Congress, in prescribing the way in which the Non-Intercourse Act was to be carried out, had not precluded any choice in the matter.[34]

Early Americans tended to think of executive "discretion" primarily as arising from legislative delegations, not from lack of legislative foresight. It might take the form of lump-sum appropriations by Congress for the operation of executive agencies, which the Federalists favored and the Republicans, preferring itemized appropriations, generally opposed. It might take the form of broad delegation of discretion to executive officers in carrying out legislation, and here also the two parties disagreed. For example, Federalists in Congress wanted to authorize the president to call men into military service "whenever he shall judge the public safety to require the measure," whereas Republicans would have required Congress to make that judgment. Federalists were willing to entrust customs collectors with the responsibility of determining which merchant ships were built so as to be readily converted into ships of war, and thus to qualify for a government subsidy, against Madison's protest that this would place "immense discretion" in the hands of those officers.[35]

American statesmen at the founding seem to have regarded executive discretion somewhat more narrowly than Locke did prerogative, but similarly to the way that they themselves regarded equity, or judicial discretion. In *Commentaries on the Constitution,* for example, Story stated that judges may consider the "spirit" of the document in interpreting it but that "the spirit is to be collected chiefly from the letter." And when the words of the document are not contradicted by anything found elsewhere in it, judges may depart from their plain meaning only when "all mankind" would agree on the "absurdity" or "injustice" of a literal application of them. As Story remarked in another work, *Commentaries on Equity Jurisprudence,* equity does not contradict or overturn law. And just as Hamilton did not favor much discretion in executive officers, neither did he approve of it in judges. "To avoid an arbitrary discretion in the courts," he wrote in *Federalist* number 78, "it is indispensable that they should be bound down by strict rules and precedents, which serve to define and point out their duty in every particular case that comes before them." Blackstone, it may be recalled, was not so restrictive as to what judges could do outside the letter of the law.[36]

If there is no right—no "prerogative"—to act "against" the law, what is a president or some other executive officer to do in circumstances that seem to require immediate action? He acts and risks the consequences. As Jefferson expressed the matter in a letter that has often been cited,

> The laws of necessity, of self-preservation, of saving our country when in danger, are of higher obligation [than "a strict observance of the written laws"]. . . . The officer who is called to act on this superior ground, does indeed risk himself on the justice of the controlling powers of the Constitution. . . . It is incumbent on those only who accept of great charges, to risk themselves on great occasions, when the safety of the nation, or some of its very high interests are at stake.[37]

In this letter, Jefferson was defending actions in three matters that came up during his presidency. In the fall of 1805, at a time when, he said, Spain was interested in selling Florida, he considered making the purchase before going to Congress for the money, in "transgression of the law," and he would have done so had he known that John Randolph would delay action in the House of Representatives until the following spring, when Spain was no longer interested in selling. In 1807, he spent unappropriated funds for military supplies when the threat of conflict with Great Britain suddenly loomed and Congress was not in session. Also in that year, James Wilkinson, the commanding general of the Louisiana Territory, arrested two of Aaron Burr's accomplices in New Orleans and sent them to the nation's capital for trial in violation of territorial law, because (so Jefferson said) Wilkinson had reason to fear that the British fleet and Burr's land forces were about to make a concerted attack on the city.[38]

Jefferson's catalogue of emergency actions could be extended. He might, for example, have mentioned his acquisition of the Louisiana Territory from France in 1803, which he thought was "an act beyond the Constitution." Or the decision of President Washington and his cabinet (of which Jefferson was a member) in 1793 to spend unappropriated money for military supplies at a tense moment in the nation's relations with France. Or the circumstances under which the Constitution had been framed and adopted. Was not the Constitutional Convention authorized only to amend the Articles of Confederation, not to change their very nature? And was it not required by the terms of the Articles to obtain the unanimous consent of the state legislatures for its proposals, not the consent of a minimum of nine state conventions elected by the people? *The Federalist* justified these departures from legality on "the transcendent and precious right of the people to 'abolish or alter their governments,' " on "the great principle of self-preservation," on "the transcendent law of nature and of nature's God, which declares that the safety and happiness of society are the objects at which all political institutions aim, and to which all such institutions must be sacrificed." *The Federalist* confirms what my quotation of Jefferson suggested: the justification for violating the laws lies in the principles of the Declaration of Independence. As knowing readers will realize, the source of these principles is Locke's *Second Treatise of Government*.[39]

The founders' notion of when it was proper for the executive to act in derogation of the laws was much less strict than that of one of our modern scholars. Arthur M. Schlesinger, Jr., it may be recalled, justified what he called "emergency prerogative" on none of the occasions I have mentioned and only two or three times in the entire course of American history.

Despite what Jefferson said, early Americans were sometimes willing to depart from the laws in situations in which neither the nation's safety nor its high interests were at stake. Recall President Adams's instructions to his naval commanders to seize ships coming from French ports (though it is possible that the president was unaware that he was acting contrary to the Non-Intercourse Act). Or consider Secretary Hamilton's suggestion to his customs collector in Providence, Rhode Island, in early 1793 that perhaps the latter had not relaxed enforcement of the revenue laws when "upon an *urgent occasion*," he might have done so. Some merchants in Providence had been complaining that the collector had been unwilling to deviate from "the plain letter of the Law" in the cases of some of these merchants. Or consider what was described at the time as the "general practice" of executive departments of taking funds appropriated for one purpose and using them for another. Although a Federalist member of Congress defended the transfers as dictated by "imperious and irresistible necessity," one wonders why, for example, it was necessary to use unappropriated funds to complete the running of a boundary line betweeen United States and Spanish territories. Convenience, not necessity, seemed to motivate Jefferson's suggestion, as president, to the governor of Virginia that the latter substitute his own means for carrying out a federal act relating to military volunteers for the "impractical" ones stipulated in the law.[40]

In bringing executive violations under "the controlling powers of the Constitution," Jefferson evidently had Congress mainly in mind. If Congress thought a violation was justified, it could, when necessary, indemnify the officer against civil or criminal action being taken against him, as Parliament had done in 1766 for those who had advised and carried out the corn embargo and as Congress was to do during the Civil War for everyone, including President Lincoln, who was involved in suspensions of the writ of habeas corpus. (I know of no instances of advance indemnification during the early decades of the Republic.) Or Congress could indemnify—reimburse—an officer for damages assessed against him in a lawsuit, as it did in the case of Captain George Little, who had made the mistake of obeying his commander in chief and not the law in capturing a vessel owned by one Barreme on its way *from* a French port in the West Indies. Probably Congress would have done the same for Jefferson had he lost the suit for trespass brought against him after he had left office for having as president ordered the seizure of a tract of land in New Orleans claimed by a private person; but the suit was dismissed on a technical point. Or, if Congress should disapprove of what an executive officer has done, it could leave him unprotected against judicial action or it could take action itself to censure or impeach and remove him from office. The president can also censure or remove from office. Hamilton may have been thinking of these possibilities when he cautioned his customs collector in Providence that any relaxation in the enforcement of the revenue laws "must always be at the peril of the officer and therefore ought to stand on manifest ground." Finally, the president might exercise the one prerogative that he clearly has to make the laws "give way," as Jefferson did when he pardoned those who had been convicted under the Sedition Act in prosecutions conducted before he became president.[41]

Political scientist Lucius Wilmerding has written that "every single one of our early statesmen agreed that acts outside the law . . . ought to be stated immediately to Congress." This goes too far. Washington and Jefferson reported their unauthorized spending to Congress (at least, Jefferson recorded that Washington planned to), and Jefferson reported General Wilkinson's arrests. But Jefferson said nothing publicly when his friends in Congress rejected his opinion that they should seek a constitutional amendment to legalize his acquisition of Louisiana after the fact, and he assured the governor of Virginia that the latter would not be challenged if he were to modify the army volunteers act, inasmuch as "no private right stands in the way and the public object is in the interest of all." And Lincoln—to look ahead once more—reported to Congress only in May 1862 that he had, with the support of his cabinet, engaged in "extraordinary proceedings" during the first months of the Civil War, which included giving large sums of money to private persons to spend for public purposes. Some of these proceedings, he said, were "without any authority of law." Lincoln belatedly acknowledged them only because the House of Representatives had singled out for censure the person who had been the secretary of war at the time they had occurred.[42]

We should amend Wilmerding's statement: executive officers must be prepared to justify acts outside the law to Congress or perhaps to their executive superior or to a court of law should the acts be questioned. It is this obligation that acknowledges the lack of a legal basis for such actions.

I end my analysis with Lincoln. Not only did he fail to divulge unauthorized acts to Congress until long after the events, but he claimed a higher authority for such acts in "the broader powers conferred by the Constitution in cases of insurrection." What he meant by this was probably revealed in his special message to Congress of July 4, 1861, shortly after the Civil War had started, where he defended his suspension of the writ of habeas corpus against the charge that he had exercised a power given by the Constitution to Congress. If he had, Lincoln said (but he was not willing to make the concession), his act was justified by his constitutional duty to see that the laws—"the whole of the laws"—were faithfully executed against resistance to them and also by his official oath to preserve the government. I cannot take up Lincoln's views in detail here, but I have revealed enough to suggest that we should look to him, not to Locke or the founders, as the source of Corwin's claim for the executive of "a broad discretion capable even of setting aside the ordinary law in the meeting of special exigencies for which the legislative power had not provided."[43]

NOTES

1. John Locke, *The Second Treatise of Government,* in *Two Treatises of Government,* ed. Peter Laslett, rev. ed. (Cambridge: Cambridge University Press, 1963). I have not retained Locke's italics in my quotations from this work in this essay.

2. Edward S. Corwin, *The President: Office and Powers, 1787–1948* 3d rev. ed. (New York: New York University Press, 1948), pp. 10, 15–16, 6–7, 182; see also p. 305.

3. Ibid., p. 82. Corwin, "War the Constitution Moulder," in Edward S. Corwin, *Presidential Power and the Constitution: Essays,* ed. Richard Loss (Ithaca, N.Y.: Cornell University Press, 1976), p. 23.

4. Corwin, *The President,* pp. 220, 103–7, 220; see also Corwin, *The President's Control of Foreign Relations* (Princeton, N.J.: Princeton University Press, 1917), p. 5, and *Total War and the Constitution* (New York: A. A. Knopf, 1947), pp. 12, 14; Corwin, *The President,* p. 317.

5. Corwin, *The President,* pp. 2, 38, 366.

6. Ibid., p. 366.

7. Joseph E. Kallenbach, *The American Chief Executive: The Presidency and the Governorship* (New York: Harper & Row, 1966), pp. 61, 448–49, 449–50; Louis W. Koenig, *The Chief Executive,* 5th ed. (New York: Harcourt Brace Jovanovich, 1986), p. 11; Arthur M. Schlesinger, Jr., *The Imperial Presidency* (New York: Popular Library, 1974), pp. 20–21, 310 (see also "Epilogue," pp. 450–51); Richard M. Pious, *The American Presidency* (New York: Basic Books, 1979), pp. 16, 44–45, 38, 45; see also pp. 47, 83–84. For other studies that follow the path opened by Corwin on the matter of prerogative (with some special turns), see Larry Arnhart, " 'The God-Like Prince': John Locke, Executive Prerogative, and the American Presidency," *Presidential Studies Quarterly* 9 (Spring 1979): 121–30; Joseph M. Bessette and Jeffrey K. Tulis, "Introduction," in *The Presidency in the Constitutional Order,* ed. Joseph M. Bessette and Jeffrey K. Tulis (Baton Rouge: Louisiana State University Press, 1981), p. 25; George C. Edwards III and Stephen J. Wayne, *Presidential Leadership: Politics and Policy Making* (New York: St. Martin's Press, 1985), p. 5; Richard H. Cox, "Executive Prerogative: A Problem for Adherents of Constitutional Government," in *E Pluribus Unum: Constitutional Principles and the Institutions of Government,* ed. Sarah B. Thurow (Lanham, Md.: University Press of America, 1988), pp. 102–22; Jeffrey Tulis, *The Rhetorical Presidency* (Princeton, N.J.: Princeton University Press, 1987), pp. 202–3.

8. James Kent, *Commentaries on American Law,* ed. O. W. Holmes, 12th ed., 4 vols. (Boston: Little, Brown, 1884); Joseph Story, *Commentaries on the Constitution of the United States,* 2 vols. (Boston: Hilliard, Gray, 1833); William Whiting, *The Government's War Powers under the Constitution of the United States* (Boston: Little, Brown, 1864; reprinted, Glorietta, N.Mex.: Rio Grande Press, n.d.); James G. Randall, *Constitutional Problems under Lincoln* (Urbana: University of Illinois Press, 1926; rev. ed., 1951); Clarence A. Berdahl, *War Powers of the Executive in the United States* (Urbana: University of Illinois Press, 1921).

9. Locke, *Second Treatise,* secs. 160, 159; Aristotle, *Rhetoric* 1774a, 27–34; Locke, *Second Treatise,* secs. 162–63.

10. Locke, *Second Treatise,* secs. 160, 164 (cf. secs. 154–58, 167), 156, 157.

11. Ibid., sec. 159.

12. Ibid., sec. 160.

13. Ibid., secs. 164–65; William Blackstone, *Commentaries on the Laws of England* (Chicago: University of Chicago Press, 1979; reprint of 1765 edition), vol. 1, introd., p. 61.

14. Blackstone, *Commentaries,* vol. 1, bk. 3, pp. 430–31. Blackstone uses the Latin *arbitrio* in referring to equity's discretion. Joseph Story, *Commentaries on Equity Jurisprudence, as Administered in England and America* (Boston: Hilliard, Gray, 1836; reprinted Arno Press, 1977), vol. 1, p. 46.

15. Blackstone, *Commentaries,* vol. 3, p. 430.

16. Thomas B. Macaulay, *The History of England, from the Accession of James II* (Philadelphia: Porter & Coates, n.d.), vol. 1, p. 39; W. S. Holdsworth, *A History of*

English Law, 2d ed. (London: Methuen, 1937), vol. 6, pp. 217–18; David Hume, *The History of England, from the Invasion of Julius Caesar to the Revolution of 1688* (New York: Liberty Classics, 1985, based on the 1778 edition), vol. 6, pp. 471–72, 474; 1 Will. & Mar. sess. 2, c. 2 (1688).

17. Locke, "The Preface," in *Two Treatises*, p. 171; Locke, *Second Treatise*, secs. 202, 206, 162.

18. Locke, *Second Treatise*, secs. 165, 166, 42, 163–64, 210, 135, 137.

19. Ibid., secs. 159, 160; *Bishops' Case*, 12 St. Tr. 183 (1688). See also Laslett, "Introduction," in Locke, *Two Treatises*, pp. 17–21.

20. *The Parliamentary History of England* (New York: Johnson Reprint Corp., n.d.; reprint of 1813 edition), vol. 16, Nov. 11, 18, 24 and Dec. 10, 1766, pp. 235–313; Nov. 24, 1766, pp. 246n, 247, 248; Lord Chatham, quoted in John Lord Campbell, *The Lives of the Lord Chancellors and Keepers of the Great Seal of England*, 2d ser. (Philadelphia: Lea and Blanchard, 1848), vol. 5, pp. 184, 218–19; "A Speech in Behalf of the Constitution against the Suspending and Dispensing Prerogative, &c," in *Parliamentary History*, Dec. 10, 1766, pp. 266–68; ibid., Nov. 18, 1766, p. 245. My attention was drawn to this debate by Lucius Wilmerding, "The President and the Law," *Political Science Quarterly* 67 (Sept. 1952): 321–38.

21. Basil Williams, *The Life of William Pitt* (London: Longmans, Green, 1914), vol. 2, p. 228.

22. Blackstone, *Commentaries,* vol. 1, pp. 243, 244, 178.

23. Hume, *History of England*, vol. 5, Appendix 4, p. 127; *Rex* v. *Hampden*, 3 St. Tr. 825 (1637); *Godden* v. *Hales*, 11 St. Tr. 1166 (1686); Locke, *Second Treatise*, secs. 159, 162, 158, 168.

24. Locke, *Second Treatise*, secs. 143, 159 (punctuation omitted), 144, 147.

25. Ibid., secs. 162, 136–37, 166, 165–66, 154, 156.

26. Blackstone, *Commentaries,* vol. 1, bk. 1, pp. 188, 192, 193, 141, 237, 193.

27. Constitution, Art. II, sec. 3; Art. II, sec. 2, cl. 2. See *Annals of Congress,* House of Representatives, 1st Cong., 1st Sess., 1789, May 19, 1789, cols. 368–84; June 16, 1789, cols. 455–79; June 17, 1789, cols. 479–512.

28. Alexander Hamilton, James Madison, and John Jay, *The Federalist* (New York: Modern Library, 1937), no. 47, pp. 319, 320; no. 48, p. 322; no. 69, pp. 450, 451; no. 73, p. 478; no. 74, p. 482; Story, *Commentaries on the Constitution,* vol. 2, secs. 1094, 1113, 1117, 1163–1167; vol. 1, secs. 841–42; vol. 2, secs. 1492, 1506; Constitution, Art. II, secs. 2(2), 3.

29. Locke, *Second Treatise*, sec. 146; Hamilton et al., *The Federalist,* no. 75, p. 486; James Madison, *Notes of Debates in the Federal Convention of 1787,* ed. Adrienne Koch (Athens: Ohio University Press, 1966), June 1, 1787, pp. 44–45; Baron de Montesquieu, *The Spirit of the Laws,* trans. Thomas Nugent (New York: Hafner Publishing Co., 1949), bk. 11, ch. 6, pp. 151–52; Alexander Hamilton, "Pacificus," No. 1, June 29, 1793, in *Letters of Pacificus and Helvidius on the Proclamation of Neutrality of 1793, by Alexander Hamilton (Pacificus) and James Madison (Helvidius)* (Washington, D.C.: J. and G. S. Gideon, 1845), pp. 6–15; James Madison, "Letters of Helvidius," No. 1, Aug. 24, 1793, ibid., pp. 53–64 (see esp. p. 62); Corwin, *The President*, p. 273.

30. Madison, "Helvidius," No. 1, *Letters of Pacificus and Helvidius,* p. 56n; Madison, "Report on the [Virginia] Resolutions, Virginia House of Delegates, 1799–1800," in James Madison, *Writings,* ed. Gaillard Hunt (New York: G. P. Putnam's Sons, 1906), vol. 6, pp. 358–59.

31. Madison, "Report on Resolutions," pp. 358–59.

32. James Wilson, *Works,* ed. Robert G. McCloskey (Cambridge, Mass.: Harvard University Press, 1967), vol. 2, p. 754 (see also pp. 755–56), cited in Wilmerding, "The President and the Law," p. 336.

33. George Washington, *Writings,* ed. John C. Fitzpatrick (Washington, D.C.: Government Printing Office, 1940), vol. 35, p. 149; Hamilton to Jeremiah Olney, Apr. 2, 1793, in Alexander Hamilton, *Papers,* ed. Harold C. Syrett et al. (New York: Columbia University Press, 1969), vol. 14, p. 277; Hamilton to James McHenry, May 17, 1798, ibid., (1974), vol. 21, pp. 461–62.

34. *Little* v. *Barreme,* 2 Cranch 170 (1804).

35. See, e.g., Leonard D. White, *The Federalists: A Study in Administrative History* (New York: Macmillan, 1948), pp. 329–30, 449; idem, *The Jeffersonians: A Study in Administrative History, 1801–1829* (New York: Macmillan, 1951), pp. 109–10; Joseph Cooper, *The Origins of the Standing Committees and the Development of the Modern House* (Houston: Rice University Studies, Summer 1970), vol. 56, no. 3, pp. 29–30, 71.

36. Story, *Commentaries on the Constitution,* vol. 1, sec. 427; Story, *Commentaries on Equity Jurisprudence,* vol. 1, p. 16; Hamilton et al., *The Federalist,* no. 78, p. 510.

37. Jefferson to J. B. Colvin, Sept. 20, 1810, in Jefferson, *Writings,* ed. Andrew A. Lipscomb and Albert E. Bergh (Washington: Thomas Jefferson Memorial Association, 1904), vol. 12, pp. 418, 421–22.

38. Ibid., pp. 418–22.

39. Jefferson to John Breckinridge, Aug. 12, 1803, in Jefferson, *Writings,* vol. 10, pp. 410–11. See Jefferson's account of the decision, in cabinet meeting entry, July 25, 1793, in *The Complete Anas of Thomas Jefferson,* ed. Franklin B. Sawvel (New York: Round Table Press, 1930), p. 145; Hamilton et al., *The Federalist,* no. 40, p. 257, and no. 43, p. 287.

40. See Hamilton to Jeremiah Olney, Apr. 2, 1793 (emphasis in original), and Jeremiah Olney to Hamilton, Mar. 28, 1793, in Hamilton, *Papers,* vol. 14, pp. 277, 214, 217; *Annals of Congress,* House of Representatives, 7th Cong., 1st Sess., 1801, Dec. 14, 1801, cols. 319–24, col. 322; Jefferson to Gov. William H. Cabell, Aug. 11, 1807, in Jefferson, *Writings,* vol. 11, pp. 319–20.

41. See Randall, *Constitutional Problems under Lincoln,* pp. 191–93; Act of Jan. 17, 1807, *Laws of the United States of America* (Washington, D.C.: Government Printing Office, 1807), vol. 8, pp. 224–25; Jefferson to Attorney General, Sept. 25, 1810, in *Writings,* vol. 12, pp. 424–27; "The Batture at New Orleans," Feb. 25, 1812, ibid., vol. 18, pp. 1–132, esp. pp. 128–32; Hamilton to Olney, in Hamilton, *Papers,* vol. 14, p. 277.

42. Wilmerding, "President and the Law," p. 324; Jefferson to Cabell, in Jefferson, *Writings,* vol. 11, p. 318; Abraham Lincoln, "To the Senate and House of Representatives," May 26, 1862, in Lincoln, *Collected Works,* ed. Roy P. Basler (New Brunswick, N.J.: Rutgers University Press, 1953), vol. 5, pp. 140–42.

43. Lincoln, "Message to Congress in Special Session," July 4, 1861, in *Collected Works,* vol. 4, pp. 429–31.

PART 3
PRECEDENTS

10

GEORGE WASHINGTON: PRECEDENT SETTER

GLENN A. PHELPS

When George Washington arrived in New York in 1789 to take his oath of office, no one doubted that he was the president of a newly constituted United States. There remained much doubt, however, as to just what this presidency *was*. A few properties of the office were clear: the method of selection, the qualifications for the office, and the length of the president's term. Ambiguity reigned, however, when the political character of the presidency was considered. As Ralph Ketcham has aptly put it, "Far from everything being settled, virtually nothing was."[1] The cryptic words of Article II, "The executive Power shall be vested in a President of the United States," offered little guidance to the first occupant of the office. What should the relationship be between the president and the other branches of the national government? Between the president and the states? Between the president and the people? What were the president's responsibilities to the Constitution itself? For Washington, then, the problem of the first presidency was not so much defined by the desire to fulfill a personal policy agenda as it was by the need to define the powers of the office and the role of the person who occupied it.[2]

Washington was aware of both the ambiguity of the constitutional text and his own potential as an explicator of that text. He shared with others of the founding generation the view that a constitution draws its life not merely from the explicit words of the written document but also from the deeds and understandings of subsequent generations.[3] Founding was an ongoing process in which customs, practices, and institutions that the Constitution was silent about would add specific meaning to the outline of 1787. Washington appreciated the importance of the stage he was about to enter. In a letter to several advisors in the spring of 1789, Washington noted, "Many things which appear of little importance in themselves and at the beginning, may have great and durable consequences from their having been established at the commencement of a new general government."[4] The veneration of the Constitution, which characterized much American thought later (and which has been carried to an extreme by the current bicentennial period of "good feelings") can lead us to forget the anxieties of Washington and his contemporaries. For them the new government was far from a sure thing. The Articles of Confederation had already been cast aside as a dismal failure, and several states also were undergoing constitutional "crises" whose outcomes were unpredictable. The republican experiment was in jeopardy, and hard choices would need to be made.

Washington clearly understood that he was in a unique position to affect those choices and, thus, the meaning of the Constitution for the future. He was, after all, the *first* president. As obvious as that statement is, we often overlook its significance. The constitutional slate was uniquely clean for him, as it never would be for his successors. As political scientist V. O. Key observed in his classic study of the American party system, much of the contemporary Constitution derives from the "persistence of original forms."[5] Certainly not all of the "forms" initiated during Washington's tenure would become ingrained in the constitutional tradition. Jefferson, for example, abandoned Washington's practice of making public addresses to Congress—a precedent not to be revived until Woodrow Wilson. Nor have subsequent presidents felt obligated to take their authority as commander in chief as literally as Washington did. None have followed the example of his conduct in the Whisky Rebellion, when he took to horse to lead the nation's troops in the field. But in other important ways the constitutional presidency of 1987 reflects choices made by the first president.

Washington came to this enterprise with formidable political resources. As the commanding general of the Continental Army, he emerged, virtually without challenge, as the one authentic *national* hero of the Revolution. The journey to relinquish his command to Congress at Annapolis and to return to his home, Mount Vernon, became a "victory tour." Towns along the route outdid themselves in their efforts to honor the retiring general with spontaneous as well as official celebrations. No American could lay a similar claim to the affections of the people. George Washington embodied the closest thing to a "cult of personality" that this nation has seen.[6]

This immense reservoir of popular support was supplemented in several ways. First, his selection by the electoral college was unanimous. Thus, his political support embraced both masses and elites. Moreover, the new Congress, while it was not partisan in the sense that it would become by 1793, was dominated by men whom Washington perceived as political allies.[7] Throughout much of 1788 he was filled by a fear that the "federal party" would not obtain control of the new government. Then, optimism bloomed as he learned of the election of more and more "friends of the Constitution"—friends who, he was convinced, shared his constitutional vision.

Curiously, most accounts of Washington's contributions to the founding emphasize his military accomplishments and his importance as a symbol for the nation-building process but minimize his substantive contributions to constitutional development. Even the most comprehensive biographies of Washington emphasize the "indispensability" of his personal authority at critical points in America's political history but make only modest claims for his constitutional accomplishments.[8] Characteristically, Washington is portrayed as a political naïf whose presidency was little more than a forum for the crucial debate between the Hamiltonians and the Jeffersonians regarding the scope and direction of the new national government. Indeed, one recent work on Washington's presidency spends more time discussing the political and economic theories of Alexander Hamilton than in discussing the accomplishments of the president.[9]

It is true that George Washington was not a political philosopher of the caliber of Jefferson, Hamilton, Madison, Wilson, Adams, Mason, and others. Despite his abiding interest in education, he was not himself well read in the classics familiar to other framers. His own reading interests leaned toward natural history and biography rather than political treatises. Many of the writings and speeches for which Washington is famous (e.g., the Farewell Address, the Circular Letter to the States, his resignation from the army) were drafted or polished by others. Add to this his desire for political consensus and his disdain of overt partisanship, and it is not difficult to conclude that the modest assessments of his presidency might well be correct.

But Fred Greenstein, in a recent work on a later president, has suggested that we take a closer look too at Washington's effectiveness and accomplishments as a leader. In his revisionist view of Dwight Eisenhower, Greenstein has demonstrated that Eisenhower's public aloofness from political controversy and his leadership style of mediation and consensus masked a coherent set of political values. Greenstein argues that Eisenhower was far more successful in shaping the national political agenda than had previously been believed.[10] Similarly, when judged by the extent to which our twentieth-century Constitution is a reflection of his presidential choices, George Washington was a more influential founder than has previously been thought.

Indeed, a close examination of Washington's writings, especially his personal letters, reveals a man with strongly felt political sentiments, especially about the purposes and procedures of a constitution. These sentiments remained remarkably consistent from the last years of the war through his tenure as president. As he remarked to James Madison, "As the first of everything, in our situation will serve to establish a precedent, it is devoutly wished on my part, that these precedents may be fixed on true principles."[11] For Washington, "founding" was an ongoing enterprise in which he intended to play a significant role—a role defined by his own sense of the "true principles" of the Constitution.

WASHINGTON AND THE RULE OF LAW

Not the least important of the constitutional norms that the first president endorsed was his commitment to the rule of law. One of the shared values of the founding generation was a commitment to constitutionalism. Lance Banning, in particular, has explained the broad acceptance of the 1787 Constitution as symptomatic of this constitutional consensus. Once the Constitution had been ratified and the new government was in place, even Antifederalists accepted its legitimacy. Their opposition politics never again challenged the authority of the Constitution; instead, it focused on the interpretation of the Constitution.[12]

Washington's attitudes firmly stamped him as a conservative republican—an ideology that saw liberty as possible only under the rule of law, that saw republicanism as flourishing only in an atmosphere of political stability. He had even explained his support for the Revolution in constitutional terms. The War for Independence was not a revolution *against* lawful authority. It was, instead, a war to restore "the rights of Americans"—rights that were being threatened by the unconstitutional actions of the British government. Explaining his actions to an old friend then living in England, Washington remarked that the Revolution "was not in the beginning, premeditated, but the result of dire necessity brought about by the persecuting spirit of the British Government." It was a "redress of grievances in a constitutional way."[13] By contrast, his later fears about the French Revolution focused on the excesses and "passions" of the revolutionaries and their unwillingness to establish law and order sufficient to safeguard "the security of that liberty."[14]

This was clearly a man unwilling to let either himself or the office he occupied become a lightning rod for efforts to undermine the rule of law. Washington's familiarity with Roman classicism had taught him that in times of crisis, republics would forever be tempted to turn to a dictator for protection. But the personalism that made a dictator attractive would eventually destroy a republic and its constitution.[15] Washington was offered the scepter more than once, most often by individuals (Hamilton) or groups (the Continental Army) with whose objectives he shared much in common. It is one thing to find men willing to uphold the rule of the law and the authority of a government when they support its policies; it is quite another to find a leader of Washington's stature willing to bear arms in defense of a government whose policies he detests, merely because it *is* the constitutional government. The inept and niggardly Continental Congress more than once drove soldiers to appeal to their commander in chief to seize the reins of power. Not only did he decline; he even sent troops to suppress his own comrades when they threatened the Congress in the Philadelphia mutiny.

Washington's criticism of the Articles of Confederation and his skepticism toward several of the state governments increased during the years before the Constitutional Convention. The nation was headed for a crisis. Nevertheless, the use of extralegal measures against constitutional governments was, for Washington, no remedy for ineffective rule. The insurrection led by Daniel Shays evoked the core of Washington's conservative feelings. The prospect that the hopes of the Revolution—self-government, republicanism, liberty under law—might vanish in a maelstrom of internecine disputes perplexed and disturbed him deeply.

> It is but the other day, that we were shedding our blood to obtain the Constitutions under which we now live; Constitutions of our own choice and making; and now we are unsheathing the sword to overturn them. The thing is so unaccountable, that I hardly know how to realize it, or to persuade myself that I am not under the illusion of a dream.[16]

Not only did Washington support the general principle of the rule of law; he had also staked a considerable amount of his jealously horded personal prestige on the drafting and ratification of the new Constitution. Thus, when he arrived in New York to accept the presidency he felt a personal responsibility for the success of the enterprise. "The destiny of the Republican model of government," he realized, was "*deeply,* perhaps *finally* staked, on the experiment entrusted to the hands of the American people"—and to his own performance as president.[17]

WASHINGTON AND SEPARATION OF POWERS

What is remarkable about Washington's commitment to the rule of law was his willingness to subordinate other firmly held political sentiments to that standard. He had confided that "there are some things in the new form [the Constitution], I will readily acknowledge, [which] never did, and I am persuaded never will, obtain my cordial approbation."[18]

Among "those things" for which Washington had little enthusiasm was separation of powers and checks and balances. His own vision of republicanism emphasized the idea of mixed government. Drawn from classical antecedents and modified by the Whig tradition, the theory of mixed government sought representation for each of the three elements of society—the monarchy, the aristocracy, and the people. Most important, in mixed government the three elements were to cooperate for the public good.[19] The British model, the King-in-Parliament, served as an example of the energy and the unity that were possible in a mixed-government state.

This view may be surprising to those who believe that all of the founders warmly endorsed the principle of separation of powers. James Madison, in *Federalist* number 51, best exemplifies this orthodoxy. Mixed government, with its emphasis on having different elements cooperate in one unified government, was replaced with a view that political power, even in republics, should be checked and balanced by a division into different departments.[20] Even many of the Antifederalists shared this commitment to the principle of separation. For them the Constitution did not go far enough in erecting sufficient safeguards against the abuse of power. More checks, not fewer, were called for.[21]

For Washington, both of these views were anathema. He remained a committed "mixed government man." His perception of the crisis of the confederacy was not that the national government lacked balance or had insufficient checks on its power. On the contrary, Washington's view was that the central government needed *fewer* limitations on its power; that it needed *fewer* obstacles to its efficient operation; that it required, in a word, "energy." The theories of Montesquieu and Hume may have been attractive to his more intellectual compatriots. But Washington, who had been exposed to the paralyzing effects of limited government during the Revolution, desired a constitution that granted powers, rather than limiting them. He thought it would be futile to create a constitutional system if it were merely to replace a government constrained by the jealousies of the states with one stalemated by internal checks and balances. "No man is a warmer advocate for proper restraints and wholesome checks in every department than I am; but I have never yet been able to discover the propriety of placing it absolutely out of the power of men to render essential services, because a possibility remains of their doing ill."[22]

These two norms—commitment to the rule of law (epitomized by the new Constitution) and a desire for unity in government (in *opposition* to the checks and balances in that Constitution)—made for some interesting and, at first glance, bewildering presidential behavior. How would a president with strong nationalist feelings and a commitment to energetic government be able to govern under a constitution that raised substantial barriers to those goals? The answer to that question reveals George Washington as a constitutional interpreter of considerable creativity. Moreover, his method of interpretation was both sensible and consistent. Whenever his responsibilities as president were stipulated by the Constitution, Washington nearly always followed the letter of the law scrupulously, sometimes even absurdly so. On the other hand, when the Constitution was silent or ambiguous, his natural inclination toward unity and cooperation led him to ignore the implicit boundaries between himself and the other branches of the national government and between himself and the American people. Ironically then, as we shall see, the roots of both the constitutional and "energetic" models of the presidency can be traced to Washington's presidency.

THE CASE OF THE UNOPENED PACKET

Consider the question of the president as legislative leader—a role expected of modern presidents. Washington conceded the constitutional primacy of Congress in domestic lawmaking ("all legislative powers herein granted shall be vested in a Congress"), therefore he was quite deferential to its prerogatives. His formal addresses to Congress rarely set out the "president's program" in a fashion we would recognize today. In his first annual address to Congress, for example, he mentioned not a single specific legislative proposal. He did note that "many interesting objects . . . will engage your attention." For example, he suggested that Congress ought to legislate in such matters as the "proper establishment of the troops," "uniformity in the currency," a "uniform rule of nationalization," "the advancement of agriculture, commerce, and manufacture," and "the promotion of science and literature."[23] Beyond such generalities, most of them little more than restatements of the enumerated powers of Article I, Washington offered no specific recommendations. He continued this pattern in all of his annual addresses to Congress.

Some scholars have interpreted this reticence as an abdication of his leadership responsibilities; they think that Washington had no substantive agenda and view his functions as purely executive. Such a claim is but partly true. In the years before his election as president, Washington wrote again and again about policies he believed essential to the health of the nation. He pleaded for an end to paper money, the full funding of the national debt as a matter of "public justice" and "national honor," broad powers to regulate and promote national commerce and manufactures, a system of roads and canals to connect the western interior to the eastern states, a liberal policy of immigration, and the use of imposts as a source of federal revenue. A glance at the fragmentary excerpts of his original, but undelivered, first Inaugural Address makes clear that this was still his domestic political agenda in 1789.[24]

Yet the record indicates that Washington did not take an active role in "politicking" for his preferences (though his supporters often did). Even during his second term, when partisanship escalated to a point where he no longer could rely on his accommodational leadership style, he still refused to involve himself directly in the legislative process or to interfere with what he saw as the rightful (constitutional) prerogatives of Congress. An interesting example of his attitude was illustrated by Washington's conduct in the slightly ludicrous case of the unopened packet. In December 1790, Washington received a packet from the French National Assembly, then in the midst of its own revolution. It was addressed to "The President and Members of the American Congress." Because the packet had been placed in his hands and because he was addressed first, Washington could have opened it without controversy. But he submitted it to the Senate for their advice: Should he open it or should Congress? The Senate decided that the president should break the seal and report back to Congress if the message warranted. "An executive who took pains of this sort to respect the authority of the legislative branch was not," Freeman commented, "likely to have a clash."[25]

From this, one might conclude that Washington was a "weak" president, intent on avoiding conflict at all costs. Such an interpretation would misread the legacy of the first presidency. This deference to Congress was actually part of a strategy for establishing a strong presidency. This was, after all, a new government, which had been established only after heated debates in the state ratifying conventions. Washington believed that the public and Congress needed to be shown that the president could be trusted. If the first president sought to usurp the Constitution for his own political ends, then the Antifederalists and their concerns about monarchical tendencies would be proven right. If, however, public confidence in the chief executive were to increase, future presidents would find it easier to take a more directive role in national policy making. As Garry Wills has noted, part of the Cincinnatus myth of Roman legend is that power must be denied before it can be *freely* exercised.[26] As we shall see, later this pattern of self-denial often led to a more activist Washington presidency.

THE INCIDENT OF THE UNPAID DRAGOONS

At the Philadelphia convention Washington supported a strong presidency. Specifically, he advocated a veto power with few limits. In one of his few recorded votes, he opposed a resolution to reduce the majority needed for override from three-fourths to two-thirds—a resolution that was approved despite his opposition.[27] Other debates considered the possibility of linking the judiciary or the Senate with the president in a Council of Revision. Although the veto power was finally placed exclusively with the chief executive, the sense of these discussions was that the veto was to be exercised as a check on "unconstitutional" legislation. Washington, who attended every session of the convention, could not have been unaware of this intention of the framers.

The president, then, had an explicit veto power. But under what circumstances was it to be exercised? And was it to be limited only to legislation of questionable constitutionality? Could a president veto acts whose policy aims he disagreed with? Washington's advisors often encouraged him to use his veto as a policy tool. This would have established the precedent for presidential involvement in the legislative process. With one important exception, he declined that opportunity. For example, Washington believed strongly that as a matter of foreign policy, tariffs and duties should be reciprocal. Nations which interfered with or discriminated against American trade ought not to be entitled to equal treatment with the "good friends" of the United States. Thus, when he received, in July 1789, a tonnage bill that did not contain these discriminations, he considered not signing the bill, as an indication of his displeasure. But he did not veto it. He eventually signed the bill when he was informed that Congress was already considering a revision that would satisfy many of his objections.[28]

August 1789 brought another bill that struck Washington as bad policy, and once again he elected not to play the role of legislative leader. Congress was about to pass legislation providing that all congressmen be paid $6 per day. Six years earlier, in his famous Circular Letter to the States, Washington had argued that governmental rewards should be proportionate "to the aids the public derives from them," an argument that allowed him then to suggest that greater rewards, either in pay or in bounty lands, for officers were justified.[29] Writing to Madison, Washington expressed his view that senators—perhaps because of their added constitutional responsibilities—ought to receive more pay than representatives and asked whether a veto would be appropriate.[30] Madison probably insisted that this was an internal matter that Congress alone should decide. At any rate, no more is known than this one cryptic note—except that no veto occurred.

While Washington thus declined to use his veto power to nullify policies he disagreed with, the assumption bill indicated that he *was* willing to consider vetoing legislation he supported if its constitutionality was questioned. Washington had long campaigned for the full payment of the national debt; at one point he even drafted his own plan for financing the debt, although this apparently was never submitted to Congress.[31] In the cabinet debate over Hamilton's funding plan, Washington never questioned its wisdom. Rather, his concerns were solely for its constitutionality.

Although he signed the bill, it is clear that he viewed the president as having a specific role as guardian of the Constitution—this in the days before John Marshall was to assert such a role for the Supreme Court.

This concern for upholding the Constitution explains the first presidential veto. The census of 1790 yielded a population figure that, when divided by the constitutionally established criterion of one representative per 30,000 persons, authorized a House of Representatives of 120 members. When one divided the figure of 30,000 into the population of each state, one was left with only 112 representatives. The congressional plan allocated the remaining seats to the eight states with the largest remainders. These "bonus" seats would have disproportionately favored the northern states. Washington, although he was concerned about the appearance of prosouthern sympathies, vetoed the bill anyway. His message to Congress explained that "the Constitution has . . . provided that the number of representatives shall not exceed 1 for every 30,000 . . . and the bill has allotted to eight of the states more than 1 for every 30,000."[32] Policy considerations offered no defense for Washington's veto; the rule of law did.

It is Washington's oft-overlooked second veto, however, that reveals his willingness to assert a more energetic presidential role, to assert his mixed-government views, and to assert a vision of the presidency much like what in recent years has been called the "two presidencies" model. Congress had passed a bill that would reduce the size of the army. In what amounted to an item veto, Washington rejected the bill because it included the dismissal of two specific companies of field military. His explanation to Congress was based, not on constitutional grounds, but on his own policy assessment. First, these military units were serving at outposts on the western frontier. Travel and communication delays in those days meant that it would be weeks before the troops could be notified of the decision, organized for demobilization (soldiers don't simply drop their gear in the mud and leave), and sent home. Yet the bill would stop their pay immediately upon the president's signature. As a soldier of the Revolution who had constantly been plagued by the grievances of unpaid troops, Washington was not about to have his administration be the source of similar indignities. Second, he believed that the provision was simply bad military policy. The frontier was the last place to turn for troop reductions. Congress agreed and immediately passed a new bill without the objectionable item.

In exercising this veto, Washington added to one of his most important contributions to constitutional development. In domestic matters he recognized the constitutional primacy of congressional prerogatives, and his deference to the legislature remained constant. But with regard to foreign affairs and military policy, the Constitution was more ambiguous as to the allocation of power. Here, cooperation, consultation, and unity would be the norm; strict separation of powers would be discarded in favor of mixed government; and collective decision making would take place in a framework of presidential leadership. More than a century and a half later, Aaron Wildavsky would give a name to this model—"the two presidencies."[33]

THE CREEK TREATY AFFAIR

Presidential leadership in foreign affairs was, perhaps, inevitable. But Washington wanted that leadership to be based upon consultation and consensus. His bias for mixed government drew upon his concerns for energy and unity in government. As commander of the Continental Army, he had both witnessed and suffered from the fragmentation of congressional power into numerous boards and committees, each guarding its prerogatives jealously. The results were, in his opinion, nearly catastrophic for the Union. Washington wanted this new constitutional government to speak and act as much as possible with one voice. A strict adherence to separation of powers could, he thought, be the Achilles' heel of the new government.

This desire for what might be best described as a "consultative presidency" can be seen in his relations with the Senate. The early months of his administration saw several attempts by Washington to institute procedures that would narrow the separation between the president and the Senate. For example, there were plans for establishing a special chamber where the Senate could meet with the president on a regular basis for consultation, especially about appointments and treaties. Washington's preference was for "oral communications" on diplomatic matters. He was comfortable with the model of shared responsibility (the Council of War) that he had employed during the Revolution, especially if these consultations could be maintained on an ongoing basis. Sensitive to the protocol problems involved in direct presidential-Senate consultations, particularly with regard to the "awkward situation" respecting the role of the vice-president, Washington thought that a permanent meeting place, separate from Congress's usual chambers, would be appropriate. When he was reviewing plans for a new capital city, he suggested that "whenever the government shall have buildings of its own, an executive chamber will no doubt be provided, where the Senate will generally attend the President."[34] Thus would the bonds between the president and the Senate be further cemented.

Whether deliberate or not, Washington's grand plan bore a strong resemblance to the king-and-council form of the British parliamentary system. He was attracted to the idea of drawing the Senate into his consultative presidency for several reasons. It was a small group (twenty-six at the time); it was composed of the "better sort of men" because of its method of appointment; and it was presumed to be free of the local, parochial interests that Washington so detested. What better instrument for joining with the president in pursuit of his nationalist vision?

The purpose and procedures of "advice and consent" are not made clear in the Constitution. It certainly means that a two-thirds vote in the Senate is needed for approval of "treaties." But does it involve presidential-Senate interaction beyond the ratification process? Washington believed that it should. In his councils of war, it was common for Washington to submit a series of proposals and questions for consideration by his general staff. As he interpreted the Constitution, this was precisely what the "advice and consent" provision encouraged him to do with the Senate. His first opportunity to put this idea to the test arose in 1789, when he decided to send some emissaries to resolve a border dispute between Georgia and the Creek Indians. He tried to call on the Senate as a kind of privy council to advise him on an appropriate strategy of negotiation. With Secretary of War Henry Knox and Vice-President John Adams in tow, Washington appeared before the Senate in person. In his message to the Senate, he said: "As it is necessary that certain principles should be fixed *previously* to forming instructions to the Commissioners, the following questions arising out of the foregoing communications are seated by the President of the United States and the *advice* of the Senate requested thereon" (my emphasis).[35] Would the Senate, he inquired, provide him with its "advice and consent" to a series of eleven questions? Vice-President Adams then read the rather involved questions to a befuddled Senate. One senator rose and, citing the noise from passing carriages, asked that the questions be read again. William Maclay, a self-appointed guardian of grass-roots republicanism who was deeply suspicious of Washington and his Federalist friends, initiated a series of motions designed to prolong the proceedings and to insist on a full written disclosure by the president of his plans. Washington's legendary temper now added to the confusion of the moment. He angrily responded that Maclay's proposals would defeat "every purpose of my coming here" and then stormed out of the chamber.[36]

Some constitutional scholars see this incident as an important precedent in establishing separation of powers.[37] It is true that no president since has asked for the collective advice of the Senate before the fact, either in treaty negotiations or on executive appointments—although the Senate has generously offered it anyway! Nor has any president visited the Senate chamber to request a face-to-face exchange of ideas. Yet Washington's efforts were not without constitutional impact. Washington continued to seek the advice of individual senators (and congressmen) on political matters—a practice all subsequent presidents have adopted with little controversy despite its apparent violation of the separation principle. Even more important, several of his advisors, most notably Hamilton and Knox, encouraged Washington to assume near-monarchical prerogatives with regard to foreign policy as his "right" under the separation-of-powers doctrine. Less out of self-denial and more out of his desire for unity in government, Washington declined. His actions thus made it more likely that the "advice and consent" function of the Senate would not become a dead letter of the Constitution.

THE CASE OF THE RELUCTANT JUDGES

Another example of Washington's commitment to unified, cooperative government that has more obviously become part of our constitutional tradition is the "cabinet idea." Congress had created several executive departments in 1789. Secretaries of those departments were clearly to have administrative responsibilities. Less clear were their responsibilities for advising the president. Washington again drew upon his wartime experiences to fashion a cabinet modeled on his personal staff. As commander in chief, he had surrounded himself with a singular assemblage of enormously talented young men—the brilliant Alexander Hamilton, the dashing Marquis de Lafayette, the diplomatic David Humphreys, the poetic John Laurens, to name but a few—who were dedicated to serving the great General. Washington could ask advice on any political question (and the General was compelled to deal with many) and he could expect useful counsel from several of his young men. As president, Washington used his cabinet less as departmental administrators and more as ministers without portfolios. Matters of foreign policy, for example, would be referred, not just to Thomas Jefferson as secretary of state, but to the entire cabinet (Alexander Hamilton, Edmund Randolph, and Henry Knox) and even to trusted friends (e.g., John Jay and James Madison) outside the executive branch. The idea of a corporate cabinet has since fallen into disuse. The administrative duties of departmental secretaries have made them less attractive as personal advisors to the president. However, modern presidents *have* found indispensable Washington's idea of a body of political advisors dedicated to serving the president, as the mushrooming growth of the White House staff suggests.

Despite Washington's commitment to a consultative presidency, an incident early in his second term has often been seen as an important precedent in affirming the principle of separation of powers. There had already been, in 1793, several challenges to American neutrality. More were anticipated. What, Washington asked the Supreme Court, would be appropriate constitutional responses to a long list of hypothetical challenges to neutrality policy? Washington saw nothing untoward in his request. He had often consulted with individual justices before, especially Chief Justice Jay, on political matters. Washington had received written "advisory opinions" from Jay and had placed him on a commission to manage the national-debt fund (a purely *executive* function). When the president left the capital on one of his tours in 1791, he had authorized the cabinet secretaries, the vice-president, *and* the chief justice to consult with each other on matters of government.[38] Washington believed that a pattern of interbranch cooperation was well established. Moreover, the crisis of 1793 presented a threat to the dignity and independence of the United States, a threat that was orchestrated by foreign powers. Was it any wonder that in such a time Washington thought a president ought to receive the best available advice from whatever quarter it might come? It was thus a shock when the Supreme Court responded:

> We have considered the previous question . . . [regarding] the lines of separation drawn by the Constitution between the three departments of the government. These being in certain respects checks upon each other and our being judges of a court in the last resort, are considerations which afford strong arguments against the propriety of our extra-judicially deciding the questions alluded to especially as the power given by the Constitution to the President, of calling on the heads of departments for opinions seems to have been *purposely* as well as expressly united to the *executive* departments.[39] (Emphasis added)

Ironically then, Washington, the advocate of mixed government, had set the stage for one of the first and strongest precedents for separation of powers—that the judicial branch will not offer advice on matters pending before the executive (or the legislature). The president did not concede the point, however. Less than a year later, he appointed John Jay as special envoy to Great Britain, where Jay subsequently helped to negotiate Jay's Treaty. Despite his previous pronouncement, Jay did not resign the chief justiceship, perceiving, perhaps, that a president's call to patriotic duty transcended the claims of strict separation—a view more consistent with Washington's sentiments. Indeed, despite the now-famous Supreme Court reply of 1793, several modern presidents have called upon federal judges to provide them with advice or to serve in an executive capacity. Franklin Roosevelt continued to consult with Felix Frankfurter after the latter had been appointed to the Supreme Court, as did Lyndon Johnson with Abe Fortas. Johnson also appointed Earl Warren to head the commission that investigated the assassination of John Kennedy. In short, Washington's vision of a unified national government continues to have a substantial claim on contemporary constitutional officials.

What all of these examples suggest is that Washington was directed by a vision of the Constitution that was also an expression of his own experience-tested political philosophy. He saw the presidency, then, as *a part of* an integrated national government, not as an institution standing *apart from* the other branches.

SOME QUESTIONS OF PRIVILEGE

We can see further examples of Washington's consultative presidency when we examine his reaction to congressional requests for information from the executive branch. In a system based upon separation of powers, we would expect a president to assert the traditional prerogatives of a sovereign king when carrying out his executive duties. Information given to Congress would be for Congress to use or husband as representatives and senators saw fit; similarly, information for the president's eyes or ears would be solely at his disposal. Neither institution would be obligated to the other, because this would imply the subordination of one to the other. So went a theory of separation prevalent at that time.

Several examples indicate that Washington was interested less in invoking executive privilege (as might be defensible under a strict interpretation of the separation principle) than in promoting unity and comity between Congress and the president. When, in 1790, the president's emissaries concluded a treaty with the Creeks (the same negotiations that had triggered Washington's ill-starred attempt at asking the Senate for advice) the question arose as to how much information should be provided to the Senate. Just the treaty? The treaty plus necessary background information? All relevant materials? His cabinet informed him that the president would be within his constitutional authority if he withheld whatever he deemed harmful to the national interest or to his own executive power. But Washington continued to be concerned about the effects of a precedent that might shatter the unity within the national government. Therefore, he decided to submit, not just his recommendations for a treaty, but all other related papers. He considered "that an unreserved . . . communication" of all such papers was "indispensably requisite for the information of Congress."[40] His only stipulation was that information that might jeopardize the national interest be reviewed in closed session.

Washington proved equally willing to share unpopular or embarrassing information with Congress. The St. Clair incident was nothing if not embarrassing. Washington had named Arthur St. Clair to command an expedition of militiamen against the Indians of the Ohio Valley. St. Clair was routed, losing more than nine hundred of his men and nearly all of his equipment. Congress insisted on an investigation and, intent on discovering scapegoats, asked the president to provide papers relating to the incident. He acceded to the House's request "for such persons, papers, and records as may be necessary to assist their inquiries."[41] He was concerned that a chief executive *might* need to keep certain sensitive papers secret in the national interest; but his inclination toward interbranch cooperation compelled him to err on the side of openness. In the end, *no* papers were withheld.

Maintaining the model of a consultative presidency was not always easy. St. Clair was not the only embarrassment to the president. Alexander Hamilton, for one, had become a lightning rod for allegations from the growing Republican faction in Congress. In 1794 Hamilton's critics at last believed they had "the goods" on him. He was accused of financial mismanagement and misappropriation of public funds and was asked to appear before Congress to answer these charges. Washington made it clear that while he would not compel Hamilton to testify, he did consider cooperation with Congress an important component of his administration. Hamilton appeared before Congress, where he defended his conduct quite successfully. This established a precedent that has remained difficult for executive officers, from Arthur St. Clair to Oliver North, to ignore.

Gouverneur Morris was also a thorn in the side of the president. A man of extreme opinions, Morris did not suffer fools lightly. As minister to France, Morris sent dispatches to Washington that were often overly generous with insulting, derogatory characterizations of French leaders. Morris's stormy relationship with the French became the focus of much gossip in the capital. Finally the Senate asked the president to provide all of the correspondence between Morris, the French government, and the State Department, apparently with an eye to forcing Morris's removal. For the first time, Washington felt compelled to withhold certain materials from the Senate. All but one of the dispatches were submitted, but several obvious deletions had been made—not unlike Richard Nixon's celebrated "expletive deleted" transcripts. It is thought that the deletions contained Morris's derogatory comments. Washington believed that releasing this information would be harmful to the "national interest" without providing a useful public purpose. The Senate did not protest, perhaps because Washington indicated that Morris would be recalled.[42]

The point, of course, is not that Washington never exercised executive privilege. As the Morris incident suggests, Washington did invoke it on occasion. When his own constitutional duties were clear, as in engaging in diplomacy with foreign governments, he could assert his prerogatives as jealously as most modern presidents. What sets Washington apart, however, is his willingness to cooperate whenever possible with Congress. Consultation, not confrontation, characterized his administrative demeanor. Executive openness, not executive privilege, was the rule rather than the exception.

MR. WASHINGTON MEETS MR. HANCOCK

To understand Washington's almost single-minded obsession about unity in the national government, one must consider again the principal political bogy in his eyes—the states. Federalism is often considered to be a substantial portion of the genius of the Constitution. As the *Federalist* pointed out, not only was the national government limited and balanced within itself; it was also limited by the allocation of powers between the states and the central government.

Washington, however, saw very little genius in federalism. His experiences during the Revolutionary War had led him to perceive state sovereignty, not as the fountainhead of liberty, but as the source of tendentiousness and petty jealousies that imperiled national unity. He summarized his thoughts on the "virtues" of state sovereignty during a dark period in the deliberations of the Philadelphia convention:

> Persuaded I am, that the primary cause of all our disorders lies in the different state governments, and in the tenacity of that power . . . the local views of each state, and separate interests, by which they are too much governed, will not yield to a more enlarged scale of politics . . . and disrespect to [the laws] of the general government, must render the situation of this great country weak, inefficient, and disgraceful.[43]

If local, "jealous" interests were allowed to obstruct the interests of the "national community," then "for what purpose do we farcically pretend to be United."[44] The confederacy, he confided to James Madison, was "thirteen sovereignties pulling against each other." This "tugging at the Federal head" would "soon bring ruin on the whole," as the dis–United States would likely fall to the predations of Europe.[45]　How, then, did this deep suspicion of state power affect Washington the president? And did his choices determine the way in which we have come to understand the role of the president today? Was he to be simply an administrator? A legislator? An exalted clerk? To some extent the president would become all of these, but the roles to which George Washington devoted most of his energies were those of head of state and national symbol. By choosing to emphasize these roles, it was clear that he wished to impress the people of the United States with the importance of establishing a sense of national identity and to impress the states with the primacy of national authority.[46]

Numerous examples suggest that Washington took the supremacy clause seriously. As commander in chief during the Revolution, he had taken to communicating to the states through circulars (a common letter transmitted to each state assembly separately). He had little choice. His position was as an agent of the states through their delegates in Congress. Even though he was commander in chief of the national army, any actions regarding American citizens could only be implemented through the states. As president of the new national government, he now saw the opportunity to establish a direct link between himself and the people of the nation. Taking his lead from the words of the Preamble, there would be no intermediary between the president and his constituency. He asserted this in numerous ways, but the precedent seems to have been asserted first with the controversy over thanksgiving proclamations. Thanksgiving proclamations and days of prayer or of fasting had been common during the war. Congress had regularly requested the several states to issue such proclamations to their citizens, the implication being, of course, that the national government lacked the constitutional authority to make such a request directly. When the first Congress under the new Constitution again decided to commemorate a day of thanksgiving, some states'-rights advocates assumed that the request would be transmitted through the state executives—a clear attempt to revive at least the constitutional *forms* of the Confederation. Washington would have none of this. Not only was his proclamation directed to the people of the United States; it also asked a special blessing for the national government and the Constitution, but *not* for the states.

He also made it clear that the president was the head of a sovereign nation and that state governments and their executives were subordinate. Two examples will suffice to make the point—one, straightforward; the other, absurd. During the notorious Citizen Genêt affair, Washington was anxious about avoiding any incidents that might reflect badly on his strategy of neutrality. One of Genêt's schemes was to outfit captured British merchantmen in American ports as French privateers. There was no American army at that point, nor were there many federal marshals. Therefore, Washington was compelled to rely on state officials for information and enforcement. The affair had an unsatisfactory end. The privateer eventually left Philadelphia because Washington lacked a navy to prevent its departure.[47] Throughout the affair, however, the president commanded Governor Thomas Mifflin to provide him with information and a sufficient number of "harbor police" to prevent any untoward happenings. Washington issued these commands as a matter of course. Mifflin never questioned the president's authority to subordinate a state governor on a matter of this sort.

The second incident is interesting, not merely as a constitutional precedent but also as a humorous example of what can happen when two enormously vain men clash over a matter of personal privilege. During his northern trip in the winter of that first presidential year, Washington expressed an interest in dining with the governor of Massachusetts—no less a personage than John Hancock. Washington understood that Hancock would call on him at his lodgings first; the two would then dine at Hancock's. When Hancock declined to visit the president, claiming ill health, Washington canceled the dinner engagement. To Washington it appeared that the governor was making a statement about sovereign authority—that a president first ought to pay his respects to a governor because of the preeminent status of states within the Union. Washington wrote Hancock:

> The President of the United States presents his best respects to the Governor, and has the honor to inform him that he shall be at home 'till 2 o'clock. The President of the United States need not express the pleasure it will give him to see the Governor; but at the same time, he most earnestly begs that the Governor will not hazard his health on the occasion.[48]

Hancock conceded, according to Woodrow Wilson's account, and arrived at Washington's lodgings "swathed . . . in flannels and borne upon men's shoulders up the stairs."[49] Silly? Perhaps. But Washington had made his point.

Interestingly, the Hancock protocol incident arose in the context of another action taken to solidify the role of president as symbol of national unity. Remembering the reluctance of some states to accept the primacy of the Continental Congress in national matters, Washington embarked upon a campaign to cement the loyalty of the American citizenry. Like a king surveying his realm, Washington made it a point to travel to every state in the Union within a few years of his inauguration. At each town the hero was greeted with enthusiastic, patriotic celebrations. By "showing the flag" (which, in a sense, was himself), the president intended to win the "hearts and minds" of Americans everywhere. He even made a point of traveling to Rhode Island shortly after that state had at last ratified the Constitution. He did so even though he had long reviled that state's noxious "paper-money junto" and anarchistic politics. His presidential tours illustrated an important irony of Washington's presidency. Most elected officials are respected because of the office they occupy. Much of their power is derived from formal instruments, such as a constitution. For the first president, that situation was reversed. Washington used his personal charisma to endow the presidency with much of its authority. That transference was the singular mission of the tours. The Constitution was legitimated for many Americans because Washington supported it; the presidency was legitimated because Americans everywhere could see the great man filling that post.

One final example of Washington's vision of the presidency as national unifier needs to be explored. The Constitution gave authority over the militia to the president as commander in chief, but it was silent as to the mode of implementation. On several occasions, Washington urged Congress to provide for the uniform training of the militia. He thought that by doing so, the loyalty of the militia would unquestioningly be directed toward the federal government. In this he was unsuccessful (though, interestingly, his idea became the basis for the National Guard and the modern, integrated armed forces), but he did successfully assert the primacy of presidential claims to use the militia as an instrument of national policy. He acknowledged that under normal circumstances the militia was a state agency. For example, on the same visit to Massachusetts that resulted in the protocol fiasco with Hancock, Washington was invited to review that state's militia. He declined—a recognition of the fact that he was not, in time of peace, the unit's commanding officer.[50]

Yet in times of national crisis, Washington made it apparent to all that the national interest transcended any state reservations about who commanded the militia. When the president ordered militia units to join in the war against the Indians of the Six Nations (under a *presidentially* appointed commander, Arthur St. Clair), he did so firmly. No objections were heard. Washington made the same point more dramatically by his actions in suppressing the Whisky Rebellion. Militia from four states (Pennsylvania, New Jersey, Maryland, and Virginia) were called out to suppress the "rebellion." Instead of appointing a commander, however, Washington himself rode to Bedford, Pennsylvania, to exercise his powers as commander in chief in the field! Although he was not really up to the physical rigors of field command, he thought it important to make the point that challenges to the sovereignty of the United States were a president's personal responsibility. Local grievances, however justified, could not be allowed to prevail over the common good—a common good that was defined and defended by national institutions of government.

THE FOUNDER AS PRESIDENT

The development of the "real" Constitution can be attributed to many individuals and events during its two-hundred-year history. Certainly that Constitution has become, in many ways, the authority for a political system quite different from that which many of the founders anticipated. Many of the specific "original forms" experimented with during Washington's tenure have been abandoned or modified since then. Nevertheless, the contributions of George Washington to the development of the Constitution have not been given their due. The constitutional norms that he chose to pursue have had a lasting influence on contemporary political arrangements.

A review of just a few of these norms suggests how "indispensable" Washington was. He acted in ways that promoted the Constitution as the supreme law of the land. Presidents from Abraham Lincoln to Richard Nixon have asserted the necessity of extraconstitutional powers, but Washington's behavior would assure that any such future claims would not be risk-free. Even a president would not be completely beyond the reach of the rule of law. His concern for "energy" in the national government made the barriers of separation of powers a semipermeable membrane—a development that would prove to be indispensable in future crisis times. Washington made clear, by both symbol and action, that the presidency was a national office, responsive to the people of the United States, not to the several states. He insisted that constitutional government needed order as well as liberty, that "virtue, frugality, and enterprise" could not prosper without a national government powerful enough to protect the "general interest." In this sense, the tradition of a restraintist president in domestic policy and an activist president in military and diplomatic matters was begun by Washington.

His presidency was not without its failures and flaws. Not all of his constitutional norms became part of the American tradition. Indeed, some of them, notably his desire for nonpartisanship and unity in national politics, did not even survive his first term. All I claim here is that George Washington continued to act as a founder long after the adjournment of the Philadelphia convention. As president, he shaped the presidency and presidential-congressional relations according to his own constitutional norms, several of which were pivotal for future generations. Was his legacy equal to that bequeathed by other founders, such as Hamilton, Madison, Jefferson, and Marshall? Perhaps not. Plainly, however, it is greater than many scholars have been willing to admit.

NOTES

1. Ralph Ketcham, *Presidents above Party: The First American Presidency, 1789–1829* (Chapel Hill: University of North Carolina Press, 1984), p. 8.

2. It would be a mistake to assume that Washington was devoid of political ideas and policy preferences. His vision of what an American republic ought to be was quite clear; it mirrored most of the goals of what would become the Federalist party. But he devoted most of his energies to the institutional problems of the presidency, not to his policy goals. See Glenn A. Phelps, "The Intention of a Framer: George Washington in 1787," paper presented to the American Political Science Association, Aug. 1985.

3. H. Jefferson Powell, "Original Understanding of Original Intent," *Harvard Law Review* 98 (1985): 885–948.

4. John Fitzpatrick, ed., *The Writings of George Washington,* 39 vols. (Washington, D.C.: Government Printing Office, 1931–44), "Queries on a Line of Conduct," May 10, 1789, 30:321 (hereafter cited as *GW*).

5. V. O. Key, *Politics, Parties and Pressure Groups* (New York: Crowell, 1969).

6. See, in particular, Garry Wills, *Cincinnatus: George Washington and the Enlightenment* (New York: Doubleday, 1984).

7. Edward Channing, "Washington and Parties, 1789–1797," *Massachusetts Historical Society Proceedings* 97 (1913): 35–44; Rudolph M. Bell, *Party and Faction in American Politics: The House of Representatives, 1789–1801* (Westport, Conn.: Greenwood Press, 1973); Glenn A. Phelps, "George Washington and the Paradox of Party," *Presidential Studies Quarterly* 15 (1989).

8. James T. Flexner, *George Washington,* 4 vols. (Boston, Mass.: Little, Brown, 1965–72); Douglas Southall Freeman, *George Washington: A Biography,* 7 vols. (New York: Scribner's, 1948–57).

9. Forrest McDonald, *The Presidency of George Washington* (Lawrence: University Press of Kansas, 1979).

10. Fred I. Greenstein, *The Hidden-Hand Presidency: Eisenhower as Leader* (New York: Basic Books, 1982).

11. *GW,* letter to James Madison, May 5, 1789, 30:311.

12. Lance Banning, "Republican Ideology and the Triumph of the Constitution, 1789 to 1793," *William and Mary Quarterly* 31 (1979): 167–88.

13. *GW,* letter to George Fairfax, July 10, 1783, 27:58.

14. *GW,* letter to Catherine Macauley, Jan. 9, 1790, 30:498.

15. See Wills, *Cincinnatus.*

16. *GW,* letter to David Humphreys, Dec. 26, 1786, 29:126.

17. *GW,* First Inaugural Address, Apr. 30, 1789, 30:294–95.

18. *GW,* letter to Edmund Randolph, Jan. 8, 1788, 29:358.

19. Gordon Wood, *The Creation of the American Republic, 1776–1787* (Chapel Hill: University of North Carolina Press, 1969), pp. 197–206.

20. Ibid., pp. 469–564.

21. Herbert Storing, *What the Anti-Federalists Were For* (Chicago: University of Chicago Press, 1981).

22. *GW,* letter to Bushrod Washington, Nov. 10, 1787, 29:316.

23. *GW,* annual address, Jan. 8, 1790, 30:491–94.

24. *GW,* undelivered Inaugural Address, Apr. 1789, 30:296–328. We have only fragments of this lengthy address. Jared Sparks, Washington's secretary, later cut up the document so that friends might have mementos of the president in his own handwriting. But the patchwork that remains does not reveal any ideas that Washington had not often repeated previously.

25. Freeman, *George Washington,* 6:302.

26. Wills, *Cincinnatus,* pp. 17–25.

27. Max Farrand, ed., *The Records of the Federal Convention of 1787,* rev. ed., 4 vols. (New Haven, Conn.: Yale University Press, 1966), 2:587.

28. *GW,* letter to David Stuart, July 1, 1787, 29:237–39.

29. *GW,* Circular Letter to the States, June 8, 1783, 26:492–93.

30. *GW,* letter to James Madison, Aug. 1789, 30:394.

31. *GW,* Finance Plan, Oct. 1789, 30:454–55.

32. Harry C. Thomson, "The First Presidential Vetoes," *Presidential Studies Quarterly* 8 (1978): 30.

33. Aaron Wildavsky, "The Two Presidencies," *Trans-Action* 4 (1966): 7–14.

34. *GW,* Sentiments, Aug. 10, 1789, 30:378.

35. *GW,* letter to the Senate, Aug. 22, 1789, 30:388.

36. William Maclay, *Sketches of Debate in the First Senate of the United States* (Harrisburg, Pa.: Lane S. Hart, 1880), pp. 122–26.

37. See, e.g., Edward S. Corwin, *The President: Office and Powers, 1787–1957,* 4th rev. ed. (New York: New York University Press, 1957), pp. 209–10; and Louis Henkin, *Foreign Affairs and the Constitution* (New York: Norton, 1972), p. 131.

38. George C. Edwards III and Stephen J. Wayne, *Presidential Leadership: Politics and Policy Making* (New York: St. Martin's Press, 1985).

39. Cited by Charles Warren in *The Supreme Court in United States History,* rev. ed., vol. 1 (Boston, Mass.: Little, Brown, 1928), pp. 110–11.

40. *GW,* letter to Congress, Aug. 12, 1790, 31:91.

41. Leonard D. White, *The Federalists: A Study in Administrative History* (New York: Macmillan, 1948), p. 80.

42. Abraham D. Sofaer, "Executive Privilege: An Historical Note," *Columbia Law Review* 75 (1975): 1318–21.

43. *GW,* letter to David Stuart, July 1, 1787, 29:238.

44. *GW,* Circular Letter to the States, June 8, 1783, 26:483–96.

45. *GW,* letter to James Madison, Nov. 5, 1786, 29:52.

46. See Seymour Martin Lipset, *The First New Nation* (New York: Basic Books, 1963), pp. 16–50.

47. Douglas S. Freeman, *Washington,* an abridgement by Richard Halwell (New York: Scribner's, 1968), pp. 625–34.

48. *GW,* letter to John Hancock, Oct. 26, 1789, 30:453.

49. Woodrow Wilson, *George Washington* (New York: Schocken, 1969), p. 282.

50. Freeman, *George Washington,* 6:243–44.

11

ALEXANDER HAMILTON
AND THE PRESIDENCY

JOHN C. KORITANSKY

When Thomas Jefferson called Alexander Hamilton the "colossus of the Federalists," he was recognizing the fact that Hamilton was *the* member of his party who articulated the comprehensive vision of republican national government and commercial society that the Federalists labored to establish.[1] Moreover, a claim might be ventured that Hamilton, as colossus of the Federalists, should be considered the chief architect of our political union. For as has often been observed, despite the fact that the Federalists would never win a national election after their defeat by the Republicans in 1800, it is remarkable how little President Jefferson dismantled the engine of central authority that Hamilton had called into being and how little Jefferson was able to alter the nation's course from the vision of commercial union that Hamilton had set forth. Nevertheless, such a claim for Hamilton's influence would be too strong. In some important respects the election of 1800 was a profound repudiation of Hamilton's political thought. We would, I think, be helped to understand our political society better if we consider both the extent to which Hamilton's political thought has been influential and also the reasons why its influence is limited.

Hamilton's political thought is especially important to students of the role of the presidency and executive administration in the American political system. Hamilton's thought regarding the proper form of government and society is directly connected with his concern for effective administration. It must be granted that Hamilton nowhere contributes anything to the development of a science of administration *per se,* nor does he even provide much in the way of that proverbial wisdom that once was taught as the way of getting things done. Leonard White, in his unsurpassed account of public administration under the Federalists, expresses some disappointment that he could not find in Hamilton's writings a set of administrative principles that White hoped and believed could at last be established through the study of public administration.[2] What explains this is that Hamilton's thoughts on public administration are not separate from his constitutional and social philosophy. For Hamilton, the study of government and the study of administration is but one study. The issues for that study are how to liberate the good sense and the natural competence of public ministers from certain kinds of confusion that Hamilton thought to be most dangerous and how to bind those ministers' self-interest and personal honor to the public welfare, as Hamilton's was seemingly bound by his own nature.[3]

Hamilton's political philosophy is presented fully in his contribution to *The Federalist Papers*. His lesser-known writings—letters and pamphlets—give some amplification illustrating specific measures towards carrying out the social policy that his *Federalist Papers* outline and defend. Of special interest in this regard are his Reports to Congress, as secretary of the Treasury, on public credit and on the state of manufactures, and his *Pacificus* pamphlets, written in defense of President Washington's authority to issue the Proclamation of Neutrality in the war between England and France in order to remove certain doubts that were left open in *The Federalist* concerning the exclusivity of the president's powers in the realm of foreign affairs.[4] In reading *The Federalist Papers,* we need to develop an eye to Hamilton's subtlety, which is imposed upon him by reason of the circumstances under which *The Federalist* was written. For one thing, *The Federalist Papers* are intended not only to interpret the Constitution faithfully and authoritatively but also to secure its ratification, so that each of the authors of *The Federalist Papers* must practice the art of expressing his more contentious points in language least likely to give offense or rhetorical advantage to their opponents. Moreover, Hamilton himself wrote only fifty-one of the eighty-five papers; the remainder were written by James Madison and, in the case of five random contributions, by John Jay.[5] With slight oversimplification we can assert that *The Federalist Papers* are the work of two minds, and while these two are careful to avoid contradicting each other, lest the Constitution itself appear to lack integrity, there are differences between them which, when developed, could and did become divisive. To grasp Hamilton's own thought, it is necessary to understand how his contribution to *The Federalist* is related to that of James Madison.

At first it appears that there is no more difference between Hamilton and Madison in *The Federalist Papers* than that imposed by the division of labor. Hamilton wrote most about the advantages of union, about the need for strong government with plenary powers, and about the make-up of the executive and the judiciary branches; whereas Madison analyzed the separation of powers between state and national governments and the checks and balances among the three branches of government; and most famously, he discussed the constitution of the House and the Senate and the theory of representation that they reflect. This is a comparison that makes Madison the more prominent member of the partnership, because in this nation the idea of representation and that of the legitimate limits of governmental power are the recurrent themes of politics, and it was Madison who addressed those themes most directly. Thus, Hamilton's contribution to *The Federalist Papers,* while more voluminous, seems to be less than Madison's in importance. Surely, nothing Hamilton wrote rivals in notoriety Madison's number 51 and, especially, number 10, papers that are sometimes said to contain the most significant American contributions to political thought. It is here that Madison cuts through the issue for his contemporaries of greatness and power versus freedom and shows how a nation can be both great in power and size and also republican and free. In this vein, Hamilton's papers look like a supplement to Madison's monumental achievement.

On closer inspection, however, Hamilton's argument in *The Federalist Papers* can be seen to have a weight of its own, and moreover, stretching the metaphor, it is Hamilton who set the founding cornerstone upon which Madison built his structure. For just in its own terms, Madison's argument is incomplete; it does not set forth the source of our national union. As every student of American government should know, Madison defines the problem of political society as that of faction and the problem of majoritarian government as majority faction which will most likely take the form of the "leveling spirit" of those many who "secretly sigh for a more equal distribution of (life's) blessings."[6] Madison's solution was to generate a large and commercial republic that would suppress the formation of a factious majority by generating a myriad of "interests" that in turn could form governing majorities only through concurrence. Moreover, such concurrent majorities would be engineered among many disparate elements by representatives of whom a certain public virtue was a realistic expectation; "a coalition of a majority of a whole society could seldom take place on any other principles than those of justice and the general good."[7]

The difficulty with Madison's celebrated argument concerns the relation of the representatives to their constituencies. On the one hand, the representatives must rather literally reflect the interests that are to form the governing majorities. They must be, in this sense, a channel of influence. On the other hand, those same representatives must be free enough of the interests they represent to rise above them and fashion them into a bargain under the aegis of justice and the general good. Representatives must both reflect and refine the variety of interests to be brought into concurrence.[8] Were the representatives to reflect only these interests, the representative assembly would itself need to be governed—the question of the source of the union of the many interests would simply have been pushed back one step. But neither does Madison's scheme work if each of the representatives assumes a Burkean posture, standing for the public interest as he sees it. That would be government by an elective aristocracy, not a popular majority. There is in practice a tension between the representatives' duty to refine and their need to reflect the interests they represent. Madison's scheme depends on an uneasy balance between the two functions of the representative.

Granted, what has been said so far does not destroy Madison's position. It could be argued that the representatives themselves must balance the two aspects of their function and that that is a realistic expectation. But the fact that the problem is not so easy to sweep aside is illustrated by the further difficulties that Madison encountered when he considered the appropriate size of the federal union and the nature of the separation of powers between the states and the national government. While what is most famous about Madison's argument is that the problem of majority faction is solvable only through *extending* the sphere of republican government, it is also true for him that we need to be concerned lest the nation get too large. In too large a nation, the proportion of representatives could no longer reflect all their constituents' particular interests. Thus, Madison had to make what today must be considered an embarrassing argument in *Federalist* number 14—that the size of the nation (in 1788) is neither too large nor too small, but just right. Nor, by the way, can Madison's argument be rescued from this embarrassment by pointing to advances in communication and travel. It is the growth of population and the complexity of the economy, rather than the physical size of the nation, that threatens the proportion of representatives to their clients that is necessary to make Madison's scheme operate.

Once we see the importance for Madison's argument of the problem that the nation might indeed grow too large for a republican form of government, and if we also see how blithely hopeful is the "solution" offered in *Federalist* number 14, then what Madison says about the separation of powers in *Federalist* number 39 appears to be an attempt to respond to this same problem on a higher level of sophistication and subtlety. In number 14 he admits that those who argue that the nation is already too large for a republican form of government would have a point, "were it proposed . . . to abolish the government of the particular states." But what saves us from this charge is that, in truth, the national government's "jurisdiction is limited to certain enumerated objects only." Madison's idea of the separation of powers is a refinement of his remark about the appropriate size of a republican government. The subtler answer to the question of size depends on the powers to be exercised and on their specific objects. Thus, the logic of his own idea of representation forces Madison to swallow the doubts he expressed in the Philadelphia convention about the possibility of limiting the national government's powers through an enumeration and to assert, in number 39, that "in this relation, then, the proposed government cannot be deemed a *national* one; since its jurisdiction extends to certain enumerated objects only, and leaves to the several states a residuary and inviolable sovereignty over all other objects."[9] While these words contain enough ambiguity to preserve the working agreement between Madison and Hamilton in *The Federalist Papers,* the implications of Madison's argument in numbers 14 and 39 would eventually drive him to break from the simpler nationalism of Hamilton and to support the party of limited government and states' rights.

But the implications of *Federalist* numbers 14 and 39 are wrong. The expansive reading of the national government's powers, especially by way of the necessary and proper clause, as interpreted by Hamilton in *Federalist* number 33 and confirmed by Chief Justice Marshall in *McCulloch* v. *Maryland,* is such that it is not possible to answer the charge that the nation is too big by pointing to the "residual and inviolable sovereignty" of the states. The states can make no claim to impede the national government from exercising powers that it deems necessary and proper merely because such exercise would violate the sphere of powers reserved to the states. The hard conclusion is that the conditions necessary for Madison's idea of representation are not met, and thus, it is not by Madison's genius that we can explain the manner and the degree to which this nation combines greatness and freedom.

The source of the contrast between Hamilton's and Madison's thought is that Hamilton rejects one of the two implicit elements in Madison's idea of representation. What I have here called the reflecting element in representation Hamilton calls "actual representation," and Hamilton goes out of his way to argue that actual representation is impossible in a pure sense, because it is flatly impossible, and that it is not an appropriate standard or even partial standard for republican government. "The idea of an actual representation of all classes of the people, by persons of each class, is altogether visionary."[10] But this observation does not lead Hamilton to recommend government by elected representatives who will devote themselves to an idea of the public interest that excludes any personal interest. Like Madison, Hamilton found the condition for effectively representative government to be met by a large and commercial republic, but not quite for the same reason. Commercialism is good, for Hamilton, not primarily because it creates a plethora of interests that will diffuse the natural and factious majority, but more important, because it will generate a new *class* of persons who will be, by reason of their particular interest, the "natural representatives" of all the many interests. This is the class of *merchants*— that is, those who neither manufacture nor mine nor farm but who earn their way by buying cheap and selling dear, as the saying goes. This class has no particular interest in the prosperity of any single industry in the nation's economy; if they are but shrewd, they will channel their resources in whatever direction promises the most profit. Hence they promote those enterprises that are the most profitable. The merchants, as a class, are like cultivators of the natural harmony of the productive arts. They facilitate and thrive off what Adam Smith called "the natural system." Indeed, so natural is the merchants' claim to be the natural representative class of a commercial society that no constitutional provision is even necessary for them to assume their rightful station! It will just happen that way for the most part.

The idea of an actual representation of the people, by persons of each class, is altogether visionary. Unless it were expressly provided in the Constitution, that each different occupation should send one or more members, the thing would never take place in practice. Mechanics and manufacturers will always be inclined, with few exceptions, to give their votes to merchants, in preference to persons of their own professions or trades. Those discerning citizens are well aware that the mechanic and manufacturing arts furnish the materials of mercantile enterprise and industry. Many of them, indeed, are immediately connected with the operations of commerce. They know that the merchant is their natural patron and friend; and they are aware that however great the confidence they may justly feel in their own good sense, their interests can be more effectively promoted by the merchant than by themselves. They are sensible that their habits in life have not been such as to give them those acquired endowments, without which in a deliberative assembly the greatest natural abilities are for the most part useless; and that the influence and weight, and superior acquirements of the merchants render them more equal to a contest with any spirit which might happen to infuse itself into the public councils, unfriendly to the manufacturing and trading inter- ests. These considerations, and many others that might be mentioned, prove, and experience confirms it, that artisans and manufacturers will commonly be disposed to bestow their votes upon merchants and those whom they recommend. We must therefore consider merchants as the natural representatives of all these classes of the community.[11]

Thus, in one stroke, Hamilton cut through Madison's dilemma. The many differing interests in a complex commercial society do not need actually to be represented individually. What government must represent is only what those interests all have in common. This general advantage, in a commercial society, is just the merchants' specific advantage—namely, a powerful economy in which the prospects for profitable exchange are high. Much as those who were renowned for their nobility and virtue represented in their own character that common good that premodern political societies strove to realize, the merchants are the natural representatives of that society that is established to facilitate each person's pursuit of his own profit.[12]

For the reason outlined above, commercialism is critical to Hamilton's solution to the problem of representation, but it should not be inferred from this that Hamilton thought commerce was the sufficient condition for good republican government. Were it so, the Articles of Confederation could have provided an adequate government for the United States. But Hamilton's *Federalist* number 6 is a powerful argument against the contention that commerce in and of itself will bring about civil peace and social harmony. "Has commerce," he asks rhetorically, "hitherto done any thing more than change the objects of war?"[13] The fuller statement of Hamilton's position is that while there is indeed a natural harmony among the productive arts, that harmony does not enforce itself with sufficient reliability in particular cases. There are situations in which one of the parties to an exchange may take advantage of an extraordinary alteration in the rate of exchange, as when a man who is dying of thirst will give all he has to the one who will sell him the only available glass of water. Such situations are, by definition, exceptions to the norm; but human ingenuity being what it is, the exceptions are legion, and their trains go on forever. So too, then, are the instances of discord and civil unrest to which commerce gives rise. For these reasons Hamilton endorsed what we would call "positive government" as necessary to preserve and even to promote "the natural system." In his early paper, the *Continentalist,* he said:

> There are some who maintain that trade will regulate itself, and it is not to be benefited by the encouragements or restraints of government. Such persons will imagine that there is no need of a common directing power. This is one of those wild speculative paradoxes, which have grown into credit among us, contrary to the uniform practice and sense of the most enlightened nations.[14]

The specific features of Hamilton's program of positive governmental measures to promote the national economy can readily be understood from a reading of his *Papers on Public Credit* and his *Report on Manufactures.* Hamilton argued in favor of a protective tariff to sustain some American industries during their infancy, and he wanted to promote industrial activity by offering a bounty for useful inventions, to be paid from the national treasury. Moreover, as is well known, he sought to establish the credit of the national government through the assumption of state debts and the funding of the entire governmental debt at par value. Finally, Hamilton sought to render the currency of the United States more stable and more available for capital investment through the aforementioned funding program and the establishment of a national bank. These programs can scarcely be mentioned today without acknowledging that they have been criticized because they tended to serve the immediate advantage of certain monied interests.[15] For example, speculators who held government bonds, having in many cases bought them at a depreciated price, would be much benefited by the assumption and refunding plans. But criticism of Hamilton's economics to the effect that some persons would benefit more from his measures than others—even if those who did so benefit were a "monied few"—is insufficient unless it also shows that the measure does not serve the public interest in the way that it is claimed to do. Hamilton admitted that his economic plans would benefit some more directly than others;[16] but he also argued that the same thing could be said against any other plan, or no plan. In defense of what he was recommending, Hamilton asserted that the public interest would be served through the generation of a vigorous capitalistic economy. Unlike some of his critics, Hamilton did not shrink from the fact that such an economy required capital and capitalists.

To return to the main argument, Hamilton's fiscal and economic program is an illustration of his general belief that the "natural system" of political economy is the foundation of healthy political community and, at the same time, that the "natural system" is not self-enforcing but needs positive governmental "encouragements and restraints" to keep it working. Thus, whereas commercialism has been shown to be the indispensable condition for Hamilton's solution to the problem of representation, the health of commercial society depends *in turn* on properly constituted political authority to supply the necessary measures. This chain of dependency would be circular if Hamilton expected that the initiative for the right kind of positive governmental measures would come from the legislative assembly, populated by a monied class of merchants that the economy would generate. But it appears that Hamilton did not rely very much on the species of political wisdom that would, at best, reside in the legislature. The advantage of the assembly of merchants is that it is able to surmount the necessary divisions in society; it can act out of accord. But even Hamilton's well-constituted assembly would not have the degree of unity or energy and duration that would be necessary for it to serve as the real agency of government. Hamilton expected that the well-constituted assembly would be able to react, with a minimum of confusion, to the initiatives that must be supplied from somewhere else—namely, from the executive branch. For this reason, Hamilton's thoughts on the nature of the executive power are his central thoughts. Moreover, for Hamilton, the key to the strength of the national government was not so much the concurrent majoritarianism that Madison describes in *Federalist* numbers 10 and 51; rather, it was the unity and the degree of independence of the executive that he himself outlined in *Federalist* numbers 67–77.

Much of the opposition to Hamilton's political program, in his own time and subsequently, centered on his defense of the independence of the executive. As for Hamilton himself, he thought that his ideas about executive independence were perfectly compatible with the fundamental liberal principles, e.g., popular sovereignty and even legislative supremacy. During his early career, Hamilton had supported the posture of Congress toward the British Parliament, and he had endorsed the American Revolution on the basis of his commitment to liberal political philosophy. In a pamphlet he wrote during that period, "A Full Vindication of the Measures of Congress," he gave his view unambiguously: "The only distinction between freedom and slavery consists in this: In the former a man is governed by laws to which he has given his consent, either in person or by his representative: In the latter he is governed by the will of another."[17] Nor did Hamilton ever retract the sentiments he had expressed on that occasion; in *Federalist* number 67 he defended the separation of the executive and legislative branches of government as necessary to maintain the distinction between a government of laws and an arbitrary government.[18] The law and the legislature must be supreme, because the law is the medium through which the people give their consent to government, and consent is the whole foundation of legitimacy.

Even though Hamilton acknowledged legislative supremacy as a formal requirement of legitimate government, the question of the degree of detail that the law must descend to in directing the executive is another. On this issue, Hamilton always defended executive discretion. Moreover, the formal supremacy of the law per se is not a principle that excludes the executive from taking the initiative for recommending policy to the legislature. Hamilton's executive would actually seize the initiative. The executive had to be the real agency of government for Hamilton, because only the executive had the requisite degree of unity that could generate the energy and rationality, at least in the administrative sense of the word, that is necessary for sound public policy. The main thrust of Hamilton's *Federalist Papers* on the executive is a defense of the executive power under the Constitution being vested in a single officer against the idea of a "dual executive" or an executive council. His discussion also contains a defense of the indefinite reeligibility of the president. On this latter point, Hamilton reveals his expectation that an indefinitely reeligible president will probably serve for an indefinite duration, thus among other advantages providing against a "mutability of measures."[19] Thus, in the interest of promoting the unitary character of government over time, Hamilton went so far as to recommend what he hoped would amount to an executive for life.

What gives Hamilton's thoughts on the proper constitution of the executive in liberal government its elegance, and at the same time what made it frightening and hateful to his Republican opponents, is the fact that Hamilton did not think that his defense of executive unity, independence, and initiative in any way compromised his commitment to government as responsible to the governed, whose consent would be expressed through law. Hamilton defended the unity of the executive as much on the grounds that it would promote responsibility as that it would comport with administrative rationality. In fact, these two considerations are merged to reveal a single idea of good government. For instance, in *Federalist* number 70, Hamilton defends executive unity by citing the "deep, solid, and ingenious" writer who says that " 'the executive power is more easily confined when it is *one.*' "[20]

> But one of the weightiest objections to a plurality in the Executive, and which lies as much against the last as the first plan, is, that it tends to conceal faults and destroy responsibility. Responsibility is of two kinds—to censure and to punishment. The first is the more important of the two, especially in an elective office. Man, in public trust, will much oftener act in such a manner as to render him unworthy of being any longer trusted, than in such a manner as to make him obnoxious to legal punishment. But the multiplication of the Executive adds to the difficulty of detection in either case. It often becomes impossible, amidst mutual accusations, to determine on whom the blame or the punishment of a pernicious measure, or series of pernicious measures, ought really to fall. It is shifted from one to another with so much dexterity, and under such plausible appearances, that the public opinion is left in suspense about the real author. The circumstances which may have led to any national miscarriage or misfortune are sometimes so complicated that, where there are a great number of actors who may have had different degrees and kinds of agency, though we may clearly see upon the whole that there has been mismanagement, yet it may be impracticable to pronounce to whose account the evil which may have been incurred is truly chargeable.[21]

In sum, the unitary executive is all alone in the spotlight. But is this a sufficient guarantee of his government's responsibility? Might we not object, in opposition to Hamilton, that a unitary executive might attempt all sorts of things that run contrary to the wishes and the interests of many people, perhaps a majority, as long as he might reasonably gamble that his misdeeds would not be deemed sufficient grounds for removing him from office? This is a natural question, but the person who asks it does not see how remarkably far-reaching Hamilton's argument is. In its fullest implications, Hamilton's argument for executive unity implies that unity is not only the necessary condition for responsible government; it is the sufficient condition as well! This surprising conclusion can be seen to follow from what has been said above if we bear in mind that what Hamilton says is the only practically possible meaning of responsibility in government must have nothing to do with "actual representation." Government is to be held responsible, not to this or that segment of the population's perceived interests, but to the general interest of the population as such; and that public interest, in the final analysis, consists in nothing but unity, in the sense of the people's freedom from social measures whereby one factious interest gains at the expense of the whole.

From the point of view of this interpretation, we can read with an enlightened eye what Hamilton wrote in *Federalist* number 68 about his degree of agreement with Alexander Pope's famous statement: "For forms of government let fools contest— / That which is best administered is best."[22] It is true that Hamilton branded Pope's statement a "political heresy," but we should note how careful Hamilton was to state his disagreement in a way that would reveal a considerable agreement. Without breaking his sentence, Hamilton follows Pope's heretical statement by saying, "yet we may safely pronounce, that the true test of a good government is its aptitude and tendency to produce a good administration."[23] In contrast to Pope's statement, forms of government are important, but they are only so insofar as they tend to promote good administration. Hamilton's response to Pope is very clever, for while he does charge Pope with heresy, he misses the point of that heresy—or rather, he actually endorses it! Surely the scandalous or heretical element in what Pope says is the suggestion that it does not matter what ends or purposes a government owns; so long as whatever it does, it does effectively and efficiently, the ends will take care of themselves. And Hamilton appears to agree. Pope had been careless—he had perhaps misused a bit of poetic license—in saying that "forms" are absolutely unimportant. Forms, in truth, have a secondary importance, as they tend to foster or hinder good administration. But the point remains that the relatively pedestrian standards of administration as such—effectiveness and efficiency—are the standards of government as a whole. It is this consideration that recommends the most important part of the formal structure of the government Hamilton is helping to establish, namely, the unitary character of the executive.

That Hamilton was able to hold forth his bold thesis about responsible government is due to his grasp, more solid and direct than that of most of his contemporaries, of what was essential to the liberal political philosophy that his generation generally adopted. His first several *Federalist Papers* on the disadvantages of the Confederation and the need for a genuine political union with a strong central government are reminiscent of Hobbes's and Locke's accounts of the inconvenience of the "state of nature" and the need for government to establish and keep the peace. And Hamilton's solution follows with appealing directness from his statement of the problem. The right of each member of the community to use force must be vested in one sovereign agency. The constitution, or "form," of that agency is, strictly speaking, for the parties to the contract to determine. But however they decide it, somewhere in the government they create, the sovereignty must come into a single point of focus, or else what they do will be in vain. Hobbes's argument for monarchy had stressed this point with force. Locke saw it too, for that matter, although Locke had also seen more clearly than Hobbes the need to veil the terrifying image of the monarch by calling for a body of legislators separate from the person of the executive.[24] The veil for Hamilton's liberal monarch was provided by those features of the Constitution that Madison stressed, in the now more celebrated *Federalist Papers*. But it was Hamilton, rather than Madison, who expressed what really held it all together. Good government *is* unitary, rational administration. The discomforting neutrality towards the ends or goals of administration contained in that statement derives from Hamilton's profound understanding of the essential neutrality of liberal political philosophy towards the question of the ultimate aims of human life. The only common good or public interest in a regime that exists only to provide the conditions under which each person may pursue his or her own idea of happiness with minimal interference is the elimination of the disturbances and threats to the public peace such as are posed by factions. Therefore, the interest of a monarch and the public interest, thus understood, are automatically woven together.

I have been arguing that there is a potential tension between Hamilton and Madison in *The Federalist Papers* regarding representation and, correspondingly, regarding the issue of executive initiative versus legislative supremacy. I do not mean to suggest by this argument that the subsequent break between Hamilton and Madison was inevitable or foreseeable, but with the benefit of hindsight it is understandable. We can see how both Hamilton and Madison would consider their subsequent political positions as being consistent with *The Federalist Papers* and therefore would accuse each other of contradiction and even perfidy. An illustration of the ambiguity in this situation is provided by the subsequent disagreement between Hamilton and Madison regarding the authority of President Washington to issue his Proclamation of Neutrality toward the conflict between England and France. Madison, in his *Helvidius Papers,* argues that the authority to issue such a statement belongs to the legislature, whereas

Hamilton, in the *Pacificus Papers,* defends President Washington. Can Hamilton's bold statement as Pacificus be seen to square with what he had said in *The Federalist?* Recently, Raoul Berger has suggested that in the *Pacificus Papers,* Hamilton finally abandoned any real attachment to the idea of legislative supremacy and that therefore he contradicted his more moderate and proper thoughts on that point in *The Federalist Papers.*[25] But this suggestion is based on a failure to understand the far-reaching implications of *The Federalist.* What is true by way of contrasting *Pacificus* with *Federalist* numbers 67–77 is that Pacificus argues that the opening words of Article II of the Constitution—"The executive Power shall be vested"—convey a positive grant of power to the president over and above what is to be inferred from the remainder of Article II; whereas in *The Federalist,* Hamilton says that the executive powers specifically enumerated in the text of Article II exhaust the president's powers. But one of the specifically enumerated powers in Article II is the power to take care that the laws be faithfully executed—and is not the Constitution itself, including its mention of "the executive Power" that is to be vested in one president, a part of the law that the president is to execute faithfully? Of course, this argument can be rightly accused of being disingenuous, for it finds a general grant of executive power within the slippery terms of a specific grant of power. But there are good reasons for us to wink at the disingenuity and accept the argument in Pacificus's behalf. When Hamilton wrote about the executive in *The Federalist,* he was responding to his readers' fear of executive tyranny, and so he veiled the most expansive possible interpretation of the executive's constitutional powers. In *Pacificus,* his purpose was to announce and vindicate the more expansive interpretation. But to pursue conflicting purposes at different times is not to be guilty of a contradiction of principles. And moreover, if we have read *The Federalist* comprehensively, we should have been prepared for what Pacificus tells us.

When Hamilton discussed the enumerated powers of the legislature in *Federalist* numbers 23–33, especially the necessary and proper clause in number 33, and again when he discussed the proposal for a bill of rights in number 84, Hamilton showed very clearly why he did not think that a government's powers could be usefully or effectively limited through specific enumerations or positive limitations. The interpretation of all specific grants and restrictions will always be conditioned by the simple requirement that a government must govern. Governments simply do what they do, to meet whatever exigencies may arise. (For that matter, Madison himself had expressed grave doubts at the Constitutional Convention whether an enumeration of the powers that the government was to have was realistically possible.) Hamilton thought that both the executive and the legislative powers would have to be interpreted to meet future exigencies.

This interpretation would require reflection on the purposes implied in the specific powers mentioned by the Constitution and on an assessment of the situation. In the specific instance discussed by Pacificus, the power to proclaim neutrality had to reside somewhere. Why not in the executive? Madison responded to Hamilton that the power to declare neutrality resided in the legislature by way of implication from its power to declare war. In either case, then, we must rely on implications. Are Madison's inferences more reliable than Hamilton's? The answer to that question depends on whether the legislature or the executive is better equipped to respond to the situation at hand. When we raise that question, the whole issue turns in Hamilton's favor.[26]

But it is not only in the field of foreign policy where, Hamilton thought, the executive ought to supply the initiative of American government. In general, Hamilton tried to make the concession to the principle of legislative supremacy that would interfere as little as possible with the power of the executive to promote rational and energetically administered policy. Legislative supremacy was considered a formal requirement of legitimacy; executive direction was an actual requirement of rationality. These two principles could both be honored without contradiction if the actual role that Congress played in government was restricted to that of ratifying, or refusing to ratify, the general features of an administration's policy. Congress might exacerbate the latent tension between the two principles of good government if it tried to hold public officers responsible to a narrow and precise definition of jurisdiction or to a very specific definition of policy. Nor would Hamilton ever be able to argue that such assertions by Congress of its authority were unconstitutional;[27] he would argue only that they were ill advised. It would be up to the president, through the exercise of executive leadership, to forestall such problems as best he could. The president, in short, was to use the strategic advantages of the office that the Constitution provided him.

Naturally, the adjustment of the principles of legislative supremacy and executive leadership required some art, for the issue is such that Hamilton could never be wholly free of the charge that he was trying to have his cake and eat it too. In fact, Jefferson accused Hamilton of playing both sides of the ambiguity about legislative supremacy: Hamilton "endeavored to place himself subject to the house when the executive should propose what he did not like, and subject to the Executive when the house should propose anything disagreeable."[28] Nevertheless, Hamilton cannot be accused of ever yielding the principle that the executive power is to be construed as deriving not from Congress's actions, but rather from the Constitution itself, and that it can set itself into motion. Moreover, inferior executive officers, albeit constituted by congressional action, may partake of such initiative in proposing measures for the general good and in interpreting the practical meaning of Congress's resolves, as the president may choose to share with *his* subordinates. Thus, for example, if Congress had not created the post of secretary of the Treasury, the president could have assumed the initiative for the Federalists' financial program. It was this initiative, rather than Congress's authority, that Secretary Hamilton exercised when he issued his *Report on Manufactures.*

For the most part, Hamilton's idea that cabinet and inferior officers that Congress created were *executive* officers, exercising an authority delegated by the president, was generally accepted even by the Republicans. There was a public argument to the contrary, but it deserves only a passing note. Congressman John Francis Mercer of Maryland was an outspoken advocate of legislative supremacy in an actual as well as a formal sense, and he argued not only that the power, for instance, to initiate a finance program belonged to Congress exclusively but also that Congress could not constitutionally delegate this power to any executive officer. Mercer held that "the power of the House to originate plans of finance . . . [is] incommunicable."[29] Hamilton could hardly take Mercer's argument seriously. Such persons as Mercer failed to read the clear constitutional requirement for the separation and coordination of the legislative and the executive branches of government. Their reading of the Constitution was blinded by their devotion to the slogan of legislative supremacy rather than being enlightened by a realistic interpretation of the requirements of rational and integral governmental policy.

The picture of United States government that emerges from reflecting on Hamilton's thoughts is that of a constitutional monarchy. Jefferson and the Republicans knew whereof they spoke when they branded Hamilton a "monarchist" and a "monocrat," even if Hamilton never himself referred to his own thought in those words after he had respectfully repudiated the avowedly monarchical stance he had taken in the Philadelphia convention. Hamilton's expectation, ultimately to be disappointed, that Washington would be reelected every four years and thus serve in effect for life would win the point for monarchy in fact, even if the word had to be suppressed from the defense of the Federalist program. Serving Washington would be a national bureaucracy that would as far as possible reflect the stamp of statesmanlike character that Washington brought to the presidency. The terms of appointment and removal from national office reveal how that character was to be promoted.

As for appointment, Leonard White has reported that Washington employed a "rule of fitness" for making his selections to the bureaucracy. By the word "fitness" he meant, not so much a technical competence for any specific office, but that kind of moral character whereby some men seem to assume an authority over others so natural that it cannot be politely contested. Just what are the exact elements of such a character is not easy to say, and neither Hamilton nor Washington ever presented an open analysis of what was meant by such expressions as "fitness of character" or "the first characters of the Union," which they used to describe those worthy of national office. Nevertheless, the standard was real—as real as the impression that Washington's own personal character made on his countrymen.[30] It would probably be easier to recognize such characters on the basis of personal experience and reputation than to define their qualifications. In fact, the most definite thing that White is able to say on this matter is that there were some factors that *excluded* a candidate from consideration. These considerations included family relationship, indolence, and drink.[31] It seems that Washington held to these rules very strictly, and by holding to them, he was better able to avoid the charge of arbitrary partiality despite the ambiguity of his positive standards. Washington and the Federalists frankly wished to erect a political nobility to staff their government. Their Republican opponents may have quarreled with the Federalists' aims and values, but they did not accuse Washington and Hamilton of using deliberately fuzzy standards to serve their own personal interests.

It would have been impossible for the executive to emerge as the central agency of American government and for him to direct the bureaucracy were it not for the fact that the president came to exercise the exclusive power to remove federal officers, in addition to his power to appoint "with advice and consent" of the Senate. The Constitution is silent about the removal power, and that silence marks the ambiguity of the issue of executive initiative versus legislative supremacy. Fortunately from Hamilton's point of view, the "decision of 1789" resolved the question in favor of the president's exclusive power to remove subordinate executive officers. The "decision of 1789" refers to the action the First Congress took when it established the Department of Foreign Affairs. The question came up in that context as to how the secretary was to be removed, and after considerable deliberation, it was decided that the power to remove would be exclusively the president's. Thereafter, the Federalists could and did assume that Congress had established the precedent that was consistent with their own interpretation of the spirit of the Constitution in this matter. It is true, as many legal scholars have noted, that in fact, the decision of 1789 contains an ambiguity, for the majority that voted to lodge the power to remove the secretary in the president exclusively was composed of at least two groups. One group was of the opinion that the power of removal was implicitly vested in the president by the terms of Article II of the Constitution and that Congress might only recognize that fact in its law. Another group took the position that Congress must itself vest the power of removal in the president if he were to have it in this case; and by way of implication, what Congress gives in one case it may deny in another, or even take back. In fact, it was not until 1926, in the case of *Myers* v. *United States,* that the president's exclusive power to remove ordinary executive officers was confirmed by the Supreme Court as valid constitutional law.[32] In that case, Chief Justice William Howard Taft based his decision on his own reading of the "decision of 1789," as well as on a general reflection of the nature of executive power under the Constitution. It would therefore be appropriate to pronounce that Hamilton's interpretation of the nature of the American executive, at least in connection with the critical issue of the power to remove bureaucratic officers, ultimately received judicial approval at the hands of the only Supreme Court justice ever to have served as president.

The exclusive power over executive removals was necessary in order to preserve the unitary character of administration. By the same token, that power would have to be used modestly. A continual rotation in office would make for two related evils: it would deprive the administration of the opportunity to develop the credentials of experience in handling public affairs, and it would also deprive the "first characters of the Union" of the motive that could be expected to lead them to public service. In this regard, Hamilton's thoughts were reflected in President Washington's practices. Washington was loath to remove any officer and did so only in cases of manifest incompetence or when faced with a kind of insubordination that seemed calculated to subvert and embarrass his administration.[33] Moreover, the partisan rivalry that bred such insubordination greatly distressed both Washington and Hamilton. In their view, men of character would be expected to aspire to public office as they aspire to a high station in life and not to vindicate a party or to line their own pockets. Public office therefore could not be considered a temporary affair, any more than one's high station or fitness of character was temporary. "The ruling passion of the noblest minds" that animated such men was a desire to be first in the eyes of their fellow citizens *because* they are able to rise above personal advantage and partisan perspective and devote themselves to the general good. This passion, in Hamilton's view, would be, for example, absolutely opposed to that raw form of ambition that seeks to use public office and power to serve one's own interests. That was the vice Burr exhibited, and Hamilton condemned and loathed him for it. Hamilton's was a nobler vision. He did not place his faith in altruism—his public servants were indeed driven by a selfish desire—but it was a desire for honor, and Hamilton knew that honor is satisfying only for those who believe themselves deserving of it. As we read Hamilton's own writings and things said about him, it is tempting to conclude that Hamilton's confidence in the political reliability of the love of honor was rooted in his familiarity with the strength of that passion in his own heart. From this point of view, it could be said, by way of summarizing his political thought, that the whole of it was an attempt to arrange political institutions so as to liberate that "ruling passion" as far as possible and to allow it to seek its own end.

CONCLUSION

Alexander Hamilton's ideas about the role of the executive and the bureaucracy in the American system of government contributed importantly to the ability of the new national government to assume its broad authority. Today, in view of the shift of our politics in the direction of a more democratic form of republicanism, his thought may still remain more right than wrong, but important qualifications must be added. Contemporary political scientists have generally conceded, some reluctantly and some with enthusiasm, that Congress cannot govern, that only the president can. The democratic element of our tradition has not dismantled the monarchical element of the Constitution; it has even made uneasy peace with it, based on the recognition of the president's advantages in pursuing progressive reforms. We remain perhaps closer to a constitutional monarchy than it is comfortable for a democracy to admit. Still, it would be wrong to say that Hamilton's constitutional philosophy has won a stealthy victory beneath appearances. In point of fact, our presidents may not serve more than two terms. Washington himself, much to Hamilton's dismay, established that critically important precedent long before the Twenty-second Amendment made it an explicit part of the Constitution. Moreover, the changes in American politics wrought by Jefferson and Jackson have rendered it all but impossible for an administration to govern the nation in the name of a fitness of character beyond all partisan interest.

What is the reason for the limited success of Hamilton's constitutional philosophy? Is it that Hamilton failed to gauge the strength of popular jealousy of executive government? Hamilton does seem to have thought that his government would be accepted if it could demonstrate its *competence* and its *convenience*. Did he, as one perceptive commentator has argued, fail to appreciate those irrational collective emotions that sometimes cause men to act against their own advantage out of devotion to abstract ideas about popular rule?[34] He was, of course, not unaware of such emotions. Toward the end of his short life, Hamilton's thoughts were much preoccupied with the growth of egalitarian idolatry. He feared that the effects of the Revolution in France would have disastrous effects on the prospects for freedom and order even in the United States. But Hamilton seems never to have been able to view the collective emotions that raged in France except with a mixture of contempt and horror. If he became more doubtful that a regime might persist if it proved its competence and convenience to the citizens' pursuit of their own self-interest, he did not imagine any other legitimate means by which a regime might win the support of its people.

For himself, Hamilton never capitulated in the erroneous translation from government rooted in the consent of the governed to government by consenting majorities. But his own political thought was vulnerable to that translation in a way that he seems not to have understood. As has been observed, Hamilton expected the "first characters of the Union" to be drawn to public service by the natural "ruling passion of the noblest minds." But there is something nonliberal about that very passion. Granted, Hamilton thought that the political aristocracy that would staff the federal government's service would *not* be an aristocracy defined either by money or by blood. The uncompromising animus against nepotism and the argument for sufficient monetary compensation were both prompted by the consideration that the new political aristocracy was to have no class interest apart from that of maintaining their honor as good rulers. In this way, Hamilton thought his political aristocracy compatible with liberal government. But, on reflection, the defense is not sufficient. Even the purely political aristocracy will have to be a proud station if it is to beckon the noblest minds. The necessary implication is that to govern is something noble and fine—nobler and finer than the pursuit of self-interest, as ordinarily understood. But how can this be, if the very purpose of government is to facilitate self-interest? There is a contradiction in holding the task of governing to be a burden, however necessary, that is borne only to facilitate private life and, on the other hand, in aspiring to govern. Theoretically, this contradiction could be resolved if the development of the political virtues that were expected of the governing class were itself taken to be the ultimate purpose of the regime. But that resolution would have called liberalism itself into question, as Jefferson sensed it was being questioned implicitly. It was precisely the illiberalism of the aspiration to govern of which Jefferson accused the Federalists, especially Hamilton. The deepest issue between the two men was not the issue of executive power or legislative supremacy or limited government. Those were essentially derivative matters, such that Jefferson could compromise his positions on all of them without letting go of the real difference between himself and his great antagonist. Jefferson accused the Federalists of encouraging men to forget that governing is a burden, rather than a prize—an honor to be borne when asked, but not sought. Against this challenge, Hamilton was without a defense. He could abandon neither what he saw as the requirements for effective, competent, high-quality administration nor his understanding of liberalism whereby the test of good government is nothing more than its capacity to administer to the needs of the citizens' pursuit of self-interest.

NOTES

This chapter is reprinted here with the permission of *Publius: The Journal of Federalism* (Spring 1979).

1. Henry Cabot Lodge, *Alexander Hamilton,* in Standard Library series, American Statesmen, vol. 7 (Boston, Mass., and New York: Houghton Mifflin, 1898), p. 273.

2. Leonard D. White, *The Federalists: A Study in Administrative History* (New York: Macmillan, 1948), chap. 37, especially the concluding paragraph on p. 478. Much light is shed on White's mature judgment on the prospects for developing a modern "science" of administration and on the relationship of his study of Hamilton to those prospects, if we reflect on his statement that "fortunately, much of the administrative art is synonymous with common sense, sound judgement, initiative, and courage—homely virtues that were doubtless as readily at hand then as now. The art was practiced, but we cannot say it was cultivated for yet a hundred years." The words suggest that for White, the study of public administration must always take its bearings from practical experience and that its usefulness will consist in providing a kind of preview of the wisdom that can only be born out by experience.

3. Hamilton confessed his heart when he wrote Henry Lee that "the public interest . . . in my eyes is sacred" (quoted by Lynton Caldwell, in *The Administrative Theories of Jefferson and Hamilton* [New York: Russell & Russell, 1964], p. 6). The reader may wish to note that Caldwell's book was originally published by the University of Chicago Press in 1944, so that Leonard White was able to refer to it, approvingly, in *The Federalists.*

4. Hamilton's explicit argument in *Pacificus* that the president derives substantive powers from the statement in Article II that "the executive power shall be vested . . ." has not been accepted as the true meaning of the Constitution on this point. But so as not to destroy Hamilton's authority altogether, the standard opinion is that there is a tension, or even a contradiction, between *Pacificus* and Hamilton's *Federalist Papers,* concerning the constitutional basis and definition of the president's powers. I will argue subsequently that at least in Hamilton's own mind, there is no incompatibility between what he says in these two sources; see pp. 298–99 above.

5. We owe this information to the scholarship of Douglass Adair, who is cited by Clinton Rossiter in his Introduction to his edition of the *Federalist Papers* (New York: New American Library, 1961), p. xi.

6. Winton U. Solberg, ed., *The Federal Convention and the Formation of the Union of the American States,* including Madison's *Notes to the Convention* (Indianapolis, Ind.: Bobbs-Merrill, 1958), p. 176.

7. *Federalist Papers* no. 51, p. 325. It might be remarked, as an aside to those who are tempted to interpret Madison as a harbinger of modern pluralist thought, that this passage reveals that Madison remained attached to the idea of the common good and hence denied the central thesis of strict pluralist thought.

8. Ibid., no. 13, p. 102.

9. Ibid., no. 39, p. 245; cf. Madison's *Notes to the Convention,* in Solberg, *Federal Convention,* p. 88.

10. *Federalist Papers* no. 35, p. 214.

11. Ibid., no. 35, pp. 214–15.

12. I realize that the word "profit" might be objected to as a narrow and even

demeaned version of the word "happiness," as it occurs in Jefferson's more sublime expression of the purpose of government to facilitate the "pursuit of happiness." But I think that the substitution is both justified and helpful. After all, what form of happiness can we imagine pursuing, *individually*, that requires government's protection, except the happiness that comes from property? On this observation it seems fair to say that Jefferson's phrase "the pursuit of happiness" is itself a sweeter but vaguer version of John Locke's more original and stricter formulation. Locke says men unite in civil society "for the mutual preservation of their lives, liberties, and estates, which I call by the general name 'property' " (*The Second Treatise of Government* [Indianapolis, Ind.: Bobbs-Merrill, 1952], p. 71).

13. *Federalist Papers* no. 6, p. 57. For an extended discussion of the difference between Hamilton and others on the question whether commerce itself tends towards peace, cf. Gerald Stourzh, *Alexander Hamilton and the Idea of Republican Government* (Stanford, Calif.: Stanford University Press, 1970), pp. 126–70.

14. Alexander Hamilton, *The Continentalist* no. 5, quoted by Caldwell in *Administrative Theories,* p. 63.

15. I have in mind Joseph Charles in particular. Charles wanted to attack Hamilton by showing that his plan for the federal government's assumption of the states' debts and for funding the entire public debt at par went beyond what was strictly necessary for clearing the public debt, and then he wanted to show that Hamilton had a much broader and more sinister motive for the plans. Charles quotes Oliver Wolcott, Hamilton's assistant secretary of the Treasury, that the *real* purpose of the financial scheme was to create a stable environment for capital investment and capitalists' profits. Wolcott said explicitly that in this country the capitalists, rather than a hereditary nobility or a clergy or a body of military officers, are to be the "engine" of the nation's life. But why is this thought sinister? We can't have capitalism without capitalists, and Charles nowhere gives us any critique of capitalism. He seems to excoriate Hamilton's views on the foundation of social union merely *because* they aid the "monied few" more directly than others and therefore are bound to destroy the "loyalty, affection and best interests of all (the nation's) citizens." But not every citizenry is so constrained by jealousy that it cannot give its loyalty and affection to a regime in which there is inequality of property. Cf. Joseph Charles, *The Origins of the American Party System* (New York: Harper & Row, 1961), pp. 7–36. Forrest McDonald has shown a shrewdness that Charles lacks when he summarily described Hamilton's financial plan as "convenient" (*The Presidency of George Washington* [Lawrence: University Press of Kansas, 1974], p. 185).

16. Hamilton, *The Continentalist,* quoted by Caldwell in *Administrative Theories,* p. 54.

17. Quoted by Stourzh in *Alexander Hamilton and the Idea of Republican Government,* p. 42.

18. *Federalist Papers* no. 67, p. 409.

19. Ibid., no. 72, p. 439.

20. Ibid., no. 70, p. 430.

21. Ibid., pp. 427–28.

22. Ibid., no. 68, p. 414.

23. Ibid.

24. I take it as pretty well established that Locke's discussion of "executive prerogative," read carefully, reveals the extent to which his doctrine of legislative supremacy is a formal requirement that can be dispensed with under severely extenuating circumstances; thus, legislative supremacy can be said to veil the

Hobbesian character of libertarian government when circumstances are more ordinary. Cf. Robert A. Goldwin, "John Locke," in *History of Political Philosophy*, ed. Leo Strauss and Joseph Cropsey (Chicago: Rand McNally & Co., 1972), pp. 477–82.

25. Raoul Berger, "The Presidential Monopoly of Foreign Relations," *Michigan Law Review* 71 (Nov. 1972): 1–33.

26. Justice George Sutherland supported this general view of the presidency in the area of foreign policy in the famous case *U.S.* v. *Curtiss Wright Corp. et al.*, 299 U.S. 304; and Berger attacks the authority of that case. The issue in the *Curtiss Wright* case is not identical to the issue in *Pacificus*, but Sutherland's general observations about the presidency are relevant. The people are sovereign in the United States, but only in their collective capacity as a nation. The effective focus of that sovereign nation of people, when it focuses for the purpose of some definite action, is the executive.

27. The question whether Congress could bind inferior executive officers to its own particular will through specifically framed legislation, in direct opposition to the president's orders to such an officer, was decided, in favor of Congress, in the important case *Kendall* v. *Stokes*, 12 Pet. 524, in 1838.

28. Quoted by Caldwell in *Administrative Theories*, p. 99.

29. Quoted by White in *Federalists*, p. 71.

30. Many have attested to Washington's physical impressiveness and to his political importance. Forrest McDonald cites the authority of John Adams that Washington "had a bearing and demeanor that inspired instant and total confidence" (*Presidency of George Washington*, p. x).

31. White, *Federalists*, p. 262.

32. *Myers* v. *U.S.*, 272 U.S. 52. The source of this account of the decision of 1789 is Edward S. Corwin, *The President: Office and Powers*, 4th ed. (New York: New York University Press, 1957), p. 87.

33. White, *Federalists*, pp. 286–88.

34. Stourzh, *Alexander Hamilton and the Idea of Republican Government*, pp. 120–22.

12
JOHN ADAMS AND THE PRESIDENCY

BRUCE MIROFF

While contemporary students of the presidency generally ignore or deride John Adams, his conception of the presidency is intriguing and, in at least one respect, pertinent. Adams employed a classical vocabulary to depict a society torn by conflict between aristocrats and democrats. He envisioned the executive as the balancing force between the contending parties, responsible, in a disinterested fashion, for the maintenance of both order and justice. Adams's executive was a curious blend of power and passivity; his hallmark was, not energy, but impartiality and integrity. As president, John Adams proved true to his theoretical prescriptions, using his executive weight against what he considered democratic excesses, through the Alien and Sedition Acts, and then against what he considered aristocratic intrigues, through his peace mission to France. Adams's version of the independent executive was infuriating to Alexander Hamilton, who became the first of a long line of critics who have condemned Adams for vanity and weakness. But Adams had wisely avoided a war and blocked Hamilton's imperial schemes; he had recognized the dangers in the Hamiltonian version of the energetic executive.

The early presidents, Adams included, operated with an exalted conception of an executive who could surmount partisanship and self-interest; as Ralph Ketcham has shown, each attempted in his own fashion to be an American republican version of Bolingbroke's "patriot king." And they were (Washington excepted) men of theoretical vision, whose presidencies would take form in light of deeply held conceptions of politics.[1]

Of these early presidents, perhaps the most intensely theoretical was John Adams. Adams's ideas about the executive were rooted in an extraordinarily wide reading of political theory and history and, in particular, echoed the idealized vision of the British monarch found in the works of Bolingbroke and Jean Louis Delolme. His practice of presidential leadership, while it was affected by factors of personality, politics, and circumstance, can be understood in large part as an exemplification of his classical conception of the executive.[2]

John Adams has received too little attention from contemporary students of the presidency. Compared especially to Washington, Hamilton, and Jefferson, he has been given scant notice; when he is discussed at all, it is ordinarily in derisive or distorted terms. Thus, Thomas Bailey, writing in *Presidential Greatness,* dismisses Adams as "temperamentally unfitted to be President" and asserts that "in some respects he was a flat failure." James David Barber suggests that among the first four presidents, Adams most closely approximates the disastrous "active-negative" type; he describes Adams as "an impatient and irascible man" who was "far more partisan than Washington" and who "presided over the new nation's first experiment in political repression."[3]

My aim in this chapter is to reconstruct Adams's conception of the executive, which is to be found scattered throughout his writings (and actions), rather than explicated at length in any single text. His conception, I contend, should neither be dismissed nor derided. In certain respects it does seem anachronistic, quite remote from the politics of the modern presidency. In other respects—particularly Adams's rejection of the energetic and aggressive executive style championed by Alexander Hamilton and his association of that style with militarism and imperial adventure—it is intriguing and still relevant.

My argument proceeds through four stages. First, I briefly sketch some of Adams's ideas about political psychology and social conflict, which establish the context for his conception of the executive. Second, I draw from Adams's writings the elements that form his conception of the executive. Third, I turn to Adams's presidency and examine several of its central incidents as commentary upon his conception of the executive. Fourth, I consider the revealing response to Adams's presidency by a far-more-familiar architect of the executive, Alexander Hamilton.

ADAMS'S CLASSICAL CONCEPTION OF THE PRESIDENCY

To understand Adams's conception of the executive, we must first look at some of his basic assumptions about political life. Adams was a lifelong student of political motives. While some of his fascination with the springs of political action derived from his own brooding Puritan introspection, Adams also believed that the development of psychological acuity was essential to the success of a "public man." As he wrote to James Warren in 1775: "There is a discernment competent to mortals by which they can penetrate into the minds of men and discover their secret passions, prejudices, habits, hopes, fears, wishes and designs. . . . A dexterity and facility of thus unravelling men's thoughts and a faculty of governing them by means of the knowledge we have of them, constitutes the principal part of the art of a politician."[4]

Among the politically relevant motives, the most attractive for Adams was disinterestedness. Commitment to public ends even at the sacrifice of personal interests was the hallmark of "civic virtue" in the classical republican tradition. In 1776, Adams had rested American hopes for republicanism upon the widespread practice of disinterestedness. Yet while he continued to admire disinterestedness—and often asserted that his own actions had manifested this austere virtue—by the 1780s he had come to believe that it was a rare phenomenon. Most of those who claimed to be sacrificing their own welfare for that of the public would, he warned, be political dissemblers. "Nothing so infallibly gulls the people and nothing more universally deceives them in the end than this pretended disinterestedness."[5]

While Adams thus believed that the "selfish passions" predominated, he was careful to differentiate between various forms of self-seeking. The form that held the greatest political potential was the love of fame. In his most extensive psychological analysis, the *Discourses on Davila,* Adams defined "the passion for distinction" as the individual's "desire to be observed, considered, esteemed, praised, believed, and admired by his fellows." While most people sought to gratify this desire through wealth or other private accomplishments, a few aimed higher: "They aim at approbation as well as attention; at esteem as well as consideration; and at admiration and gratitude, as well as congratulation. . . . This last description of persons is the tribe out of which proceed your patriots and heroes, and most of the great benefactors to mankind."[6]

Having abandoned any expectation of widespread civic virtue, Adams looked to the political leadership of an elite driven by the love of fame. If the political order would reward actions productive of public advantages with resplendent honors and grateful applause, the energy derived from the love of fame would vitalize the Republic. Adams is best known for advocating balanced institutions that check the passions, but for *this* passion his prescription was different. He wanted it to be "gratified, encouraged, and arranged on the side of virtue."[7]

Unfortunately, other "selfish passions" were more prevalent than the love of fame. Uppermost, according to Adams, were ambition and avarice. Neither ambition nor avarice could be arranged on the side of virtue, for what they shared was self-aggrandizement at the expense of the common good. Ambition aimed at power or office without regard for the public welfare. Avarice corrupted political life by turning public business into the handmaiden of personal greed for wealth. The balanced institutions that

Adams ceaselessly advocated were defenses against the powerful forces of ambition and avarice.

For John Adams, the centerpiece of constitutional wisdom was the idea of balance. A republic could survive, he believed, only if it established an equilibrium between three social orders: the body of the people, the aristocracy, and the "monarchical" element. His three bulky volumes, *A Defence of the Constitutions of Government of the United States of America*, laboriously tracked down the guises under which balanced government had functioned.

Adams was especially concerned with the role of the aristocracy. He did not restrict the term to a hereditary order. To Jefferson, he wrote: "The five pillars of aristocracy are beauty, wealth, birth, genius, and virtues. Any one of the three first can at any time overbear any one or both of the two last." To John Taylor, he explained, "By aristocracy, I understand all those men who can command, influence, or procure more than an average of votes." Adams believed that regardless of the egalitarian dreams of his epoch, an aristocracy—or what we would call an elite—would be found in every society.[8]

His critics charged that Adams was a devotee of aristocracy, yet he could assail aristocrats with a ferocity that rivaled that of Thomas Paine. Haughty, imperious aristocrats were, Adams observed, usually able to get the better of the common people. They could trade upon the people's sense of inferiority in their presence. And if a lofty demeanor was not enough to attain the aristocrats' objectives, they were quite capable of shifting to low tricks, for the "multitude have always been credulous, and the few are always artful." Ordinarily more than a match for the people in any simple form of government, aristocracy would swiftly prove its oppressiveness once it had the opportunity. But it would also prove its instability, for aristocratic pride would engender rivalries among the leading families that would divide and torment a polity.[9]

If this elite was both dangerous and irrepressible, it was also potentially valuable. Adams argued that although ability and wisdom might originate in any part of society, the greatest concentration of learning and talent was to be found among the social and economic elite. The aristocracy "is the brightest ornament and glory of the nation, and may always be made the greatest blessing of society, if it be judiciously managed in the constitution." The institutional home for the aristocracy, Adams urged, ought to be a senate. Set off by themselves in a senate, the aristocrats could no longer overawe or manipulate the common people. And they could offer valuable services to the Republic. They would be the bulwark of property against unjust leveling schemes among the people; they would be a potent barrier against executive despotism, as aristocratic pride responded vigorously to any executive who grasped for dominion. Hedged in by the popular assembly on one side and the executive on the other, aristocratic passions would, in a properly constructed senate, be able to promote only desirable public ends.[10]

Although Adams's institutional prescriptions for the elite were out of kilter with the emerging American understanding of a constitutional order, his insights into the role that elites would play in American life remain impressive. The same cannot be said for his view of the American people. His voracious readings in classical and European history, and his erudition in political theory, proved to be a trap for Adams when he attempted to gauge the political impulses of the mass of Americans. Steeped in European categories, he was unable to grasp the moderation of the American people.

Adams held to a fearful view of the American people. Although his standpoint towards the people was neither hostile nor unsympathetic, he worried about their propensity to rush to political extremes. Like the aristocracy, the common people were prone to their own particular set of political vices. One popular vice was credulity. Without the capacity to discern who their true friends were, the people often invested their trust in demagogues. The popular vice that most terrified Adams, however, was envy. In a balanced constitution, where passions could only flow in demarcated channels, the people would learn to respect talent, virtue, birth, and wealth. Thrown together with the aristocrats in a singular and unbounded political arena, on the other hand, popular envy would flourish. The aristocrats still might succeed in overawing or tricking the multitude, but if they failed, the multitude were sure to be despoiled.

Warning repeatedly against the horrors of "simple democracy," Adams advocated what he believed to be genuine democracy, by which he meant a popular assembly sharing power with an aristocratic senate and a monarchical executive. Just as a senate delimited and fructified aristocratic passions, so would a popular assembly bring out the best qualities of the people. The assembly would be the home for their legitimate political interests and activities.

BALANCED GOVERNMENT

The executive was the linchpin in John Adams's theory of balanced government. Equilibrium between aristocracy and democracy was not, in his view, a mechanical arrangement, but rather a political achievement. It would demand the commitment and talent of the executive to maintain a balance in the face of contending forces that constantly threatened to upset it.

Adams's attempts to show the American people what kind of executive they required met with considerable incomprehension. His difficulties stemmed in part from his impolitic language, for he refused to cast aside the classical usages and to adapt his words to the current fashion. An equally serious impediment to understanding was the extent of Adams's deviation from both sides of the prevailing debate in the new United States about the character of a republican executive. If his proposed executive was far too powerful and regal to please the Antifederalists and their successors, it was too nonpartisan and passive to impress those whose model of the executive derived from James Wilson and Alexander Hamilton.

Adams was impatient with the radical Whig animus against executive power. To deny the need for this power was to ignore the propensities of human nature and the regularities of human history. "There is a strong and continual effort, in every society of men, arising from the constitution of their minds, towards a kingly power." He was further impatient with the prevailing obsession about shunning the vocabulary of monarchy, believing that it distracted political theorizing from the essence of the phenomenon which monarchy named.

> Everybody knows that the word monarchy has its etymology in the Greek . . . and signifies single rule or authority in one. This authority may be limited or unlimited, of temporary or perpetual duration. . . . Nevertheless, as far as it extends, and as long as it lasts, it may be called a monarchical authority with great propriety, by any man who is not afraid of a popular clamor and a scurrilous abuse of words.[11]

Although Adams strongly opposed unlimited executive authority, he believed that in a balanced government a "monarchical" figure was indispensable, for it was this figure who would ultimately uphold the balance. Detached from the contending classes and parties, Adams's executive would prevent anyone from obtaining a dominant position. "Neither the poor nor the rich should ever be suffered to be masters. They should have equal power to defend themselves; and that their power may be always equal, there should be an independent mediator between them, always ready, always able, and always interested to assist the weakest."[12]

Edward Handler has suggested that Adams set out two mutually inconsistent descriptions of the executive: in one, the executive served as a mediator between the aristocracy and the people, while in the other, the executive championed the people's cause against the aristocracy. Both descriptions of the executive can be found in Adams, but their apparent inconsistency dissolves once his view of the political struggle between aristocrats and democrats is recalled. Because conflict between the few and the many jeopardized political equilibrium, the executive sometimes had to assume the role of "a third party, whose interest and duty it [is] to do justice to the other two." Because the aristocracy ordinarily brought to this conflict superior resources and wiles, the executive sometimes had to act as "the natural friend of the people, and the only defense which they or their representatives can have against the avarice and ambition of the rich and distinguished citizens."[13]

What was most striking about Adams's conception of the executive was not the shifting roles this figure would have to assume in order to maintain the political balance; it was the unusual blend of power and passivity that would characterize his actions. Adams wanted to vest in an American president all of the essential prerogatives of the British monarch. The chief magistrate that he favored would possess an unencumbered power in making appointments, treaties, and wars and would be armed with an absolute veto over the products of legislative action. Yet Adams believed that this panoply of powers would be used sparingly and defensively, for the executive, unlike the senate or assembly, was not given to aggression.[14]

The defensiveness and passivity that characterized this conception become clearer when Adams's executive figure is contrasted with the chief magistrates proposed by James Wilson and Alexander Hamilton. Wilson was the foremost architect of a strong and unitary executive in the Constitutional Convention, where he highlighted the "energy, dispatch, and responsibility" such an executive would provide. Hamilton, in his famous *Federalist* number 70, further developed this notion by his demonstration that "all men of sense will agree in the necessity of an energetic Executive." Adams agreed with much of the case for a unitary executive. He wrote in the *Defence* that "the unity, the secrecy, the dispatch of one man has no equal." He endorsed the idea, shared by Wilson and Hamilton, that unity ensured responsibility and that "the attention of the whole nation should be fixed upon one point." What was lacking in Adams was the emphasis upon executive energy. The driving, dominating, committed executive, whose lineaments were most visible in the ideas and actions of Hamilton, was the opposite of what Adams wanted.[15]

When Adams spoke of the executive's motives, he adopted different tones than those he employed to describe aristocratic or democratic motives. Ambition and avarice typically drove the few and the many; in the best of institutional arrangements, their desire for fame might come to play a significant part. Writing about the executive, however, Adams seemed to assume that either disinterestedness or the love of fame would be uppermost. Standing apart from the passions of the aristocratic and democratic parties, the executive as mediator was supposed to "calm and restrain the ardor of both." Favoring neither the interests of the few nor the interests of the many, but seeking instead to do "justice to all sides," the executive would become a rallying point for "the honest and virtuous of all sides." Adams's executive was thus to be a figure marked, not by energy, but by impartiality and integrity.[16]

Serving as the balancing force between social classes, political parties, and legislative branches, the executive might have to move with decisiveness and firmness. Yet, since he lacked any interest or program of his own, his characteristic stance was to wait. His power would be held in abeyance until he had to defend the weaker party against the stronger, or until a line of action opened up that was independent of either party and conducive to the national welfare. Adams's executive did not, therefore, search out opportunities for action or grasp at instruments for aggression.

In light of this conception, it was not surprising that Adams wanted to base American national defense on a strong navy or that he was disturbed by Hamilton's dream of a professional American army. With a strong navy, the executive might assure the defense of the nation's territory and commerce against European depredations. But Adams was reluctant to see a large army recruited in America, regarding it as a seductive tool for executive and national aggression.

The emphasis on impartiality and integrity and the fear of aggressive and partisan energy were also evident in Adams's perspective on executive appointments. Adams adhered to the classical republican objective of attracting the most meritorious individuals to public service and rewarding them with lustrous public honors. What jeopardized this objective was class and factional animosity. If the people or the legislature were given the responsibility of awarding offices and distributing honors, factional rivalries would polarize the Republic. In contrast, "when the emulation of all the citizens looks up to one point, like the rays of the circle from all parts of the circumference, meeting and uniting in the center, you may hope for uniformity, consistency, and subordination."[17]

By proposing that the executive alone should dispense political offices and honors, Adams made it easy for his critics to assail him as the champion of a royal court in American garb. But his concern here was not, in fact, with patronage and influence. Rather, he wanted to draw upon the executive's impartial judgment of men's characters to select the most deserving for offices of public trust. Presidents of the United States, he insisted, "must look out for merit wherever they can find it; and talent and integrity must be a recommendation to office, wherever they are seen, though differing in sentiments from the president."[18]

When Adams applied his theoretical conception of the executive—rooted in his classical commitment to a government that balanced social orders as well as institutions—within the context of American politics, he ran into a host of frustrations. He considered the executive he proposed for America as benign, especially towards the people, but he could never convince "old Whigs" of his perspective.

During the Revolution, Adams himself had shared, to some extent, in the Whiggish mistrust of magisterial power and prominence. By the time of the *Defence* and the United States Constitution, however, Adams was unequivocal in his support for a strong executive. Flying in the face of revolutionary sensibilities, he incautiously argued that America should acknowledge its status, under the new Constitution, as a "monarchical republic." While Hamilton was employing all his cleverness, in *Federalist* number 69, to demonstrate how the new president bore hardly any resemblance to the British king, Adams was insisting to Roger Sherman on their likeness.

> The duration of our president is neither perpetual nor for life; it is only for four years; but his power during those four years is much greater than that of an avoyer, a consul, a doge, a stadtholder, nay, than a king of Poland; nay, than a king of Sparta. I know of no first magistrate in any republican government, excepting England and Neuchatel, who possesses a constitutional dignity, authority, and power comparable to his.[19]

Adams endorsed presidential power, and he regretted that it had been compromised by admitting the aristocratic Senate to a share in such executive functions as appointments and treaty making. Reacting to the new Constitution, he wrote to Jefferson in December 1787: "You are afraid of the one—I, of the few. . . . You are apprehensive of monarchy; I, of aristocracy. I would therefore have given more power to the President and less to the Senate." Criticizing the Senate's part in appointments, Adams predicted to Sherman that it would "weaken the hands of the executive, by lessening the obligation, gratitude, and attachment of the candidate to the president, by dividing his attachment between the executive and legislative, which are natural enemies. . . . The president's own officers, in a thousand instances, will oppose his just and constitutional exertions, and screen themselves under the wings of their patrons and party in the legislature."[20]

Adams hoped for an independent president who would not be dragged into class and partisan strife. He tried repeatedly to impress upon the American people the necessity for executive independence. "The people cannot be too careful in the choice of their presidents; but when they have chosen them, they ought to expect that they will act their own independent judgments, and not be wheedled or intimidated by factious combinations of senators, representatives, heads of departments, or military officers."[21]

It was desirable, in Adams's estimation, that the choice of the executive be consensual, as it had been in the case of Washington. He dreaded partisan division over so preeminent a leader: "His person, countenance, character, and actions are made the daily contemplation and conversation of the whole people. Hence arises the danger of a division of this attention. Where there are rivals for the first place, the national attention and passions are divided, and thwart each other." Once partisan strife had emerged and jeopardized his own succession to the presidential chair, Adams concealed his disappointment with the sardonic observation that this was only one more verification of his much-maligned theory of politics. Writing to his wife in February 1796, he pointed out that "the first situation is the great object of contention—the center and main source of all emulation, as the learned Dr. Adams teaches in all his writings, and everybody believes him, though nobody will own it."[22]

But he could never reconcile himself to the connection between political parties and the presidency. Rather than understanding parties as a base of political support, and thus as an aid to a president's effectiveness, Adams continued to espouse the executive's independence and to regard parties as weakening him. He cited not only his own experience as president but also that of his successors to bolster this view. Contemplating the state of the presidency under James Madison, Adams could find only a pathetic dependency. The president, he told Benjamin Rush, had become "a mere head of wood. A mere football, kicked and tossed by Frenchmen, Englishmen, or rather Scotchmen, and ignorant, mischievous boys."[23]

Adams's conception of the independent executive, with its echoes of the idealized British monarch advocated by Bolingbroke and described by Delolme, was already somewhat anachronistic by the time of his own administration. In the era of Jefferson and his heirs, its "monarchical" imagery would render it even more unfashionable. Yet Adams remained convinced that only this kind of executive would serve the public good. In a poignant but futile gesture, the elderly Adams exhorted the American people to rally behind the presidency and to liberate it from its captivity to the party system.

> People of the United States! You know not half the solicitude of your presidents for your happiness and welfare, nor a hundredth part of the obstructions and embarrassments they endure from intrigues of individuals of both parties. You must support them in their independence, and turn a deaf ear to all the false charges against them.[24]

THE ADAMS PRESIDENCY

For a commentary upon Adams's conception of the executive, one of the most instructive places to look is his own presidency. Assuming the presidency of a young republic caught between two warring giants abroad, with increasingly antagonistic domestic parties accusing each other of allegiance to one of those foreign giants, Adams stepped into a situation straight out of his earlier theoretical writings.

> The parties of rich and poor, of gentlemen and simplemen, unbalanced by some third power, will always look out for foreign aid, and never be at a loss for names, pretexts, and distinctions. Whig and Tory, Constitutionalist and Republican, Anglomane and Francomane, Athenian and Spartan, will serve the purpose as well as Guelph and Ghibelline. The great desideratum in a government is a distinct executive power, of sufficient strength and weight to compel both these parties, in turn, to submit to the laws.[25]

Adams would attempt to act the part of the independent executive throughout his presidency. That part would prove an ordeal for him. Standing alone in his cherished independence, he would attract hostile fire from partisans on both sides. Yet, in his own terms at least, he could claim success on several counts. To examine Adams's independent executive in action, I will consider two of the major events of his presidency, the Alien and Sedition Acts and the peace mission to France in 1799, plus one minor but revealing incident, the Fries pardon.

The Alien and Sedition Acts are, of course, the chief stigma on the record of the Adams administration. This attempt, during the "quasi-war" with France, to proscribe and punish critics of the government has earned the near-universal condemnation of historians, political scientists, and civil libertarians. Adams's part in the repressive episode certainly merits criticism. Yet it is important to look carefully both at the specific role he played in the history of the Alien and Sedition Acts and at his understanding of that role.

The Alien and Sedition Acts were not shaped by John Adams. As John C. Miller has observed, they were not "administration measures in the sense that they were recommended by the President." The legislation was devised by Federalists in Congress. "These laws," Miller has written, "were the work of the Federalist party, acting out of fear of 'Jacobinism,' admiration of the stern repressive measures taken by the British government—and under the fervent conviction that the good of the country required the rooting out of all French sympathizers."[26]

If the Alien and Sedition Acts were the fault of a whole party (the only prominent Federalist to oppose them was John Marshall, who doubted their expediency), Adams's culpability was nonetheless substantial. As the proponent of executive independence, he should have steered clear of measures with such partisan implications. Instead, he shaped the climate in which the legislation was enacted by delivering his bellicose addresses after the XYZ affair. He signed the legislation willingly, and he authorized the use of the Alien Act for deportations and the Sedition Act for prosecutions of his journalistic critics.

But Adams refrained from a policy of sweeping repression. The zealot of repression was Timothy Pickering, secretary of state and the most forceful of the "High Federalists" in Adams's cabinet. It was Pickering who searched through Republican newspapers for evidence of sedition and pressed for prompt prosecutions. Although Adams sometimes concurred with Pickering's choice of victims, at other times, Adams restrained the secretary of state.

Adams approved the enforcement of the Alien Act in a handful of cases. But no one was actually deported under this statute. As James Morton Smith has concluded, "The chief reason for the record of nonenforcement was the determination of John Adams to give the law a much stricter interpretation than the Federalist extremists desired. Refusing to become a rubber stamp to the zealots in his Cabinet, . . . he preferred to retain the power of final decision rather than to sign blank warrants which Pickering and his colleagues might use as they pleased." Adams was also resistant to the most blatantly partisan uses of the Sedition Act. He would not countenance any effort to ensnare Vice-President Jefferson in the machinery of repression. John C. Miller has argued that Adams "was better than his party: although he approved of both the Alien and Sedition Acts, he never advocated the prostitution of these laws to party purposes."[27]

From Adams's perspective, the Alien and Sedition Acts were not supposed to be the tools of a party. They were instruments of self-preservation for a republic threatened by a foreign power and its domestic adherents. They aimed, not at legitimate public discourse, but at the licentious and false rhetoric with which democratic extremists stirred up popular passions. When the Republican journalist Thomas Cooper interpreted the policies of the Adams administration as signaling a plan of executive usurpation, the president's response was: "A meaner, a more artful, or a more malicious libel has not appeared. As far as it alludes to me, I despise it; but I have no doubt it is a libel against the whole government, and as such ought to be prosecuted." The independent executive could, in Adams's conception, become a repressive—though not a partisan—figure, employing his "strength and weight to compel" the democratic party "to submit to the laws."[28]

The aristocratic party too would, in its turn, be compelled "to submit to the laws." The ascendancy of the High Federalists, premised upon the likelihood of a war with France, would be fatally undermined by Adams's decision to send a peace mission to France in 1799. Their plans for military power, imperial adventure, and political supremacy would be confounded by Adams's unexpected move. Having collaborated with the aristocratic party in repressing democratic licentiousness, the independent executive would shift his stance and set about to thwart aristocratic intrigue.

Initially, Adams's view of the French threat largely coincided with the position of the High Federalists, who looked to Alexander Hamilton for leadership. After the brazen insult to the United States of the XYZ affair, Adams appeared to rule out further efforts at negotiation and to rally the American people for a confrontation with France. Indeed, on several occasions he considered asking Congress for a declaration of war. Yet, for a number of reasons, he hesitated. Instead of all-out war, there would be the Alien and Sedition Acts, a rapid build-up of the army and navy, and a state of "quasi-war" on the seas between the United States and France.

But the agreement between Adams and the High Federalists was fragile. Whereas Adams had wanted to impress the French with American naval preparedness, Federalists in Congress presented him with a large army. Adams's unhappiness with this army was then exacerbated by a lengthy intrigue over the chain of command. George Washington, appointed by Adams to head the "new army," stipulated that he would not begin active duty until actual hostilities impended; in the meantime, Alexander Hamilton must be second in command. When Adams resisted placing Hamilton above officers who had previously outranked him, Hamilton's partisans in the cabinet (Pickering, James McHenry, and Oliver Wolcott) schemed behind Adams's back and eventually prevailed upon Washington to face down the president.[29]

Adams was forced to accept an army dominated by a man he regarded as the arch aristocratic intriguer in the United States and the ambitious leader of a "British faction." And Adams was progressively made aware of the army's dangerous potential, for Hamilton and his associates were nurturing imperial dreams. Hamilton's letters during this period reveal his belief that with the decisive rupture between the United States and France, "tempting objects will be within our grasp." As well as employing "the land force" to guard against a possible French invasion, the United States "ought certainly to look to the possession of the Floridas and Louisiana— and we ought to squint at South America." For an expedition southward, Hamilton proposed a British fleet and an American army, and he made plain who would be its guiding presence. "The command in this case would very naturally fall upon me."[30]

Hamilton's army also had possible domestic uses. Richard H. Kohn has argued that contrary to the assumption of most historians, there is no evidence that the High Federalists planned to crush their Republican adversaries with armed force. Yet Hamilton and his colleagues were certainly aware of the power of intimidation that a large and exclusively Federalist army offered. Responding to the Kentucky and Virginia resolutions, Hamilton proposed a military reassertion of national authority: "When a clever force has been collected, let them be drawn towards Virginia, for which there is an obvious pretext—and then let measures be taken to act upon the laws and put Virginia to the test of resistance. This plan will give time for the fervor of the moment to subside, for reason to resume the reins, and by dividing its enemies will enable the government to triumph with ease."[31]

Although Hamilton had gained effective control of the army, the appointment of officers and the recruitment of troops still required presidential action. Adams seems to have chosen deliberately to dally with the measures necessary for the army build-up. While proceeding expeditiously with the construction of naval vessels, the president dragged his feet on army matters. In a letter to Hamilton, Secretary of War McHenry reported a typical instance of Adams's delaying tactics: "Your instructions are and have been some days with the President. . . . I spoke to him yesterday, on the subject: he had not considered them, and seemed to insinuate the affair need not be hurried."[32]

But it was not enough for Adams to impede the formation of Hamilton's army; as long as war with France remained a distinct possibility, events might still play into Hamilton's hands. Fearful, as he would later claim, of a possible civil war and increasingly persuaded, from the reports of his diplomats in Europe as well as the recently returned Elbridge Gerry, that the French were now interested in resuming negotiations, Adams decided to make the most dramatic move of his presidency. On February 18, 1799, he nominated William Vans Murray as a peace envoy to France. Adams had come to this decision by himself, without consulting his cabinet. He saw no reason to seek the counsel of men whose opposition he anticipated and whose loyalty he distrusted.

Adams's decision stunned and outraged the High Federalists. A committee of Federalist senators soon called upon the president and asked him to withdraw the nomination. Adams bridled at their approach, protesting that these senators were interfering with the executive's duties. As one of the senators, Theodore Sedgwick, reported, "during the conversation [Adams] declared, repeatedly, that to defend the executive against oligarchic influence, it was indispensable, that he should insist, on a decision on the nomination." At one point, Adams went so far as to threaten to resign if the Senate balked him—which would have made Jefferson the president! Eventually, it was agreed that the peace mission would be enlarged by adding two more envoys.[33]

It was to be another eight months before two envoys would sail for France (Vans Murray was already in the Netherlands). Some commentators have blamed Adams for this delay, criticizing him for vacillation and an inability to follow through after a "statesmanlike gesture." Others have contended that the delay was deliberate, that Adams waited on a clarification of the murky political situation in France and the completion of naval construction. In any case, Adams did finally dispatch the mission, in the face of a last, desperate effort by the High Federalists to forestall it. And with its dispatch, the hopes of the High Federalists were irrevocably blasted.[34]

Public opinion embraced the turn toward peace. The "new army" was disbanded; Hamilton was returned to civilian life. As Richard H. Kohn has observed: " To save himself and the nation from . . . a dangerous course, Adams had exploded Hamilton's dreams." The United States made peace with France and thus weathered a crisis that could have destroyed the Republic. But the cost, to Adams, was high. One wing of the Federalist party became fiercely hostile to him. His Republican adversaries were vindicated by the collapse of the High Federalist program. Adams thus went down to defeat in the election of 1800 (albeit narrowly), with the bitter satisfaction of a great but unrewarded service to his country.[35]

Before that defeat there was a coda, in which Adams once more acted the part of the independent executive. The taxes levied by the Federalists in Congress to pay for military build-up had produced a minor rebellion in eastern Pennsylvania. The most prominent character in this rebellion, John Fries, was arrested for leading a party of armed men to free two tax evaders from prison. Charged with treason, Fries was tried (twice), convicted, and sentenced to be hanged. Most Federalists applauded the sentence as an example of judicial rigor useful for cowing disorderly elements in the population. Linking this rebellion to the earlier Whisky Rebellion in western Pennsylvania, they were not disposed to be merciful. As Hamilton later put it, "Two insurrections in the same state . . . demonstrated a spirit of insubordination or disaffection which required a strong corrective."[36]

Adams, however, refused to use Fries's death as an emblem of order. Adams concluded that Fries had been guilty of riotous behavior but that his crime did not warrant so grave a charge as treason—or so severe a punishment. Hence, Adams overrode the unanimous advice of his cabinet in May 1800 and pardoned Fries. Adams had chosen, he informed Attorney General Charles Lee, to "take on myself alone the responsibility of one more appeal to the humane and generous natures of the American people."[37]

True to his theoretical prescriptions, Adams employed his presidential power as an instrument of balance. During the first half of his term, he directed most of his efforts against what he took to be the excesses of the democratic, or "French," party. Facing what he considered familiar democratic vices—demagoguery, licentiousness, turbulence—he was ready to utilize the heavy hand of repression. Halfway through the term, having become persuaded of the dangers attendant on a war with France, upon which all of the Hamiltonians' plans hinged, Adams carried out a dramatic reversal which thwarted the aristocratic, or "British," party. Facing familiar aristocratic vices—intrigue, manipulation, grandiose ambition— he was ready to circumvent the intriguers, to overcome their manipulations, and to puncture their imperious visions. Adams hardly conducted these shifts in policy flawlessly. Yet their character was not an indication of weakness or vacillation; it was a reflection of his commitment to fulfill the responsibilities of the independent executive.

Adams's conduct as the independent executive was infuriating and incomprehensible to the champion of the energetic executive, Alexander Hamilton. As Hamilton found his own energies bottled up by Adams's actions, his criticisms became increasingly scathing. While these criticisms were fueled by personal frustration, they also served to measure the distance between the two men's respective conceptions of the executive. Many modern commentators have judged Adams's presidency by the Hamiltonian desideratum of energy and have pronounced it weak. The first commentator to offer that pronouncement was Alexander Hamilton.

Hamilton had not wanted Adams to be president. He had even made efforts in 1796 to supplant him with Thomas Pinckney. However, for the first year and a half of the Adams administration, Hamilton was not dissatisfied with Adams's presidency. After delineating the features of the energetic executive in *The Federalist Papers* and personally infusing energy into the executive handling of financial, diplomatic, and military affairs under President Washington, Hamilton was now officially on the sidelines, a New York lawyer at last making money for his family. But his protégés and adherents held the cabinet posts of state, war, and treasury, and the leading Federalist legislators turned to him for guidance. The one actor whom he could not directly counsel was the president; but John Adams, during this period, seemed of a like mind with Hamilton. Thus, Hamilton wrote to Rufus King: "I believe there is no danger of want of firmness in the Executive. If he is not ill-advised he will not want prudence."[38]

In the period of national excitement and war fever that followed the public disclosure of the XYZ affair, Hamilton approved of Adams's spirited posture but feared that Adams might become carried away with martial ardor. Complaining to Secretary of the Treasury Wolcott that one of Adams's addresses contained a statement that was "intemperate and revolutionary," Hamilton worried that the president "may run into indiscretion. This will do harm to the Government, to the cause, and to himself. Some hint must be given, for we must make no mistakes."

Hamilton regarded himself as far more cool and controlled than Adams, and more cognizant of the need for care in directing public opinion toward firmness and vigor.[39]

As we have seen, the conflict between Hamilton and Adams first took shape over Hamilton's rank in the "new army." Hamilton's frustration with Adams slowly mounted as Hamilton began to put together this army. The successful selection of officers for a large force, he observed, "depends on the President—and on that success the alternative of some or no energy." But Hamilton was coming to doubt the president's competency for executive duties. Adams, he thought, was a theorist rather than a man of action. To Rufus King, Hamilton observed: "You know . . . how widely different the business of government is from the speculation of it, and the energy of the imagination, dealing in general propositions, from that of execution in detail."[40]

The president's delaying tactics continued to dog Hamilton's indefatigable efforts to bring his army into existence. Hamilton looked to his friends in the cabinet for assistance. He wrote to Secretary of War McHenry: "If the Chief is too desultory, his Ministers ought to be more united and steady and well settled in some reasonable system of measures." But Hamilton's appeals were unavailing; hobbled by administrative failures in addition to Adams's resistance, the "new army" never attained its mandated size. "Less than half the authorized number of men ever enlisted, so each regiment limped along, . . . perpetually understrength."[41]

Hamilton's criticism of Adams for lacking executive energy extended beyond army matters to the Alien and Sedition Acts. While Hamilton had not played a part in the genesis of the repressive legislation, he was more eager than the president to see it vigorously enforced. Complaining about Adams's performance to Senator Jonathan Dayton, Hamilton proclaimed:

> But what avail laws which are not executed? Renegade aliens conduct more than one of the most incendiary presses in the United States—and yet in open contempt and defiance of the laws they are permitted to continue their destructive labors. Why are they not sent away? . . . Vigor in the Executive is at least as necessary as in the legislative branch. If the President requires to be stimulated, those who can approach him ought to do it.[42]

When the "desultory" Adams made an unexpected move to announce a new peace mission to France, imperiling Hamilton's military plans and imperial visions, the general was hardly more pleased with him. Adams was not credited with energy but was castigated for passion; his decision was attributed to vanity and petulance. "Our measures, from the first cause, are too much the effect of momentary impulse. Vanity and jealousy exclude all counsel. Passion wrests the helm from reason."[43]

The final straw for Hamilton was Adams's dismissal of McHenry and Pickering from the cabinet. No longer able to control his anger at the intrigues that had swirled around him, Adams lashed out at McHenry in a personal interview. Among the accusations he hurled at the secretary of war was subservience to Hamilton, whom Adams called "the greatest intriguant in the world." When McHenry sent Hamilton an account of the interview, Hamilton replied that Adams "is more mad than I ever thought him and, I shall soon be led to say, as wicked as he is mad."[44]

Even before receiving accounts of the cabinet purge, Hamilton had concluded that he could not support Adams for reelection. Along with some of his associates, Hamilton developed a strategy whereby the Federalist vice-presidential candidate, Charles C. Pinckney, might gain more electoral votes than Adams and become president. Once Adams's supporters learned of this plan and began to denounce it as the work of a "British faction," Hamilton decided to vindicate his own actions and to expose Adams's defects in a detailed letter. Facing the possibility that this letter might irreparably split the Federalists, Hamilton insisted that Adams had "already disorganized and in a great measure prostrated the Federal Party."[45]

Hamilton's letter—which did more to diminish his own reputation than that of Adams—restated his prior complaints and added some new ones. "Not denying to Mr. Adams patriotism and integrity, and even talents of a certain kind, I should be deficient in candor, were I to conceal the conviction, that he does not possess the talents adapted to the administration of government, and that there are great and intrinsic defects in his character, which unfit him for the office of Chief Magistrate." Adams's personal flaws were repeatedly underscored. He was proclaimed to be "a man of an imagination sublimated and eccentric . . . ," possessing "a vanity without bounds, and a jealousy capable of discoloring every object."[46]

In a lengthy critique of Adams's peace mission, Hamilton set out to demonstrate that the president's diplomacy was "wrong, both as to mode and substance." A nation animated by a spirit of patriotic enthusiasm had been plunged from its "proud eminence" by an impulsive decision. Refusing to take counsel from his own constitutional ministers, the president had reversed his own prior stance and waived the chief point of national honor by sending a mission to France. He had compounded his original error—the nomination of Vans Murray—by later ordering the envoys to sail without proper assurances from the French Directory. "Thus, on every just calculation, whatever may be the issue, the measure, in reference either to our internal or foreign affairs, even to our concerns with France, was alike impolitic."[47]

After reviewing other alleged misdeeds of the president—for example, the firings of McHenry and Pickering and the pardoning of Fries— Hamilton concluded that Adams had gravely weakened the young American Republic. "Let it be added, as the necessary effect of such conduct, that he has made great progress undermining the ground which was gained for the government by his predecessor, and that there is real cause to apprehend, it might totter, if not fall, under his future auspices." Hamilton interpreted Adams's presidency as a disastrous mixture of lassitude and caprice. But the majority of contemporary historians have—in my view, correctly—regarded Hamilton's plans during this period for high-toned authority, military power, and imperial expansion as the real danger to the survival of the Republic. Adams was, as Hamilton charged, vain and jealous at times. But Adams kept his eye always on the paramount duty of the independent executive: preserving the Republic from the external and internal forces that threatened to corrupt or destroy it.[48]

CONCLUSION

John Adams's conception of the independent executive was classical, derived chiefly from Roman republicanism and Bolingbroke's idea of a patriot king. It was also premodern, lacking a sense both of executive initiative and of executive partisanship. While deserving to be understood and respected on its own terms, it rests on conceptions of society and government that American political thought long ago discarded. The partisanship against which Adams repeatedly warned has been a fixture of presidential politics since at least the time of Andrew Jackson. One can sympathize with Adams's search for a position above parties, given the intemperance of partisan conflict in the 1790s, but it was a futile quest. Because Adams had few active supporters and numerous enemies, his independent stance left him the vulnerable target of more partisan leaders.

What I have called Adams's unusual blend of power and passivity also seems antique. The unencumbered powers he wished to grant to the president hardly appear benign in light of memorable presidential aggrandizements. The history of the presidency has been marked by occasional acts of disinterestedness and numerous examples of the love of fame. Yet ambition and even avarice have been too prominent to permit us the trust in executive intentions that Adams possessed. The passivity of Adams's executive is more ambiguous in its historical resonance. It can point to a healthy sense of restraint in presidential decision making, yet it also entails the loss of opportunities for constructive and progressive action.

Where Adams's conception and practice of executive leadership are most pertinent is in the questioning of the uses of energy. Adams's deepest commitment was to the preservation of the Republic and its central values. He therefore feared energy that was turned to the purposes of militarism and imperial adventure. Stifling his own bellicose feelings, he blocked an aggressive and powerful elite by insisting upon peace. Contemporary students of American politics can find an unexpected wisdom in John Adams's view of the executive. Generally enamored of Hamiltonian energy, they can find a salutary corrective in the ideas and the example of a man who recognized its dangers.

NOTES

An earlier version of this chapter appeared in *Presidential Studies Quarterly* 17 (Spring 1987). It is reprinted here by permission of the author. The following acronyms are used in the notes:

WJA *The Works of John Adams,* edited by Charles Francis Adams. 10 vols. Boston, Mass.: Charles C. Little & James Brown, 1851–56.

PAH *The Papers of Alexander Hamilton,* edited by Harold C. Syrett and Jacob Cooke. 17 vols. New York: Columbia University Press, 1961–79.

1. Ralph Ketcham, *President above Party: The First American Presidency, 1789–1829* (Chapel Hill: University of North Carolina Press, 1984).

2. On Adams's debts to Bolingbroke and Delolme see Zoltan Haraszti, *John Adams and the Prophets of Progress* (New York: Grosset & Dunlap, 1952), pp. 49–79; Manning Dauer, *The Adams Federalists* (Baltimore, Md.: Johns Hopkins Press, 1953), p. 44; Joyce Appleby, "The New Republican Synthesis and the Changing Political Ideas of John Adams," *American Quarterly* 25 (1973): 578–95; Ketcham, *Presidents above Party,* pp. 94–95.

3. Thomas A. Bailey, *Presidential Greatness* (New York: Appleton-Century, 1966), p. 269; James David Barber, *The Presidential Character* (Englewood Cliffs, N.J.: Prentice-Hall, 1972), p. 14.

4. John Adams, *Papers of John Adams,* ed. Robert J. Taylor (Cambridge, Mass.: Harvard University Press, 1979), vol. 3, p. 238. For a discussion of how Adams linked his political psychology to a republican politics centering around meritorious action see Bruce Miroff, "John Adams: Merit, Fame and Political Leadership," *Journal of Politics* 48 (1986): 116–32.

5. Quoted by Haraszti in *John Adams and the Prophets of Progress,* p. 207.

6. *WJA,* 6:232, 248.

7. Ibid., p. 246.

8. Lester J. Cappon, ed., *The Adams-Jefferson Letters* (New York: Simon & Schuster, 1971), p. 371; *WJA,* 6:451.

9. *WJA,* 4:292.

10. Ibid., p. 397.

11. Ibid., 6:165, 473.

12. Ibid., 9:570.

13. Edward Handler, *America and Europe in the Political Thought of John Adams*

(Cambridge, Mass.: Harvard University Press, 1964), pp. 66–67; *WJA*, 6:340, 4:585.

14. For Adams's description of appropriate executive powers see *WJA*, 6:430–31.

15. Max Farrand, ed., *The Records of the Federal Convention of 1787*, 4 vols. (New Haven, Conn.: Yale University Press, 1937), 1:65; Clinton Rossiter, ed., *The Federalist Papers* (New York: New American Library, 1961), p. 423; *WJA*, 4:585, 586.

16. *WJA*, 6:533, 340–41.

17. Ibid., p. 256.

18. Ibid., p. 539.

19. Ibid., p. 430.

20. *Adams-Jefferson Letters*, p. 213; *WJA*, 6:435.

21. *WJA*, 9:302.

22. Ibid., 6:255–56; Adams Papers, Massachusetts Historical Society, microfilm reel 381.

23. John A. Schutz and Douglass Adair, eds., *The Spur of Fame: Dialogues of John Adams and Benjamin Rush, 1805–1813* (San Marino, Calif.: Huntington Library, 1966), p. 232.

24. *WJA*, 6:539.

25. Ibid., 5:473.

26. John C. Miller, *Crisis in Freedom: The Alien and Sedition Acts* (Boston, Mass.: Little, Brown, 1951), pp. 71, 72–73.

27. James Morton Smith, *Freedom's Fetters: The Alien and Sedition Laws and American Civil Liberties* (Ithaca, N.Y.: Cornell University Press, 1956), p. 175; Miller, *Crisis in Freedom*, p. 134.

28. *WJA*, 9:13–14. For a sympathetic treatment of Adams's role with respect to the Alien and Sedition Acts see Page Smith, *John Adams* (Garden City, N.Y.: Doubleday, 1962), vol. 2, pp. 975–78.

29. For accounts of how the issue of the army alienated Adams from the High Federalists see Dauer, *Adams Federalists*, pp. 145–49; Stephen G. Kurtz, *The Presidency of John Adams* (Philadelphia: University of Pennsylvania Press, 1957), pp. 307–31; Richard H. Kohn, *Eagle and Sword: The Federalists and the Creation of the Military Establishment in America, 1783–1802* (New York: Free Press, 1975), pp. 219–38.

30. *PAH*, 22:389, 23:227, 22:154.

31. Kohn, *Eagle and Sword*, pp. 249–52; *PAH*, 22:453.

32. *PAH*, 22:472.

33. Ibid., p. 503.

34. For an argument that the delay reflected Adams's personal weaknesses see Peter Shaw, *The Character of John Adams* (Chapel Hill: University of North Carolina Press, 1976), pp. 260–65. For an argument that the delay was deliberate and justifiable see Stephen G. Kurtz, "The French Mission of 1799–1800: Concluding Chapter in the Statecraft of John Adams," *Political Science Quarterly* 80 (1965): 543–57.

35. Kohn, *Eagle and Sword*, p. 272.

36. *PAH*, 25:225.

37. *WJA*, 9:60.

38. *PAH*, 21:26.

39. Ibid., p. 485.

40. Ibid., 22:168, 192.

41. Ibid., 23:227; Kohn, *Eagle and Sword,* p. 248.

42. *PAH,* 23:604.

43. Ibid., 24:168.

44. Ibid., pp. 557, 573.

45. Ibid., 25:60.

46. Ibid., pp. 186, 190.

47. Ibid., pp. 207–21.

48. Ibid., p. 233; for a vigorous defense of Hamilton's conduct during the Adams administration see Forrest McDonald, *Alexander Hamilton: A Biography* (New York: W. W. Norton, 1979), pp. 329–53.

13
THOMAS JEFFERSON AND THE PRESIDENCY

GARY J. SCHMITT

Thomas Jefferson's varied and divergent statements concerning the nature and extent of executive power seem to defy interpretation. Evidence can be gathered to support the proposition that Jefferson was a determined foe of Hamilton's conception of the chief executive or that he was an active partisan of that view. My argument here is that as opportunities arose, Jefferson set out to revise the public understanding of the formal powers of the president and, in so doing, moved away from his earlier position on the extent of those powers. Jefferson's purpose was to check what he perceived to be the dangerous "monarchic" designs of the Federalists and, in turn, to reinvigorate the republican spirit of the regime. At the same time, Jefferson did not discard his appreciation for the necessity of resorting at times to an enlarged executive authority. How Jefferson set about to balance these elements in his revised conception of the presidency raises, in a direct fashion, key questions about the role of executive power in a popular government dedicated to the rule of law.

In spite of the wide expanse of the Atlantic, the outbreak in 1793 of war in Europe between Great Britain and France seemed almost certain to entangle the young United States—an involvement it could ill afford. To avoid this, President Washington issued on April 22 what has come to be known as the Neutrality Proclamation; it declared that American policy would be impartial toward the warring European states. Opponents of the policy were quick to criticize the proclamation as an unconstitutional exercise of presidential power.

Alexander Hamilton, then secretary of the Treasury, wasted no time in coming to Washington's defense. Writing under the pseudonym "Pacificus," Hamilton argued that the president was legally justified in issuing the proclamation based on powers inherent in the executive office. Hamilton's theorizing about the powers of the presidency led Jefferson to write James Madison in the hope that his good friend and political ally might pen a rebuttal to those "most striking heresies." Madison, writing as "Helvidius," did just that, rejecting Hamilton's arguments about the sweeping nature of the president's executive power.

From the tone and character of Jefferson's letter to Madison, it is not difficult to conclude that the secretary of state saw himself as playing the part of Whig statesman to Hamilton's Tory villain: "Nobody answers him and his doctrines will therefore be taken as confessed. For God's sake, my dear Sir, take up your pen, select the most striking heresies, and cut him to pieces in face of the public."[1] Jefferson himself, of course, never disabused anyone who held that view. Indeed, he fed such interpretations by writing letters such as this:

> Were parties here divided by a greediness for office, as in England, to take a part with either would be unworthy of a reasonable or moral man, but where the principle of difference is as substantial and as strongly pronounced as between the republicans and the Monocrats of our country, I hold it as honorable to take a firm & decided part, and as immoral to pursue a middle line, as between the parties of Honest men, & Rogues into which every country is divided.[2]

The stark division in political principles drawn by Jefferson in this letter was nothing new for most of his contemporaries. Most educated Americans had adopted one or another of the two opposed interpretations of British history—the Whig or the Tory. Both versions were defined largely in terms of the rise and fall of the Crown. For the Whigs, history began with an idyllic Anglo-Saxon society in which democracy ruled and liberty reigned. Its undoing dates from the time of the Norman Conquest and the imposition of a monarchy more befitting slaves than free men. For eighteenth-century Whigs, the history of England was nearly synonymous with the history of the struggle to limit and control this alien imposition on the body politic. In sharp contrast, Tory historians maintained that the "golden age" of Anglo-Saxon history was in fact marked more by chaos and barbarism than by real freedom. For them, the monarchy was critical in maintaining social stability and political order in England; the executive power of the Crown was the shield behind which true liberty—civil liberty—could flourish. Jefferson, in couching his sentiments in language evoking the deepest sentiments of Whig history, appears to have appropriated its rhetoric to define the partisan struggles then taking place in the new regime.[3]

For Jefferson, a Whig reading of history provided insight not only into British affairs but into the young nation's as well. America had been largely spared the disease of ministerial corruption associated with the English

Crown. When it had begun to take hold on these shores, the American Revolution had effectively uprooted it. Yet the Revolution, according to Jefferson and his followers, was in this matter in danger of being sabotaged by the machinations of Hamilton and his friends. To buttress his claims, Jefferson repeatedly referred to a conversation that he said took place among Vice-President Adams, Hamilton, and himself during the first days of Washington's administration. By Jefferson's account, the question arose as to which form of government was best. To no one's surprise, Jefferson suggested the agrarian republic. Adams, to Jefferson's chagrin, claimed that monarchy was better and that the British system of government, if it could be purged of its corruption, would be the best that man could do. Hamilton, to the consternation of both, maintained that it was, in fact, only corruption that made the British government work and that, moreover, it was, as it stood, the most perfect system of government.[4]

By Jefferson's account, such talk was not all that rare. Upon his return from Paris, where he had been the United States minister to France and an active "witness" to the fall of the *ancien régime,* Jefferson settled into his new cabinet post and the political society that accompanied it. To his surprise, the table talk he found in the nation's capital was often the opposite of what he expected: "I cannot describe the wonder and mortification with which the table conversations filled me. . . . A preference of kingly over republican government was evidently the sentiment. . . . I found myself for the most part the only advocate on the Republican side of the Question."[5] For Jefferson, the Federalists were all too receptive to the idea of "kingly" government.

How genuinely surprised Jefferson was at this turn of events is difficult to determine. In a letter written to John Adams, long after the partisan rupture between the Federalists and the Republicans, Jefferson ascribed that political division to the very nature of man: "The same political parties which now agitate the U.S. have existed thro' all time . . . in fact the terms whig and tory belong to natural, as well as to civil history. They denote the temper and constitution of mind of different individuals."[6] Jefferson apparently believed that the partisan struggle that had marked the country within its first decade was not traceable to anything so idiosyncratic as the personalities or individuals involved. Jefferson claimed that he had told Adams at the time that theirs was "no personal contest": "Two systems of principles on the subject of government divide our fellow citizens into two parties. With one of these you concur, and I with the other. . . . Were we both to die to-day, to-morrow two other names would be in the place of ours, without any change in the motion of the machinery."[7] In short, the contest between himself and Hamilton, the Republicans and the Federalists, was, in Jefferson's view, the inevitable collision of Tories and Whigs over political first principles.

Inevitable or not, for Jefferson's Republicans, "the victory of 1800 has rescued the nation from the threat of monarchic subversion."[8] The new president seemed determined to put an end to the pretensions of rank that had attached themselves to the Oval Office. For example, instead of riding around the capital in a coach and four with liveried outriders, as Washington had done, Jefferson chose to ride his own horse, accompanied by a single servant. As for his personal attire, it was republican to the core—simple and unpretentious. Indeed, so unpretentious was his dress as chief executive that some foreign dignitaries, accustomed as they were to the fashions and mores of the courts of Europe, believed that this former envoy to the court of France had deliberately chosen to affront them by wearing such attire when they met. This, combined with Jefferson's decision to host dinners at which it seemed that all distinctions and rank were ignored, gave social life in the capital a decidedly republican cast.

Jefferson carried out this role with the Congress as well. For example, prior to his first term in office, Presidents Washington and Adams had delivered the constitutionally mandated annual address to the Congress in person. For Jefferson and the Republicans, this practice recalled rather too strongly the British monarch's address at the opening of Parliament. This president would submit his annual message in writing and, in doing so, evidence due deference.[9]

Such deference was a key element in the Republicans' plans to curtail the wide discretion and power previously exercised by presidents. In place of that discretion, the Republicans intended to substitute a party program which, while implemented by the president, would be controlled by Congress and sanctioned by popular election.[10] Executive prerogatives and monarchic practices were to give way to the sentiments of the people and the will of their representatives. According to Edward S. Corwin, "Jefferson's conception of executive power came finally to be more Whig than that of the British Whigs themselves in subordinating it to 'the supreme legislative power.' "[11]

JEFFERSON'S CONCEPTION OF EXECUTIVE POWER

Corwin was not the first to hold this opinion. It was John Marshall's view, expressed while the election of 1800 was pending in the House, that were Jefferson chosen, he would "embody himself in the House of Representatives," thereby "weakening the office of the President."[12] This was evidently the common judgment among Jefferson's opponents—with one notable exception.

That exception was Alexander Hamilton. Hamilton, a cabinet colleague of Jefferson's, was in a position to know. After all, he was privy to most of the counsel offered by the secretary of state to Washington. To the general charge put forward by Marshall, Hamilton had the following to say:

> It is not true, as is alleged, that he is for confounding all the powers in the House of Representatives. It is a fact which I have frequently mentioned, that while we were in the administration together, he was generally for a large construction of the Executive authority and not backward to act upon it in cases which coincided with his views. Let it be added that in his theoretic ideas he has considered as improper the participation of the Senate in the Executive Authority.[13]

From Hamilton's point of view, whatever the Republican rhetoric, Jefferson was not to be counted among those who held simple-minded Whig convictions.

That Jefferson was a strong supporter of "Executive Authority" should not have been a surprise. Jefferson, as governor of Virginia during the War of Independence, was intimately familiar with the tribulations of running a government under a constitution marked by antiexecutive features. As Robert Johnstone notes, Jefferson's being "responsible for defending his state against invasion caused him to have a dread of executive responsibility without power and of legislative omnipotence without responsibility."[14]

Jefferson's experiences while governor of Virginia were not unique. By the time of the Constitutional Convention, there seemed to be a general recognition that the fundamentally Whiggish state constitutions drafted in the wake of the Declaration of Independence were as incapable of governing well as the monarchy they replaced.[15] According to Jefferson, it was "no alleviation" that the powers of governing are "exercised by a plurality of hands, and not by a single one. . . . 173 despots" are "surely . . . as oppressive as one."[16]

If Jefferson had any doubt of the need for a vigorous, independent executive authority, such doubt was largely overwhelmed by his firsthand association with the incompetence displayed daily by the Congress of the Articles of Confederation. The Articles made no provision for an independent executive; the Congress was its own. But because of its plural composition, the Congress exhibited a threatening lack of energy and dispatch in prosecuting the war and an almost equally fatal want of secrecy and decisiveness in conducting the nation's foreign affairs. The more perceptive of the founders recognized that these failings did not lie with particular members of Congress. To a large degree, the Congress was just being the Congress.[17] By the time of the Constitutional Convention, it had become abundantly clear to a large segment of the framers that the national government, however it was finally configured, required an independent executive authority.[18]

Jefferson was not slow to come to this opinion. He joined the Congress in 1783 and within a relatively brief period concluded that it was both "rational and necessary" for the national government to have an independent executive arm. Jefferson reaffirmed this judgment the next year while serving as a member of a committee specifically charged with seeing how best to conduct the government's business during the summer months of 1784. Jefferson's proposal was to divide it into two, legislative and executive. If nothing else, such an alignment would, as least temporarily, quiet the "quarreling and bickering" by giving the government "a single Arbiter for ultimate decision."[19]

By the time of the Constitutional Convention, Jefferson had been sent by the government to be its minister to the court of France. As a result, he was not among that close circle of Virginians who were active in planning for Philadelphia. Nevertheless, Jefferson made known his desires. Specifically, he hoped that the delegates would reach beyond their more limited instructions on amending the Articles of Confederation and attempt a "broader reformation" of the government. According to Jefferson, a critical element in such reform was the adoption, in some form, of the doctrine of separation of powers. Creation of an independent executive authority would limit the Congress's "meddl[ing]" and confine it to "what should be legislative" and "enable the Federal head to exercise the powers given it, to best advantage."[20] "I think it very material to separate in the hands of Congress the Executive and Legislative powers. . . . The want of it has been the source of more evil than we have ever experienced from any other cause."[21]

By 1787, Jefferson clearly viewed the adoption of separation of powers, and with it an independent executive branch, as a rational division of the government's labor. What is not evident is Jefferson's understanding of exactly what powers should be exercised by the executive authority, especially in a republican form of government.

At first glance, Jefferson's definition of executive power seems markedly Whiggish:

> By executive powers, we mean no reference to those powers exercised under our former government by the crown as of its prerogative, nor that these shall be the standard of what may or may not be deemed the rightful powers of the governor. We give them those powers only, which are necessary to execute the laws (and administer the government), and which are not in their nature either legislative or judiciary.[22]

Rhetorically, at least, the thrust of Jefferson's attempt at delineating the executive sphere is to limit it.

Yet the hole in this attempt to fence in the executive is Jefferson's use of the phrase "and which are not in their nature either legislative or judiciary." The looseness of this construction leaves its meaning open to interpretation. Jefferson himself said that it was a matter whose "application . . . must be left to reason."

Nevertheless, it was not a matter to which little thought had been given. Every educated eighteenth-century American would have read Locke's and Montesquieu's discussion of the executive. In particular, Jefferson's claim that the executive's power includes those things neither legislative nor judicial would almost certainly have evoked in his reader's mind Locke's treatment of the wide range of powers associated with the conduct of foreign affairs, what he called the "federative" powers. These powers, according to Locke, were in theory separate from the executive but were his in practice.[23]

Jefferson appears to have had in mind something like Locke's discussion of the federative powers. In clarifying his definition, Jefferson explicitly excludes the "prerogative powers," such as erecting courts, fairs, markets, and the like. Left unsaid, but clearly implied, is the thought that these are powers exercised by monarchs, justified on conventional grounds but not appropriate for executives in a republican form of government. These Jefferson would "expressly deny" the executive. What remains on his list, however, are precisely those powers that Locke would have described as being federative, powers integral to the conduct of foreign affairs: the power to declare war, conclude peace, contract alliances, and direct the military.[24]

Jefferson's broad conception of executive power before the Constitutional Convention is consistent with the views he expressed when holding the position of secretary of state during Washington's administration. As a member of the cabinet, Jefferson was not, as Hamilton later pointed out, shy to argue for a "large construction of the Executive authority" nor "backward to act upon it."

Jefferson, of course, was not unmindful of Congress's prerogatives under the new constitution. On the other hand, he showed no Whiggish inclination to bring the president's powers under the simple control of a "supreme Legislature." Quite the opposite. In 1793, for example, Jefferson, as secretary of state, met with Edmond Charles Genêt, envoy to the United States from the First French Republic. Jefferson, the former United States minister to Paris, was on the whole sympathetic to Genêt's effort to move the United States toward a role more supportive of France in its war with Great Britain. The problem facing Genêt was that President Washington had earlier issued a proclamation stating that the nation's policy was strict neutrality between the two belligerent powers, this in spite of a standing treaty of friendship with France. Yet even in this instance,

Jefferson would hear nothing that suggested that the president's powers are anything less than complete in themselves:

> "[Genêt] asked if they [Congress] were not sovereign." I told him no. . . . "But," said he, "at least, Congress are bound to see that the treaties are observed." I told him no . . . the President is to see that treaties are observed. "If he decides against the treaty, to whom is a nation to appeal?" I told him the Constitution had made the President the last appeal.[25]

While it is to be expected that a secretary of state would respond to a foreign envoy in such unequivocal terms, Jefferson in fact maintained this stance vis-à-vis Congress as well. Washington and his cabinet officers were often asked by Congress to supply papers and memoranda to support the administration's decisions and policies. The administration typically complied with such requests. However, Washington's cabinet was not slow to come to the opinion that if the national interest so required, the president had the discretion to withhold material requested by the legislature.

The issue first arose after the stunning defeat of General Arthur St. Clair by the Wabash Indians in late 1791. The House committee created to investigate the defeat requested that Secretary of War Henry Knox turn over all papers connected to St. Clair's campaign. According to Jefferson, Washington called his cabinet together to discuss the request "because it was the first example, and he wishes so far as it should become a precedent, it should be rightly conducted."

Jefferson then noted that Washington believed that "there might be papers of so secret a nature, as that they ought not to be given up." In a subsequent cabinet meeting, called to resolve the administration's final position on the request, Jefferson reported that while the Congress might properly "institute inquiries" and "call for papers generally," the executive had every right "to refuse those, the disclosure of which would injure the public." Jefferson showed no signs that he disagreed with the administration's position; indeed, his notes outline a brief based on a famous debate in the British Parliament, in the case of Sir Robert Walpole, which supported the proposition that the executive authority had such discretion.[26]

Even in those areas in which the Constitution gives the Senate a share of the executive's responsibilities, Jefferson consistently argued for a reading to the president's advantage. For example, in the case of appointments, Jefferson would brook little interference from the upper house of Congress. Writing to Washington early in his first administration, Jefferson advised him that "the Senate is not supposed by the Constitution to be acquainted with the concerns of the Executive Department. It was not intended that these should be communicated, nor can they therefore be qualified to judge of the necessity which calls for a mission to any particular place, or of the particular grade. . . . All of this is left to the President. They are only to see that no unfit person be employed."[27]

Jefferson appears to have had a similarly limited view of the Senate's role in regard to treaty making. The early days of Washington's presidency were punctuated with instances of his consulting the Senate prior to the start of negotiations. Historians have typically read Washington's behavior in these instances as adherence to the constitutional mandate of receiving not only the Senate's consent but also its advice. According to Jefferson, however, Washington's "habit of consulting the Senate previously" was a matter of common sense rather than constitutional prescription. Jefferson believed that it was "prudent to consult them" since "their subsequent ratification would be necessary."[28]

As Jefferson's words imply, it might be prudent at times *not* to consult. Jefferson seemed to believe that the president retained, as circumstances required, the discretion as to when and how to involve the upper house. Events did intervene to end Washington's practice of prior consultation. It became clear that the need for what *The Federalist* called "qualities . . . indispensable in the management of foreign negotiations [and which] point out the Executive as the most fit agent in these transactions" would lead Washington to abandon his habit of conferring with the Senate.[29] One of those "qualities" was a better capability of keeping things secret. In 1793, Washington had the secretary of state begin and conclude negotiations with the western Indians without consulting the Senate over the terms of the treaty. According to Jefferson, "We all thought if the Senate should be consulted and consequently appraised of our line, it would become known to [British Minister George] Hammond, and we should lose all chance of saving anything more at the treaty than our ultimatum."[30] Jefferson never suggested that this precedent was in any way constitutionally objection-able—indeed, he participated in making it.

Time after time, Jefferson, as Washington's secretary of state, partici-pated in making decisions that upheld the independence and the pre-rogatives of the nation's chief executive. There is no indication that he did so in an uninformed way or for reasons of simple political calculation. From the evidence at hand, Jefferson's rationale for supporting the newly formed office of the president was based on his principled understanding of the nature of the executive authority. As he wrote to Washington: "The transaction of business with foreign nations is Executive altogether. It belongs then to the head of the department, *except* as to such portions of it as are specially submitted to the Senate. *Exceptions* are to be construed strictly."[31] In Jefferson's view, whatever remnants of Whiggish sentiment had found their way into the Constitution were strictly conventional, although perhaps prudent, limitations on the natural and correct scope of the executive's power.[32]

Even on the issue that led to the great debate between "Pacificus" and "Helvidius"—the Proclamation of Neutrality—Jefferson agreed with his cabinet colleagues that the proclamation should be issued. He nowhere, even in his letters to Madison, suggests that Washington did not have the authority to make the declaration that he did. Moreover, to Washington's query of his cabinet whether the Congress should be called back in session early to consider this matter, Jefferson reported that the cabinet had "decided negatively." From this decision, Jefferson did not dissent. Whatever his ultimate concern regarding Hamilton and the "Monocrats," Jefferson never officially objected to Washington's assertion of authority, and he never publicly registered the smallest complaint.[33]

JEFFERSON'S EXERCISE OF PRESIDENTIAL POWER

Jefferson, who had joined the administration in the spring of 1790, left at the end of 1793. By early 1798, he was describing a key difference between the two fledgling American political parties as being the Republicans' apparent affinity for the Congress and the Federalists' for the presidency.[34] Given those preferences, it was certainly to be expected that the victory of Jefferson and the Republicans in 1800 would signal a major change in the pattern of executive-legislative relations that had been established by the Federalist administrations of Washington and Adams. What Jefferson himself described as the "Revolution of 1800" was looked to not only to alter the relationship between the federal and state governments but also to shift power from the second branch of the federal government to the first.[35]

In fact, little seemed to change. This so frustrated John Randolph, a leading Republican orator and majority leader in the House, that he bitterly declared that there were only

> two parties in all States—the *ins and outs;* the *ins* desirous so to construe the charter of the Government as to give themselves the greatest possible degree of patronage and wealth; and the *outs* striving to construe it so as to circumscribe . . . their adversaries' power. But let the *outs* get in . . . and you will find their Constitutional scruples and arguments vanish like dew before the morning sun.[36]

Randolph's opinion that the difference between the Federalist administrations of Washington and Adams and the first Republican administration was less than revolutionary is shared by others. According to Leonard D.

White, a student of both Federalist and Republican administrations, "Jefferson fully maintained in practice the Federalist conception of the executive power."[37] White has been seconded by Abraham Sofaer, who has found that between the two, "little changed." Indeed, if anything, Jefferson "probably increased the powers of the President at the expense of Congress."[38]

There is little reason to object to these assessments of Jefferson's presidency; for the most part, they accurately portray his practice. However, there are some things that cannot be so easily accounted for if one simply equates Jefferson's behavior while president with that of his Federalist predecessors.

The first of these was Jefferson's handling of the military expedition against Tripoli. The pasha of Tripoli, dissatisfied with the amount of tribute he was exacting from the United States, had begun again to threaten American shipping in the Mediterranean late in Adams's term. Upon taking office, Jefferson ordered a navy squadron under the command of Commodore Richard Dale to the Mediterranean to protect the nation's property and ships. In early August, an American schooner, the *Enterprise,* encountered a Tripolitan cruiser, which, after three hours of battle, was captured, stripped of its guns, and allowed to drift back to its home port.

Jefferson reported the *Enterprise*'s victory in his first annual message to the Congress. After describing why he had sent the squadron to the Mediterranean, he recounted the engagement and the eventual release of the Tripolitan ship. He justified the cruiser's release thus:

> Unauthorized by the Constitution, without the sanction of Congress, to go beyond the line of defense, the vessel, being disabled from committing further hostilities, was liberated with its crew. The Legislature will doubtless consider whether, by authorizing measures of offence also, they will place our force on an equal footing with that of its adversaries. I communicate all material information on this subject, that, in the exercise of this important function confided by the Constitution to the Legislature exclusively, their judgment may form itself on a knowledge and consideration of every circumstance of weight.[39]

On reading Jefferson's justification, Hamilton went on the attack. Writing in the *New York Evening Post* as "Lucius Crassus," Hamilton argued that attempts to draw such fine distinctions were chimerical. When one nation openly waged war against another, a declaration of war was hardly required. It was, according to Hamilton, "a very extraordinary position" that "between two nations there may exist a state of complete war on the one side and of peace on the other."[40]

Hamilton was not the only one who would have found Jefferson's reason for turning the pasha's ship loose "extraordinary." So must have his cabinet. In mid May, prior to the expedition's departure, the cabinet met to discuss the question of precisely what actions the navy squadron could take against the Tripolitans if it were attacked. The near-unanimous position of the cabinet—the only dissent coming from Attorney General Levi Lincoln—was that once an act of war had been perpetrated against the American ships, a state of war existed. From that point on, the squadron could, without question, search for and destroy the enemy's vessels wherever they could find them. And it was these orders that were cut for Commodore Dale.[41]

The historical truth is that the *Enterprise* cut the Tripolitan corsair free for operational reasons. Dale had ordered the captain of the American schooner to make his way to Malta for supplies for the squadron and not to waste valuable time by going out of his way to chase, capture, or sink the Tripolitan ships. There was nothing in the administration's orders to Dale or in Dale's to his subordinate that suggested that the *Enterprise* was legally bound to act as it did. Jefferson created the account he put forward in the annual message out of whole cloth, weaving novel threads into the constitutional fabric.[42]

Waging war with the Barbary pirates was not the only occasion on which Jefferson exhibited a talent for constitutional legerdemain. The second important instance is found in connection with his administration's purchase of the Louisiana Territory from France in 1803.

At the time, the purchase itself was hailed not only because of its size and the potential it held for the country but chiefly because it, in the words of Jefferson, "remove[d] from us the greatest source of danger to our peace."[43] By gaining control of both the inland waterways and the port of New Orleans, Jefferson had with one stroke largely secured peace in the West. For his administration, the underlying issue was one of national security rather than of territory.

While Jefferson was adamant as to the necessity of the purchase, he nevertheless entertained questions concerning its legality. This is not all that surprising, since strict constructionists within his own party were bound to point out that there was no specific grant of authority in the Constitution allowing the government to make territorial acquisitions of any dimensions—never mind one that would double the size of the country. In January 1803, just prior to Monroe's going to France to complete negotiations with Napoleon, Jefferson asked his cabinet about the constitutionality of the "proposed bargain" with France.[44]

Attorney General Levi Lincoln was the first to submit a reply. So convoluted was Lincoln's opinion that Jefferson turned to Secretary of the Treasury Albert Gallatin for his views. Gallatin "assumed a constitutional position which was virtually indistinguishable from the liberal construction of his predecessor Hamilton." Gallatin's position was:

> 1st. That the United States as a nation have an inherent right to acquire territory.
>
> 2nd. That whenever that acquisition is by treaty, the same constituted authorities in whom the treaty-making power is vested have a constitutional right to sanction the acquisition.
>
> 3rd. That whenever the territory has been acquired, Congress have the power either of admitting into the Union as a new state, or of annexing to a State with the consent of that State, or of making regulations for the government of such territory.

Jefferson accepted Gallatin's analysis: "You are right in my opinion . . . there is no constitutional difficulty."[45]

Within Jefferson's official family, the constitutional question about the purchase was never really an issue. However, the president showed little inclination to state his case publicly along the lines Gallatin had argued and to which Jefferson had agreed. Again, Jefferson was apparently not above a little constitutional dissembling. To John Dickinson he wrote: "The general government has no powers but such as the constitution has given it; and it has not given it a power of holding foreign territory, and still less of incorporating it into the Union."[46] To his political ally and Republican stalwart Senator John Breckinridge of Kentucky, Jefferson made the following argument:

> The Executive in seizing the fugitive occurrence which so much advances the good of their country, have done an act beyond the Constitution. The Legislature in casting behind them metaphysical subtleties, and risking themselves like faithful servants, must ratify to pay for it, and throw themselves on their country for doing for them unauthorized what we know they would have done for themselves had they been in a situation to do it. It is the case of a guardian, investing the money of his ward in purchasing an important adjacent territory; and saying to him when of age, I did this for your good. I pretend to no right to bind you: you may disavow me, and I must get out of the scrape as I can: I thought it my duty to risk myself for you.[47]

These and similar letters were written in July and August 1803. On August 17, however, Jefferson received word from the United States minister in Paris, Robert Livingston, that Napoleon was having second thoughts about the wisdom of selling Louisiana and was now looking for some pretense to void the agreement. Jefferson reacted to this news by concluding that nothing should be done which might give France an excuse to rescind the accord. Writing to his secretary of state, James Madison, Jefferson stated; "I infer that the less we say about constitutional difficulties respecting Louisiana the better."[48] In the end, Jefferson made no further attempt to provoke a constitutional debate; nor, it should be added, did he attempt to publicize his private view that there was, "no constitutional difficulty."

A third episode worth reviewing was generated by the British warship *Leopard*'s attack on the American frigate *Chesapeake* in the summer of 1807. In late June, the British ship pulled alongside the *Chesapeake* as it left Hampton Roads, Virginia. The captain of the fifty-gun *Leopard* ordered the smaller United States vessel to stop and submit to a search for British deserters. The *Chesapeake*'s captain at first refused. The *Leopard* then opened fire and disabled the *Chesapeake,* in the process killing and wounding some twenty seamen. The United States frigate was then searched by the British, who impressed four of its crew.

News of the engagement caused an enormous uproar in the United States. Because war with Britain seemed imminent, Jefferson acted to prepare the country. In early July, he issued a proclamation excluding British warships from American waters. In late July, he ordered that all money that had been appropriated for the nation's fortifications and that remained available be used solely for fortifying New York, Charleston, and New Orleans. In addition, and most significantly, he ordered the purchase of 500 tons of saltpetre, 100 tons of sulphur, and sufficient timber for building 100 gunboats. Of these latter purchases, not a single dime had been authorized or appropriated by Congress.[49]

Congress went back into session in late October. In his annual message, Jefferson communicated to Congress the steps he had taken. He made no attempt to hide what he had done, nor did he make any attempt to justify it constitutionally. Quite the opposite, Jefferson pleaded necessity in light of "the emergencies threatening" the nation:

> The moment our peace was threatened, I deemed it indispensable to secure a greater provision of those articles of military stores with which our magazines were not sufficiently furnished. To have awaited a previous and special sanction by law would have lost occasions which might not be retrieved. . . . I trust that the legislature, feeling the same anxiety for the safety of our country, so materially advanced by this precaution, will approve, when done, what they would have seen so important to be done, if then assembled.[50]

Jefferson's actions did not go unchallenged. Randolph decried the president's deeds as being at odds with "the true old Whig doctrine." Congressman John Smilie, as did other House members, came to the president's defense: "Every gentleman knew that there were cases in which this form must be dispensed with, and in this instance he thought the circumstances of the case justified the measures adopted."[51]

Randolph believed Smilie's defense and Jefferson's action to be Republican "heresy." What it was, was a bold assertion of executive prerogative, the power to ignore the law if an emergency so dictates. Or, as the Whig theorist John Locke described it:

> For the Legislators not being able to foresee, and provide, by Laws, for all, that may be useful to the Community, the Executor of the Laws, having the power in his hands, has by the common Law of Nature, a right to make use of it . . . where the municipal Law has given no direction, till the Legislature can conveniently be assembled to provide for it. . . . This power to act according to discretion, for the publick good, without the prescription of law, and sometimes even against it, *is* that which is called *Prerogative.*[52]

Jefferson's decision to resort to prerogative is important to note; however, it is equally important that he made absolutely no attempt to give it the slightest constitutional justification.

Jefferson's actions in this instance can be usefully compared with Abraham Lincoln's in 1861. In the wake of his election in 1860, seven southern states seceded from the Union. After his inauguration the following March, Lincoln issued a call for Congress to reconvene, and he undertook a series of actions, the propriety of which constitutional historians have long debated. While Lincoln believed that circumstances clearly justified the steps he took, he also went to great lengths to provide a constitutional argument for what he had done, invoking not only the commander-in-chief clause and the take-care clause but also his presidential oath.[53]

Lincoln claimed that the Constitution authorizes the president to take extraordinary measures, otherwise not lawful, in such grave circumstances. His argument was not that "the Constitution is different" in such times but that "its application" may be.[54] Circumstances demand different things of a government. In making this case, Lincoln was not advancing a novel constitutional doctrine. *The Federalist* had laid down as axiomatic that "a power equal to every possible contingency must exist somewhere in the government."[55]

CONCLUSION

Jefferson's presidency, according to the biographer and historian Dumas Malone, "was much the most complicated part of Jefferson's career."[56] To one degree or another, Jefferson confounded friends and foes alike, frustrating such principled opposites as Randolph and Hamilton.

While we know that Jefferson understood both the need for executive power and the strength of its embodiment in Article II of the Constitution, we also know that by the end of Washington's term, Jefferson had become concerned that through the office of the presidency the Federalists were "maneuvering" the citizenry into a "form of government, the principal branches of which may be beyond their control."[57] Even though Jefferson was never explicit on the point, it can be plausibly conjectured that to meet his concern he undertook to drain from the presidency as much of its formidable formal powers as was practical. This stratagem can be inferred not only from instances such as those discussed above but also from such other decisions as Jefferson's setting for himself a limit of two terms in office—undermining to some degree his formal powers with the creation of the "lame-duck" term.

The substance of this endeavor was reflected in the style of his administration, by his "substituting what may be called 'republican simplicity' for Washington's 'republican dignity.'" Under Jefferson there would be "no great dinners, weekly receptions, personally delivered messages to Congress, none of the formalities that Jefferson associated with the monarchic executive."[58]

While in each of the three cases described above there are less esoteric reasons available to explain Jefferson's behavior, it is equally possible that he was moved to act as he did in these instances because he had concluded before taking office that the presidency, under the pressure of events and the influence of Hamilton, had become more powerful than he judged consistent with republican government. While Jefferson understood the constitutional potential for an expanded exercise of executive power, he was nevertheless surprised perhaps both by the degree and by the swiftness with which it came to the fore, and also by the eagerness with which some saw it employed. Had what Jefferson expected to be exceptional become, by the end of Washington's second term, the norm?[59]

Jefferson would not have objected to Hamilton's axiom in *The Federalist* that "energy in the executive is a leading character in the definition of good government."[60] However, he must have questioned its constant and exclusive application. Because for Jefferson "a free government is of all others the most energetic," a single-minded and continual reliance on the formal instrumentalities of presidential authority by the Federalists betrayed their serious disregard for the republican basis of the polity.[61] Moreover, broad readings of the president's powers gave vent to that dangerous "preference of kingly over republican government," which Jefferson had found espoused at dinner tables throughout the nation's capital. To make reliance on the formal powers of the executive more difficult, he hoped, in addition to some revisionism, to employ a stratagem, where feasible, of strict constitutional construction:

> When an instrument admits two constructions, the one safe, the other dangerous, the one precise, the other indefinite, I prefer that which is safe and precise. . . . Our peculiar security is in possession of a written Constitution. Let us not make it a blank paper by construction.[62]

The point is not that Jefferson did not appreciate that there would be times when a president would need to exercise extraordinary power. While he was apparently willing to see the formal scope of executive discretion trimmed back, Jefferson was also willing to advance in bold fashion the doctrine of extraconstitutional executive prerogative. It was this theory that he advanced, after having left office, to justify his purchase of Louisiana:

> A strict observance of the written law is doubtless *one* of the high duties of a good citizen, but it is not *the highest*. The laws of necessity, of self preservation, of saving our country when in danger, are of higher obligation. To lose our country by a scrupulous adherence to written law, would be to lose the law itself, with life, liberty, property and all those who are enjoying them with us; thus absurdly sacrificing the end to the means.[63]

In short, Jefferson understood as well as Hamilton did the need for a potentially expansive executive authority; what they came to disagree about—if the conjecture above is correct—was what form such power might take and the ease and occasion on which it might be exercised. Jefferson presumably believed that if one could revise and scale down the formal, constitutional powers of the president while at the same time granting him, as circumstances warranted, the right to exercise extraconstitutional powers, one would make the use of such powers less likely.

Hamilton's rebuttal would certainly be that while presidents might initially be reluctant to exercise such powers, their reluctance was sure to dissipate over time. As Madison stated in *The Federalist*, "every precedent . . . is a germ of unnecessary and multiplied repetitions."[64] What is initially extraordinary becomes ordinary through use. Moreover, Hamilton would argue that a resort to extraconstitutional powers was not conducive to the preservation of the public's deference to the idea of the rule of law. It is difficult to maintain respect for the rule of law in citizens and presidents alike when in the most critical instances they are publicly reminded of its radical insufficiency. As Hamilton had written in *The Federalist*:

Wise politicians will be cautious about fettering the government with restrictions that cannot be observed, because they know that every breach of the fundamental laws, though dictated by necessity, impairs that sacred reverence which ought to be maintained in the breast of rulers towards the constitution of a country, and forms a precedent for other breaches where the same plea of necessity does not exist at all, or is less urgent and palpable.[65]

In pointing toward a less imposing executive authority which nevertheless might break the bonds of the law as necessity dictated, Jefferson believed he was devising a presidency more in tune with the nation's republican character and less susceptible of abuse. Hamilton might have countered that necessity is often in the eye of the beholder and would have doubted whether such a presidential regime was in fact more likely to promote the rule of law and maintain republican mores.[66] Perhaps only someone as intimate with ambition as Hamilton was could understand the dangers inherent in Jefferson's design.

NOTES

This chapter has been reprinted by permission from *Publius: The Journal of Federalism* 17 (Spring 1987).

1. Thomas Jefferson, *Writings,* ed. Paul L. Ford, 10 vols. (New York: G. P. Putnam's, 1892–99), 6:338.
2. Ibid., 7:43.
3. See Forrest McDonald, *The Presidency of Thomas Jefferson* (Lawrence: University Press of Kansas, 1976), pp. 20, 33.
4. Ibid., p. 20.
5. Jefferson, *Writings,* 1:160.
6. *The Adams-Jefferson Letters,* ed. Lester J. Cappon, 2 vols. (Chapel Hill: University of North Carolina Press, 1959), 2:332.
7. Jefferson, *Writings,* 9:296. Jefferson is recounting his conversation with Adams more than a decade later, in 1811.
8. James P. Ceaser, *Presidential Selection* (Princeton, N.J.: Princeton University Press, 1979), p. 89.
9. See Robert M. Johnstone, Jr., *Jefferson and the Presidency* (Ithaca, N.Y.: Cornell University Press, 1978), pp. 58–59.
10. See Ceaser, *Presidential Selection,* pp. 103, 121.
11. Edward S. Corwin, *The President: Office and Powers, 1787–1984: A History and Analysis of Practice and Opinion,* 5th rev. ed. (New York: New York University Press, 1984), p. 18.
12. Ibid.
13. Alexander Hamilton, *Works,* ed. Henry C. Lodge, 12 vols. (New York: G. P. Putnam's, 1904), 10:413.

14. Johnstone, *Jefferson,* p. 53. See, in general, Merrill D. Peterson, *Thomas Jefferson and the New Nation* (New York: Oxford University Press, 1970), pp. 166ff; and John S. Pancake, *Thomas Jefferson and Alexander Hamilton* (Woodbury, N.Y.: Barron's, 1974), pp. 79ff.

15. See Charles C. Thach, Jr., *The Creation of the Presidency, 1775–1789: A Study in Constitutional History* (Baltimore, Md.: Johns Hopkins University Press, 1923), pp. 49–52.

16. Jefferson, *Writings,* 3:223.

17. John Jay wrote to Jefferson in 1787, "Those inconveniences arise not from personal disqualifications, but from the nature and construction of government"; see *The Correspondence and Public Papers of John Jay,* ed. Henry P. Johnston, 3 vols. (New York: G. P. Putnam's, 1890–93), 3:223.

18. See Thach, *Creation,* pp. 55–75.

19. Louis Fisher, *President and Congress* (New York: Free Press, 1972), p. 263.

20. Thomas Jefferson, *Papers,* ed. Julian P. Boyd, 20 vols. (Princeton, N.J.: Princeton University Press, 1954–), 10:603.

21. Ibid., 11:679.

22. Ibid., 6:298–99.

23. See Locke, *Second Treatise,* chap. 12, sec. 148; and Montesquieu, *Spirit of the Laws,* bk. 11, chap. 6.

24. Jefferson, *Papers,* 6:299. Jefferson's discussion is in the context of a proposal for a new state constitution. Jefferson's focus here is on the powers to be held by the governor under Virginia's new constitution. What he states is that these "other" powers are exercised "under the authority of the confederation" and, as such, fall outside the office of the state's chief executive. However, that he considers these "other" powers to be executive in nature is clear from the context of the discussion and from his statement that "in all cases" where those powers are not exercised by the Confederation, "they shall be exercised by the governor."

25. "Minutes of Conversation," July 10, 1793, *International Law Digest,* ed. John B. Moore, 8 vols. (Washington, D.C.: Government Printing Office, 1906), 4:680–81.

26. See Abraham D. Sofaer, *War, Foreign Affairs and Constitutional Power: The Origins* (Cambridge, Mass.: Ballinger, 1976), pp. 81–82.

27. Johnstone, *Jefferson,* p. 62.

28. Jefferson, *Writings,* 1:294.

29. Alexander Hamilton, James Madison, and John Jay, *The Federalist Papers,* ed. Clinton Rossiter (New York: New American Library, 1961), no. 75, p. 45; see also no. 64, p. 393.

30. Thomas Jefferson, *The Complete Anas of Thomas Jefferson,* ed. Franklin B. Sawvel (New York: Round Tables, 1903), pp. 108–11.

31. Jefferson, *Writings,* 5:161–62.

32. See text to note 13 above.

33. See Sofaer, *War,* pp. 111–16.

34. Dumas Malone, *Jefferson the President: First Term* (Boston, Mass.: Little, Brown, 1970), p. xviii.

35. Sofaer, *War,* pp. 168–69.

36. *Annals of Congress,* vol. 20, p. 70.

37. Leonard D. White, *The Jeffersonians: A Study in Administrative History, 1801–1829* (New York: Macmillan, 1951), p. 30.

38. Sofaer, *War,* pp. 169, 224.

39. *Annals of Congress,* vol. 11, pp. 11–12.

40. Sofaer, *War,* p. 212.

41. Ibid., pp. 209–10, 212–13.

42. Jefferson took a similar line with regard to military action against Morocco in 1802—again, against the stated position of his cabinet; Sofaer, *War,* pp. 221–24.

43. Malone, *Jefferson the President: First Term,* p. 284.

44. Ibid., p. 311.

45. Ibid., p. 312.

46. Jefferson, *Writings,* 8:262.

47. Ibid., pp. 244ff.

48. Malone, *Jefferson the President: First Term,* pp. 314–15.

49. Sofaer, *War,* p. 172.

50. *Annals of Congress,* vol. 17, pp. 14–17.

51. Ibid., pp. 822, 826.

52. Locke, *Second Treatise,* chap. 14, secs. 159 and 160.

53. "Message for Congress," 4 July 1861, *Collected Works,* ed. Roy P. Basler, 9 vols. (New Brunswick, N.J.: Rutgers University Press, 1953), 4:429–30, 440; and "First Inaugural Address," Mar. 4, 1861, ibid., pp. 265, 270.

54. Ibid., 6:302.

55. *Federalist* no. 26, p. 170.

56. Malone, *Jefferson the President: First Term,* p. xiii.

57. Jefferson, *Writings,* 7:280; see also ibid., 7:435 and the following reported statement by Madison: "I deserted Colonel Hamilton, or rather Colonel H. deserted me; in a word, the divergence between us took place—from his wishing to *administration,* or rather to administer the Government (these were Mr. M's very words), into what he thought it ought to be" (quoted in Memoranda by Trist, Sept. 27, 1834, reprinted in *The Records of the Federal Convention of 1787,* ed. Max Farrand, 4 vols. (New Haven, Conn.: Yale University Press, 1966), 3:534.

58. Robert Scigliano, "The Constitutional Governments of Hamilton and Jefferson," paper presented at the annual meeting of the American Political Science Association, New Orleans, Aug. 29–Sept. 1, 1985, p. 15.

59. To some extent, the enumerated powers found in Article II are deceiving in that they appear understated. By themselves, they do not explain the particular primacy the presidency has had in the governmental system since 1789. What helps to explain this fact is the presidency's radically different institutional characteristics, especially its unity of office. Because of its unique features, it enjoys—as the framers largely intended—the capacity of acting with the greatest expedition, secrecy, and effective knowledge. As a result, when certain stresses, particularly in the area of foreign affairs, are placed on the nation, it will "naturally" rise to the forefront. Since those stresses existed at the beginning, it is not surprising that "the framework for executive-congressional relations developed during the first eight years differs more in degree than in kind from the present framework" (Sofaer, *War,* p. 127). See also Alexis de Tocqueville, *Democracy in America,* vol. 1, pt. 1, chap. 8, "Accidental Causes that May Increase the Influence of the Executive Power."

60. *Federalist* no. 70, p. 423.

61. Jefferson, *Writings,* 9:201. "By weakening the presidential office in comparison with the original constitutional design and certainly in comparison with the status it held under Washington and Adams, the Republicans had brought about the situation in which energy, if it were to come from the executive, would have to rely on a non-institutional source" (Ceaser, *Selection,* p. 102).

62. Jefferson, *Writings,* 8:247.
63. Jefferson, *Writings,* 9:279.
64. *Federalist* no. 41, p. 257.
65. *Federalist* no. 25, p. 167.
66. Interview with Richard Nixon by David Frost, *New York Times,* May 20, 1977, p. A-16.

14
JAMES MADISON AND THE PRESIDENCY

RALPH KETCHAM

No problem of politics troubled James Madison more than limiting the powers of government, no power of government seemed harder to limit than executive power, and no time so dangerously tended to enlarge executive power, he averred, as wartime. Thus, when he saw the United States imperiled by war in 1793 and found Alexander Hamilton extending executive power to "proclaim" neutrality and to meet foreign threats of force with force, Madison was greatly alarmed:

> In war, a physical force is to be created; and it is the executive will, which is to direct it. In war, the public treasures are to be unlocked; and it is the executive hand which is to dispense them. In war, the honours and emoluments of office are to be multiplied; and it is the executive patronage under which they are to be enjoyed. It is in war, finally, that laurels are to be gathered; and it is the executive brow they are to encircle. The strongest passions and most dangerous weaknesses of the human breast; ambition, avarice, vanity, the honourable or venial love of fame, are all in conspiracy against the desire and duty of peace.

In general, Madison argued, even under a constitution of limited powers, "every power that can be deduced from [it], will be deduced, and exercised sooner or later by those who have an interest in so doing. . . . A people . . . who are so happy as to possess the inestimable blessing of a free and defined constitution cannot be too watchful against the introduction, nor too critical in tracing the consequences, of new principles and new constructions, that may remove the landmarks of power."

On the other hand, Madison had a keen sense of the constructive uses of power in a republican government. As an ardent "nationalist" during the

1780s, for example, he had again and again sought to enlarge the powers of the Continental Congress, to remove frustrating causes of inaction, and to combat the strong tendency among many revolutionaries, mindful of British excesses before 1776, to equate freedom with the absence of governmental power. To the end of his long life, when he defended the Union against Calhoun's theory of nullification, Madison understood the good use, in the interests of the people, that could be made of power in a republican government. In more than half a century of experience in government, often under constitutions he had played a major role in drafting, Madison sought to devise and use executive power in ways that would at once enable actions in the public interest and deter the tendency toward abuse and tyranny. This was always for him the vital balance of republican government.

Madison had an early lesson in executive impotence as a member of the Virginia Council of State, 1778–79, when not only did the executive have very little power overall, but the governor was forbidden to act except with the approval of his eight-member council. The delays and inability to act in the exigencies of war eventually convinced Madison that the construction of the executive department was "the worst part of a bad Constitution." The same executive weakness existed in the Continental Congress. Standing committees conducted much of the executive business; but they were plagued by uncertain authority, dispersed responsibility, rotating personnel, and spotty attendance. Madison supported the creation of "executive departments" of foreign affairs, finance, war, and marine in February 1781, and he sought to fill the new offices with able men. He was, in fact, never among the suspicious people who supposed that any person who had been given the power to do anything would invariably act badly. Such a proposition, when applied indiscriminately to officials who derive their election or appointment from the people, Madison later charged, "impeached the fundamental principle" of republican government by holding that officers chosen by the people would "immediately and infallibly betray the trust committed to them."

As a supporter both of increased national power and of effective executive authority, Madison came biased to the Constitutional Convention of 1787. In deference to Edmund Randolph's fear of a unitary executive (such was "the foetus of monarchy," he asserted), Madison at first went along with a proposal for a plural executive. Because executive authority was monarchical even in most "mixed constitutions" of the day and because the colonies had felt most tyranny from executive power, Randolph and the delegates had had little constructive experience with it, and they sensed in it great potential danger. James Wilson saw sooner than others, though, that in a republic where even executive power rested, directly or indirectly, on the people, there might be less to fear in its exercise than under a monarchy. The more clearly the executive was held responsible to the people, Wilson argued, the more power he could safely be given. This view suited Madison's sober optimism that a self-governing system could be devised that would exercise power wisely; it also suited his sense of the need for vigor and responsibility in government. Thus, he supported a single executive, his power to appoint officials in his department, his powers as commander in chief and in foreign affairs, his long term in office, and his eligibility for reelection.

Election of the executive posed a seemingly insoluble problem. Madison shared some of George Mason's fear that to allow election directly by the people was like referring "a trial of colours to a blind man" and Gouverneur Morris's counterfear that if a legislative body were to choose the executive, "it will be like the election of a pope by a conclave of cardinals." Madison eventually supported the electoral-college scheme as a hedge against both dangers.

Madison's sensitivity to both executive needs and executive excesses emerged most acutely in his remarks on the war power. He did, as has so often been noted during our era of undeclared wars, support the change in the power of Congress from that to "make" war to that to "declare" war, in order to leave "to the Executive the power to repel sudden attacks." A month later, however, he sought to give the Senate exclusive power to make treaties of peace because the president "would necessarily derive so much power and importance from a state of war that he might be tempted, if authorized, to impede a treaty of peace." Altogether, however, the executive power as it emerged from the convention suited Madison as a reasonable compromise between the needs of authority and of limitation.

II

Everything depended, of course, upon the early precedents established and the conduct of the first presidents. George Washington's vast prestige gave crucial support to the dignity and authority of the office, most of which Madison supported. In fact, as Washington's chief advisor during the critical years 1788 and 1789, Madison had a large role in the organization of the executive department, its etiquette, and its relations with the other departments. Especially critical was Madison's defense in the House of Representatives of the president's inherent power to remove his appointees from office. Madison scorned arguments that the president should be denied such power because he would infallibly abuse it by removing faithful public servants: such fears, and the consequent denials of power, would hopelessly hamstring governments. Rather, he insisted upon the more basic, self-regulating "principle of unity and responsibility in the

Executive department, which was intended for the security of liberty and the public good. If the President alone should possess the power of removal from office, those employed in the execution of the law will be in their proper situation, and the chain of dependence therefore terminates in the supreme body, namely, in the people." That is, the president needed to have the power of removal for profoundly republican reasons: the people would then be able to hold him responsible for the malfeasance of his appointees and could then be justified in refusing him reelection (or in extreme cases, even impeach him) for inefficiency or corruption in his department. One can imagine, of course, the excuses that would have emanated from the Oval Office during the Watergate era had not this principle of responsibility been early enjoined on the presidency.

The precision of Madison's understanding of a proper, republican executive authority is sharpened when set beside his rejection of what to him were unrepublican supports. John Adams had argued for a grand title for the president before the Senate and had written to a friend that "a royal or at least a princely title will be found indispensably necessary to maintain the reputation, authority, and dignity of the President. His Highness, or, if you will, His Most Benign Highness, is the correct title," Adams insisted, "that will comport with his constitutional prerogatives and support his state in the minds of our own people or foreigners." Such titles, Madison responded later in the House of Representatives, "are not very reconcilable with the nature of our Government or the genius of the people. . . . Instead of increasing, they diminish the true dignity and importance of a Republic. . . . The more simple, the more Republican we are in our manners, the more rational dignity we shall acquire." The only title needed, he suggested, was simply "the President of the United States."

In these two speeches, Madison showed his keen concern that the executive office be suited inherently to the nature of a republic, that is, to a system of government whose vital principles were to maintain both a responsibility to the will of the people and a capacity to execute their expressed will. Within this conception it was positively pernicious to introduce the monarchical trappings of pompous titles, "splendid tinsel or gorgeous robe." This harked back to the reverence for the person of the monarch, rather than depending on the republican principle of "rational dignity." By 1789 Madison had achieved a maturing idea of what it meant to exercise executive power in a republican government.

This conception sharpened his apprehension of the uses to which Hamilton and other Federalists sought to put the executive department during the 1790s. Madison, although he had greatly admired Washington and had worked closely with Hamilton for many years, was first amazed and then appalled at what the executive department had become under Hamilton's guidance. Madison's sympathies for a vigorous executive, for an efficient civil service, and for a sound public credit led him to support many of Hamilton's proposals taken individually, but it was the totality Madison opposed. The growth of the executive branch, especially the Treasury Department, allowed its secretary to take the initiative. To this power Hamilton quite candidly added the force and support he could derive from granting privilege to bankers and merchants. Sharing the largess and financial prospects with congressmen and their friends, furthermore, gave him great influence in the legislature. These consolidating moves, mobilized under the doctrine of loose construction devised to legitimize the National Bank, instituted, in Madison's view, a veritable "phalanx." Far from being an executive branch that would take its lead in policy from the legislature and be the *executor* of its will, as republican theory required, the machine Hamilton had created would lead and dominate the nation. The parallel between the means George III and his ministers had used to control Parliament during the 1770s and Hamilton's own conception of himself as a proconsul or prime minister on the order of Richelieu or Colbert or the Elder Pitt was all too apparent. The ease and speed with which Hamilton achieved this model of executive, under the Constitution, was a sobering lesson for Madison. Phrases about separation of power, and even what he thought were explicit limitations, seemed to mean little when confronted by a person of Hamilton's energy, wile, and brilliance. Thus, Madison resorted to two additional reliances. First, he stepped back from his ardent nationalism of the 1780s to favor both limited federal power in general vis-à-vis the states and a stricter interpretation of the powers of Congress and of the executive. Second, he saw reluctantly that a party devoted to a republican restraint or mildness in the conduct of government, yet organized to gain power, might be a vital part of a scheme of self-government capable of preserving the benefits of that ideal.

Federalist response to the renewal of war between France and Great Britain in 1793—arguments that the president, not Congress, could "proclaim" neutrality (the counterpart, after all, to declaring war), calls for building up the armed forces, special diplomatic missions, higher taxes, and so on—further frightened Madison because the "needs" of war so perfectly promoted the executive tendencies Hamilton had already set in motion. It also seemed to Madison that American "monocrats" (as Jeffersonian Republicans increasingly, though unfairly, termed the Federalists) used shrill accounts of the excesses of the French Revolution in 1793/94 to slander republicanism generally and to strengthen ties with England that would draw American government and society closer to its aristocratic, imperial model. When Hamilton gathered an army in the fall of 1794 to suppress the "Whisky Rebellion," Madison saw in the making "a formidable attempt . . . to establish the principle that a standing army was necessary for *enforcing the law*." After Hamilton had persuaded

Washington to criticize publicly the democratic societies that had mush-roomed in opposition to Federalist policies in 1794/95, Madison retorted that "in the nature of republican government the censorial power is in the people over the government, and not in the government over the people." Executive arrogance heightened, in Madison's opinion, in the debate over Jay's Treaty in the House of Representatives in 1796. The Federalist Roger Griswold insisted that, having received the approval of the president and of the Senate, the treaty "is become law, and the House of Representatives have nothing to do with it, but provide for its execution." Washington also refused to let the House see papers related to the negotiation of the treaty under an early version of the doctrine of executive privilege (but quite different from that asserted by Richard Nixon and his Watergate lawyer, James St. Clair, in 1974). This, to Madison, made a mockery of republican principles and showed clearly the inherently encroaching nature of executive power. More and more, he gravitated toward political response: to be safe, executive power had to be in the hands of people who were more faithful to republican principles than were Hamilton, John Adams, Timothy Pickering, and even the revered Washington.

During Adams's administration, Madison continued to fret and fume over executive excess. He saw in the president's florid addresses during the war crisis of 1798 only "violent passions and heretical politics," and he labeled the Alien Act "a monster that must forever disgrace its parents." "Perhaps it is a universal truth," he wrote Jefferson in an early parallel to the Church Committee's condemnations of the domestic activities of the CIA in 1976, "that the loss of liberty at home is to be charged to provisions against danger real or pretended from abroad." In the Report on the Virginia Resolutions (1800), Madison castigated an enlargement of the executive by "excessive augmentation of . . . offices, honors and emolu-ments" that seemed bent on "the transformation of the republican system of the United States into a monarchy."

Jefferson's victory in 1801, then, was for Madison the end of an exceedingly dangerous era in the growth or, more accurately, the degrada-tion of the Republic. He had witnessed the Constitution he had largely helped draft (and had enthusiastically recommended to his countrymen) used, indeed abused, in ways he was sure would destroy the whole notion of free self-government. The chief engine for this ruin, built by Hamilton from a domestic coalition of mercantile, antirepublican forces and a consolidation spurred by foreign danger, was the executive department. As Madison noted repeatedly during the 1790s, such a tendency was no surprise to anyone familiar with the history of Rome and other republics. He entered Jefferson's cabinet, then, with both a keen sense of the need for legitimate executive authority arising from his experience of the 1780s and an intense apprehension of the dangers of executive excess born of his observation of Hamilton's executive "phalanx" during the 1790s. Madison knew now that the Constitution made room for both the legitimacy and the excess. Only a proper republican management, faithful to the rights and needs of a free people, could ensure the former and prevent the latter. This was the grounds for the politicization of both Madison and Jefferson.

III

Service in Jefferson's cabinet had the not surprising effect of reviving Madison's sense of the legitimate use of executive power. So much so, in fact, that more doctrinaire Republicans, such as John Randolph of Roanoke, saw Madison as a dangerous "crypto-Federalist," betraying Jeffersonian principles. Madison, however, was discriminating. He agreed thoroughly with Jefferson and Gallatin that a prime Republican responsibility was to reduce the apparatus of federal government, especially of the executive department. But as Jefferson stated in his first Inaugural Address, among the "essential principles of our government [was] . . . the preservation of the general government in its whole constitutional vigor" that it might, among other things, encourage agriculture and "commerce as its handmaid." The new president also called for "the support of state governments in all their rights, as the most competent administrations of our domestic concerns, and the surest bulwarks against anti-republican tendencies; . . . the supremacy of the civil over the military authority; [and] economy in the public expense, that labor might be lightly burdened."

Madison undertook his own campaign for "mild" government by firing one of the eight clerks in the State Department (its entire personnel in 1801) and by abandoning virtually all ceremony in conducting his office. He approved Republican measures to reduce the diplomatic establishment, lower the number of federal employees, put the national debt "on the road to extinction," diminish the military, reduce taxes, and repeal the Federalist Judiciary Act of 1801. He agreed, however, that Federalist institutions that had proven useful, such as the National Bank, could remain undisturbed, and he participated willingly in the informal leadership Jefferson exercised through his influence over key members of Congress. Even Gallatin, who had an especially keen sense of the "why and how" of "republicanizing" the executive department, sought earnestly to sustain institutions that would make it possible for the federal government to lead, or at least guide, the nation. The republican theory of executive power, then, was not a heedless dismantling that would make governing itself virtually impossible; rather, it would alter the tone and manner of executive authority to make it consistent with the very essence of republicanism—that is, to be "mild" rather than imperious.

In two major events of Jefferson's presidency, the Louisiana Purchase and the Embargo, Madison showed his willingness to use executive power to achieve important republican ends. He agreed with Gallatin that the Louisiana Purchase was constitutional because "the existence of the United States as a nation presupposes the power enjoyed by every nation of extending their territory by treaties" and that the Constitution clearly gave the executive the authority to conduct such treaties. The critically important republicanizing results of the Louisiana Purchase—the doubling of agricultural lands, the removal of great power rivalry from the Mississippi Valley, and the reduction thus permitted in defense expenditures—more than compensated for a departure from the letter of Jefferson's self-imposed strict constructionism. Madison appreciated Jefferson's scruples, and he supported the plan to seek a constitutional amendment to validate the purchase, if achievable; but he saw, too, that it would be falsely republican to forfeit the benefits of the purchase to maintain a narrow, doctrinaire consistency.

The Embargo was a similarly bold effort to achieve a momentous republican breakthrough—nothing less than a substitution of economic pressure for war in international relations—by the orderly processes of a law passed by Congress and its faithful administration by the executive department. Jefferson and Madison, however, both underestimated the sectional inequity of the measure and the consequent unwillingness of the nation to accept the required sacrifices, and he overestimated the dependence of international trade (especially Britain's) on American exports. Thus, the enforcement of the Embargo and the apparent need for its long-range continuance soon entailed a considerable extension of executive power. Gallatin, who was in charge of enforcing the Embargo, reported that to make it effective, measures "equally dangerous and odious" would be needed: "not a single vessel shall be permitted to move without the special permission of the executive," collectors would have to "be invested with the general power of seizing property anywhere . . . without being liable to personal suits," and "a little army" would have to patrol the Canadian border. Such measures, of course, appalled Gallatin, but even more dangerous, he thought, was to "display our impotence to enforce our laws." At this point, the Republican leaders, Madison most reluctantly, made a revealing decision. They gave up a policy proven ineffective in its intended objective and, even worse, sure seriously to erode republican values if persisted in in the face of widespread public opposition. They resisted the temptations to prove determination and "creditability" by enlarging executive authority and to overpower rather than conciliate deep-felt opposition. The contrast with less scrupulously republican exercises of executive power is both obvious and significant.

Madison thus began his own presidency facing immense difficulties. He was forced, furthermore, to accept dictation from Congress about the make-up of his cabinet. In many ways, these were unhapppy appointments, but they also reveal more of Madison's conception of executive power. To him, recognizing, even acceding to, congressional pressures seemed somehow republican in spirit; or to put it conversely, Madison saw danger in an executive so far from, so independent of, congressional opinion as to find himself defying it. As all the world watched to see what the new Republic would do as it faced Armageddon, Madison felt obliged to resist Caesarism, proconsulism, or, more precisely, Hamiltonianism of any kind. He was unable to envision how, in the manner of a Lincoln or a Churchill or a Roosevelt, the chief executive of a democratic nation might, in emergencies, necessarily move away from strictly republican modes and act with vigor, high-handedness, and even ruthlessness to defend the nation. Madison's hesitation is a credit to his republican earnestness, but his ineptitude is a mark of his failure to grasp a realistic corollary of republican government. Thus, rather than face the known and manifest threats to every principle of free government, Madison chose, deliberately, to accept the dangers of weak and divided, even compromised, councils. Although this may seem overscrupulous, even misguided and foolish in retrospect, in the unsettled state of government after only twenty years under the new Constitution, Madison's caution is understandable. Hamilton's possible courses under similar circumstances—either to have seized the reins and permanently subordinated Congress and other sources of opposition or to have given a vigorous but benign direction to events— reveal either the reality of Madison's concern or the virtue of a more imperious course. The fact that we can plausibly conjecture both alternatives illustrates the dangerous uncertainties that were present.

Relations between Madison and the so-called War Hawk Congress that met in November 1811 further reveal both Madison's view of executive power and his use of it. The War Hawks—Henry Clay, John C. Calhoun, William Lowndes, Felix Grundy, Peter B. Porter, and others—were influential, not in dragging the president out of a paralysis of indecision or in propelling him and the nation into an unnecessary imperialism, but in supplying leadership in Congress and in the country that could give effect to a policy the president thought vital to national survival. Through the frustrating winter of 1811/12, Madison was pleased that Congress moved haltingly to some of his recommended war preparations (not enough or not altogether proper ones, but better than nothing) and that speeches and newspaper editorials rallied public opinion for the impending trial of strength. Madison and his new secretary of state, James Monroe, worked closely with congressional committees "to moderate the zeal and impatience of the ultra belligerent men, and to stimulate the more moderate and forbearing" in order, Madison's private secretary remembered, to carry a declaration of war when the time came, "by a large and influential majority."

Whatever can be said of Madison's prudence and skill in achieving a congressional majority for war, however, his organization of the executive department and of the armed forces, for which he had clear and direct responsibility, left much to be desired. The War and Navy departments had, besides, as Senator William H. Crawford noted, secretaries "incapable of discharging the duties of their office," no assistant secretaries, and less than a dozen clerks each to organize a far-flung war effort. Further, no staff officers in either service were attached to the departments in Washington to aid in planning and liaison; orders had to go directly from the incompetent secretaries to officers in the field. Although Congress's refusal to authorize and pay for such officials, the Senate's rejection of some nominees, and other nominees' refusal to serve must bear some of the blame, a resourceful, determined president might have prevailed by cleverness, browbeating, and sheer will power—one needs only to imagine Andrew Jackson in the White House in 1812 to grasp the possibilities. But to these very real difficulties and to Madison's personal liabilities must be added the same republican scrupulousness that prevented him from dealing more forcefully with Congress. If Congress did not provide explicitly for a more potent war machine and if citizens were not willing to rush to the colors, it was not the president's task, or even within his powers, to compel a different path. Indeed, to have so acted would, from Madison's perspective, have fundamentally and perhaps fatally altered the very nature of constitutional government in the still-young nation. Thus he took the nation into war *knowing* it was divided and ill prepared and depending, naively, on its ability to mobilize and rise to the occasion once war had been declared. Madison failed to discern a path both forceful and republican—perhaps the most difficult of all balances to achieve, and one that has, in the tendency toward overemphasis on force and efficiency, often been the path to both frontal assaults on freedom and the cancerous growth of what Arthur M. Schlesinger, Jr., has called "The Imperial Presidency." No friend of free government who has observed the Johnson and Nixon presidencies can be unmindful of, or unsympathetic toward, Madison's dilemma as the clouds of war gathered.

IV

The conduct of the war proved as difficult and perilous as moving toward it had been. Instead of sustaining the "mild" republican government undertaken in 1801, war reversed its direction. As he had feared, Secretary of the Treasury Gallatin found himself forced to be "a mere financier, to become a contriver of taxes, a dealer in loans, a seeker of resources for the purpose of supporting useless baubles, of increasing the number of idle and dissipated members of the community, of fattening contractors, pursers, and agents, and of introducing in all its ramifications that system of patronage, corruption, and rottenness" the Republicans had so long resisted. Even a "just war" was deeply antithetical to cherished republican values.

Madison's patient endurance of a nearly treasonable opposition to the war and his careful protection of civil liberties during it, however, most precisely reveal his standing as a republican executive. When the Federalists made open, skilled, strenuous, and often shrill opposition to the administration's every move, they encouraged, Madison thought, both at home and abroad, the belief that war would not be seriously prepared for, finally declared, or effectively fought. The result, noted the Pennsylvania Congressman Jonathan Roberts, was that "all along [there was] an idea cherished by the opposition, that the [Republicans] would not have nerve enough to meet the war." This, Roberts concluded, "mainly induced Britain to persist in her aggressions. If she could have been made to believe . . . that we were a united people, and would act as such, war might have been avoided." A London newspaper put the matter even more bluntly: "In every measure of the [American] government, the [Federalist] faction have rallied in opposition, and urged the [British] Ministry to persist in their Orders." Madison thus felt, with some justification, that had his administration received full and loyal support from the whole country, his republican faith in measures short of war might have prevailed. He also realized, paradoxically and ruefully, that this republican *end*, of preserving national integrity and interests without war, had been frustrated at least in part by his fidelity to the republican *means* of allowing full freedom to dissidents. The tension, of course, was inherent and one that Madison had struggled with since experiencing similar frustrations in Congress during the Revolutionary War. Then, as now, genuine devotion to free self-government has often been revealed in a willingness to accept difficulties and obstructions in order to persist more fundamentally in the methods of freedom in pursuing a goal. Events in Washington in 1973/74, and in New Delhi in 1975, for example, attest to this need.

Once the war had begun, Madison faced a series of largely New England–based obstructions: to recruiting officers, to mobilization of militia, to tax collectors, to credit needs, to court orders, to trade regulations, and even to movements of the federal army and navy. It was not only uncongenial personally and in principle for Madison to move harshly against these enervating resistances; it was very nearly practically impossible as well. The federal system itself, which in Madison's own theory was the *only* republican way to govern a nation as large as the United

States, gave state officials a multitude of ways to obstruct the national conduct of the war. Furthermore, republican theory forbade stifling the opposition or summarily denying civil liberties even during wartime; to do so was tantamount to losing the essential point (a free society) at the beginning and by default.

Although the repulse of the British forces in the Champlain Valley and before Baltimore in September 1814 ended the immediate threat of conquest and ultimately persuaded Wellington and other British leaders to accept a stand-off peace agreement, months passed before Madison had sure evidence of the British reaction. In the meantime, an enlarged war seemed likely amid heightened domestic difficulties. Although Rufus King led Federalists in Congress to a loyal if grudging support of the war effort, extremists, still vociferous and strong, reacted differently. To King's plea for support of the administration, Gouverneur Morris retorted: "How often, in the name of God, will you agree to be cheated? What are you to gain by giving Mr. Madison Men and Money? . . . An union of the commercial states to take care of themselves, leaving the War, its expense and its debts to those choice spirits so ready to declare and so eager to carry it on, seems to be now the only rational course."

Vice-President Gerry's death in November 1814, accompanied by Federalist schemes to elect King president pro tem of the Senate and thus put him next in line for the presidency, as well as hints, even hopes, that Madison might "quietly sleep with the late vice-president," did little to bolster national morale. Not surprisingly, one visitor in Washington found Madison's thoughts and conversation "full of the New England sedition." To an old friend, Madison unburdened himself with expressions of presidential bitterness matched, one suspects, only by Lyndon Johnson's frustrated rage at opponents of the Vietnam War. Madison wrote:

> You are not mistaken in viewing the conduct of the Eastern States as the source of our greatest difficulties in carrying on the war; as it is certainly the greatest, if not the sole, inducement with the enemy to persevere in it. The greater part of the people in that quarter have been brought by their leaders, aided by their priests, under a delusion scarcely exceeded by that recorded in the period of witchcraft; and the leaders are daily becoming more desperate in the use they make of it. Their object is power. If they could obtain it by menaces, their efforts would stop there. These failing, they are ready to go to every length.

In this atmosphere, Madison faced more New England resistance to war measures. Massachusetts refused to send militia to meet a British invasion of Maine, Vermont smugglers drove herds of cattle into Canada to feed British troops, Connecticut Federalists talked of a New England army free from federal control, and the Massachusetts legislature called for a convention to plan regional "self-defense" and to decide whether "to lay the foundation for a radical reform in the national compact," a resolution that led to the Hartford Convention of December 1814. Secretary of War James Monroe found these moves so threatening that he sent the hero of Lundy's Lane, Colonel Thomas Jesup, to Hartford, ostensibly as a recruiting officer but actually as a federal agent to watch for possible treason and rebellion. Jesup's unreassuring reports caused Monroe to authorize New York's Governor Daniel D. Tompkins and General Robert Swartwout to send in loyal troops in case of a New England uprising. Only the triumph of relative moderates at the Hartford Convention persuaded Monroe and Madison to relax from a posture of armed preparedness against potential domestic insurrection.

All this watchful concern by the administration, however, occurred without whipping up the public against the dissenters, without attempting to interfere with the Hartford Convention, and without any special declarations of emergency or other measures that might have led to detentions, strictures on the press, threats to public meetings, or other curtailments of civil liberties. It might be argued, of course, that to praise such restraint is to make a virtue of necessity, since the degree of disaffection in New England was such that Madison could not have coerced the home territory of Daniel Shays even if he had tried. Perhaps, and at the very least, some stiff fighting might have ensued, but the temptation and probably the force for a repressive policy existed. For the time being at least, British forces in Canada were discouraged and quiescent as attention focused on New Orleans, so the veterans of Plattsburg and the Niagara Frontier, now battle-tested and under vigorous, young leadership, were available for service. A few regiments, marched to Hartford or Springfield or even Boston, might have cowed the dissidents and emboldened national sentiment in the region. Furthermore, politically the Republicans might have relished an opportunity to brand their foes as traitors and perhaps discredit them for a generation. Again, one need only imagine what Hamilton, who had mobilized an army against the whisky rebels, or Jackson, who would threaten and sign the Force Act (to say nothing of the examples of Cromwell, Lord Salisbury, Bismarck, and Kemal Ataturk at other times and places), might have done in New England in 1814 to see the point.

V

In any case, Madison's course was consistent with his theory of republican government and, especially, of the use of executive power. Although in the last extremity he might have suspended civil liberties or even marched in the army, even to have had to do so would for him have been a stunning, profoundly sorrowful defeat—a "victory" in such an effort would have had only a bitter taste. Foreign war, with the mobilization, waste, restriction, suffering, and bloodshed it entailed, was blow enough to Madison's view of republicanism; but to have acted as a tyrant within his own country would have been to default grievously and utterly. Madison's willingness to act firmly to sustain Washington's army in 1780/81 and his support of Jackson in the nullification crisis provide clear evidence of his willingness to defend the nation with force if necessary. He probably would also have approved of Lincoln's understanding and defense of the Union in 1861, but these were indeed extremities from which he held back as much as possible, both personally and in principle. The image of Madison as a mild-mannered, self-effacing, indecisive, even "withered little applejohn" of a man is in part caricature and in part an accurate description of his personality and appearance; but it is also part of his conception of the republican leader. To be imperious or domineering or grand was to him simply inappropriate in a president who was the agent of the people, the follower of Congress in matters of policy, and the creature of the Constitution in the definition of his powers. In this sense, Madison's conduct of the War of 1812, with all its difficulties, indecisiveness, and failures, was an ultimate triumph in that republican government emerged confirmed and strengthened.

Madison failed to resolve painful dilemmas during his presidency, and he lacked the proconsular decisiveness often useful to a wartime executive; but he was well aware of the realities he confronted, and moreover, he had profound, principled reasons for the course he took. His experience during the 1780s left him a firm though watchful friend of executive authority and responsibility—a view, by the way, that reemerged in his remarkable seventh annual message of December 1815, in which he recommended a national bank, a small but professional defense force, a selective protective tariff, internal improvements, and a national university. Deeply disturbing to him, however, were the actual and potential uses of executive power, even under a supposedly limiting constitution, as Hamilton had demonstrated during the 1790s. This refocused Madison's sense of what a consistently *republican* executive had to be. During Jefferson's administration, the president and his two chief cabinet officers had a creative and propitious opportunity to work out the parameters of a faithfully republican leadership. Thus impressed with both the dangers and the opportunities, Madison entered his own presidency with guidelines firmly in mind. Thomas Bailey's criticism of Madison for not being "a dynamic leader of men," which of course is true, in part misses the point, because Madison had solid grounds for not wanting the president to be everlastingly such a "dynamic" leader. In every one of his critical relationships and decisions—in bringing the nation face-to-face with war, in dealing with Congress, in organizing his cabinet, and in enduring a near-treasonable dissent—he acted in view of *republican* principles of executive leadership. To do otherwise, he believed, would be to default in advance, to "lose" the war by waging it incongruously, whatever the clauses of its terminating treaty. Madison won the War of 1812, basically, by his republican conduct of it. As France's Minister Sérurier put it in February 1815, "three years of warfare have been a trial of the capacity of [American] institutions to sustain a state of war, a question . . . now resolved to their advantage."

In the spring of 1974, when Richard Nixon was at bay in the Oval Office, editing the White House tapes, Richard Harris reflected insightfully on a speech the president had made on the 165th anniversary of the birth of Abraham Lincoln. Nixon had sought in the speech, which he had delivered at the Lincoln Memorial, surrounded by the chiseled words of his predecessor, to evoke comparisons between the Great Emancipator and himself. Noting that in 1974 the United States was "the strongest nation in the world, the richest nation by far in the world, and a nation greatly respected all over the world," Nixon stated that Lincoln "would have asked, as we must ask ourselves, how will history look back on our time? What did we do with our strength? What did we do with our wealth?" Then, quoting Lincoln's phrase about the United States' being "the last, best hope of the earth," Nixon supposed his predecessor would have agreed that "we had a destiny far beyond this great nation, looking out over the whole wide world." Actually, of course, in speaking of a "last, best hope," Lincoln had had in mind the domestic example of ending slavery, not a world crusade. "The fiery trial through which we pass will light us down, in honor or dishonor, to the latest generation," he had said, pointing out that to preserve the Union in its republican character was the fundamental war aim.

Nixon's attempted comparison, ludicrous and self-serving, nevertheless highlights the essential nature of Madison's view of executive power. Nixon was willing to subordinate republican modes in order to pursue grand schemes of geopolitics and to conduct his high office in almost any way necessary to retain his political power. The first intention may have had its noble aspects, but as Nixon pursued it, it entailed fatal ramifications at home, while the second goal was simply a grotesque perversion of every republican premise. Lincoln, on the other hand, had a keen sense of the inherent nature of free government, both in his insistence that slavery be "put on a course toward ultimate extinction" and in his relatively unrepressive conduct of an agonizing civil war. Although Madison did not possess the poignant humaneness and sense of humor that made Lincoln's presidency a spiritual triumph and he also lacked Lincoln's gift for making the surgical decision, Madison's kinship with Lincoln rather than with

Nixon is obvious. Both the architect and the savior of the Union knew that to be a faithfully republican chief executive is to embody republican principles in both the routine and "crisis" conduct of the office. Madison gradually evolved an understanding of what this meant as he helped to fashion the presidency, moved toward it in his own public career, and then carried out his executive duties in time of war, international turmoil, and domestic disharmony.

This understanding of how executive power, long thought to be inherently monarchical, had to become implicitly republican was the most critical insight into the operational meaning of free government to emerge from the Revolutionary Era. And in our day of Watergate tapes, "covert surveillance," and the Church Committee Report on the CIA and the FBI, which have revealed an "imperial presidency" in all its malignant arrogance dwelling within constitutional forms, this conception and use of executive power may be Madison's most significant contribution to our concern to grasp anew the basic tenets of American democratic government.

This chapter is reprinted, with permission, from *Virginia Quarterly Review* 54, no. 1 (Winter 1978).

ALEXANDER HAMILTON'S
FEDERALIST ESSAYS ON THE
EXECUTIVE, NUMBERS 69–73

Alexander Hamilton, a brilliant New York attorney, had been a top military aide to General George Washington during the American Revolution. He was a delegate to the Constitutional Convention of 1787 in Philadelphia, and his was one of the strongest voices for a strengthened national government and a powerful and independent president. His own home state, however, contained many who were skeptical about the newly proposed constitution. They had doubts about many things, among them the idea of a strong president who could be reelected every four years and who would operate without an executive council.

Hamilton, joined by James Madison and John Jay, wrote eighty-five newspaper essays now collectively known as *The Federalist Papers,* explaining and defending the constitution fashioned in Philadelphia. These essays were written in the months leading up to the New York State ratifying convention. Doubtless they constituted a deliberate attempt to persuade New Yorkers to ratify the constitution. Hamilton's two fellow delegates from New York to the Constitutional Convention had left early because of their opposition. New York's highly visible and popular governor, George Clinton, was a vigorous opponent as well. Hamilton wrote ten essays specifically clarifying the proposed new presidency, its term, powers, and accountability. Five of the most important essays are reproduced in full in the following pages.

Here you will read how Hamilton compared the president with the king of England and the governor of New York. Hamilton made an especially effective case in *Federalist* number 70 for the need for energy in the executive department. He pleaded too for a four-year term with the opportunity for reelection. He strenuously opposed any limitation on the number of terms a president may serve. He also made a strong case for permitting the president a partial veto over legislation.

These essays convey a flavor of the debates that took place in New York and elsewhere during the ratifying struggles of 1788. Hamilton helpfully summed up many of the chief criticisms of the Antifederalists and then proceeded to dismiss them as exaggerated or unfounded. In the process Hamilton occasionally overstated his own case and in places he suggested that certain presidential powers or responsibilities would prove to be unimportant, whereas the opposite has turned out to be the case. Still, these excellent essays are essential reading for any student of the invention of the American presidency. Along with the notes from the Constitutional Convention and the debates from the ratifying conventions, they provide the best approximation of what most of the framers intended the presidency to become. They should not be taken as the only or the final word on these decisions, but they must surely be taken into account as the authoritative views of one of the most important of the framers.

These five essays were all written and published in March of 1788. Four months later New York ratified the constitution. Some have argued that these essays influenced the ratification in New York and Virginia, if only because they became an authoritative "debater's handbook" of the Federalist positions. Others are less sure about this claim. In any event, these pamphlet essays have become a classic and remain one of the best expositions of the early thinking about the role of the president in republican government. I have supplied short introductory titles.—ED.

FEDERALIST NUMBER 69.
COMPARING THE PRESIDENT
WITH KINGS AND GOVERNORS

I proceed now to trace the real characters of the proposed executive, as they are marked out in the plan of the convention. This will serve to place in a strong light the unfairness of the representations which have been made in regard to it.

The first thing which strikes our attention is, that the executive authority, with few exceptions, is to be vested in a single magistrate. This will scarcely, however, be considered as a point upon which any comparison can be grounded; for if, in this particular, there be a resemblance to the king of Great Britain, there is not less a resemblance to the Grand Seignior, to the khan of Tartary, to the Man of the Seven Mountains, or to the governor of New York.

That magistrate is to be elected for *four* years; and is to be re-eligible as often as the people of the United States shall think him worthy of their confidence. In these circumstances there is a total dissimilitude between *him* and a king of Great Britain, who is an *hereditary* monarch, possessing the crown as a patrimony descendible to his heirs forever; but there is a close analogy between *him* and a governor of New York, who is elected for *three* years, and is re-eligible without limitation or intermission. If we consider how much less time would be requisite for establishing a dangerous influence in a single state, than for establishing a like influence throughout the United States, we must conclude that a duration of *four* years for the chief magistrate of the Union is a degree of permanency far less to be dreaded in that office, than a duration of *three* years for a corresponding office in a single state.

The president of the United States would be liable to be impeached, tried, and, upon conviction of treason, bribery, or other high crimes or misdemeanors, removed from office; and would afterwards be liable to prosecution and punishment in the ordinary course of law. The person of the king of Great Britain is sacred and inviolable; there is no constitutional tribunal to which he is amenable, no punishment to which he can be subjected without involving the crisis of a national revolution. In this delicate and important circumstance of personal responsibility, the president of Confederated America would stand upon no better ground than a governor of New York, and upon worse ground than the governors of Maryland and Delaware.

The president of the United States is to have power to return a bill, which shall have passed the two branches of the legislature, for reconsideration; and the bill so returned is to become a law, if, upon that reconsideration, it be approved by two thirds of both houses. The king of Great Britain, on his part, has an absolute negative upon the acts of the two houses of Parliament. The disuse of that power for a considerable time past does not affect the reality of its existence; and is to be ascribed wholly to the crown's having found the means of substituting influence to authority, or the art of gaining a majority in one or the other of the two houses, to the necessity of exerting a prerogative which could seldom be exerted without hazarding some degree of national agitation. The qualified negative of the president differs widely from this absolute negative of the British sovereign; and tallies exactly with the revisionary authority of the council of revision of this state, of which the governor is a constituent part. In this respect the power of the president would exceed that of the governor of New York, because the former would possess, singly, what the latter shares with the chancellor and judges; but it would be precisely the same with that of the governor of Massachusetts, whose constitution, as to this article, seems to have been the original from which the convention have copied.

The president is to be the "commander-in-chief of the army and navy of the United States, and of the militia of the several States, when called into the actual service of the United States. He is to have power to grant reprieves and pardons for offences against the United States, *except in cases of impeachment;* to recommend to the consideration of Congress such measures as he shall judge necessary and expedient; to convene, on extraordinary occasions, both houses of the legislature, or either of them, and, in case of disagreement between them *with respect to the time of adjournment,* to adjourn them to such time as he shall think proper; to take care that the laws be faithfully executed; and to commission all officers of the United States." In most of these particulars, the power of the president will resemble equally that of the king of Great Britain and of the governor of New York. The most material points of difference are these:—*First.* The president will have only the occasional command of such part of the militia of the nation as by legislative provision may be called into the actual service of the Union. The king of Great Britain and the governor of New York have at all times the entire command of all the militia within their several jurisdictions. In this article, therefore, the power of the president would be inferior to that of either the monarch or the governor. *Secondly.* The president is to be commander-in-chief of the army and navy of the United States. In this respect his authority would be nominally the same with that of the king of Great Britain, but in substance much inferior to it. It would amount to nothing more than the supreme command and direction of the military and naval forces, as first general and admiral of the Confederacy; while that of the British king extends to the *declaring* of war and to the *raising* and *regulating* of fleets and armies,—all which, by the Constitution under consideration, would appertain to the legislature. The governor of New York, on the other hand, is by the constitution of the state vested only with the command of its militia and navy. But the constitutions of several of the states expressly declare their governors to be commanders-in-chief, as well of the army as navy; and it may well be a question, whether those of New Hampshire and Massachusetts, in particular, do not, in this instance, confer larger powers upon their respective governors, than could be claimed by a president of the United States. *Thirdly.* The power of the president, in respect to pardons, would extend to all cases, *except those of impeachment.* The governor of New York may pardon in all cases, even in those of impeachment, except of treason and murder. Is not the power of the governor, in this article, on a calculation of political consequences, greater than that of the president? All conspiracies and plots against the government, which have not been matured into actual treason, may be screened from punishment of every kind, by the interposition of the prerogative of pardoning. If a governor of New York, therefore, should be at the head of any such conspiracy, until the design had been ripened into actual hostility he could insure his accomplices and adherents an entire impunity. A president of the Union, on the other hand, though he may even pardon treason, when prosecuted in the ordinary course of law, could shelter no offender, in any degree, from the effects of impeachment and conviction. Would not the prospect of a total indemnity for all the preliminary steps be a greater temptation to undertake and persevere in an enterprise against the public liberty, than the mere prospect of an exemption from death and confiscation, if the final execution of the design, upon an actual appeal to arms, should miscarry? Would this last expectation have any influence at all, when the probability was computed, that the person who was to afford that exemption might himself be involved in the consequences of the measure, and might be incapacitated by his agency in it from affording the desired impunity? The better to judge of this matter, it will be necessary to recollect, that, by the proposed Constitution, the offence of treason is limited "to levying war upon the United States, and adhering to their enemies, giving them aid and comfort"; and that by the laws of New York it is confined within similar bounds. *Fourthly.* The president can only adjourn the national legislature in the single case of disagreement about the time of adjournment. The British monarch may prorogue or even dissolve the Parliament. The governor of New York may also prorogue the legislature of this state for a limited time; a power which, in certain situations, may be employed to very important purposes.

The president is to have power, with the advice and consent of the Senate, to make treaties, provided two-thirds of the senators present concur. The king of Great Britain is the sole and absolute representative of the nation in all foreign transactions. He can of his own accord make treaties of peace, commerce, alliance, and of every other description. It has been insinuated, that his authority in this respect is not conclusive, and that his conventions with foreign powers are subject to the revision, and stand in need of the ratification, of Parliament. But I believe this doctrine was never heard of, until it was broached upon the present occasion. Every jurist of that kingdom, and every other man acquainted with its Constitution, knows, as an established fact, that the prerogative of making treaties exists in the crown in its utmost plentitude; and that the compacts entered into by the royal authority have the most complete legal validity and perfection, independent of any other sanction. The Parliament, it is true, is sometimes seen employing itself in altering the existing laws to conform them to the stipulations in a new treaty; and this may have possibly given birth to the imagination, that its cooperation was necessary to the obligatory efficacy of the treaty. But this parliamentary interposition proceeds from a different cause: from the necessity of adjusting a most artificial and intricate system of revenue and commercial laws, to the changes made in them by the operation of the treaty; and of adapting new provisions and precautions to the new state of things, to keep the machine from running into disorder. In this respect, therefore, there is no comparison between the intended power of the president and the actual power of the British sovereign. The one can perform alone what the other can do only with the concurrence of a branch of the legislature. It must be admitted, that, in this instance, the power of the federal executive would exceed that of any state executive. But this arises naturally from the sovereign power which relates to treaties. If the Confederacy were to be dissolved, it would become a question, whether the executives of the several states were not solely invested with that delicate and important prerogative.

The president is also to be authorized to receive ambassadors and other public ministers. This, though it has been a rich theme of declamation, is more a matter of dignity than of authority. It is a circumstance which will be without consequence in the administration of the government; and it was far more convenient that it should be arranged in this manner, than that there should be a necessity of convening the legislature, or one of its branches, upon every arrival of a foreign minister, though it were merely to take the place of a departed predecessor.

The president is to nominate, and, *with the advice and consent of the Senate,* to appoint ambassadors and other public ministers, judges of the Supreme Court, and in general all officers of the United States established by law, and whose appointments are not otherwise provided for by the Constitution. The king of Great Britain is emphatically and truly styled the fountain of honor. He not only appoints to all offices, but can create offices. He can confer titles of nobility at pleasure; and has the disposal of an immense number of church preferments. There is evidently a great inferiority in the power of the president, in this particular, to that of the British king; nor is it equal to that of the governor of New York, if we are to interpret the meaning of the constitution of the state by the practice which has obtained under it. The power of appointment is with us lodged in a council, composed of the governor and four members of the Senate, chosen by the Assembly. The governor *claims,* and has frequently *exercised,* the right of nomination, and is *entitled* to a casting vote in the appointment. If he really has the right of nominating, his authority is in this respect equal to that of the president, and exceeds it in the article of the casting vote. In the national government, if the Senate should be divided, no appointment could be made; in the government of New York, if the council should be divided, the governor can turn the scale, and confirm his own nomination. If we compare the publicity which must necessarily attend the mode of appointment by the president and an entire branch of the national legislature, with the privacy in the mode of appointment by the governor of New York, closeted in a secret apartment with at most four, and frequently with only two persons; and if we at the same time consider how much more easy it must be to influence the small number of which a council of appointment consists, than the consider-able number of which the national Senate would consist, we cannot hesitate to pronounce that the power of the chief magistrate of this state, in the disposition of offices, must, in practice, be greatly superior to that of the chief magistrate of the Union.

Hence it appears that, except as to the concurrent authority of the president in the article of treaties, it would be difficult to determine whether that magistrate would, in the aggregate, possess more or less power than the governor of New York. And it appears yet more unequivocally, that there is no pretence for the parallel which has been attempted between him and the king of Great Britain. But to render the contrast in this respect still more striking, it may be of use to throw the principal circumstances of dissimilitude into a closer group.

The president of the United States would be an officer elected by the people for *four* years; the king of Great Britain is a perpetual and *hereditary* prince. The one would be amenable to personal punishment and disgrace; the person of the other is sacred and inviolable. The one would have a *qualified* negative upon the acts of the legislative body; the other has an *absolute* negative. The one would have a right to command the military and naval forces of the nation; the other, in addition to this right, possesses that of *declaring* war, and of *raising* and *regulating* fleets and armies by his own authority. The one would have a concurrent power with a branch of the legislature in the formation of treaties; the other is the *sole possessor* of the power of making treaties. The one would have a like concurrent authority in appointing to offices; the other is the sole author of all appointments. The one can confer no privileges whatever: the other can make denizens of aliens, noblemen of commoners; can erect corporations with all the rights incident to corporate bodies. The one can prescribe no rules concerning the commerce or currency of the nation; the other is in several respects the arbiter of commerce, and in this capacity can establish markets and fairs, can regulate weights and measures, can lay embargoes for a limited time, can coin money, can authorize or prohibit the circulation of foreign coin. The one has no particle of spiritual jurisdiction; the other is the supreme head and governor of the national church! What answer shall we give to those who would persuade us that things so unlike resemble each other? The same that ought to be given to those who tell us that a government, the whole power of which would be in the hands of the elective and periodical servants of the people, is an aristocracy, a monarchy, and a despotism.

FEDERALIST NUMBER 70.
THE NEED FOR ENERGY
AND A SINGLE EXECUTIVE

There is an idea, which is not without its advocates, that a vigorous executive is inconsistent with the genius of republican government. The enlightened well-wishers to this species of government must at least hope that the supposition is destitute of foundation; since they can never admit its truth, without at the same time admitting the condemnation of their own principles. Energy in the executive is a leading character in the definition of good government. It is essential to the protection of the community against foreign attacks; it is not less essential to the steady administration of the laws; to the protection of property against those irregular and high-handed combinations which sometimes interrupt the ordinary course of justice; to the security of liberty against the enterprises and assaults of ambition, of faction, and of anarchy. Every man the least conversant in Roman story, knows how often that republic was obliged to take refuge in the absolute power of a single man, under the formidable title of Dictator, as well against the intrigues of ambitious individuals who aspired to the tyranny, and the seditions of whole classes of the community whose conduct threatened the existence of all government, as against the invasions of external enemies who menaced the conquest and destruction of Rome.

There can be no need, however, to multiply arguments or examples on this head. A feeble executive implies a feeble execution of the government. A feeble execution is but another phrase for a bad execution; and a government ill executed, whatever it may be in theory, must be, in practice, a bad government.

Taking it for granted, therefore, that all men of sense will agree in the necessity of an energetic executive, it will only remain to inquire, what are the ingredients which constitute this energy? How far can they be combined with those other ingredients which constitute safety in the republican sense? And how far does this combination characterize the plan which has been reported by the convention?

The ingredients which constitute energy in the executive are, first, unity; secondly, duration; thirdly, an adequate provision for its support; fourthly, competent powers.

The ingredients which constitute safety in the republican sense are, first, a due dependence on the people; secondly, a due responsibility.

Those politicians and statesmen who have been the most celebrated for the soundness of their principles and for the justice of their views, have declared in favor of a single executive and a numerous legislature. They have, with great propriety, considered energy as the most necessary qualification of the former, and have regarded this as most applicable to power in a single hand; while they have, with equal propriety, considered the latter as best adapted to deliberation and wisdom, and best calculated to conciliate the confidence of the people and to secure their privileges and interests.

That unity is conducive to energy will not be disputed. Decision, activity, secrecy, and dispatch will generally characterize the proceedings of one man in a much more eminent degree than the proceedings of any greater number; and in proportion as the number is increased, these qualities will be diminished.

This unity may be destroyed in two ways: either by vesting the power in two or more magistrates of equal dignity and authority; or by vesting it ostensibly in one man, subject, in whole or in part, to the control and cooperation of others, in the capacity of counsellors to him. Of the first, the two consuls of Rome may serve as an example; of the last, we shall find examples in the constitutions of several of the states. New York and New Jersey, if I recollect right, are the only states which have intrusted the executive authority wholly to single men. Both these methods of destroying the unity of the executive have their partisans; but the votaries of an executive council are the most numerous. They are both liable, if not to equal, to similar objections, and may in most lights be examined in conjunction.

The experience of other nations will afford little instruction on this head. As far, however, as it teaches any thing, it teaches us not to be enamoured of plurality in the executive. We have seen that the Achæans, on an experiment of two prætors, were induced to abolish one. The Roman history records many instances of mischiefs to the republic from the dissensions between the consuls, and between the military tribunes, who were at times substituted for the consuls. But it gives us no specimens of any peculiar advantages derived to the state from the circumstance of the plurality of those magistrates. That the dissensions between them were not more frequent or more fatal, is matter of astonishment, until we advert to the singular position in which the republic was almost continually placed, and to the prudent policy pointed out by the circumstances of the state, and pursued by the consuls, of making a division of the government between them. The patricians engaged in a perpetual struggle with the plebeians for the preservation of their ancient authorities and dignities; the consuls, who were generally chosen out of the former body, were commonly united by the personal interest they had in the defence of the privileges of their order. In addition to this motive of union, after the arms of the republic had considerably expanded the bounds of its empire, it became an established custom with the consuls to divide the administration between themselves by lot—one of them remaining at Rome to govern the city and its environs, the other taking the command in the more distant provinces. This expedient must, no doubt, have had great influence in preventing those collisions and rivalships which might otherwise have embroiled the peace of the republic.

But quitting the dim light of historical research, attaching ourselves purely to the dictates of reason and good sense, we shall discover much greater cause to reject than to approve the idea of plurality in the executive, under any modification whatever.

Wherever two or more persons are engaged in any common enterprise or pursuit, there is always danger of difference of opinion. If it be a public trust or office, in which they are clothed with equal dignity and authority, there is peculiar danger of personal emulation and even animosity. From either, and especially from all these causes, the most bitter dissensions are apt to spring. Whenever these happen, they lessen the respectability, weaken the authority, and distract the plans and operation of those whom they divide. If they should unfortunately assail the supreme executive magistracy of a country, consisting of a plurality of persons, they might impede or frustrate the most important measures of the government, in the most critical emergencies of the state. And what is still worse, they might split the community into the most violent and irreconcilable factions, adhering differently to the diffferent individuals who composed the magistracy.

Men often oppose a thing, merely because they have had no agency in planning it, or because it may have been planned by those whom they dislike. But if they have been consulted, and have happened to disapprove, opposition then becomes, in their estimation, an indispensable duty of self-love. They seem to think themselves bound in honor, and by all the motives of personal infallibility, to defeat the success of what has been resolved upon contrary to their sentiments. Men of upright, benevolent tempers have too many opportunities of remarking, with horror, to what desperate lengths this disposition is sometimes carried, and how often the great interests of society are sacrificed to the vanity, to the conceit, and to the obstinacy of individuals, who have credit enough to make their passions and their caprices interesting to mankind. Perhaps the question now before the public may, in its consequences, afford melancholy proofs of the effects of this despicable frailty, or rather detestable vice, in the human character.

Upon the principles of a free government, inconveniences from the source just mentioned must necessarily be submitted to in the formation of the legislature; but it is unnecessary, and therefore unwise, to introduce them into the constitution of the executive. It is here too that they may be most pernicious. In the legislature, promptitude of decision is oftener an evil than a benefit. The differences of opinion, and the jarrings of parties in that department of the government, though they may sometimes obstruct salutary plans, yet often promote deliberation and circumspection, and serve to check excesses in the majority. When a resolution too is once taken, the opposition must be at an end. That resolution is a law, and resistance to it punishable. But no favorable circumstances palliate or atone for the disadvantages of dissension in the executive department. Here, they are pure and unmixed. There is no point at which they cease to operate. They serve to embarrass and weaken the execution of the plan or measure to which they relate, from the first step to the final conclusion of it. They constantly counteract those qualities in the executive which are the most necessary ingredients in its composition,—vigor and expedition, and this without any counterbalancing good. In the conduct of war, in which the energy of the executive is the bulwark of the national security, every thing would be to be apprehended from its plurality.

It must be confessed that these observations apply with principal weight to the first case supposed—that is, to a plurality of magistrates of equal dignity and authority, a scheme, the advocates for which are not likely to form a numerous sect; but they apply, though not with equal, yet with considerable weight to the project of a council, whose concurrence is made constitutionally necessary to the operations of the ostensible executive. An artful cabal in that council would be able to distract and to enervate the whole system of administration. If no such cabal should exist, the mere diversity of views and opinions would alone be sufficient to tincture the exercise of the executive authority with a spirit of habitual feebleness and dilatoriness.

But one of the weightiest objections to a plurality in the executive, and which lies as much against the last as the first plan, is, that it tends to conceal faults and destroy responsibility. Responsibility is of two kinds—to censure and to punishment. The first is the more important of the two, especially in an elective office. Man, in public trust, will much oftener act in such a manner as to render him unworthy of being any longer trusted, than in such a manner as to make him obnoxious to legal punishment. But the multiplication of the executive adds to the difficulty of detection in either case. It often becomes impossible, amidst mutual accusations, to determine on whom the blame or the punishment of a pernicious measure, or series of pernicious measures, ought really to fall. It is shifted from one to another with so much dexterity, and under such plausible appearances, that the public opinion is left in suspense about the real author. The circumstances which may have led to any national miscarriage or misfortune are sometimes so complicated that, where there are a number of actors who may have had different degrees and kinds of agency, though we may clearly see upon the whole that there has been mismanagement, yet it may be impracticable to pronounce to whose account the evil which may have been incurred is truly chargeable.

"I was overruled by my council. The council were so divided in their opinions that it was impossible to obtain any better resolution on the point." These and similar pretexts are constantly at hand, whether true or false. And who is there that will either take the trouble or incur the odium, of a strict scrutiny into the secret springs of the transaction? Should there be found a citizen zealous enough to undertake the unpromising task, if there happen to be collusion between the parties concerned, how easy it is to clothe the circumstances with so much ambiguity, as to render it uncertain what was the precise conduct of any of those parties?

In the single instance in which the governor of this state is coupled with a council—that is, in the appointment to offices, we have seen the mischiefs of it in the view now under consideration. Scandalous appointments to important offices have been made. Some cases, indeed, have been so flagrant that ALL PARTIES have agreed in the impropriety of the thing. When inquiry has been made, the blame has been laid by the governor on the members of the council, who, on their part, have charged it upon his nomination; while the people remain altogether at a loss to determine, by whose influence their interests have been committed to hands so unqualified and so manifestly improper. In tenderness to individuals, I forbear to descend to particulars.

It is evident from these considerations, that the plurality of the executive tends to deprive the people of the two greatest securities they can have for the faithful exercise of any delegated power, *first,* the restraints of public opinion, which lose their efficacy, as well on account of the division of the censure attendant on bad measures among a number, as on account of the uncertainty on whom it ought to fall; and, *secondly,* the opportunity of discovering with facility and clearness the misconduct of the persons they trust, in order either to their removal from office, or to their actual punishment in cases which admit of it.

In England, the king is a perpetual magistrate; and it is a maxim which has obtained for the sake of the public peace, that he is unaccountable for his administration, and his person sacred. Nothing, therefore, can be wiser in that kingdom, than to annex to the king a constitutional council, who may be responsible to the nation for the advice they give. Without this, there would be no responsibility whatever in the executive department— an idea inadmissible in a free government. But even there the king is not bound by the resolutions of his council, though they are answerable for the advice they give. He is the absolute master of his own conduct in the exercise of his office, and may observe or disregard the counsel given to him at his sole discretion.

But in a republic, where every magistrate ought to be personally responsible for his behavior in office, the reason which in the British Constitution dictates the propriety of a council, not only ceases to apply, but turns against the institution. In the monarchy of Great Britain, it furnishes a substitute for the prohibited responsibility of the chief magistrate, which serves in some degree as a hostage to the national justice for his good behavior. In the American republic, it would serve to destroy, or would greatly diminish, the intended and necessary responsibility of the chief magistrate himself.

The idea of a council to the executive, which has so generally obtained in the state constitutions, has been derived from that maxim of republican jealousy which considers power as safer in the hands of a number of men than of a single man. If the maxim should be admitted to be applicable to the case, I should contend that the advantage on that side would not counterbalance the numerous disadvantages on the opposite side. But I do not think the rule at all applicable to the executive power. I clearly concur in opinion, in this particular, with a writer whom the celebrated Junius pronounces to be "deep, solid, and ingenious," that "the executive power is more easily confined when it is ONE"; that it is far more safe there should be a single object for the jealousy and watchfulness of the people; and, in a word, that all multiplication of the executive is rather dangerous than friendly to liberty.

A little consideration will satisfy us, that the species of security sought for in the multiplication of the executive, is unattainable. Numbers must be so great as to render combination difficult, or they are rather a source of danger than of security. The united credit and influence of several individuals must be more formidable to liberty, than the credit and influence of either of them separately. When power, therefore, is placed in the hands of so small a number of men, as to admit of their interests and views being easily combined in a common enterprise, by an artful leader, it becomes more liable to abuse, and more dangerous when abused, than if it be lodged in the hands of one man; who, from the very circumstance of his being alone, will be more narrowly watched and more readily suspected, and who cannot unite so great a mass of influence as when he is associated with others. The Decemvirs of Rome, whose name denotes their number, were more to be dreaded in their usurpation than any ONE of them would have been. No person would think of proposing an executive much more numerous than that body; from six to a dozen have been suggested for the number of the council. The extreme of these numbers is not too great for an easy combination; and from such a combination America would have more to fear than from the ambition of any single individual. A council to a magistrate, who is himself responsible for what he does, are generally nothing better than a clog upon his good intentions, are often the instruments and accomplices of his bad, and are almost always a cloak to his faults.

I forbear to dwell upon the subject of expense; though it be evident that if the council should be numerous enough to answer the principal end aimed at by the institution, the salaries of the members, who must be drawn from their homes to reside at the seat of government, would form an item in the catalogue of public expenditures too serious to be incurred for an object of equivocal utility. I will only add that, prior to the appearance of the Constitution, I rarely met with an intelligent man from any of the states, who did not admit, as the result of experience, that the UNITY of the executive of this state was one of the best of the distinguishing features of our constitution.

FEDERALIST NUMBER 71.
THE FOUR-YEAR TERM OF OFFICE

Duration in office has been mentioned as the second requisite to the energy of the executive authority. This has relation to two objects: to the personal firmness of the executive magistrate, in the employment of his constitutional powers; and to the stability of the system of administration which may have been adopted under his auspices. With regard to the first, it must be evident, that the longer the duration in office, the greater will be the probability of obtaining so important an advantage. It is a general principle of human nature, that a man will be interested in whatever he possesses, in proportion to the firmness or precariousness of the tenure by which he holds it; will be less attached to what he holds by a momentary or uncertain title, than to what he enjoys by a durable or certain title; and, of course, will be willing to risk more for the sake of the one, than for the sake of the other. This remark is not less applicable to a political privilege, or honor, or trust, than to any article of ordinary property. The inference from it is, that a man acting in the capacity of chief magistrate, under a consciousness that in a very short time he *must* lay down his office, will be apt to feel himself too little interested in it to hazard any material censure or perplexity, from the independent exertion of his powers, or from encountering the ill-humors, however transient, which may happen to prevail, either in a considerable part of the society itself, or even in a predominant faction in the legislative body. If the case should only be, that he *might* lay it down, unless continued by a new choice, and if he should be desirous of being continued, his wishes, conspiring with his fears, would tend still more powerfully to corrupt his integrity, or debase his fortitude. In either case, feebleness and irresolution must be the characteristics of the station.

There are some who would be inclined to regard the servile pliancy of the executive to a prevailing current, either in the community or in the legislature, as its best recommendation. But such men entertain very crude notions, as well of the purposes for which government was instituted, as of the true means by which the public happiness may be promoted. The republican principle demands that the deliberate sense of the community should govern the conduct of those to whom they intrust the management of their affairs; but it does not require an unqualified complaisance to every sudden breeze of passion, or to every transient impulse which the people may receive from the arts of men, who flatter their prejudices to betray their interests. It is a just observation, that the people commonly *intend* the PUBLIC GOOD. This often applies to their very errors. But their good sense would despise the adulator who should pretend that they always *reason right* about the *means* of promoting it. They know from experience that they sometimes err; and the wonder is that they so seldom err as they do, beset, as they continually are, by the wiles of parasites and sycophants, by the snares of the ambitious, the avaricious, the desperate, by the artifices of men who possess their confidence more than they deserve it, and of those who seek to possess rather than to deserve it. When occasions present themselves, in which the interests of the people are at variance with their inclinations, it is the duty of the persons whom they have appointed to be the guardians of those interests, to withstand the temporary delusion, in order to give them time and opportunity for more cool and sedate reflection. Instances might be cited in which a conduct of this kind has saved the people from very fatal consequences of their own mistakes, and has procured lasting monuments of their gratitude to the men who had courage and magnanimity enough to serve them at the peril of their displeasure.

But however inclined we might be to insist upon an unbounded complaisance in the executive to the inclinations of the people, we can with no propriety contend for a like complaisance to the humors of the legislature. The latter may sometimes stand in opposition to the former, and at other times the people may be entirely neutral. In either supposition, it is certainly desirable that the executive should be in a situation to dare to act his own opinion with vigor and decision.

The same rule which teaches the propriety of a partition between the various branches of power, teaches us likewise that this partition ought to be so contrived as to render the one independent of the other. To what purpose separate the executive or the judiciary from the legislative, if both the executive and the judiciary are so constituted as to be at the absolute devotion of the legislative? Such a separation must be merely nominal, and incapable of producing the ends for which it was established. It is one thing to be subordinate to the laws, and another to be dependent on the legislative body. The first comports with, the last violates, the fundamental principles of good government; and, whatever may be the forms of the Constitution, unites all power in the same hands. The tendency of the legislative authority to absorb every other, has been fully displayed and illustrated by examples in some preceding numbers. In governments purely republican, this tendency is almost irresistible. The representatives of the people, in a popular assembly, seem sometimes to fancy that they are the people themselves, and betray strong symptoms of impatience and disgust at the least sign of opposition from any other quarter; as if the exercise of its rights, by either the executive or judiciary, were a breach of their privilege and an outrage to their dignity. They often appear disposed to exert an imperious control over the other departments; and as they commonly have the people on their side, they always act with such momentum as to make it very difficult for the other members of the government to maintain the balance of the Constitution.

It may perhaps be asked, how the shortness of the duration in office can affect the independence of the executive on the legislature, unless the one were possessed of the power of appointing or displacing the other. One answer to this inquiry may be drawn from the principle already re-marked—that is, from the slender interest a man is apt to take in a short-lived advantage, and the little inducement it affords him to expose himself, on account of it, to any considerable inconvenience or hazard. Another answer, perhaps more obvious, though not more conclusive, will result from the consideration of the influence of the legislative body over the people; which might be employed to prevent the re-election of a man who, by an upright resistance to any sinister project of that body, should have made himself obnoxious to its resentment.

It may be asked also, whether a duration of four years would answer the end proposed; and if it would not, whether a less period, which would at least be recommended by greater security against ambitious designs, would not, for that reason, be preferable to a longer period, which was, at the same time, too short for the purpose of inspiring the desired firmness and independence of the magistrate.

It cannot be affirmed, that a duration of four years, or any other limited duration, would completely answer the end proposed; but it would contribute towards it in a degree which would have a material influence upon the spirit and character of the government. Between the commence-ment and termination of such a period, there would always be a considerable interval, in which the prospect of annihilation would be sufficiently remote, not to have an improper effect upon the conduct of a man indued with a tolerable portion of fortitude; and in which he might reasonably promise himself, that there would be time enough before it arrived, to make the community sensible of the propriety of the measures he might incline to pursue. Though it be probable that, as he approached the moment when the public were, by a new election, to signify their sense of his conduct, his confidence, and with it his firmness, would decline; yet both the one and the other would derive support from the opportunities which his previous continuance in the station had afforded him, of establishing himself in the esteem and good-will of his constituents. He might, then, hazard with safety, in proportion to the proofs he had given of his wisdom and integrity, and to the title he had acquired to the respect and attachment of his fellow-citizens. As, on the one hand, a duration of four years will contribute to the firmness of the executive in a sufficient degree to render it a very valuable ingredient in the composition; so, on the other, it is not enough to justify any alarm for the public liberty. If a British House of Commons, from the most feeble beginnings, *from the mere power of assenting or disagreeing to the imposition of a new tax,* have, by rapid strides, reduced the prerogatives of the crown and the privileges of the nobility within the limits they conceived to be compatible with the principles of a free government, while they raised themselves to the rank and consequence of a coequal branch of the legislature; if they have been able, in one instance, to abolish both the royalty and the aristocracy, and to overturn all the ancient establishments, as well in the church as state; if they have been able, on a recent occasion, to make the monarch tremble at the prospect of an innovation attempted by them, what would be to be feared from an elective magistrate of four years' duration, with the confined authorities of a president of the United States? What, but that he might be unequal to the task which the Constitution assigns him? I shall only add, that if his duration be such as to leave a doubt of his firmness, that doubt is inconsistent with a jealousy of his encroachments.

FEDERALIST NUMBER 72.
THE IMPORTANCE OF RE-ELIGIBILITY

The administration of government, in its largest sense, comprehends all the operations of the body politic, whether legislative, executive, or judiciary; but in its most usual and perhaps in its most precise signification, it is limited to executive details, and falls peculiarly within the province of the executive department. The actual conduct of foreign negotiations, the preparatory plans of finance, the application and disbursement of the public moneys in conformity to the general appropriations of the legislature, the arrangement of the army and navy, the direction of the operations of war,—these, and other matters of a like nature, constitute what seems to be most properly understood by the administration of government. The persons, therefore, to whose immediate management these different matters are committed, ought to be considered as the assistants or deputies of the chief magistrate, and on this account, they ought to derive their offices from his appointment, at least from his nomination, and ought to be subject to his superintendence. This view of the subject will at once suggest to us the intimate connection between the duration of the executive magistrate in office and the stability of the system of administration. To reverse and undo what has been done by a predecessor, is very often considered by a successor as the best proof he can give of his own capacity and desert; and in addition to this propensity, where the alteration has been the result of public choice, the person substituted is warranted in supposing that the dismission of his predecessor has proceeded from a dislike to his measures; and that the less he resembles him, the more he will recommend himself to the favor of his constituents. These considerations, and the influence of personal confidences and attachments, would be likely to induce every new president to promote a change of men to fill the subordinate stations; and these causes together could not fail to occasion a disgraceful and ruinous mutability in the administration of the government.

With a positive duration of considerable extent, I connect the circumstance of re-eligibility. The first is necessary to give to the officer himself the inclination and the resolution to act his part well, and to the community time and leisure to observe the tendency of his measures, and thence to form an experimental estimate of their merits. The last is necessary to enable the people, when they see reason to approve of his conduct, to continue him in his station, in order to prolong the utility of his talents and virtues, and to secure to the government the advantage of permanency in a wise system of administration.

Nothing appears more plausible at first sight, nor more ill-founded upon close inspection, than a scheme which in relation to the present point has had some respectable advocates,—I mean that of continuing the chief magistrate in office for a certain time, and then excluding him from it, either for a limited period or forever after. This exclusion, whether temporary or perpetual, would have nearly the same effects, and these effects would be for the most part rather pernicious than salutary.

One ill effect of the exclusion would be a diminution of the inducements to good behavior. There are few men who would not feel much less zeal in the discharge of a duty, when they were conscious that the advantages of the station with which it was connected must be relinquished at a determinate period, than when they were permitted to entertain a hope of *obtaining,* by *meriting,* a continuance of them. This position will not be disputed so long as it is admitted that the desire of reward is one of the strongest incentives of human conduct; or that the best security for the fidelity of mankind is to make their interest coincide with their duty. Even the love of fame, the ruling passion of the noblest minds, which would prompt a man to plan and undertake extensive and arduous enterprises for the public benefit, requiring considerable time to mature and perfect them, if he could flatter himself with the prospect of being allowed to finish what he had begun, would, on the contrary, deter him from the undertaking, when he foresaw that he must quit the scene before he could accomplish the work, and must commit that, together with his own reputation, to hands which might be unequal or unfriendly to the task. The most to be expected from the generality of men, in such a situation, is the negative merit of not doing harm, instead of the positive merit of doing good.

Another ill effect of the exclusion would be the temptation to sordid views, to peculation, and, in some instances, to usurpation. An avaricious man, who might happen to fill the office, looking forward to a time when he must at all events yield up the emoluments he enjoyed, would feel a propensity, not easy to be resisted by such a man, to make the best use of the opportunity he enjoyed while it lasted, and might not scruple to have recourse to the most corrupt expedients to make the harvest as abundant as it was transitory; though the same man, probably, with a different prospect before him, might content himself with the regular perquisites of his situation, and might even be unwilling to risk the consequences of an abuse of his opportunities. His avarice might be a guard upon his avarice. Add to this that the same man might be vain or ambitious, as well as avaricious. And if he could expect to prolong his honors by his good conduct, he might hesitate to sacrifice his appetite for them to his appetite for gain. But with the prospect before him of approaching an inevitable annihilation, his avarice would be likely to get the victory over his caution, his vanity, or his ambition.

An ambitious man, too, when he found himself seated on the summit of his country's honors, when he looked forward to the time at which he must descend from the exalted eminence for ever, and reflected that no exertion of merit on his part could save him from the unwelcome reverse; such a man, in such a situation, would be much more violently tempted to embrace a favorable conjuncture for attempting the prolongation of his power, at every personal hazard, than if he had the probability of answering the same end by doing his duty.

Would it promote the peace of the community, or the stability of the government to have half a dozen men who had had credit enough to be raised to the seat of the supreme magistracy, wandering among the people like discontented ghosts, and sighing for a place which they were destined never more to possess?

A third ill effect of the exclusion would be, the depriving the community of the advantage of the experience gained by the chief magistrate in the exercise of his office. That experience is the parent of wisdom, is an adage the truth of which is recognized by the wisest as well as the simplest of mankind. What more desirable or more essential than this quality in the governors of nations? Where more desirable or more essential than in the first magistrate of a nation? Can it be wise to put this desirable and essential quality under the ban of the Constitution, and to declare that the moment it is acquired, its possessor shall be compelled to abandon the station in which it was acquired, and to which it is adapted? This, nevertheless, is the precise import of all those regulations which exclude men from serving their country, by the choice of their fellow-citizens, after they have by a course of service fitted themselves for doing it with a greater degree of utility.

A fourth ill effect of the exclusion would be the banishing men from stations in which, in certain emergencies of the state, their presence might be of the greatest moment to the public interest or safety. There is no nation which has not, at one period or another, experienced an absolute necessity of the services of particular men in particular situations; perhaps it would not be too strong to say, to the preservation of its political existence. How unwise, therefore, must be every such self-denying ordinance as serves to prohibit a nation from making use of its own citizens in the manner best suited to its exigencies and circumstances! Without supposing the personal essentiality of the man, it is evident that a change of the chief magistrate, at the breaking out of a war, or at any similar crisis, for another, even of equal merit, would at all times be detrimental to the community, inasmuch as it would substitute inexperience to experience, and would tend to unhinge and set afloat the already settled train of the administration.

A fifth ill effect of the exclusion would be, that it would operate as a constitutional interdiction of stability in the administration. By *necessitating* a change of men, in the first office of the nation, it would necessitate a mutability of measures. It is not generally to be expected, that men will vary and measures remain uniform. The contrary is the usual course of things. And we need not be apprehensive that there will be too much stability, while there is even the option of changing; nor need we desire to prohibit the people from continuing their confidence where they think it may be safely placed, and where, by constancy on their part, they may obviate the fatal inconveniences of fluctuating councils and a variable policy.

These are some of the disadvantages which would flow from the principle of exclusion. They apply most forcibly to the scheme of a perpetual exclusion; but when we consider that even a partial exclusion would always render the readmission of the person a remote and precarious object, the observations which have been made will apply nearly as fully to one case as to the other.

What are the advantages promised to counterbalance these disadvantages? They are represented to be: 1st, greater independence in the magistrate; 2d, greater security to the people. Unless the exclusion be perpetual, there will be no pretence to infer the first advantage. But even in that case, may he have no object beyond his present station, to which he may sacrifice his independence? May he have no connections, no friends, for whom he may sacrifice it? May he not be less willing, by a firm conduct, to make personal enemies, when he acts under the impression that a time is fast approaching, on the arrival of which he not only MAY, but MUST, be exposed to their resentments, upon an equal, perhaps upon an inferior, footing? It is not an easy point to determine whether his independence would be most promoted or impaired by such an arrangement.

As to the second supposed advantage, there is still greater reason to entertain doubts concerning it. If the exclusion were to be perpetual, a man of irregular ambition, of whom alone there could be reason in any case to entertain apprehension, would, with infinite reluctance, yield to the necessity of taking his leave forever of a post in which his passion for power and preeminence had acquired the force of habit. And if he had been fortunate or adroit enough to conciliate the good-will of the people, he might induce them to consider as a very odious and unjustifiable restraint upon themselves, a provision which was calculated to debar them of the right of giving a fresh proof of their attachment to a favorite. There may be conceived circumstances in which this disgust of the people, seconding the thwarted ambition of such a favorite, might occasion greater danger to liberty, than could ever reasonably be dreaded from the possibility of a perpetuation in office, by the voluntary suffrages of the community, exercising a constitutional privilege.

There is an excess of refinement in the idea of disabling the people to continue in office men who had entitled themselves, in their opinion, to approbation and confidence; the advantages of which are at best speculative and equivocal, and are overbalanced by disadvantages far more certain and decisive.

FEDERALIST NUMBER 73.
SALARY AND THE VETO POWER

The third ingredient towards constituting the vigor of the executive authority, is an adequate provision for its support. It is evident that, without proper attention to this article, the separation of the executive from the legislative department would be merely nominal and nugatory. The legislature, with a discretionary power over the salary and emoluments of the chief magistrate, could render him as obsequious to their will as they might think proper to make him. They might, in most cases, either reduce him by famine, or tempt him by largesses, to surrender at discretion his judgment to their inclinations. These expressions, taken in all the latitude of the terms, would no doubt convey more than is intended. There are men who could neither be distressed nor won into a sacrifice of their duty; but this stern virtue is the growth of few soils; and in the main it will be found that a power over a man's support is a power over his will. If it were necessary to confirm so plain a truth by facts, examples would not be wanting, even in this country, of the intimidation or seduction of the executive by the terrors or allurements of the pecuniary arrangements of the legislative body.

It is not easy, therefore, to commend too highly the judicious attention which has been paid to this subject in the proposed Constitution. It is there provided that "The President of the United States shall, at stated times, receive for his service a compensation *which shall neither be increased nor diminished during the period for which he shall have been elected;* and he *shall not receive within that period any other emolument* from the United States, or any of them." It is impossible to imagine any provision which would have been more eligible than this. The legislature, on the appointment of a president, is once for all to declare what shall be the compensation for his services during the time for which he shall have been elected. This done, they will have no power to alter it, either by increase or diminution, till a new period of service by a new election commences. They can neither weaken his fortitude by operating on his necessities, nor corrupt his integrity by appealing to his avarice. Neither the Union, nor any of its members, will be at liberty to give, nor will he be at liberty to receive, any other emolument than that which may have been determined by the first act. He can, of course, have no pecuniary inducement to renounce or desert the independence intended for him by the Constitution.

The last of the requisites to energy, which have been enumerated, are competent powers. Let us proceed to consider those which are proposed to be vested in the president of the United States.

The first thing that offers itself to our observation, is the qualified negative of the president upon the acts or resolutions of the two houses of the legislature; or, in other words, his power of returning all bills with objections, to have the effect of preventing their becoming laws, unless they should afterwards be ratified by two thirds of each of the component members of the legislative body.

The propensity of the legislative department to intrude upon the rights, and to absorb the powers, of the other departments, has been already suggested and repeated; the insufficiency of a mere parchment delineation of the boundaries of each, has also been remarked upon; and the necessity of furnishing each with constitutional arms for its own defence, has been inferred and proved. From these clear and indubitable principles results the propriety of a negative, either absolute or qualified, in the executive, upon the acts of the legislative branches. Without the one or the other, the former would be absolutely unable to defend himself against the depredations of the latter. He might gradually be stripped of his authorities by successive resolutions, or annihilated by a single vote. And in the one mode or the other, the legislative and executive powers might speedily come to be blended in the same hands. If even no propensity had ever discovered itself in the legislative body to invade the rights of the executive, the rules of just reasoning and theoretic propriety would of themselves teach us, that the one ought not to be left to the mercy of the other, but ought to possess a constitutional and effectual power of self-defence.

But the power in question has a further use. It not only serves as a shield to the executive, but it furnishes an additional security against the enaction of improper laws. It establishes a salutary check upon the legislative body, calculated to guard the community against the effects of faction, precipitancy, or of any impulse unfriendly to the public good, which may happen to influence a majority of that body.

The propriety of a negative has, upon some occasions, been combated by an observation, that it was not to be presumed a single man would possess more virtue and wisdom than a number of men; and that unless this presumption should be entertained, it would be improper to give the executive magistrate any species of control over the legislative body.

But this observation, when examined, will appear rather specious than solid. The propriety of the thing does not turn upon the supposition of superior wisdom or virtue in the executive, but upon the supposition that the legislature will not be infallible; that the love of power may sometimes betray it into a disposition to encroach upon the rights of other members of the government; that a spirit of faction may sometimes pervert its deliberations; that impressions of the moment may sometimes hurry it into measures which itself, on maturer reflection, would condemn. The primary inducement to conferring the power in question upon the executive is, to enable him to defend himself; the secondary one is to increase the chances in favor of the community against the passing of bad laws, through haste, inadvertence, or design. The oftener the measure is brought under examination, the greater the diversity in the situations of those who are to examine it, the less must be the danger of those errors which flow from want of due deliberation, or of those missteps which proceed from the contagion of some common passion or interest. It is far less probable, that culpable views of any kind should infect all the parts of the government at the same moment and in relation to the same object, than that they should by turns govern and mislead every one of them.

It may perhaps be said that the power of preventing bad laws includes that of preventing good ones; and may be used to the one purpose as well as to the other. But this objection will have little weight with those who can properly estimate the mischiefs of that inconstancy and mutability in the laws, which form the greatest blemish in the character and genius of our governments. They will consider every institution calculated to restrain the excess of law-making, and to keep things in the same state in which they happen to be at any given period, as much more likely to do good than harm; because it is favorable to greater stability in the system of legislation. The injury which may possibly be done by defeating a few good laws, will be amply compensated by the advantage of preventing a number of bad ones.

Nor is this all. The superior weight and influence of the legislative body in a free government, and the hazard to the executive in a trial of strength with that body, afford a satisfactory security that the negative would generally be employed with great caution; and there would oftener be room for a charge of timidity than of rashness in the exercise of it. A king of Great Britain, with all his train of sovereign attributes, and with all the influence he draws from a thousand sources, would, at this day, hesitate to put a negative upon the joint resolutions of the two houses of Parliament. He would not fail to exert the utmost resources of that influence to strangle a measure disagreeable to him, in its progress to the throne, to avoid being reduced to the dilemma of permitting it to take effect, or of risking the displeasure of the nation by an opposition to the sense of the legislative body. Nor is it probable, that he would ultimately venture to exert his prerogatives, but in a case of manifest propriety, or extreme necessity. All well-informed men in that kingdom will accede to the justness of this remark. A very considerable period has elapsed since the negative of the crown has been exercised.

If a magistrate so powerful and so well fortified as a British monarch, would have scruples about the exercise of the power under consideration, how much greater caution may be reasonably expected in a president of the United States, clothed for the short period of four years with the executive authority of a government wholly and purely republican?

It is evident that there would be greater danger of his not using his power when necessary, than of his using it too often or too much. An argument, indeed, against its expediency, has been drawn from this very source. It has been represented, on this account, as a power odious in appearance, useless in practice. But it will not follow, that because it might be rarely exercised, it would never be exercised. In the case for which it is chiefly designed, that of an immediate attack upon the constitutional rights of the executive, or in a case in which the public good was evidently and palpably sacrificed, a man of tolerable firmness would avail himself of his constitutional means of defence, and would listen to the admonitions of duty and responsibility. In the former supposition, his fortitude would be stimulated by his immediate interest in the power of his office; in the latter, by the probability of the sanction of his constituents, who, though they would naturally incline to the legislative body in a doubtful case, would hardly suffer their partiality to delude them in a very plain case. I speak now with an eye to a magistrate possessing only a common share of firmness. There are men who, under any circumstances, will have the courage to do their duty at every hazard.

But the convention have pursued a mean in this business, which will both facilitate the exercise of the power vested in this respect in the executive magistrate, and make its efficacy to depend on the sense of a considerable part of the legislative body. Instead of an absolute negative, it is proposed to give the executive the qualified negative already described. This is a power which would be much more readily exercised than the other. A man who might be afraid to defeat a law by his single VETO, might not scruple to return it for reconsideration; subject to being finally rejected only in the event of more than one third of each house concurring in the sufficiency of his objections. He would be encouraged by the reflection, that if his opposition should prevail, it would embark in it a very respectable proportion of the legislative body, whose influence would be united with his in supporting the propriety of his conduct in the public opinion. A direct and categorical negative has something in the appearance of it more harsh, and more apt to irritate, than the mere suggestion of argumentative objections to be approved or disapproved by those to whom they are addressed. In proportion as it would be less apt to offend, it would be more apt to be exercised; and for this very reason, it may in practice be found more effectual. It is to be hoped that it will not often happen that improper views will govern so large a proportion as two thirds of both branches of the legislature at the same time; and this, too, in spite of the counterposing weight of the executive. It is at any rate far less probable that this should be the case, than that such views should taint the resolutions and conduct of a bare majority. A power of this nature in the executive, will often have a silent and unperceived, though forcible, operation. When men, engaged in unjustifiable pursuits, are aware that obstructions may come from a quarter which they cannot control, they will often be restrained by the bare apprehension of opposition, from doing what they would with eagerness rush into, if no such external impediments were to be feared.

This qualified negative, as has been elsewhere remarked, is in this state vested in a council, consisting of the governor, with the chancellor and judges and the Supreme Court, or any two of them. It has been freely employed upon a variety of occasions, and frequently with success. And its utility has become so apparent, that persons who, in compiling the Constitution, were violent opposers of it, have from experience become its declared admirers.

I have in another place remarked, that the convention, in the formation of this part of their plan, had departed from the model of the constitution of this state, in favor of that of Massachusetts. Two strong reasons may be imagined for this preference. One is that the judges, who are to be the interpreters of the law, might receive an improper bias, from having given a previous opinion in their revisionary capacities; the other is that by being often associated with the executive, they might be induced to embark too far in the political views of that magistrate, and thus a dangerous combination might by degrees be cemented between the executive and judiciary departments. It is impossible to keep the judges too distinct from every other avocation than that of expounding the laws. It is peculiarly dangerous to place them in a situation to be either corrupted or influenced by the executive.

SELECTED BIBLIOGRAPHY

Benton, Wilbourne E., ed. *1787: Drafting the U.S. Constitution.* 2 vols. College Station: Texas A & M University Press, 1986.

Berger, Raoul. *Executive Privilege: A Constitutional Myth.* Cambridge, Mass.: Harvard University Press, 1974.

————. *Impeachment: The Constitutional Problems.* Cambridge, Mass.: Harvard University Press, 1973.

Bessette, Joseph M., and Tulis, Jeffrey, eds. *The Presidency in the Constitutional Order.* Baton Rouge: Louisiana State University Press, 1981.

Bowen, Catherine D. *Miracle at Philadelphia: The Story of the Constitutional Convention.* Boston, Mass.: Little, Brown, 1966.

Cooke, Jacob E., ed. *The Federalist* by Alexander Hamilton, James Madison, and John Jay. Cleveland, Ohio: Meridian Books, 1961.

Corwin, Edward S. *The President: Office and Powers, 1787–1984: A History and Analysis of Practice and Opinion,* 5th rev. ed. New York: New York University Press, 1984.

————. *Presidential Power and the Constitution: Essays,* ed. Richard Loss. Ithaca, N.Y.: Cornell University Press, 1976.

Cronin, Thomas E. *The State of the Presidency.* 2d ed. Boston, Mass.: Little, Brown, 1980.

Curtis, George. *A History of the Origin, Formation, and Adoption of the Constitution of the United States.* New York: Harper and Bros., 1958.

Elliot, Jonathan, ed. *The Debates in the Several State Conventions on the Adoption of the Federal Constitution.* Philadelphia: J. P. Lippincott, 1861; republished in 5 vols. New York: Burt Franklin, 1974.

Farrand, Max, ed. *The Records of the Federal Convention of 1787.* 4 vols., rev. ed. New Haven, Conn.: Yale University Press, 1966.

Fisher, Louis. *Constitutional Conflicts between Congress and the President.* Princeton, N.J.: Princeton University Press, 1985.

Fitzpatrick, John Clement, ed. *The Diaries of George Washington, 1748–1799.* 4 vols. Boston, Mass.: Houghton Mifflin, 1925.

Hart, James. *The American Presidency in Action, 1789: A Study in Constitutional History.* New York: Macmillan, 1948.

————. *The Ordinance Making Powers of the President of the United States.* Baltimore, Md.: Johns Hopkins University Press, 1925.

Henkin, Louis. *Foreign Affairs and the Constitution.* Mineola, N.Y.: Foundation Press, 1972.

Humbert, W. H. *The Pardoning Power of the President.* Washington, D.C.: American Council on Public Affairs, 1941.

Jensen, Merrill. *The Documentary History of the Adoption of the Federal Constitution.* Madison: University of Wisconsin Press, 1976–84.

——. *The New Nation: A History of the United States during the Confederation, 1781–1789.* New York: Knopf, 1950.

Jillson, Calvin C. *Constitution Making: Conflict and Consensus in the Federal Convention of 1787.* New York: Agathon Press, 1988.

Kallenbach, Joseph E. *The American Chief Executive: The Presidency and Governorship.* New York: Harper & Row, 1961.

Kelley, Alfred H., and Winfred A. Harbison. *The American Constitution: Its Origins and Development.* 5th ed. New York: W. W. Norton and Company, 1976.

Ketcham, Ralph. *James Madison: A Biography.* New York: Macmillan, 1971.

——. *Presidents above Party: The First American Presidency, 1789–1829.* Chapel Hill: University of North Carolina Press, 1984.

Kurland, Philip B., and Ralph Lerner, eds. *The Founders' Constitution.* 5 vols. Chicago: University of Chicago Press, 1987.

Labovitz, John R. *Presidential Impeachment.* New Haven, Conn.: Yale University Press, 1978.

Levy, Leonard W., ed. *Essays on the Making of the Constitution.* New York: Oxford University Press, 1969.

Levy, Leonard W. *Original Intent and the Framers' Constitution.* New York: Macmillan, 1988.

Locke, John. "The Second Treatise of Government," in *Two Treatises of Government,* ed. Peter Laslett, rev. ed. Cambridge: Cambridge University Press, 1963.

Long, Breckenridge. *The Genesis of the Constitution of the United States of America.* New York, 1926.

Lowi, Theodore. *The Personal President.* Ithaca, N.Y.: Cornell University Press, 1985.

Madison, James. *Notes of Debates in the Federal Convention of 1787,* ed. Adrienne Koch. Athens: Ohio University Press, 1966.

Main, Jackson Turner. *The Antifederalists: Critics of the Constitution, 1781–1788.* Chapel Hill: University of North Carolina Press, 1961.

Mason, Edward C. *The Veto Power.* Boston, Mass.: Ginn & Co., 1890.

McDonald, Forrest. *Alexander Hamilton: A Biography.* New York: W. W. Norton, 1979.

——. *Novus Ordo Seclorum: The Intellectual Origins of the Constitution.* Lawrence: University Press of Kansas, 1985.

——. *The Presidency of George Washington.* Lawrence: University Press of Kansas, 1974.

McLaughlin, Andrew. *The Foundations of American Constitutionalism.* New York: New York University Press, 1932.

Miller, John C. *The Federal Era, 1789–1901.* New York: Harper, 1960.

Morris, Richard B. *The Forging of the Union, 1781–1789.* New York: Harper & Row, 1987.

——. *Witnesses at the Creation: Hamilton, Madison, Jay and the Constitution.* New York: New American Library, 1985.

——. *The New Nation: A History of the U.S. during the Confederation, 1781–1789.* New York: Knopf, 1950.

Neustadt, Richard. *Presidential Power.* New York: John Wiley, 1960.

Peterson, Merrill D. *Thomas Jefferson and the New Nation.* New York: Oxford University Press, 1970.

Pious, Richard M. *The American Presidency.* New York: Basic Books, 1979.

Rakove, Jack N. *The Beginnings of National Politics: An Interpretive History of the Continental Congress.* Baltimore, Md.: Johns Hopkins University Press, 1979.

Robinson, Donald L. *"To the Best of My Ability": The President and the Constitution.* New York: Norton, 1987.

Rossiter, Clinton. *1787: The Grand Convention.* New York: Macmillan, 1966.

Rutland, Robert A. *The Ordeal of the Constitution: The Antifederalists and the Ratification Struggle of 1787–1788.* Norman: Oklahoma University Press, 1966.

Sanders, Jennings B. *The Evolution of the Executive Departments of the Continental Congress, 1774–1789.* Chapel Hill: University of North Carolina Press, 1935.

Schlesinger, Arthur M., Jr. *The Imperial Presidency.* Boston: Houghton Mifflin, 1973.

Slaughter, Thomas P. *The Whiskey Rebellion.* New York: Oxford University Press, 1986.

Sofaer, Abraham D. *War, Foreign Affairs and Constitutional Power: The Origins.* Cambridge, Mass.: Ballinger, 1976.

Spitzer, Robert J. *The Presidential Veto.* Albany: State University of New York Press, 1988.

Storing, Herbert J. *The Complete Anti-Federalist.* 7 vols. Chicago: University of Chicago Press, 1981.

———. *What the Anti-Federalists Were For.* Chicago: University of Chicago Press, 1981.

Thach, Charles C., Jr. *The Creation of the Presidency, 1775–1789: A Study in Constitutional History.* Baltimore, Md.: Johns Hopkins Press, 1923.

Tulis, Jeffrey K. *The Rhetorical Presidency.* Princeton, N.J.: Princeton University Press, 1987.

Warren, Charles. *The Making of the Constitution.* Boston: Little, Brown and Co., 1928; republished New York: Barnes and Noble, 1967.

White, Leonard D. *The Federalists: A Study in Administrative History.* New York: Macmillan, 1948.

Wills, Garry. *Cincinnatus: George Washington and the Enlightenment.* Garden City, N.Y.: Doubleday, 1984.

Wood, Gordon S. *The Creation of the American Republic, 1776–1787.* Chapel Hill: University of North Carolina Press, 1969.

Wormuth, Francis D., and Edwin B. Firmage. *To Chain the Dog of War: The War Power of Congress in History and Law.* Dallas, Tex.: Southern Methodist University Press, 1986.

INDEX